CCNA®
Certificat[i]
Practice Tests

Exam 200-301 v1.1
Second Edition

CCNA®
Certification
Practice Tests
Exam 200-301 v1.1
Second Edition

Jon Buhagiar

A Wiley Brand

Acknowledgments

I would like to thank my wife, Teresa. She has had so much patience during the writing of this book. I would also like to thank the many people who made this book possible, including the following: Kenyon Brown at Wiley Publishing for giving me the opportunity to write this book; Kim Wimpsett, for working with me as the developmental editor and making the entire project seamless; Saravanan Dakshinamurthy, for helping with production editing and guiding me through the process; Ben Piper, for serving as technical reviewer to ensure I didn't miss any details; and Elizabeth Welch, for the many edits that helped make this book a polished product. Thank you to the many other people I've never met who worked behind the scenes to make this book a success.

Acknowledgments

About the Author

Jon Buhagiar, BS/ITM, MCSE, CCNA, is an information technology professional with two decades of experience in higher education and the private sector.

Jon is currently the director of information technology at RareMed Solutions. In this role, he manages projects related to the IT infrastructure and cloud services that serve multiple pharmacies operated by RareMed Solutions. In addition, he is responsible for the technology that supports hundreds of care specialists who raise the quality of life for many patients all over the world.

Jon was previously the supervisor of network operations at Pittsburgh Technical College, where he managed the data center, network infrastructure operations, and IT operations and was involved in managing projects supporting the quality of education at the college. He also served as an adjunct instructor in the college's School of Information Technology department, where he taught courses for Microsoft and Cisco certification. Jon has been an instructor for 20+ years with several colleges in the Pittsburgh area since the introduction of the Windows NT MCSE in 1998.

Jon earned a bachelor of science degree in information technology management from Western Governors University. He also achieved an associate degree in business management from Pittsburgh Technical College. His most recent certifications are Windows Server Microsoft Certified Solutions Expert (MCSE) and the Cisco Certified Network Associate (CCNA) certification. Other certifications include CompTIA Network+, CompTIA A+, and CompTIA Project+.

In addition to his professional and teaching roles, Jon has authored the *CCNA Routing and Switching Practice Tests: Exam 100-105, Exam 200-105, and Exam 200-125* (Sybex, 2017); *CompTIA Network+ Review Guide: Exam N10-007, 4th Edition* (Sybex, 2018), and *CompTIA A+ Deluxe Study Guide: Exam 220-1102* (Sybex, 2022), *CompTIA Network+ Study Guide: Exam N10-009 (Sybex Study Guide),* along with Todd Lammle (Sybex, 2024). He has also served as the technical editor for the second edition of the *CompTIA Cloud+ Study Guide* (Sybex, 2016); *CCNA Security Study Guide: Exam 210-260* (Sybex, 2018); *CCNA Cloud Complete Study Guide: Exam 210-451 and Exam 210-455* (Sybex, 2018); *CCNP Enterprise Certification Study Guide: Implementing* (Sybex, 2018); *Operating Cisco Enterprise Network Core Technologies: Exam 300-401* (Sybex, 2020). Jon has spoken at several conferences about spam and email systems. He is an active radio electronics hobbyist and has held a ham radio license for the past 20 years, KB3KGS. He experiments with electronics and has a strong focus on the Internet of Things (IoT).

About the Technical Editor

Ben Piper is a consultant and instructor who has authored multiple books and taught more than 20 training courses covering cloud, networking, programming, and DevOps. You can contact Ben by visiting his website: `https://benpiper.com`.

Contents

Introduction   *xiii*

Chapter   1   **Network Fundamentals (Domain 1)**   **1**

Chapter   2   **Network Access (Domain 2)**   **43**

Chapter   3   **IP Connectivity (Domain 3)**   **85**

Chapter   4   **IP Services (Domain 4)**   **137**

Chapter   5   **Security Fundamentals (Domain 5)**   **159**

Chapter   6   **Automation and Programmability (Domain 6)**   **189**

Chapter   7   **Practice Exam 1**   **207**

Chapter   8   **Practice Exam 2**   **229**

Appendix   **Answers to Review Questions**   **249**

    Chapter 1: Network Fundamentals (Domain 1)   250
    Chapter 2: Network Access (Domain 2)   277
    Chapter 3: IP Connectivity (Domain 3)   301
    Chapter 4: IP Services (Domain 4)   332
    Chapter 5: Security Fundamentals (Domain 5)   344
    Chapter 6: Automation and Programmability (Domain 6)   363
    Chapter 7: Practice Exam 1   377
    Chapter 8: Practice Exam 2   389

Index   *403*

Introduction

CCNA Certification Practice Tests: Exam 200-301 is a companion volume to the *CCNA Certification Study Guide*. If you're looking to test your knowledge before you take the CCNA exam, this book will help you by providing a combination of 1,200 questions that cover the CCNA objectives.

If you're just starting to prepare for the CCNA exam, I highly recommend that you start with *CCNA Certification Study Guide, Volume 1* and *CCNA Certification Study Guide, Volume 2*, both by Todd Lammle (Sybex, 2024), to help you learn about each of the objectives covered in the CCNA exam. Once you're ready to test your knowledge, use this book to find places where you may need to study more or practice for the exam itself.

Since it is a companion to the *CCNA Certification Study Guide* books for Exam 200-301, this book is designed to be similar to taking the CCNA certification exam. It contains scenarios and standard multiple-choice questions similar to those you may encounter in the certification exam itself. The book contains eight chapters: six objective-centric chapters with 100 to 250 questions, weighted by the objectives, and two chapters that contain 100-question practice tests to simulate taking the exam. The bulk of the questions are in the IP Connectivity objective.

Cisco's Network Certification

It used to be that to secure the holy grail of Cisco certifications—the Cisco Certified Internetwork Expert (CCIE)—you passed only one written test before being faced with a grueling, formidable hands-on lab. This intensely daunting, all-or-nothing approach made it nearly impossible to succeed and predictably didn't work out too well for most people. Cisco responded to this issue by creating a series of new certifications, which not only made it easier to eventually win the highly coveted CCIE prize, but gave employers a way to accurately rate and measure the skill levels of prospective and current employees. This exciting paradigm shift in Cisco's certification path truly opened doors that few were allowed through before!

Beginning in 1998, obtaining the Cisco Certified Network Associate (CCNA) certification was the first milestone in the Cisco certification climb, as well as the official prerequisite for each of the more advanced levels. Today, the Cisco CCNA exam remains as important in the scheme of Cisco certification as it was 20+ years ago. Of course, you can imagine that what we learned two decades ago has changed significantly, and so has the current Cisco CCNA exam. The CCNA exam is less focused on routing and switching than prior exams and more focused on a wider spectrum of technologies. The technologies include virtualization, wireless, and software-defined networking, just to name a few.

In May 2023, Cisco made an exciting and welcomed announcement about their certification offerings. The news is that the exam numbers no longer change, from exam to exam! This truly is exciting news for everyone who is in the midst of studying for a CCNA. Cisco has adopted a new policy of point releases for their exams when there is less than 20% of changes to the objectives. The current CCNA exam is now version 1.1 for the 200-301, which means that less than 20% changed since the last version of 1.0 of the 200-301. If more than 20% changes from exam to exam, then the major version will change to version 2.0, 3.0, and beyond.

> The prior CCNA exam of 200-301 was retroactively assigned the version of v1.0.

The news gets even better because Cisco has published exactly what has changed from version 1.0 to version 1.1 for the 200-301 exam. In the future, when the minor or major version changes, Cisco is committed to publishing the delta objectives for each revision. The exam number will never change for these versions, so you can stay on pace for obtaining your certification.

Since the last release of the CCNA certification exam 200-301 v1.0, Cisco has retired the Cisco Certified Entry Network Technician (CCENT). You are now required to take the CCNA certification in one exam (200-301 v1.1), and there are no prerequisites and no separate parts as there were in the past CCNA exams. Cisco has introduced an entry-level exam called the Cisco Certified Support Technician (CCST) Networking Exam. The CCST exam is aimed at entry-level technicians who support and maintain Cisco equipment. The CCST has not replaced the CCENT, and rest assured, the CCNA is still the benchmark for network professionals.

Cisco Certified Network Associate (CCNA)

For the uninitiated, the CompTIA A+ and Network+ certifications aren't official prerequisites, but know that Cisco does expect you to have that type and level of experience before embarking on your Cisco certification journey. If you are just starting out on the journey of Cisco certification and prefer to stick with Cisco-centric material, a good starting point is the book *CCNA Certification Study Guide, Volume 1: Exam 200-301* by Todd Lammle (Sybex, 2024), which includes many of the introductory topics you are expected to know by the time you start the CCNA exam process.

All of this gets us to the current day, when the climb to Cisco supremacy got much harder again. The fact that the certification process is getting harder really works better for you in the long run, because that which is harder to obtain only becomes that much more valuable when you finally do, right? Yes, indeed!

The CCNA (200-301) exam is extremely hard and covers a lot of material, so you have to really know your stuff. Taking a Cisco class or spending months with hands-on experience is definitely a requirement to succeed when faced with this monster! However, the CCNA certification is the most popular Cisco certification by far because it's the most sought-after certification by all employers.

And once you have your CCNA, you don't have to stop there—you can choose to continue and achieve an even higher certification, called the Cisco Certified Network Professional (CCNP). There are various certifications, and each one focuses on a specialty area. The CCNP Enterprise certification is still the most popular, with the Security certification coming in at a close second. And I've got to tell you that the Data Center certification is quickly catching up. Also good to know is that anyone with a CCNP specialty certification has all the skills and knowledge needed to attempt the notoriously dreaded but coveted CCIE specialty lab. But just becoming a CCNA can land you that job you've dreamed about, and that's what this book is all about: helping you get and keep a great job!

Why Become a CCNA?

Cisco, like Microsoft and other vendors that provide certification, has created the certification process to give administrators a set of skills and to equip prospective employers with a way to measure those skills or match certain criteria. And as you probably know, becoming a CCNA is certainly the initial, key step on a successful journey toward a new, highly rewarding, and sustainable networking career.

The CCNA program was created to provide a solid introduction, not only to switching and IP connectivity but also to internetworking in general, making it helpful to you in areas not exclusively Cisco's. And regarding today's certification process, it's not unrealistic that network managers—even those without Cisco equipment—require Cisco certifications for their job applicants. Rest assured, if you make it through the CCNA and are still interested in Cisco and internetworking, you're headed down a path to certain success!

What Skills Do You Need to Become a CCNA?

This CCNA exam (200-301) tests a candidate for the knowledge and skills required to successfully install, operate, and troubleshoot a small branch office network to a medium-sized enterprise network. The exam includes questions on the operation of IP data networks, LAN switching technologies, IPv6, IP routing technologies, IP services, network device security, and basic troubleshooting. The exam also includes questions on physical and network security, network troubleshooting, and WAN technologies. We also see wireless technology added as an objective, since many networks today consist of wired and wireless technologies.

This CCNA exam has also added an objective domain to consider the expanse of virtualized networking. Both private and public cloud-based networks are included in this objective domain. The CCNA exam added the objective domain of automation and programmability to accommodate this real-world requirement. Much of what we do today must scale and be reproducible with expected results.

How Do You Become a CCNA?

All you have to do is pass the CCNA exam (200-301). Oh, but don't you wish it were that easy? True, it's just one test, but it's a whopper, and to pass it you must possess enough knowledge to understand what the test writers are saying, and you need to know everything I mentioned previously! Hey, it's hard, but it can be done!

Where Do You Take the Exams?

You may take the CCNA or any Cisco exam at any of the Pearson VUE authorized testing centers. For information, check www.pearsonvue.com or call 877-404-EXAM (3926).

To register for a Cisco exam, follow these steps:

1. Determine the number of the exam you want to take. (The CCNA exam is 200-301 v1.1.)

2. Register with the nearest Pearson VUE testing center. At this point, you will be asked to pay for the exam in advance. As of this writing, the CCNA exam is $300. The exams must be taken within one year of payment. You can schedule exams up to six weeks in advance or as late as the day you want to take it—but if you fail a Cisco exam, you must wait five days before you will be allowed to retake it. If something comes up and you need to cancel or reschedule your exam appointment, contact Pearson VUE at least 24 hours in advance.

3. When you schedule the exam, you'll get instructions regarding all appointment and cancellation procedures, the ID requirements, and information about the testing-center location.

Pearson VUE has recently introduced OnVUE online proctored exams. Currently on their registration page they urge you to schedule an OnVUE online proctored exam that can be taken from the comfort of your home.

Tips for Taking Your Cisco Exams

The Cisco exams contain about 50–60 questions and must be completed in about 120 minutes or less. This information can change per exam. You must get a score of about 85 percent to pass this exam, but again, each exam can be different.

Many questions on the exam have answer choices that at first glance look identical, especially the syntax questions! So remember to read through the choices carefully because close just doesn't cut it. If you get commands in the wrong order or forget one measly character, you'll get the question wrong. So, practice; do the hands-on exercises found at the end of each chapter in the books *CCNA Certification Study Guide, Volume 1*, and *CCNA Certification Study Guide, Volume 2* by Todd Lammle (Sybex, 2024), and perform them over and over again until they feel natural to you.

Also, never forget that the right answer is the Cisco answer. In many cases, more than one appropriate answer is presented, but the correct answer is the one that Cisco recommends. On the exam, you will always be told to pick one, two, or three options, never "choose all that apply." The Cisco exam may include the following test formats:

- Multiple-choice single answer
- Multiple-choice multiple answers
- Drag-and-drop
- Router simulations

Cisco proctored exams will not show the steps to follow in completing a router interface configuration, but they do allow partial command responses. For example, show run, sho running, or sh running-config would be acceptable.

Here are some general tips for exam success:

- Arrive early at the exam center so you can relax and review your study materials.
- Read the questions carefully. Don't jump to conclusions. Make sure you're clear about exactly what each question asks. "Read twice, answer once," is what I always tell my students.

- When answering multiple-choice questions that you're not sure about, use the process of elimination to get rid of the obviously incorrect answers first. Doing this greatly improves your odds if you need to make an educated guess.

- You can no longer move forward and backward through the Cisco exams, so double-check your answer before clicking Next since you can't change your mind.

After you complete an exam, you'll get immediate, online notification of your pass or fail status, a printed examination score report that indicates your pass or fail status, and your exam results by section. (The test administrator will give you the printed score report.) Test scores are automatically forwarded to Cisco within five working days after you take the test, so you don't need to send your score to them. If you pass the exam, you'll receive confirmation from Cisco, typically within two to four weeks, sometimes a bit longer.

How to Use This Book and the Interactive Online Learning Environment and Test Bank

This book includes over 1,000 practice test questions, which will help you get ready to pass the CCNA exam. The interactive online learning environment that accompanies *CCNA Certification Practice Tests: Exam 200-301, Second Edition* provides a robust test bank to help you prepare for the certification exams and increase your chances of passing them the first time! By using this test bank, you can identify weak areas up front and then develop a solid studying strategy using each of these testing features.

The test bank also offers two practice exams. Take these practice exams just as if you were taking the actual exam (without any reference material). When you've finished the first exam, move on to the next one to solidify your test-taking skills. If you get more than 90 percent of the answers correct, you're ready to take the certification exams.

You can access the Sybex interactive online test bank at www.wiley.com/go/sybextestprep.

Like all exams, the CCNA certification from Cisco is updated periodically and may eventually be retired or replaced. At some point after Cisco is no longer offering this exam, the old editions of our books and online tools will be retired. If you have purchased this book after the exam was retired, or are attempting to register in the Sybex online learning environment after the exam was retired, please know that we make no guarantees that this exam's online Sybex tools will be available once the exam is no longer available.

CCNA (200-301 v1.1) Exam Objectives

Exam objectives are subject to change at any time without prior notice and at Cisco's sole discretion. Please visit Cisco's certification website, www.cisco.com/c/en/us/training-events.html, for the latest information on the CCNA exam. Tables 1–6 cover the CCNA (200-301 v1.1) exam objectives.

TABLE 1   1.0 Network Fundamentals (20%)

Objective	Chapter
1.1 Explain the role and function of network components	1
1.1.a Routers	1
1.1.b Layer 2 and Layer 3 switches	1
1.1.c Next-generation firewalls and IPS	1
1.1.d Access points	1
1.1.e Controllers	1
1.1.f Endpoints	1
1.1.g Servers	1
1.1h PoE	
1.2 Describe characteristics of network topology architectures	1
1.2.a Two-tier	1
1.2.b Three-tier	1
1.2.c Spine-leaf	1
1.2.d WAN	1
1.2.e Small office/home office (SOHO)	1
1.2.f On-premises and cloud	1
1.3 Compare physical interface and cabling types	1
1.3.a Single-mode fiber, multimode fiber, copper	1
1.3.b Connections (Ethernet shared media and point-to-point)	1

Objective	Chapter
1.4 Identify interface and cable issues (collisions, errors, mismatch duplex, and/or speed)	1
1.5 Compare TCP to UDP	1
1.6 Configure and verify IPv4 addressing and subnetting	1
1.7 Describe private IPv4 addressing	1
1.8 Configure and verify IPv6 addressing and prefix	1
1.9 Compare IPv6 address types	1
1.9.a Unicast (global, unique local, and link local)	1
1.9.b Anycast	1
1.9.c Multicast	1
1.9.d Modified EUI 64	1
1.10 Verify IP parameters for Client OS (Windows, Mac OS, Linux)	1
1.11 Describe wireless principles	1
1.11.a Nonoverlapping Wi-Fi channels	1
1.11.b SSID	1
1.11.c RF	1
1.11.d Encryption	1
1.12 Explain virtualization fundamentals (server virtualization, containers, and VRFs)	1
1.13 Describe switching concepts	1
1.13.a MAC learning and aging	1
1.13.b Frame switching	1
1.13.c Frame flooding	1
1.13.d MAC address table	1

TABLE 2   2.0 Network Access (20%)

Objective	Chapter
2.1 Configure and verify VLANs (normal range) spanning multiple switches	2
2.1.a Access ports (data and voice)	2
2.1.b Default VLAN	2
2.1.c InterVLAN Connectivity	2
2.2 Configure and verify interswitch connectivity	2
2.2.a Trunk ports	2
2.2.b 802.1Q	2
2.2.c Native VLAN	2
2.3 Configure and verify Layer 2 discovery protocols (Cisco Discovery Protocol and LLDP)	2
2.4 Configure and verify (Layer 2/Layer 3) EtherChannel (LACP)	2
2.5 Interpret basic operations of Rapid PVST+ Spanning Tree Protocol	2
2.5.a Root port, root bridge (primary/secondary), and other port names	2
2.5.b Port states and roles	2
2.5.c PortFast	2
2.5.d Root guard, loop guard, BPDU filter, and BPDU guard	2
2.6 Describe Cisco Wireless Architectures and AP modes	2
2.7 Describe physical infrastructure connections of WLAN components (AP, WLC, access/trunk ports, and LAG)	2
2.8 Describe network device management access (Telnet, SSH, HTTP, HTTPS, console, and TACACS+/RADIUS, and cloud managed)	2
2.9 Interpret the wireless LAN GUI configuration for client connectivity, such as WLAN creation, security settings, QoS profiles, and advanced settings	2

TABLE 3   3.0 IP Connectivity (25%)

Objective	Chapter
3.1 Interpret the components of a routing table	3
3.1.a Routing protocol code	3
3.1.b Prefix	3
3.1.c Network mask	3
3.1.d Next hop	3
3.1.e Administrative distance	3
3.1.f Metric	3
3.1.g Gateway of last resort	3
3.2 Determine how a router makes a forwarding decision by default	3
3.2.a Longest prefix match	3
3.2.b Administrative distance	3
3.2.c Routing protocol metric	3
3.3 Configure and verify IPv4 and IPv6 static routing	3
3.3.a Default route	3
3.3.b Network route	3
3.3.c Host route	3
3.3.d Floating static	3
3.4 Configure and verify single area OSPFv2	3
3.4.a Neighbor adjacencies	3
3.4.b Point-to-point	3
3.4.c Broadcast (DR/BDR selection)	3
3.4.d Router ID	3
3.5 Describe the purpose, functions, and concepts of first hop redundancy protocol	3

TABLE 4   4.0 IP Services (10%)

Objective	Chapter
4.1 Configure and verify inside source NAT using static and pools	4
4.2 Configure and verify NTP operating in a client and server mode	4
4.3 Explain the role of DHCP and DNS within the network	4
4.4 Explain the function of SNMP in network operations	4
4.5 Describe the use of syslog features including facilities and levels	4
4.6 Configure and verify DHCP client and relay	4
4.7 Explain the forwarding per-hop behavior (PHB) for QoS such as classification, marking, queuing, congestion, policing, shaping	4
4.8 Configure network devices for remote access using SSH	4
4.9 Describe the capabilities and function of TFTP/FTP in the network	4

TABLE 5   5.0 Security Fundamentals (15%)

Objective	Chapter
5.1 Define key security concepts (threats, vulnerabilities, exploits, and mitigation techniques)	5
5.2 Describe security program elements (user awareness, training, and physical access control)	5
5.3 Configure device access control using local passwords	5
5.4 Describe security password policy elements, such as management, complexity, and password alternatives (multifactor authentication, certificates, and biometrics)	5
5.5 Describe IPsec remote access and site-to-site VPNs	5
5.6 Configure and verify access control lists	5
5.7 Configure Layer 2 security features (DHCP snooping, dynamic ARP inspection, and port security)	5
5.8 Compare authentication, authorization, and accounting concepts	5
5.9 Describe wireless security protocols (WPA, WPA2, and WPA3)	5
5.10 Configure and verify WLAN within the GUI using WPA2 PSK	5

TABLE 6   6.0 Automation and Programmability (10%)

Objective	Chapter
6.1 Explain how automation impacts network management	6
6.2 Compare traditional networks with controller-based networking	6
6.3 Describe controller-based and software defined architectures (overlay, underlay, and fabric)	6
6.3.a Separation of control plane and data plane	6
6.3.b Northbound and southbound APIs	6
6.4 Explain AI (generative and predictive) and machine learning in network operations	6
6.5 Describe characteristics of REST-based APIs (Authentication types, CRUD, HTTP verbs, and data encoding)	6
6.6 Recognize the capabilities of configuration management mechanisms, such as Ansible and Terraform	6
6.7 Recognize components of JSON-encoded data	6

CCNA (200-301 v1.1) Exam Delta Objectives

Studying to take a Cisco exam takes time, lots of time! Understandably, we can find ourselves in the middle of studying for one exam, such as the prior CCNA (200-301 v1.0) exam, only to find out it is being retired and replaced with the CCNA (200-301 v1.1). To maintain your momentum, you will find yourself frantically looking at what exactly changed from the past exam to the current exam. For this purpose, I have included the delta exam objectives in this book. These delta objectives are the new or changed objectives that were not present on the prior exam or were not emphasized in the prior exam. This section is only a guide for you to prepare for the transition to the current certification of CCNA (200-301 v1.1). This section is not the only portion you must study in addition to the prior study material.

Exam objectives are subject to change at any time without prior notice and at Cisco's sole discretion. Please visit Cisco's certification website (www.cisco.com/c/en/us/training-events.html) for the latest information on the CCNA (200-301 v1.1) exam. Table 7 covers the differences between the prior CCNA (200-301 v1.0) exam and the new CCNA (200-301 v1.1) exam objectives.

TABLE 7 Delta objectives

Objective	Version
2.5 Interpret basic operations of Rapid PVST+ Spanning Tree Protocol 　2.5.a Root port, root bridge (primary/secondary), and other port names 　2.5.b Port states and roles 　2.5.c PortFast	1.0
2.5 Interpret basic operations of Rapid PVST+ Spanning Tree Protocol 　2.5.a Root port, root bridge (primary/secondary), and other port names 　2.5.b Port states and roles 　2.5.c PortFast 　2.5.d Root guard, loop guard, BPDU filter, and BPDU guard	1.1
2.8 Describe AP and WLC management access (Telnet, SSH, HTTP, HTTPS, console, and TACACS+/RADIUS)	1.0
2.8 Describe network device management access (Telnet, SSH, HTTP, HTTPS, console, TACACS+/RADIUS, and cloud managed)	1.1
6.4 Compare traditional campus device management with Cisco DNA Center enabled device management	1.0
6.4 Explain AI (generative and predictive) and machine learning in network operations	1.1
6.5 Describe characteristics of REST-based APIs (CRUD, HTTP verbs, and data encoding)	1.0
6.5 Describe characteristics of REST-based APIs (authentication types, CRUD, HTTP verbs, and data encoding)	1.1
6.6 Recognize the capabilities of configuration management mechanisms, such as Puppet, Chef, and Ansible	1.0
6.6 Recognize the capabilities of configuration management mechanisms, such as Ansible and Terraform	1.1

Using This Book to Practice

This book is composed of eight chapters. Each of the first six chapters covers a domain, with a variety of questions that can help test your real-world, scenario, and best practices networking knowledge. The final two chapters are complete practice exams that can serve as timed practice tests to help determine if you're ready for the CCNA exam.

I recommend taking the first practice exam to help identify where you may need to spend more study time and then using the domain-specific chapters to test where your domain knowledge is weak. Once you're ready, take the second practice exam to make sure you've covered all the material and are ready to attempt the CCNA exam.

The book is separated into eight chapters, six chapters to reflect the major objectives and two chapters with practice tests:

Chapter 1: Network Fundamentals (Domain 1)

Chapter 2: Network Access (Domain 2)

Chapter 3: IP Connectivity (Domain 3)

Chapter 4: IP Services (Domain 4)

Chapter 5: Security Fundamentals (Domain 5)

Chapter 6: Automation and Programmability (Domain 6)

Chapter 7: Practice Exam 1

Chapter 8: Practice Exam 2

How to Contact the Publisher

If you believe you have found a mistake in this book, please bring it to our attention. At John Wiley & Sons, we understand how important it is to provide our customers with accurate content, but even with our best efforts an error may occur.

In order to submit your possible errata, please email it to our Customer Service Team at wileysupport@wiley.com with the subject line "Possible Book Errata Submission."

Chapter

1

Network Fundamentals (Domain 1)

THE CCNA EXAM TOPICS COVERED IN THIS PRACTICE TEST INCLUDE THE FOLLOWING:

✓ **1.0 Network Fundamentals**

- **1.1** Explain the role and function of network components

  - 1.1.a Routers

  - 1.1.b Layer 2 and Layer 3 switches

  - 1.1.c Next-generation firewalls and IPS

  - 1.1.d Access points

  - 1.1.e Controllers

  - 1.1.f Endpoints

  - 1.1.g Servers

  - 1.1.h PoE

- **1.2** Describe the characteristics of network topology architectures

  - 1.2.a Two-tier

  - 1.2.b Three-tier

  - 1.2.c Spine-leaf

  - 1.2.d WAN

  - 1.2.e Small office/home office (SOHO)

  - 1.2.f On-premises and cloud

- **1.3** Compare physical interface and cabling types

  - 1.3.a Single-mode fiber, multimode fiber, copper

  - 1.3.b Connections (Ethernet shared media and point-to-point)

1.4   Identify interface and cable issues (collisions, errors, mismatch duplex, and/or speed)

1.5   Compare TCP to UDP

1.6   Configure and verify IPv4 addressing and subnetting

1.7   Describe private IPv4 addressing

1.8   Configure and verify IPv6 addressing and prefix

1.9   Compare IPv6 address types

    1.9.a Unicast (global, unique local, and link local)

    1.9.b Anycast

    1.9.c Multicast

    1.9.d Modified EUI 64

1.10   Verify IP parameters for Client OS (Windows, Mac OS, Linux)

1.11   Describe wireless principles

    1.11.a Nonoverlapping Wi-Fi channels

    1.11.b SSID

    1.11.c RF

    1.11.d Encryption

1.12   Explain virtualization fundamentals (server virtualization, containers, and VRFs)

1.13   Describe switching concepts

    1.13.a MAC learning and aging

    1.13.b Frame switching

    1.13.c Frame flooding

    1.13.d MAC address table

1. How many broadcast domains are present in the network in the following figure?

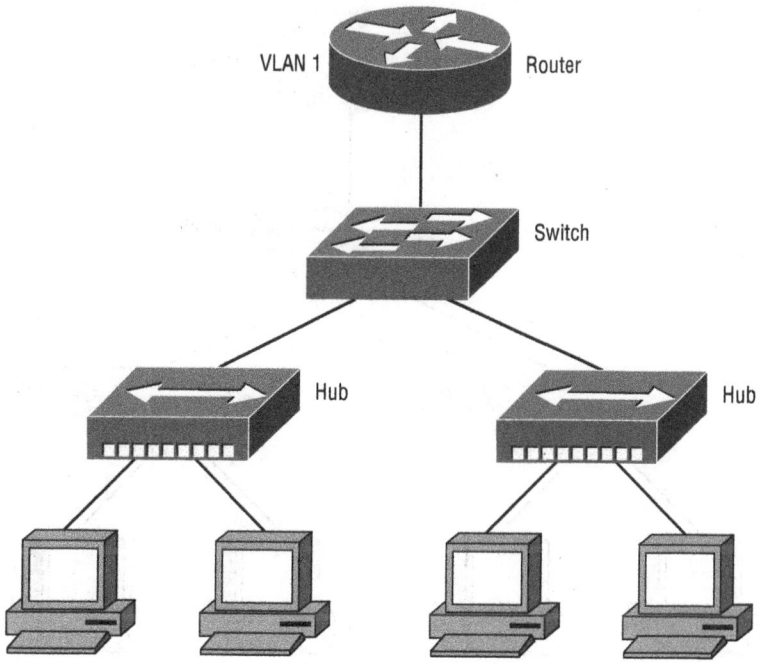

A. One broadcast domain
B. Two broadcast domains
C. Three broadcast domains
D. Seven broadcast domains

2. How many potential collision domains are present in the network in the following figure?

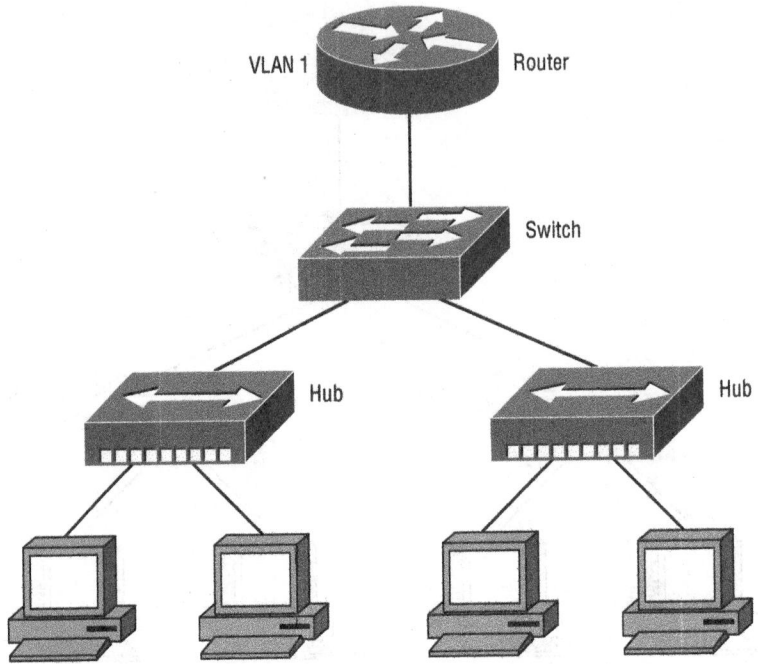

A. One collision domain

B. Two collision domains

C. Three collision domains

D. Seven collision domains

3. Which statement is true about collision domains?

A. All computers in the collision domain have the potential to have a frame collision.

B. All computers in the collision domain have the potential to receive layer 2 broadcast messages.

C. All computers in the collision domain have the potential to receive layer 3 broadcast messages.

D. All computers in the collision domain are set to 10 Mb/s full-duplex.

4. In the following figure, which would be true if the hub was replaced with a switch?

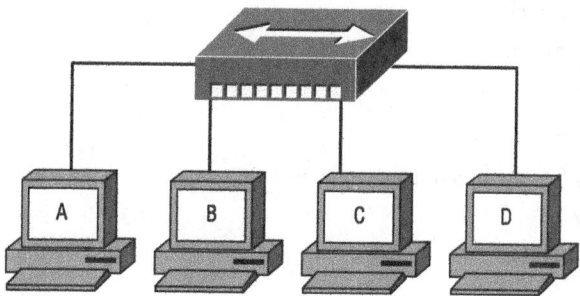

   A. The number of collision domains would increase.
   B. The number of collision domains would decrease.
   C. The number of broadcast domains would increase.
   D. The number of broadcast domains would decrease.

5. Considering the following figure, which of the following is a correct statement?

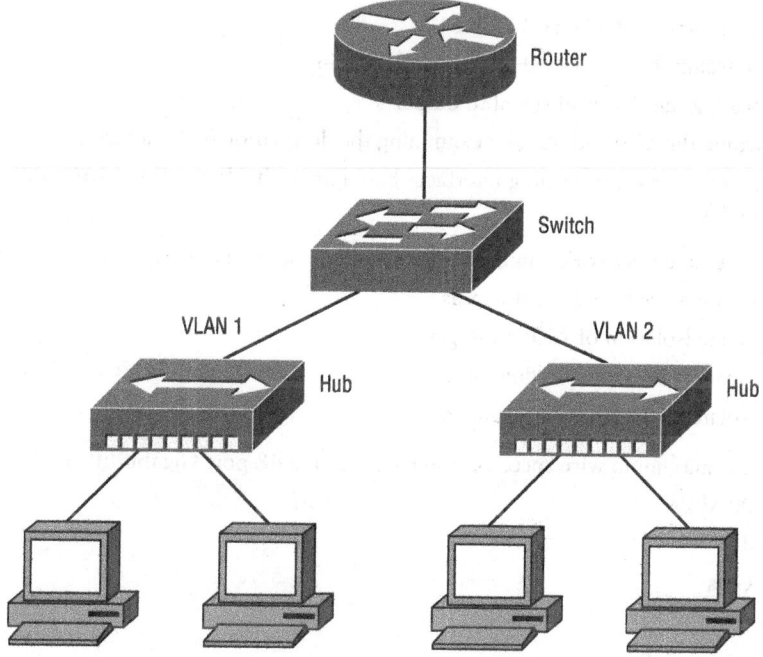

   A. One collision domain exists with one broadcast domain.
   B. Two collision domains exist with one broadcast domain.
   C. Three collision domains exist with two broadcast domains.
   D. Seven collision domains exist with two broadcast domains.

6. Which component acts as a distribution switch for the physical data center?
    A. Top of Rack switch
    B. End of Row switch
    C. Core switch
    D. Virtual switch

7. Which advantage(s) are gained using switches?
    A. Low latency
    B. Software switching
    C. High cost
    D. All of the above

8. Which is a correct statement when hubs are replaced with switches?
    A. The replacement increases collision domains.
    B. The replacement decreases collision domains.
    C. The replacement increases broadcast domains.
    D. The replacement decreases broadcast domains.

9. Which is a function of a layer 2 switch?
    A. Forwarding the data based on logical addressing
    B. Repeating the electrical signal to all ports
    C. Learning the MAC address by examining the destination MAC addresses
    D. Determining the forwarding interfaces based upon the destination MAC address and tables

10. What is a reason a network administrator would segment a network with a switch?
    A. To create more broadcast domains
    B. To create isolation of ARP messages
    C. To create fewer collision domains
    D. To isolate traffic between segments

11. What is the maximum wire speed of a single port on a 48-port Gigabit Ethernet switch?
    A. 1,000 Mb/s
    B. 2 Gb/s
    C. 48 Gb/s
    D. 96 Gb/s

12. Which statement describes the microsegmentation that a switch provides?
    A. All of the ports on the switch create a single collision domain.
    B. Each port on the switch segments broadcasts.
    C. Each port on the switch creates its own collision domain.
    D. Each port on the switch creates an isolation for layer 2 broadcasts.

13. Given the information in the following figure, which statement is true when Computer A needs to communicate with Computer F?

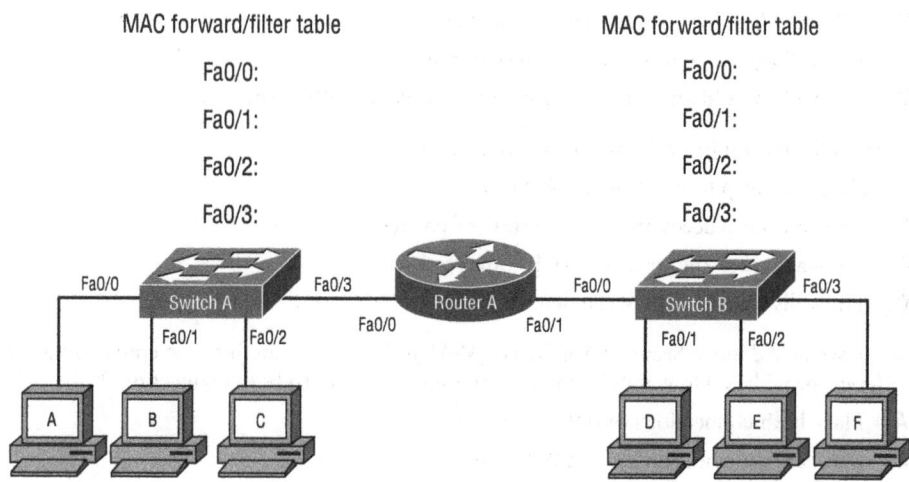

MAC forward/filter table   MAC forward/filter table

Fa0/0:   Fa0/0:

Fa0/1:   Fa0/1:

Fa0/2:   Fa0/2:

Fa0/3:   Fa0/3:

A. Switch A and Switch B will flood the frame across all ports.

B. Only Switch A will flood the frame across all ports.

C. Only Switch B will flood the frame across all ports.

D. Switch A will flood the frame across all ports; Switch B will forward traffic only to Computer F's port.

14. When firewalls are placed in a network, which zone contains Internet-facing services?

A. Outside zone

B. Enterprise network zone

C. Demilitarized zone

D. Inside zone

15. According to best practices, what is the proper placement of a firewall?

A. Only between the internal network and the Internet

B. At key security boundaries

C. In the DMZ

D. Only between the DMZ and the Internet

16. Which is a false statement about firewalls?

A. Firewalls can protect a network from external attacks.

B. Firewalls are commonly deployed to protect a network from internal attacks.

C. Firewalls can provide stateful packet inspection.

D. Firewalls can control application traffic.

17. Which of the following statements does not represent the logical management of a firewall?

   A. All physical access to the firewall should be tightly controlled.

   B. All firewall policies should be documented.

   C. Firewall logs should be regularly monitored.

   D. Firewalls should allow traffic by default and deny traffic explicitly.

18. What is the reason firewalls are considered stateful?

   A. Firewalls keep track of the zone states.

   B. Firewalls keep accounting on the state of packets.

   C. Firewalls track the state of a TCP conversation.

   D. Firewalls transition between defense states.

19. You have an Adaptive Security Appliance (ASA) and two separate Internet connections via different providers. How could you apply the same policies to both connections?

   A. Place both connections into the same zone.

   B. Place each connection into an ISP zone.

   C. Apply the same ACL to both of the interfaces.

   D. Each connection must be managed separately.

20. Why should servers be placed in the DMZ?

   A. To allow unrestricted access by Internet clients

   B. To allow access to the Internet and the internal network

   C. To allow the server to access the Internet

   D. To restrict the server to the Internet

21. Which type of device will detect but not prevent unauthorized access?

   A. Firewall

   B. IPS

   C. IDS

   D. Honeypots

22. Which term describes what it is called when more than one wireless access point (WAP) covers the same SSID?

   A. Broadcast domain

   B. Basic service set

   C. Extended service set

   D. Wireless mesh

23. Which protocol allows a Lightweight AP (LWAP) to forward data to the wired LAN?

    A. Spanning Tree Protocol (STP)

    B. Bridge Protocol Data Units (BPDUs)

    C. Orthogonal Frequency Division Multiplexing (OFDM)

    D. Control and Provisioning of Wireless Access Points (CAPWAP)

24. Which component allows wireless clients to roam between access points and maintain authentication?

    A. Basic service set

    B. Extended service set

    C. Wireless LAN controller

    D. Service set ID

25. Why would you use Multiprotocol Label Switching (MPLS) as a connectivity option?

    A. You need support for multicast packets.

    B. You need support for both IPv4 and IPv6 packets.

    C. You need a high amount of bandwidth.

    D. You require encryption.

26. What is a service-level agreement (SLA) for network connectivity?

    A. It is an agreement of bandwidth between the ISP and the customer.

    B. It is a quality of service agreement between the ISP and the customer.

    C. It is an agreement of uptime between the ISP and the customer.

    D. All of the above.

27. Which is a valid reason to implement a wireless LAN controller?

    A. Centralized authentication

    B. The use of autonomous WAPs

    C. Multiple SSIDs

    D. Multiple VLANs

28. Which allows for seamless wireless roaming between access points?

    A. Single SSID

    B. Single service set

    C. 802.11ac

    D. Wireless LAN controller

29. Which is one of the critical functions that a wireless LAN controller performs?

    A. Allows autonomous WAPs

    B. Synchronizes the WAPs with the same IOS

    C. Triangulates users for location lookups

    D. Allows for the use of all frequency channels

30. Which should be performed at the core layer?

   A. Routing

   B. Supporting clients

   C. Configuring ACLs

   D. Switching

31. Which network topology design has a centralized switch connecting all of the devices?

   A. Star topology

   B. Full-mesh topology

   C. Partial-mesh topology

   D. Hybrid topology

32. Which is a direct benefit of a full-mesh topology?

   A. Increased bandwidth

   B. Increased redundancy

   C. Decreased switch count

   D. Increased complexity

33. Where is the hybrid topology most commonly seen in the three-tier design model?

   A. Core layer

   B. Distribution layer

   C. Access layer

   D. Routing layer

34. Where is the full-mesh topology commonly seen in the three-tier design model?

   A. Core layer

   B. Distribution layer

   C. Access layer

   D. Routing layer

35. Where is the star topology most commonly seen in the three-tier design model?

   A. Core layer

   B. Distribution layer

   C. Access layer

   D. Routing layer

36. Which topology does the collapsed core layer switch use in a two-tier design model?

   A. Star topology

   B. Full-mesh topology

   C. Partial-mesh topology

   D. Hybrid topology

37. The two-tier design model contains which layer switches?

    A. Core, distribution, and access

    B. Core and distribution

    C. Distribution and access

    D. Internet, core, distribution, and access

38. You have one campus, which contains 2,000 PCs, and each edge switch will contain 25 to 40 PCs. Based on this layout, which design model should be used?

    A. Collapsed core model

    B. Three-tier model

    C. DOD model

    D. Access model

39. Which is an accurate statement about the collapsed core design concept?

    A. It is best suited for large-scale networks.

    B. It allows for better bandwidth.

    C. It is best suited for small enterprises.

    D. It bottlenecks bandwidth.

40. Access layer switches in the three-tier design model perform which task?

    A. Connect to other switches for redundancy

    B. Connect to users

    C. Connect campuses

    D. Connect to the Internet

41. Distribution layer switches in the three-tier design model perform which task?

    A. Connect to other switches for redundancy

    B. Connect to users

    C. Connect campuses

    D. Connect to the Internet

42. Core layer switches in the three-tier design model perform which task?

    A. Connect to other switches for redundancy

    B. Connect to users

    C. Connect to campuses

    D. Connect to the Internet

43. You have four campuses, each containing 500 PCs, and each edge switch will contain 20 to 30 PCs. Based on this layout, which design model should be used?

    A. Collapsed core model

    B. Three-tier model

    C. DoD model

    D. Access model

44. Which layer in the three-tier model should the redistribution of routing protocols be performed?

  A. Core layer

  B. Distribution layer

  C. Access layer

  D. Routing layer

45. Which layer in the three-tier model should the collision domains be created?

  A. Core layer

  B. Distribution layer

  C. Access layer

  D. Routing layer

46. In Cisco's three-tier architecture, the links between the distribution layer switches indicate what kind of topology?

  A. Full-mesh topology

  B. Partial-mesh topology

  C. Star topology

  D. Ring topology

47. Which technology provides for a hub-and-spoke design?

  A. E-Tree services

  B. Wireless WAN

  C. E-Line services

  D. E-LAN services

48. Which is a typical use case for hub-and-spoke WAN design?

  A. Connections for an enterprise spread over a metropolitan area

  B. Connections for an Internet service provider to its customers

  C. Connections between two or more corporate locations

  D. Connection internally inside of a service provider's network

49. Which WAN connectivity technology is always configured in a hub-and-spoke topology?

  A. IPsec

  B. MPLS

  C. DMVPN

  D. Metro Ethernet

50. Which subprotocol inside of the PPP suite is responsible for authentication?

  A. MPLS

  B. NCP

  C. LCP

  D. ACP

51. Which encapsulation protocol is used to transmit data over serial links?

A. PPPoE

B. HDLC

C. MPLS

D. X.25

52. Which authentication method used with PPP uses a nonce (random number) to hash the password and prevent replay attacks?

A. PAP

B. PSAP

C. CHAP

D. LDAP

53. Which subprotocol inside of the PPP suite facilitates multilink connections?

A. MPLS

B. NCP

C. LCP

D. ACP

54. Which is a benefit of using MLPPP?

A. Simplified layer 3 configuration

B. Does not require routing protocols

C. Does not require authentication protocols

D. Provides end-to-end encryption

55. Which configuration will create the multilink interface for an MLPPP connection to an adjoining router?

A.
```
RouterA(config)#interface multilink 1
RouterA(config-if)#encapsulation ppp
RouterA(config-if)#ppp multilink
RouterA(config-if)#ip address 192.168.1.1 255.255.255.0
RouterA(config-if)#ppp multilink group 1
```

B.
```
RouterA(config)#interface multilink 1
RouterA(config-if)#ppp multilink
RouterA(config-if)#ip address 192.168.1.1 255.255.255.0
```

C.
```
RouterA(config)#interface multilink 1
RouterA(config-if)#encapsulation ppp multilink
```

D.
```
RouterA(config)#interface multilink 1
RouterA(config-if)#ip address 192.168.1.1 255.255.255.0
RouterA(config-if)#ppp multilink group 1
```

56. You need to set up PPP authentication for RouterA. The adjoining router is named RouterB, and both routers will have a matching password of *cisco*. Which commands will achieve this?

- **A.** `RouterA(config)#username RouterA password cisco`

  `RouterA(config)#interface serial 0/1/0`

  `RouterA(config-if)#ppp authentication chap pap`

- **B.** `RouterA(config)#username RouterB password cisco`

  `RouterA(config)#interface serial 0/1/0`

  `RouterA(config-if)#ppp authentication chap pap`

- **C.** `RouterA(config)#username RouterA cisco`

  `RouterA(config)#interface serial 0/1/0`

  `RouterA(config-if)#ppp authentication chap pap`

- **D.** `RouterA(config)#username RouterA password cisco`

  `RouterA(config)#interface serial 0/1/0`

  `RouterA(config-if)#authentication chap pap`

57. In the following figure, what does the line LCP closed mean?

```
RouterA#show interface s0/3/0
Serial0/0 is up, line protocol is down
  Hardware is PowerQUICC Serial0/0
  Internet address is 10.0.1.1/24
  MT 1500 bytes, BW 1544 kbit, DLY 20000 usec,
  reliability 233/255. txload 1/255, rxload 1/255
  Encapsulation PPP, loopback not set
  Keepalive set (10 sec)
  LCP Closed
  Closed IPCP, CDPCP
```

- **A.** The LCP process has completed.
- **B.** The router does not have an IP address configured.
- **C.** The serial line is disconnected.
- **D.** The LCP process has not completed.

58. You have obtained an ADSL circuit at a remote office for central office connectivity. What will you need to configure on the remote office router?

- **A.** Metro Ethernet
- **B.** PPPoE
- **C.** PPP
- **D.** MPLS

59. Amazon Web Services (AWS) and Microsoft Azure are examples of what?

- **A.** Public cloud providers
- **B.** Private cloud providers
- **C.** Hybrid cloud providers
- **D.** Dynamic cloud providers

60. You are looking to create a fault-tolerant colocation site for your servers at a cloud provider. Which type of cloud provider would you be searching for?

   A. PaaS

   B. IaaS

   C. SaaS

   D. BaaS

61. Which is not a NIST criterion for cloud computing?

   A. Resource pooling

   B. Rapid elasticity

   C. Automated billing

   D. Measured service

62. Which term describes the type of cloud an internal IT department hosting virtualization for a company would host?

   A. Public cloud

   B. Elastic cloud

   C. Private cloud

   D. Internal cloud

63. What is the role of a cloud services catalog?

   A. It defines the capabilities for the cloud.

   B. It defines the available VMs for creation in the cloud.

   C. It defines the available VMs running in the cloud.

   D. It defines the drivers for VMs in the cloud.

64. A hosted medical records service is an example of which cloud model?

   A. PaaS

   B. IaaS

   C. SaaS

   D. BaaS

65. A hosted environment that allows you to write and run programs without having to manage the underlying operating system is an example of which cloud model?

   A. PaaS

   B. IaaS

   C. SaaS

   D. BaaS

66. Which cloud connectivity method allows for seamless transition between public clouds?

    A. MPLS VPN

    B. Internet VPN

    C. Intercloud exchange

    D. Private WAN

67. Which option is not a consideration when converting to an email SaaS application if the majority of users are internal?

    A. Internal bandwidth usage

    B. External bandwidth usage

    C. Location of the users

    D. Branch office connectivity to the Internet

68. You purchase a VM on a public cloud and plan to create a VPN tunnel to the cloud provider. Your IP network is 172.16.0.0/12, and the provider has assigned an IP address in the 10.0.0.0/8 network. What virtual network function (VNF) will you need from the provider to communicate with the VM?

    A. Virtual switch

    B. Virtual firewall

    C. Virtual router

    D. Another IP scheme at the provider

69. Which protocol would you use to synchronize the VM in the public cloud with an internal time source at your premises?

    A. DNS

    B. rsync

    C. NTP

    D. VPN

70. Which cable type would you use to connect a switch to a switch?

    A. Straight-through cable

    B. Crossover cable

    C. Rolled cable

    D. Shielded cable

71. Which fiber optic standard utilizes a 50 micron core?

    A. UTP

    B. Multimode

    C. Single-mode

    D. STP

72. Which type of cable would be used to connect a computer to a switch for management of the switch?

   A. Straight-through cable

   B. Crossover cable

   C. Rollover cable

   D. Shielded cable

73. Which specification for connectivity is currently used in data centers for lower cost and simplicity?

   A. 10GBase-T

   B. 40GBase-T

   C. 10GBase-CX

   D. 100GBase-TX

74. If you had an existing installation of Cat5e on your campus, what is the highest speed you could run?

   A. 10 Mb/s

   B. 100 Mb/s

   C. 1 Gb/s

   D. 10 Gb/s

75. Which statement is correct about straight-through cables and crossover cables?

   A. Crossover cables are wired with pins 1 through 8 on one side and 8 through 1 on the other side.

   B. Crossover cables are wired with the 568B specification on both sides.

   C. Straight-through cables are wired with the 568B specification on one side and the 568A specification on the other side.

   D. Crossover cables are wired with the 568B specification on one side and the 568A specification on the other side.

76. In the following figure, PPP is negotiating the username and password for the adjacent router. You are debugging PPP on the local router. What needs to be done to fix the problem?

```
*Feb  3 12:23:57.559: Se0:3 PAP: I AUTH-REQ id 25 Len 18 from "PAPUSER"
*Feb  3 12:23:57.559: Se0:3 PPP: Phase is FORWARDING
*Feb  3 12:23:57.559: Se0:3 PPP: Phase is AUTHENTICATING
*Feb  3 12:23:57.559: Se0:3 PAP: Authenticating peer PAPUSER
*Feb  3 12:23:57.559: Se0:3 PAP: O AUTH-NAK id 25 Len 32 msg is
```

   A. Configure PAP on this router.

   B. Configure PPP encapsulation on this router.

   C. Verify that the local username matches the adjacent router's hostname and the passwords match.

   D. Verify that the remote username matches the adjacent router's hostname and the passwords match.

77. Which device is responsible for adding the label to an MPLS packet?

    A. Customer edge (CE) router

    B. Provider edge (PE) router

    C. Customer premise switch

    D. Label switch routers (LSR)

78. What is the term that defines the end of the provider's responsibility and the beginning of the customer's responsibility?

    A. CPE

    B. CO

    C. Local loop

    D. Demarc

79. What is the speed of a DS1 connection in North America?

    A. 2.048 Mb/s

    B. 44.736 Mb/s

    C. 1.544 Mb/s

    D. 622.08 Mb/s

80. Which command would you run to diagnose a possible line speed or duplex issue?

    A. `show speed`

    B. `show duplex`

    C. `show interface status`

    D. `show diagnostics`

81. In the following figure, what can you conclude about the interface or node?

```
Switch#sh int fastEthernet 0/2
FastEthernet0/2 is down, line protocol is down (disabled)
  Hardware is Lance, address is 000a.f36c.1502 (bia 000a.f36c.1502)
[output cut]
   956 packets input, 193351 bytes, 0 no buffer
   Received 956 broadcasts, 0 runts, 0 giants, 0 throttles
   0 input errors, 0 CRC, 0 frame, 0 overrun, 0 ignored, 0 abort
   0 watchdog, 0 multicast, 0 pause input
   0 input packets with dribble condition detected
   2357 packets output, 263570 bytes, 0 underruns
   0 output errors, 0 collisions, 10 interface resets
   0 babbles, 457 late collision, 0 deferred
   0 lost carrier, 0 no carrier
   0 output buffer failures, 0 output buffers swapped out
```

    A. The interface is shut down.

    B. The interface is negotiated at half-duplex.

    C. There is a duplex mismatch on the interface.

    D. The cabling is shorted on the interface.

82. In the following figure, what can you conclude about the interface or node?

```
Switch#sh interfaces fastEthernet 0/2
FastEthernet0/2 is administratively down, line protocol is down (disabled)
  Hardware is Lance, address is 000a.f36c.1502 (bia 000a.f36c.1502)
[output cut]
    956 packets input, 193351 bytes, 0 no buffer
    Received 956 broadcasts, 0 runts, 0 giants, 0 throttles
    0 input errors, 0 CRC, 0 frame, 0 overrun, 0 ignored, 0 abort
    0 watchdog, 0 multicast, 0 pause input
    0 input packets with dribble condition detected
    2357 packets output, 263570 bytes, 0 underruns
    0 output errors, 0 collisions, 10 interface resets
    0 babbles, 0 late collision, 0 deferred
    0 lost carrier, 0 no carrier
    0 output buffer failures, 0 output buffers swapped out
```

A. The interface is shut down.

B. The interface is negotiated at half-duplex.

C. There is a duplex mismatch on the interface.

D. The cabling is shorted on the interface.

83. You have just resolved a problem and now need to monitor the problem on the interface. How would you reset the error counts for a single interface?

A. `reset counters interface fast 0/1`

B. `clear interface fast 0/1`

C. `clear counters interface fast 0/1`

D. `clear statistics interface fast 0/1`

84. In the following figure, what can you conclude about the interface or node?

```
Switch#sh interfaces fastEthernet 0/1
FastEthernet0/1 is down, line protocol is down (disabled)
  Hardware is Lance, address is 000a.f36c.1501 (bia 000a.f36c.1501)
[output cut]
    956 packets input, 193351 bytes, 0 no buffer
    Received 956 broadcasts, 0 runts, 0 giants, 0 throttles
    0 input errors, 0 CRC, 0 frame, 0 overrun, 0 ignored, 0 abort
    0 watchdog, 0 multicast, 0 pause input
    0 input packets with dribble condition detected
    2357 packets output, 263570 bytes, 0 underruns
    0 output errors, 0 collisions, 10 interface resets
    0 babbles, 0 late collision, 0 deferred
    0 lost carrier, 0 no carrier
    0 output buffer failures, 0 output buffers swapped out
```

A. The interface is shut down.

B. The interface is negotiated at half-duplex.

C. The interface is operating normally.

D. The cable is disconnected for the node.

85. A router is connected to the switch via a Fast Ethernet interface. Intermittently you experience an outage. What should be done first to remedy the problem? Refer to the following figure.

```
 |
interface FastEthernet0/2
  switchport mode access
  switchport access vlan 5
  switchport nonegotiate
[output cut]
```

   A. The speed and duplex should be set statically.

   B. Change the VLAN to a less crowded VLAN.

   C. Change the switchport mode to a trunk.

   D. Set the switchport to auto-negotiate.

86. In the following figure, what can you conclude about the interface or node?

```
Switch#sh int fastEthernet 0/2
FastEthernet0/2 is up, line protocol is up (connected)
  Hardware is Lance, address is 000a.f36c.1502 (bia 000a.f36c.1502)
BW 10000 Kbit, DLY 1000 usec,
    reliability 255/255, txload 220/255, rxload 80/255
  Encapsulation ARPA, loopback not set
  Keepalive set (10 sec)
  Full-duplex, 10Mb/s
[output cut]
    956 packets input, 193351 bytes, 0 no buffer
    Received 956 broadcasts, 0 runts, 0 giants, 0 throttles
    0 input errors, 0 CRC, 0 frame, 0 overrun, 0 ignored, 0 abort
    0 watchdog, 0 multicast, 0 pause input
    0 input packets with dribble condition detected
    2357 packets output, 263570 bytes, 0 underruns
    0 output errors, 0 collisions, 10 interface resets
    0 babbles, 0 late collision, 0 deferred
    0 lost carrier, 0 no carrier
    0 output buffer failures, 0 output buffers swapped out
```

   A. There are no problems with the interface.

   B. The interface is auto-negotiating speed and duplex.

   C. There are a large number of broadcasts.

   D. The node needs a faster network interface.

87. You have statically set an interface to 100 Mb/s full-duplex. However, the device you are plugging in will not work. Which command(s) would you use to set speed and duplex back to auto-negotiate?

   A. `speed auto`

       `duplex auto`

   B. `speed autonegotiate`

       `duplex autonegotiate`

   C. `switchport autonegotiate`

   D. `interface autonegotiate`

88. You have auto-negotiation turned off on the node, but it is turned on at the switch's interface connecting the node. The interface is a 10/100/1000 Mb/s interface and the node is 100 Mb/s full-duplex. What will the outcome be when you plug in the node?

  A. The switch interface will be set to the 100 Mb/s full-duplex.

  B. The switch interface will be set to the 100 Mb/s half-duplex.

  C. The switch interface will be set to the 10 Mb/s full-duplex.

  D. The switch interface will be set to the 10 Mb/s half-duplex.

89. You plug a 100 Mb/s hub into a switch. What is the expected outcome?

  A. The switch interface will be set to the 100 Mb/s full-duplex.

  B. The switch interface will be set to the 100 Mb/s half-duplex.

  C. The switch interface will be set to the 10 Mb/s full-duplex.

  D. The switch interface will be set to the 10 Mb/s half-duplex.

90. You want to see the status of all speed and duplex negotiations for all interfaces. Which command would you use?

  A. `show run`

  B. `show interfaces counters`

  C. `show interfaces status`

  D. `show counters interfaces`

91. Flow control can typically be found at which layer of the OSI?

  A. Transport layer

  B. Network layer

  C. Data Link layer

  D. Session layer

92. Which protocol requires the programmer to deal with lost segments?

  A. SSL

  B. TCP

  C. UDP

  D. NMS

93. Which is a correct statement about the Transmission Control Protocol (TCP)?

  A. TCP is a connectionless protocol.

  B. TCP allows for error correction.

  C. TCP is faster than UDP.

  D. TCP allows for retransmission of lost segments.

94. Which statement correctly describes what happens when a web browser initiates a request to a web server?

  A. The sender allocates a port dynamically above 1024 and associates it with the request.

  B. The receiver allocates a port dynamically above 1024 and associates it with the request.

  C. The sender allocates a port dynamically below 1024 and associates it with the request.

  D. The receiver allocates a port dynamically below 1024 and associates it with the request.

95. Which protocol and port number is associated with SMTP?

  A. UDP/69

  B. UDP/68

  C. UDP/53

  D. TCP/25

96. How does TCP guarantee delivery of segments to the receiver?

  A. Via the destination port

  B. TCP checksums

  C. Window size

  D. Sequence and acknowledgment numbers

97. When a programmer decides to use UDP as a transport protocol, what is a decision factor?

  A. Redundancy of acknowledgment is not needed.

  B. Guaranteed delivery of segments is required.

  C. Windowing flow control is required.

  D. A virtual circuit is required.

98. Which mechanism allows for programs running on a server (daemons) to listen for requests through the process called binding?

  A. Headers

  B. Port numbers

  C. MAC address

  D. Checksums

99. Which is a correct statement about sliding windows used with TCP?

  A. The window size is established during the three-way handshake.

  B. Sliding windows allow for data of different lengths to be padded.

  C. It allows TCP to indicate which upper-layer protocol created the request.

  D. It allows the router to see the segment as urgent data.

100. Why does DNS use UDP for queries?

    A. DNS requires acknowledgment of the request for auditing.

    B. The requests require flow control of UDP.

    C. DNS requests are usually small and do not require connections setup.

    D. DNS requires a temporary virtual circuit.

101. What is required before TCP can begin sending segments?

    A. Three-way handshake

    B. Port agreement

    C. Sequencing of segments

    D. Acknowledgment of segments

102. Which class is the IP address 172.23.23.2?

    A. Class A

    B. Class B

    C. Class C

    D. Class D

103. Which is the default subnet mask for a Class A address?

    A. 255.0.0.0

    B. 255.255.0.0

    C. 255.255.255.0

    D. 255.255.255.255

104. Which address is a multicast IP address?

    A. 221.22.20.2

    B. 223.3.40.2

    C. 238.20.80.4

    D. 240.34.22.12

105. Which is true of the IP address 135.20.255.255?

    A. It is a Class A address.

    B. It is a broadcast address.

    C. It is the default gateway address.

    D. It has a default mask of 255.0.0.0.

106. What is the CIDR notation for a subnet mask of 255.255.240.0?

    A. /19

    B. /20

    C. /22

    D. /28

107. You have been given an IP address network of 203.23.23.0. You are asked to subnet it for two hosts per network. What is the subnet mask you will need to use to maximize networks?

- **A.** 255.255.255.252
- **B.** 255.255.255.248
- **C.** 255.255.255.240
- **D.** 255.255.255.224

108. You have been given an IP address network of 213.43.53.0. You are asked to subnet it for 22 hosts per network. What is the subnet mask you will need to use to maximize networks?

- **A.** 255.255.255.252
- **B.** 255.255.255.248
- **C.** 255.255.255.240
- **D.** 255.255.255.224

109. Which valid IP is in the same network as 192.168.32.61/26?

- **A.** 192.168.32.59
- **B.** 192.168.32.63
- **C.** 192.168.32.64
- **D.** 192.168.32.72

110. You are setting up a network in which you need 15 subnetworks. You have been given a network address of 153.20.0.0, and you need to maximize the number of hosts in each network. Which subnet mask will you use?

- **A.** 255.255.224.0
- **B.** 255.255.240.0
- **C.** 255.255.248.0
- **D.** 255.255.252.0

111. An ISP gives you an IP address of 209.183.160.45/30 to configure your end of the serial connection. Which IP address will be on the side at the ISP?

- **A.** 209.183.160.43/30
- **B.** 209.183.160.44/30
- **C.** 209.183.160.46/30
- **D.** 209.183.160.47/30

112. In the following figure, what needs to be changed for Computer A to successfully communicate with Computer B (assume the least amount of effort to fix the problem)?

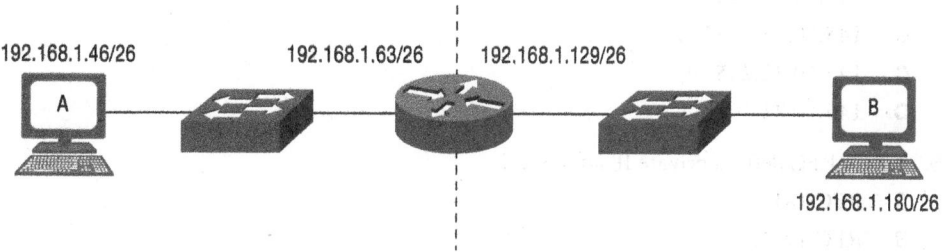

192.168.1.46/26   192.168.1.63/26   192.168.1.129/26

A   B

192.168.1.180/26

    A. Computer A needs to have its IP address changed.

    B. Computer B needs to have its IP address changed.

    C. The default gateway IP address for Computer A needs to be changed.

    D. The default gateway IP address for Computer B needs to be changed.

113. In the following figure, what needs to be changed for Computer A to successfully communicate with Computer B (assume the least amount of effort to fix the problem)?

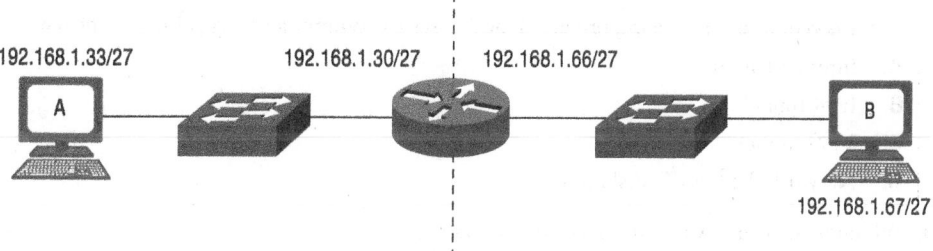

192.168.1.33/27   192.168.1.30/27   192.168.1.66/27

A   B

192.168.1.67/27

    A. Computer A needs to have its IP address changed.

    B. Computer B needs to have its IP address changed.

    C. The default gateway IP address for Computer A needs to be changed.

    D. The default gateway IP address for Computer B needs to be changed.

114. Which subnet does host 131.50.39.23/21 belong to?

    A. 131.50.39.0/21

    B. 131.50.32.0/21

    C. 131.50.16.0/21

    D. 131.50.8.0/21

115. A computer has an IP address of 145.50.23.1/22. What is the broadcast address for that computer?

  A. 145.50.254.255

  B. 145.50.255.255

  C. 145.50.22.255

  D. 145.50.23.255

116. Which RFC defines private IP addresses?

  A. RFC 1819

  B. RFC 1911

  C. RFC 1918

  D. RFC 3030

117. What is a major reason to use private IP addressing?

  A. It allows for the conservation of public IP addresses.

  B. Since private IP addresses are nonroutable on the Internet, they are secure.

  C. It keeps communications private.

  D. It allows easier setup than public IP addresses.

118. What is required when using private IP addresses to communicate with Internet hosts?

  A. Internet router

  B. IPv4 tunnel

  C. VPN tunnel

  D. Network Address Translation

119. Which is the Class A private IP address range?

  A. 10.0.0.0/8

  B. 10.0.0.0/12

  C. 172.16.0.0/12

  D. 10.0.0.0/10

120. Which is the Class B private IP address range?

  A. 10.0.0.0/8

  B. 10.0.0.0/12

  C. 172.16.0.0/12

  D. 10.0.0.0/10

121. Which is the Class C private IP address range?

  A. 192.168.1.0/24

  B. 192.168.0.0/24

  C. 192.168.0.0/16

  D. 192.168.0.0/12

122. You plug a laptop into a network jack. When you examine the IP address, you see 169.254.23.43. What can you conclude?

A. The network jack is not working.

B. Your laptop has a static IP address configured.

C. The network is configured properly.

D. The DHCP server is down.

123. You want to put a web server online for public use. Which IP address would you use?

A. 192.168.34.34

B. 172.31.54.3

C. 10.55.33.32

D. 198.168.55.45

124. Who is the governing body that distributes public IP addresses?

A. IANA

B. RFC

C. IAB

D. IETF

125. Which protocol allows multicast switches to join computers to the multicast group?

A. ICMP

B. IGMP

C. IPMI

D. IPGRP

126. Why is IPv6 needed in the world today?

A. It does not require NAT to operate.

B. The IPv4 public address space is exhausted.

C. IPv4 is considered legacy, and IPv6 is the replacement.

D. IPv6 does not support subnetting.

127. How many bits is an IPv6 address?

A. 32 bits

B. 64 bits

C. 128 bits

D. 256 bits

128. You have two facilities and both use IPv6 addressing internally. However, both facilities are connected to the Internet via IPv4. What is one recommended method you can use to communicate between the facilities over the Internet?

   A. Dedicated leased line

   B. Frame Relay

   C. Dual stack

   D. 6to4 tunnel

129. Which command is required on a router to support IPv6 static addressing?

   A. `ipv6 address`

   B. `ipv6 routing`

   C. `ipv6 enable`

   D. `ipv6 unicast-routing`

130. Which command would you use on an interface to set the IPv6 address?

   A. `ip address 2001:0db8:85aa:0000:0000:8a2e:1343:1337`

   B. `ipv6 address 2001:0db8:85aa:0000:0000:8a2e:1343:1337`

   C. `ip address 2001:0db8:85aa:0000:0000:8a2e:1343:1337/64`

   D. `ipv6 address 2001:0db8:85aa:0000:0000:8a2e:1343:1337/64`

131. Which field of the IPv6 header allows for a dual-stack host to decide which stack to process the packet in?

   A. Version field

   B. Flow label

   C. Source address

   D. Destination address

132. You want to see all of the interfaces on a router configured with IPv6. Which command would you use?

   A. `show ipv6 interfaces brief`

   B. `show ip interfaces brief`

   C. `show interfaces status`

   D. `show ip addresses`

133. Which is a valid shortened IPv6 address for 2001:0db8:0000:0000:0000:

8a2e:0000:1337?

   A. 2001:db8:0000::8a2e::1337

   B. 2001:db8:::8a2e:0000:1337

   C. 2001:db8::8a2e::1337

   D. 2001:db8::8a2e:0:1337

134. Which is the correct expansion for the IPv6 address 2001::456:0:ada4?

   A. 2001:0000:0000:0456:0000:ada4

   B. 2001:0000:0000:0000:456:0000:ada4

   C. 2001:0000:0000:0000:0000:0456:0000:ada4

   D. 2001:0000:0000:0000:0456:0000:0000:ada4

135. In the IPv6 address 2001.0db8:1234:0016:0023:8080:2345:88ab/64, what is the subnet quartet?

   A. 1234

   B. 0016

   C. 0023

   D. 8080

136. What is the network prefix for the IPv6 address 2001.db8::8080:2345:88ab/64?

   A. 2001:db8::/64

   B. 2001:0db8:8080:2345/64

   C. 2001:0db8:0000:8080/64

   D. 2001:0db8:0000:2345/64

137. You need to verify connectivity to the IPv6 address fc00:0000:0000:0000:0000:0000:0000:0004. Which command would you use?

   A. `ping fc00::4`

   B. `ping fc::4`

   C. `ping ipv6 fc00::4`

   D. `ping ipv6 fc::4`

138. Which method is used to direct communications to a single host?

   A. Unicast

   B. Broadcast

   C. Multicast

   D. Anycast

139. Which protocol uses broadcasting at layer 3?

   A. ARP

   B. DHCP

   C. IGMP

   D. SNMP

140. Which method is used to direct communications to all computers in a subnet?

   A. Unicast

   B. Broadcast

   C. Multicast

   D. Anycast

141. You work for an ISP. The American Registry for Internet Numbers (ARIN) has given you the 2001:0db8:8/34 IP address block. How many /48 blocks can you assign to your customers?

   A. 32,768

   B. 16,384

   C. 8,192

   D. 4,096

142. What protocol/process in IPv6 replaces the IPv4 ARP process?

   A. NDP (NS/NA)

   B. DAD (NS/NA)

   C. SLAAC (RS/RA)

   D. ARPv6 (NS/NA)

143. Which address is a global unicast address?

   A. fe80:db80:db01:ada0:1112::1

   B. 2005:acd:234:1132::43

   C. fd00:ac34:34b:8064:234a::7

   D. ff00:101:4ab0:3b3e::10

144. For global unicast addresses, which part of the address is allotted by the regional Internet registry (RIR) for the corresponding region?

   A. First 23 bits

   B. First 32 bits

   C. First 48 bits

   D. First 64 bits

145. Which address is a unique local address?

   A. fe80:db80:db01:ada0:1112::1

   B. 2005:acd:234:1132::43

   C. fd00:ac34:34b:8064:234a::7

   D. ff00::10

146. Which IPv6 address type is similar to IPv4 RFC 1918 addresses?

    A. Link-local addresses

    B. Global unicast addresses

    C. EUI-64 addresses

    D. Anycast addresses

147. Which address is a link-local address?

    A. fe80:db80:db01:ada0:1112::1

    B. 2005:acd:234:1132::43

    C. fd00:ac34:34b:8064:234a::7

    D. ff00:101:4ab0:3b3e::10

148. Which method is used to direct communications to the IP address that is closest to the source?

    A. Unicast

    B. Broadcast

    C. Multicast

    D. Anycast

149. Which command would configure a single anycast address on a router's interface?

    A. `ip address 2001:db8:1:1:1::12/64`

    B. `ipv6 address 2001:db8:1:1:1::12/64 anycast`

    C. `ipv6 anycast address 2001:db8:1:1:1::12/128`

    D. `ipv6 address 2001:db8:1:1:1::12/128 anycast`

150. Which method is used to direct communications to a group of computers that subscribe to the transmission?

    A. Unicast

    B. Broadcast

    C. Multicast

    D. Anycast

151. Which address is a multicast address?

    A. fe80:db80:db01:ada0:1112::1

    B. 2005:acd:234:1132::43

    C. fd00:ac34:34b:8064:234a::7

    D. ff00::10

152. You are using the EUI-64 method of allocating the host portion of the IPv6 addresses. The MAC address of the host is f423:5634:5623. Which is the correct IP address that will be calculated for a network ID of fd00:1:1::?

   A. fd00:0001:0001:0000:f623:56ff:fe34:5623/64

   B. fd00:0001:0001:0000:f423:56ff:fe34:5623/64

   C. fd00:0001:0001:0000:fffe:f623:5634:5623/64

   D. fd00:0001:0001:0000:f623:56ff:ff34:5623/64

153. Which address is a EUI-64 generated address?

   A. 2001:db8:33::f629:58fe:ff35:5893/64

   B. fd00:4:33::f680:45ca:ac3b:5a73/64

   C. 2001:db8:aa::f654:56ff:fe34:a633/64

   D. 2001:db8:17:fffe:f623::ff34:5623/64

154. Which command would use the MAC address for the host portion of the IPv6 address on a router interface?

   A. `ip address eui-64 2001:db8:1234::/64`

   B. `ip address 2001:db8:1234::/64 mac-address`

   C. `ipv6 address 2001:db8:1234::/64 eui-64`

   D. `ipv6 address 2001:db8:1234::/64 mac`

155. Which command on Windows will allow you to verify your IP address, subnet mask, default gateway, and MAC address?

   A. `ipconfig`

   B. `ipstatus`

   C. `ipconfig /all`

   D. `hostname`

156. Which command on Windows will allow you to verify the path a packet gets routed through on the network?

   A. `tracert 198.78.34.2`

   B. `ping 198.78.34.2`

   C. `traceroute 198.78.34.2`

   D. `route print`

157. Your DNS administrator has changed the DNS entry for RouterB. You clear the DNS cache on RouterA and ping `routerb.sybex.com` from RouterA, but you still ping the original address prior to the change. All other DNS addresses work fine and the entry resolves correctly on your laptop. What is the problem?

   A. The router is configured to the wrong DNS server.

   B. RouterA has a host entry configured.

   C. The DNS administrator made an error.

   D. The domain name of the router is incorrect.

158. You have configured a router to point to the DNS server with the IP address 10.2.2.2 and configured the domain name of `sybex.com`. However, you cannot resolve the host `routerb.sybex.com`. Which Windows command will help you verify the DNS name resolution?

    A. `ping routerb.sybex.com`

    B. `tracert routerb.sybex.com`

    C. `nslookup routerb.sybex.com`

    D. `dig routerb.sybex.com`

159. Which Windows command will allow you to see the DHCP server that has configured the client computer with an IP address?

    A. `ipconfig`

    B. `ipconfig /all`

    C. `ipconfig /showclassid`

    D. `ipstatus`

160. You have configured a DHCP server on a router interface. You test a Windows client and receive the address 169.254.24.56. What can you conclude?

    A. You have successfully configured the scope of 169.254.24.0/24.

    B. The client had a static IP address of 169.254.24.0/24 configured.

    C. The DHCP server is not configured properly and the client has configured itself with a link-local address.

    D. The DHCP server is configured for APIPA.

161. Which is the contention method 802.11 wireless uses?

    A. CSMA/CA

    B. CSMA/CD

    C. DSSS

    D. OFDM

162. In the 2.4 GHz spectrum for 802.11, which channels are nonoverlapping?

    A. Channels 1, 3, and 11

    B. Channels 1, 3, and 6

    C. Channels 1, 6, and 11

    D. Channels 1 through 6

163. You are designing a wireless network for an office building. The building has a large number of tenants who utilize wireless already. Which protocol will least likely overlap with wireless channels the tenants are currently using?

    A. 802.11b

    B. 802.11g

    C. 802.11n

    D. 802.11ac

164. Which wireless encryption protocol uses a 24-bit initialization vector?

 A. WPA

 B. WEP

 C. WPA2

 D. WPA3

165. Which wireless standard does not use a preshared key for authentication?

 A. WPA

 B. WPA2

 C. WEP

 D. WPA2 Enterprise

166. When designing a wireless network, which would be a compelling reason to use 5 GHz?

 A. 5 GHz can go further.

 B. 5 GHz allows for more clients.

 C. There are 24 nonoverlapping channels.

 D. There is less interference on 5 GHz.

167. Which wireless frequency spectrum is shared with Bluetooth?

 A. 900 MHz

 B. 2.4 GHz

 C. 5 GHz

 D. All of the above

168. Which 802.11 standard functions strictly on 2.4 GHz?

 A. 802.11g

 B. 802.11n

 C. 802.11a

 D. 802.11ac

169. Which allows for the distribution of compute resources such as CPU and RAM to be distributed over several operating systems?

 A. Physical server

 B. Hypervisor

 C. Virtual machine

 D. Virtual network

170. Which option describes a VM best?

 A. An operating system that is running directly on hardware

 B. An operating system that is running with dedicated hardware

 C. An operating system that is running on reduced hardware features

 D. An operating system that is decoupled from the hardware

171. What is the physical hardware used in virtualization called?

    A. Host

    B. VM

    C. Hypervisor

    D. Guest

172. Which component connects the VM NIC to the physical network?

    A. vNIC

    B. Trunk

    C. Virtual switch

    D. NX-OS

173. Which of the following is a virtual network function (VNF) device?

    A. Virtual switch

    B. Virtual firewall

    C. Database server

    D. File server

174. You need to scale out some web servers to accommodate load. Which method would you use?

    A. Add vCPUs

    B. Add vRAM

    C. Add DNS

    D. Add SLBaaS

175. Which is a correct statement about MAC addresses?

    A. Organizationally unique identifiers (OUIs) create a unique MAC address.

    B. The first 24 bits of a MAC address are specified by the vendor.

    C. The IEEE is responsible for MAC address uniqueness.

    D. If the I/G bit is set to 1, then the frame identifies a broadcast or multicast.

176. Which command would you use to diagnose a problem with frames that are not getting forwarded to the destination node on a switch?

    A. `show route`

    B. `show mac address-table`

    C. `show mac table`

    D. `show interface`

177. Which mechanism does a switch employ to stop switching loops?

    A. Port channels

    B. Spanning Tree Protocol (STP)

    C. Ether channels

    D. Trunks

178. Which is a consequence of not using loop avoidance with layer 2 switching?

    A. Duplicate unicast frames

    B. Broadcast storms

    C. MAC address thrashing

    D. All of the above

179. Which switching method checks the CRC checksum as the frame is received by the switch?

    A. Cut-through mode

    B. Frag-free mode

    C. Store-and-forward mode

    D. Fast switching

180. Which switch mode operation reads only the first 64 bytes before making a switching decision?

    A. Cut-through mode

    B. Fragment-free mode

    C. Store-and-forward mode

    D. Fast switching

181. A user is complaining of extremely long logon times. Using the following figure, what can you conclude?

```
Switch#sh interfaces fastEthernet 0/1
FastEthernet0/1 is up, line protocol is up (connected)
  Hardware is Lance, address is 000a.f36c.1501 (bia 000a.f36c.1501)
[output cut]
     956 packets input, 193351 bytes, 0 no buffer
     Received 956 broadcasts, 0 runts, 0 giants, 0 throttles
     0 input errors, 0 CRC, 235 frame, 0 overrun, 0 ignored, 0 abort
     0 watchdog, 0 multicast, 0 pause input
     0 input packets with dribble condition detected
     2357 packets output, 263570 bytes, 0 underruns
     0 output errors, 212 collisions, 10 interface resets
     0 babbles, 0 late collision, 0 deferred
     0 lost carrier, 0 no carrier
     0 output buffer failures, 0 output buffers swapped out
```

    A. The connection to the computer needs to be upgraded to 100 Mb/s.

    B. The connection to the computer has wiring issues.

    C. The NIC in the attached computer is going bad and needs replacement.

    D. The interface or computer is running at half-duplex.

182. How are MAC addresses learned and associated with the port?

    A. Destination MAC address learning

    B. Source MAC address learning

    C. Port listen/learning

    D. Frame type learning

183. In the following figure, what will happen if the computers on ports Fa0/1 (Computer A) and Fa0/4 (Computer B) are swapped?

```
Mac Address Table
---------------------------------

Vlan  Mac Address       Type      Ports
----  -----------------  --------  ----------
1     0001.6c58.486e    STATIC    Fa0/1
1     0001.6c58.5606    DYNAMIC   Fa0/2
1     0001.6c58.486e    DYNAMIC   Fa0/3
1     0001.6c58.5406    DYNAMIC   Fa0/4
```

A. Computer A's frames will only be forwarded to port Fa0/1.

B. Computer A's frames will be forwarded to ports Fa0/1 and Fa0/4.

C. Computer A's frames will only be forwarded to port Fa0/4.

D. Computer B's frames will be forwarded to all ports.

184. In the following figure, what will happen if the computers on ports Fa0/2 (Computer A) and Fa0/3 (Computer B) are swapped?

```
Mac Address Table
---------------------------------

Vlan  Mac Address       Type      Ports
----  -----------------  --------  ----------
1     0001.6c58.486e    STATIC    Fa0/1
1     0001.6c58.5606    DYNAMIC   Fa0/2
1     0001.6c58.486e    DYNAMIC   Fa0/3
1     0001.6c58.5406    DYNAMIC   Fa0/4
```

A. Computer A's frames will only be forwarded to port Fa0/2.

B. Computer A's frames will be forwarded to port Fa0/2 and Fa0/3.

C. Computer A's frames will only be forwarded to port Fa0/3.

D. Computer B's frames will be forwarded to all ports.

185. What is the default MAC address aging time for dynamic entries on most switches?

A. 30 seconds

B. 60 seconds

C. 300 seconds

D. 500 seconds

186. Refer to the following figure. Which statement is true about the computer with a MAC address of 0001.6c58.24ae?

```
          Mac Address Table
          ..............................

     Vlan  Mac Address      Type     Ports
     .....  ..................  ........  ...........
     1     0001.6c58.486e   STATIC   Fa0/1
     1     0001.6c58.5606   DYNAMIC  Fa0/2
     1     0001.6c58.486e   DYNAMIC  Fa0/3
     1     0001.6c58.5406   DYNAMIC  Fa0/4
     1     0001.6c58.2323   DYNAMIC  Gi0/1
     1     0001.6c58.2325   DYNAMIC  Gi0/1
     1     0001.6c58.24ae   DYNAMIC  Gi0/1
```

   A. The computer is directly connected to Gi0/1.

   B. The computer is directly connected to Fa0/1.

   C. The computer is connected to another switch on Gi0/1.

   D. The MAC address table is thrashed due to a loop.

187. What information is added to the MAC address table when a frame is received on an interface?

   A. Destination MAC address of the frame and incoming port number

   B. Source MAC address of the frame and incoming port number

   C. Destination MAC address of the frame and outgoing port number

   D. Source MAC address of the frame and outgoing port number

188. You need to change the default MAC address aging time on a switch to 400 seconds. Which command would you use?

   A. `set mac aging 400`

   B. `mac aging-time 400 seconds`

   C. `mac-address-table aging-time 400`

   D. `mac address-aging 400`

189. How do switches forward frames only to the destination computer?

   A. Forward/filter decisions based on the MAC address table

   B. Forward/filter decisions based on the routing table

   C. Flooding ports for the destination MAC address

   D. Broadcasting for the MAC address

190. Referring to the following figure, what will happen when a frame destined for 0001.6c58.486f enters the switch?

```
Mac Address Table
................................

Vlan Mac Address      Type     Ports
.....  ....................   ........  ..........
 1     0001.6c58.486f  DYNAMIC  Fa0/1
 1     0001.6c58.5606  DYNAMIC  Fa0/2
 1     0001.6c58.486e  DYNAMIC  Fa0/3
```

A. The frame will be forwarded to the uplink port.

B. The frame will be forwarded to all active ports except the one on which it was received.

C. The frame will be dropped.

D. The frame will be forwarded to a MAC address of ffff.ffff.ffff.

191. Given the information in the following figure, which statement is true when Computer A needs to communicate with Computer C?

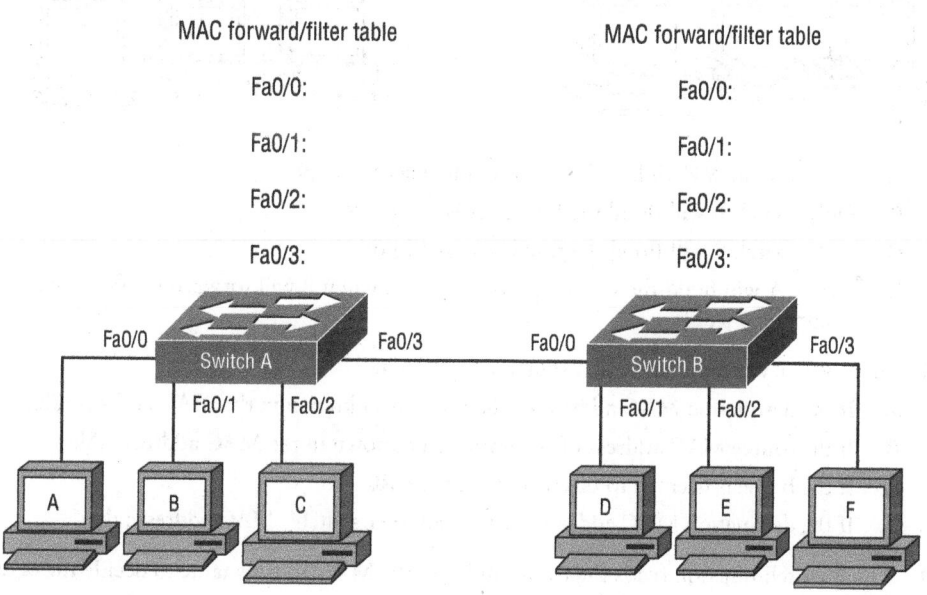

A. Switch A and Switch B will flood the frame across all ports.

B. Only Switch A will flood the frame across all ports.

C. Only Switch B will flood the frame across all ports.

D. Switch A will forward traffic only to Computer C's port.

192. Given the information in the following figure, which statement is true when Computer A needs to communicate with Computer F?

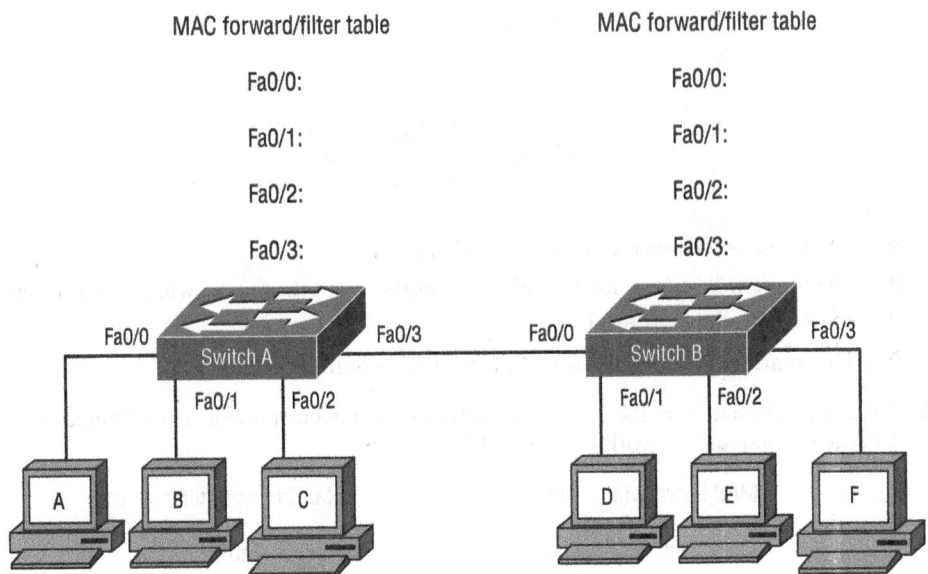

MAC forward/filter table   MAC forward/filter table

Fa0/0:   Fa0/0:

Fa0/1:   Fa0/1:

Fa0/2:   Fa0/2:

Fa0/3:   Fa0/3:

- **A.** Switch A and Switch B will flood the frame across all ports.
- **B.** Only Switch A will flood the frame across all ports.
- **C.** Only Switch B will flood the frame across all ports.
- **D.** Switch A will flood the frame across all ports. Switch B will forward traffic only to Computer F's port.

193. Under which circumstance will a switch drop a frame?

- **A.** If the destination MAC address of the frame is unknown in the MAC address table
- **B.** If the source MAC address of the frame is unknown in the MAC address table
- **C.** If the frame is deemed to be corrupt via the CRC
- **D.** If the destination MAC address exists in another switch's MAC address table

194. Which switch function reads the frame and uses the MAC address table to decide the egress interface for the frame?

- **A.** Forward/filter
- **B.** Address learning
- **C.** Loop avoidance
- **D.** Frame flooding

195. In the following figure, what will happen first at the switch when Computer A wants to send Computer B a message?

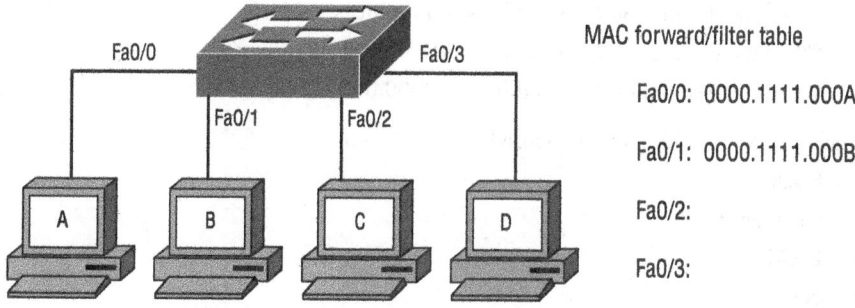

MAC forward/filter table

Fa0/0: 0000.1111.000A

Fa0/1: 0000.1111.000B

Fa0/2:

Fa0/3:

   A. The switch will forward the frame to all ports on the switch.

   B. The switch will direct communication to port Fa0/1.

   C. The switch will record Computer A's MAC address on port Fa0/0.

   D. The switch will record Computer B's MAC address on port Fa0/1.

196. In the following figure, what will happen first when Computer A wants to send Computer B a message?

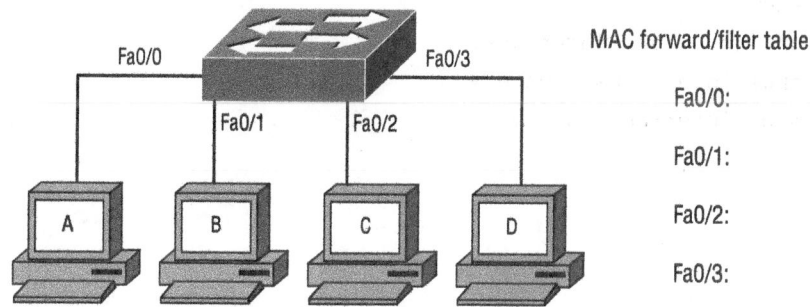

MAC forward/filter table

Fa0/0:

Fa0/1:

Fa0/2:

Fa0/3:

   A. The switch will forward the frame to all ports on the switch.

   B. The switch will direct communication to port Fa0/1.

   C. The switch will record computer A's MAC address on port Fa0/0.

   D. The switch will record computer B's MAC address on port Fa0/1.

197. Which statement is true of an ARP request entering into a switch?

   A. The source MAC address of the frame will be all *f*s.

   B. The destination MAC address of the frame will be all *f*s.

   C. The switch will only forward the ARP request to the port for the destination computer.

   D. The switch will respond directly back with an ARP reply.

198. Under what circumstance will a switch flood a frame to all ports on the switch?

   A. When the source MAC address is unknown by the switch

   B. When the destination MAC address is a multicast address

   C. When the destination MAC address is unknown by the switch

   D. When the destination MAC address is 0000.0000.0000

199. Where are MAC address tables stored?

   A. Flash

   B. CPU registers

   C. RAM

   D. NVRAM

200. Which command will allow you to see the MAC address table?

   A. show mac

   B. show mac address-table

   C. show cam table

   D. show mac table

201. Which command will display all connected ports on a switch and include descriptions?

   A. show ports

   B. show counters interfaces

   C. show interfaces counters

   D. show interfaces status

Chapter

2

Network Access (Domain 2)

THE CCNA EXAM TOPICS COVERED IN THIS PRACTICE TEST INCLUDE THE FOLLOWING:

✓ **2.0   Network Access**

2.1   Configure and verify VLANs (normal range) spanning multiple switches

2.1.a Access ports (data and voice)

2.1.b Default VLAN

2.1.c InterVLAN Connectivity

2.2   Configure and verify interswitch connectivity

2.2.a Trunk ports

2.2.b 802.1Q

2.2.c Native VLAN

2.3   Configure and verify Layer 2 discovery protocols (Cisco Discovery Protocol and LLDP)

2.4   Configure and verify (Layer 2/Layer 3) EtherChannel (LACP)

2.5   Interpret basic operations of Rapid PVST+ Spanning Tree Protocol

2.5.a Root port, root bridge (primary/secondary), and other port names

2.5.b Port states and roles

2.5.c PortFast

2.5.d Root guard, loop guard, BPDU filter, and BPDU guard

2.6   Describe Cisco Wireless Architectures and AP modes

2.7   Describe physical infrastructure connections of WLAN components (AP, WLC, access/trunk ports, and LAG)

2.8 Describe network device management access connections (Telnet, SSH, HTTP, HTTPS, console, and TACACS+/RADIUS, and cloud managed)

2.9 Interpret the wireless LAN GUI configuration for client connectivity, such as WLAN creation, security settings, QoS profiles, and advanced settings

1. You are trying to reprovision a switch in a different part of your network. However, you still see the old VLANs configured from the old network. How can you rectify the problem?

   A. Upgrade the IOS.

   B. Type **erase startup-config**, confirm it, and reload.

   C. Type **clear vlan**, confirm it, and reload.

   D. Delete vlan.dat, confirm it, and reload.

2. What is the normal range for VLANs before you must use extended VLAN IDs?

   A. VLAN 1 through 1001

   B. VLAN 1 through 1002

   C. VLAN 1 through 1005

   D. VLAN 2 through 1002

3. Which is a benefit to converting a network from a flat layer 2 network to a routed layer 3 VLAN-enabled network?

   A. Increased collision domains for increased bandwidth

   B. Reduced complexity of design and operations

   C. Flexibility of user management and design

   D. Decreased number of broadcast domains for increased bandwidth

4. You have configured a new VLAN 9 and applied it to the interface. However, you find that the computer still remains in VLAN 1. What is the problem? Refer to the following figure.

   ```
   Switch#sh run
   Building configuration...
   [output cut]
   !
   interface FastEthernet0/2
    switchport access vlan 9
    switchport mode trunk
    switchport nonegotiate
    spanning-tree portfast
   !
   ```

   A. The switchport is configured with **switchport nonegotiate**.

   B. The switchport is configured as a trunk and dot1q trunking is intervening.

   C. The switchport is configured as a trunk and the native VLAN is VLAN 1.

   D. Spanning-tree PortFast is configured and defaulting to VLAN 1.

5. What is the extended VLAN range?

   A. VLAN 1002 to 4096

   B. VLAN 1006 to 4096

   C. VLAN 1006 to 4094

   D. VLAN 1006 to 4092

6. Which command(s) will delete a VLAN?

   A. `vlan database`
     `no vlan 9`

   B. `vlan database`
     `delete vlan 9`

   C. `no vlan 9`

   D. `vlan 9 delete`

7. Which is a correct statement about frames and VLANs?

   A. Broadcast frames are sent to ports that are configured in different VLANs.

   B. Unicast frames that are not in the MAC address table are flooded to all ports in all VLANs.

   C. The ports that link switches together must be access links.

   D. Frames with a destination MAC that are not in the MAC address table are flooded to only ports in the respective VLAN.

8. What is the normal range of VLANs that can be modified on a Cisco switch with default configuration?

   A. VLAN 1 to 1002

   B. VLAN 1 to 1001

   C. VLAN 2 to 1002

   D. VLAN 2 to 1001

9. Static VLANs are being used on a switch's interface. Which of the following statements is correct?

   A. Nodes use a VLAN policy server.

   B. Nodes are assigned VLANs based on their MAC address.

   C. Nodes are unaware of the VLAN in which they are configured.

   D. All nodes are in the same VLAN.

10. A switch is configured with a single VLAN of 12 for all interfaces. All nodes auto-negotiate at 100 Mb/s full-duplex. What is true if you add an additional VLAN to the switch?

   A. The switch will decrease its bandwidth due to overhead.

   B. The switch will increase its count of collision domains.

   C. The switch will now require a router.

   D. The switch will increase its bandwidth due to broadcast domains.

11. What is a direct benefit of adding VLANs?

   A. An increase of broadcast domains while decreasing collision domains

   B. An increase of broadcast domains while increasing collision domains

   C. A decrease of broadcast domains while decreasing collision domains

   D. A decrease of broadcast domains while increasing collisions domains

12. Which statement describes dynamic VLANs?

    A. The access port is switched into the respective VLAN based on user credentials.

    B. The access port is switched into the respective VLAN based on the computer's IP address.

    C. The access port is switched into the respective VLAN based on the computer's MAC address.

    D. The access port is switched into the respective VLAN based on security ACLs.

13. You have changed the name of VLAN 3, and you now want to check your change. Which command will you enter to verify the name change?

    A. `show vlans`

    B. `show interface vlan 3`

    C. `show run`

    D. `show vlan id 3`

14. Which of the following is a true statement if you have changed the MTU on a VLAN to support jumbo frames?

    A. If a normal MTU of 1528 is used, the switch will not forward the traffic.

    B. Once jumbo frames are configured, nothing more needs to be done. Clients will autodetect the new MTU and use jumbo frames.

    C. Changing the MTU is an easy and effective method for raising speed.

    D. For jumbo frames to be effective, all devices on the VLAN, including switches, must support them.

15. Which is a benefit of implementing VLANs with a layer 3 router?

    A. VLANs can span multiple switches.

    B. Implementing routed VLANs will decrease the broadcast domains.

    C. ACLs can be employed to secure VLANs.

    D. All of the above.

16. You have created a VLAN for the Research department. Now you need to configure an interface on the switch for the newly created VLAN. Which command will configure the interface for the respective VLAN?

    A. `switchport vlan research`

    B. `switchport access vlan research`

    C. `switchport access vlan 9`

    D. `switchport vlan 9`

17. You are installing a VoIP phone on the same interface as an existing computer. Which command will allow the VoIP phone to switch traffic onto its respective VLAN?

    A. `switchport voice vlan 4`

    B. `switchport vlan voice 4`

    C. `switchport voip vlan 4`

    D. `switchport access vlan 4 voice`

18. Which type of port removes the VLAN ID from the frame before it egresses the interface?

    A. Access port

    B. Trunk port

    C. Voice port

    D. Native port

19. Which of the following is a true statement about static access ports?

    A. An access port can carry VLANs via tagging.

    B. A client computer can request the VLAN to be placed in.

    C. A client computer cannot see any VLAN tagging information.

    D. A client computer can see the VLAN tagging information.

20. You have been tasked to configure an interface with a VLAN ID of 8 and support a VoIP phone on VLAN 6. Which commands would achieve the goal?

    A. `switchport vlan 8`

        `switchport vlan 6 voip`

    B. `switchport mode access vlan 8`

        `switchport voice vlan 6`

    C. `switchport access vlan 8`

        `switchport voice vlan 6`

    D. `switchport access vlan 8 voice 6`

21. In the following figure, you have configured a port for a phone on an existing port for a computer. However, after you are done, only the phone works. What might be the problem?

```
Switch#sh run
Building configuration...
[output cut]
!
interface FastEthernet0/5
  switchport access vlan 8
  switchport voice vlan 4
  switchport mode trunk
  switchport nonegotiate
  spanning-tree portfast
!
```

    A. The phone is misconfigured.

    B. The computer is misconfigured.

    C. The `switchport nonegotiate` command is stopping the computer from negotiating a connection.

    D. The switchport mode needs to be configured as an access port.

22. When you are protecting an interface with port security, to which mode should you set the switchport?

   A. Access mode

   B. Dynamic mode

   C. Trunk mode

   D. Voice mode

23. Which VLAN is the default VLAN used to configure all switches from the factory?

   A. VLAN 999

   B. VLAN 1002

   C. VLAN 1005

   D. VLAN 1

24. You want to delete VLAN 1 for security reasons. However, the switch will not let you. What is the reason you cannot delete VLAN 1?

   A. The VLAN is still configured on a port.

   B. The VLAN serves as the switch's main management IP.

   C. The VLAN is protected from deletion.

   D. The VLAN is still configured as a native VLAN on a trunk.

25. Why is it recommended that you do not use VLAN 1?

   A. It is not a production VLAN.

   B. It cannot be routed via an SVI.

   C. It cannot participate in VTP transfers.

   D. It shouldn't be used for security reasons.

26. You attempt to configure a VLAN with a new name. You receive the error `Default VLAN 1 may not have its name changed.` What is wrong?

   A. The VLAN is used on interfaces currently.

   B. The VLAN is protected from any changes.

   C. The VLAN is being referenced by its name in interface configuration.

   D. You are not in the VLAN database when committing the change.

27. You have configured a new VLAN 12 and applied it to the interface. However, you find that the computer still remains in VLAN 1. Which command will fix the issue? Refer to the following figure.

```
Switch#sh run
Building configuration...
[output cut]
!
interface FastEthernet0/4
  switchport access vlan 12
  switchport mode trunk
  switchport nonegotiate
  spanning-tree portfast
!
```

   A. `switchport native vlan 12`

   B. `no switchport nonegotiate`

   C. `switchport mode access`

   D. `no spanning-tree portfast`

28. What is the command to verify a VLAN and the port(s) it is associated with?

   A. `show vlans`

   B. `show vlan`

   C. `show access vlan`

   D. `show vlan database`

29. You are configuring a Catalyst 9200 switch, a VLAN is not configured yet, and you mistakenly configure it on an interface with the command `switch access vlan 12`. What will happen?

   A. The command will error.

   B. The command will complete and update the VLAN database.

   C. The command will complete, but before forwarding can happen, the VLAN must be manually created.

   D. The command will need to be negated and performed after the VLAN is manually created.

30. You have been asked to segment the network for an R&D workgroup. The requirement is to allow the R&D group access to the existing servers, but no other VLANs should be able to access R&D. How can this be achieved with maximum flexibility?

   A. Create a new VLAN, configure a routed SVI interface, and apply ACLs to the VLAN.

   B. Create a new VLAN, configure a routed SVI interface, and apply extended ACLs to the R&D switchports.

   C. Create a new VLAN, and install a new R&D server in the new VLAN.

   D. Create a new VLAN, and trunk the existing file server for both the production and R&D networks.

31. You have just installed a Cisco VoIP phone, and it will not provision. Referring to the following figure, what needs to be changed?

```
Switch#sh run
Building configuration...
[output cut]
!
interface FastEthernet0/4
  switchport access vlan 12
  switchport voice vlan 4
  switchport mode access
  no cdp enable
  switchport nonegotiate
  spanning-tree portfast
!
```

A. CDP needs to be enabled.

B. Spanning-tree PortFast needs to be removed.

C. The interface is configured with `switchport nonegotiate`.

D. The interface needs to be configured as a trunk.

32. You need to verify that an interface is in the proper VLAN. Which command will display the status of the interface, the VLAN configured, and the operational mode?

A. `show vlan`

B. `show running-config`

C. `show interfaces`

D. `show interfaces switchport`

33. You configured VLAN on an interface, but it is not working. After looking at the VLAN database, you find it has been disabled. Which command will enable the VLAN?

A. `Switch#enable vlan 3`

B. `Switch(config)#enable vlan 3`

C. `Switch#no shutdown vlan 3`

D. `Switch(config)#vlan 3`
    `Switch(config-vlan)#no shutdown`

34. Which command will show the operational mode of only Fa0/3?

A. `show interfaces`

B. `show interfaces switchport`

C. `show interfaces FastEthernet 0/3 switchport`

D. `show interfaces status | i 0/3`

35. The guest VLAN is not allowing traffic to be routed. What is the cause of the problem? Refer to the following figure.

```
Switch#sh vlan

VLAN Name                             Status    Ports
---- -------------------------------- --------- -------------------------------
1    default                          active    Fa0/1, Fa0/2, Fa0/3, Fa0/4
                                                Fa0/5, Fa0/6, Fa0/7, Fa0/8
                                                Fa0/9, Fa0/10, Fa0/11, Fa0/12
                                                Fa0/13, Fa0/14, Fa0/15, Fa0/16
                                                Fa0/17, Fa0/18, Fa0/19, Fa0/20
                                                Fa0/21, Fa0/22, Fa0/23, Gig0/2
2    office                           active
3    production                       active
4    voip                             active
5    guests                           act/lshut Fa0/24
1002 fddi-default                     active
1003 token-ring-default               active
[output cut]
```

A. The VLAN interface is shut down.

B. The VLAN is disabled.

C. The guest ports are not in the proper VLAN.

D. There is a problem elsewhere.

36. You need to create a new VLAN 5 called office and apply it to interface Fa0/4. Which commands will you need to enter?

A. `Switch(config)#vlan 5`

`Switch(config-vlan)#name office`

`Switch(config-vlan)#exit`

`Switch(config)#interface fast 0/4`

`Switch(config-if)#switchport access vlan 5`

B. `Switch(config)#vlan 5`

`Switch(config-vlan)#name office`

`Switch(config-vlan)#exit`

`Switch(config)#interface fast 0/4`

`Switch(config-if)#switchport access vlan office`

C. `Switch(config)#vlan 5 office`

`Switch(config)#interface fast 0/4`

`Switch(config-if)#switchport access vlan 5`

D. `Switch(config)#vlan 5 name office`

`Switch(config)#interface fast 0/4`

`Switch(config-if)#switchport access vlan 5`

37. In the following figure, what is wrong with VLAN 4?

```
Switch#sh vlan

VLAN Name                             Status    Ports
---- --------------------------       --------- -------------------------------
1    default                          active    Fa0/1, Fa0/2, Fa0/3, Fa0/4
                                                 Fa0/5, Fa0/6, Fa0/7, Fa0/8
                                                 Fa0/9, Fa0/10, Fa0/11, Fa0/12
                                                 Fa0/13, Fa0/14, Fa0/15, Fa0/16
                                                 Fa0/17, Fa0/18, Fa0/19, Fa0/20
                                                 Fa0/21, Fa0/22, Fa0/23, Gig0/2
2    office                           active
3    production                       active
4    VLAN0004                         active
5    guests                           act/lshut Fa0/24
1002 fddi-default                     active
1003 token-ring-default               active
[output cut]
```

A. The VLAN is shut down.

B. The VLAN is unnamed.

C. The VLAN was created on a non-Cisco switch.

D. The VLAN is suspended.

38. A VLAN was created on another non-Cisco switch. You look at the current VLAN database, but the VLAN is not in the VLAN database. What must be done to correct the issue?

A. Set the correct trunking protocol between the switches.

B. Create the VLAN manually.

C. Configure VTP on both switches.

D. Assign the VLAN to an interface on the other switch.

39. You have just configured the network in the following figure. The commands you have entered configured the VLAN database and assigned the VLAN IDs to the interfaces. You cannot communicate between VLAN 2 and VLAN 4, but communication within VLAN 4 works. What is wrong?

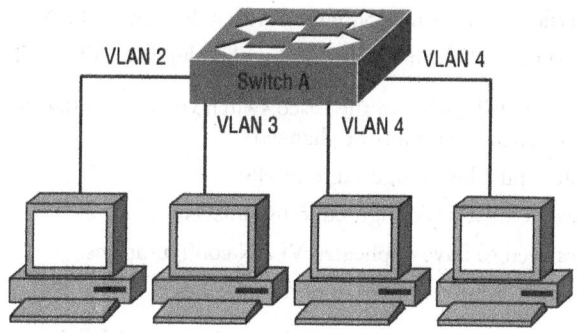

   A. The VLANs must be enabled via the command no shutdown.

   B. The network requires routing between the VLANs.

   C. The VLANs require VTP to be configured.

   D. The interfaces are administratively shut down by default and need to be enabled via no shutdown.

40. An administrator calls you and states they believe an interface is down on a router you maintain. Which command will show only the interface, the IP address configured, and the status of the interface?

   A. show ip interface

   B. show interface

   C. show ip interface brief

   D. show interface brief

41. Which statement is true about the following figure?

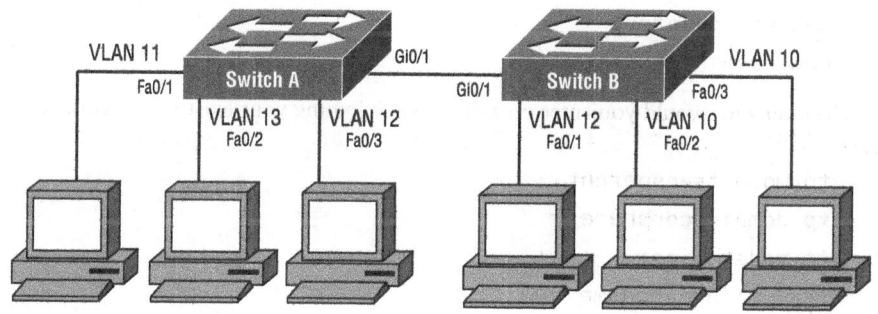

    A. Switch A interface Gi0/1 is configured as an access switchport to Switch B interface Gi0/1.

    B. Switch A interface Gi0/1 and Switch B interface Gi0/1 are both configured as trunk switchports.

    C. Switch B interface Fa0/1 is misconfigured with a duplicate VLAN ID.

    D. Switch A interface Fa0/3 is misconfigured with a duplicate VLAN ID.

42. You have connected a Dell switch to the Cisco switch you are configuring and you cannot get a trunk between the two. What must be changed?

    A. The Dell switch must be configured to use ISL.

    B. The Cisco switch must be configured to use 802.1Q.

    C. Both switches need to have duplicated VLAN configurations.

    D. VTP needs to be configured on each of the switches.

43. You need to view all of the trunks on a switch and verify that they have the proper trunking protocols configured. Which command will display the information?

    A. `show interfaces brief`

    B. `show interfaces trunk`

    C. `show switchport trunk`

    D. `show switchport brief`

44. What is the default VTP mode all switches are configured as by default?

    A. Server

    B. Client

    C. Transparent

    D. Master

45. You need to verify the VTP mode on a switch. Which command will display the information?

    A. `show vtp`

    B. `show vtp status`

    C. `show vtp counters`

    D. `show running-config`

46. Which commands would you enter on a new switch joining your existing network to configure VTP?

    A. `vtp mode transparent`
        `vtp domain corpname`

    B. `vtp mode client`
        `vtp domain corpname`

    C. `vtp domain corpname`

    D. `vtp client`
        `vtp corpname`

47. You need to remove VLANs 2 through 4 from the allowed list on a trunk interface. Which command will remove only these VLANs without interruption to the network?

 A. `switchport trunk remove vlan 2-4`

 B. `switchport remove vlan 2-4`

 C. `switchport trunk allowed vlan remove 2-4`

 D. `switchport trunk allowed remove vlan 2-4`

48. You have a list of allowed VLANs over an existing trunk. You need to set the allowed list back to default. Which command will perform this without interruption? Refer to the following figure.

```
Current configuration : 202 bytes
!
interface FastEthernet0/32
 description Switch A to Switch B
 switchport trunk encapsulation dot1q
 switchport trunk native vlan 2
 switchport trunk allowed vlan 4,6,12,15
 switchport mode trunk
end
```

 A. `no switchport trunk allowed`

 B. `no switchport trunk allowed all`

 C. `no switchport trunk allowed 1-4096`

 D. `switchport trunk allowed vlan all`

49. You need to add VLAN 4 to the allowed list on a trunk interface. Currently VLANs 5 through 8 are allowed. Which command will add only this VLAN without interruption to the network?

 A. `switchport trunk allowed vlan add 4`

 B. `add allowed vlan 4`

 C. `switchport trunk add vlan 4`

 D. `switchport trunk allowed add vlan 4`

50. You try to configure the command `switchport mode trunk` on an interface. However, you see the error message `Command rejected: An interface whose trunk encapsulation is Auto cannot be configured to trunk mode.` What command will fix the issue?

 A. `switchport mode trunk manual`

 B. `no switchport mode dynamic auto`

 C. `switchport trunk encapsulation dot1q`

 D. `no switchport trunk encapsulation auto`

51. What is the function of VTP?

 A. VTP allows for dynamic trunking between links.

 B. VTP allows for propagation of the VLAN database.

 C. VTP detects trunk encapsulation and negotiates trunks.

 D. VTP allows for propagation of the trunking database.

52. Which VTP mode will not allow the switch to participate in VTP traffic but will forward VTP traffic?

A. Server mode

B. Transparent mode

C. Proxy mode

D. Client mode

53. You have just configured a trunk between two switches, Switch A and Switch B. The trunk operates as normal. However, there are minor issues with some of the switch traffic. What might be the problem? Refer to the following figure.

```
SwitchA# show interface fastethernet 3/1 switchport
Name: Fa3/1
Switchport: Enabled
Administrative Mode: trunk
Operational Mode: trunk
Administrative Trunking Encapsulation: dot1q
Operational Trunking Encapsulation: dot1q
Negotiation of Trunking: On
Access Mode VLAN: 1 (default)
Trunking Native Mode VLAN: 1 (default)
Voice VLAN: none
Administrative private-vlan host-association: none
Administrative private-vlan mapping: none
Administrative private-vlan trunk native VLAN: none
Administrative private-vlan trunk encapsulation: dot1q
Administrative private-vlan trunk normal VLANs: none
Administrative private-vlan trunk private VLANs: none
Operational private-vlan: none
Trunking VLANs Enabled: ALL
Pruning VLANs Enabled: 2-1001
Capture Mode Disabled
Capture VLANs Allowed: ALL
```

```
Switch B# show interface gi 1/1 switchport
Name: Gi1/1
Switchport: Enabled
Administrative Mode: trunk
Operational Mode: trunk
Administrative Trunking Encapsulation: dot1q
Operational Trunking Encapsulation: dot1q
Negotiation of Trunking: On
Access Mode VLAN: 1 (default)
Trunking Native Mode VLAN: 10 (inactive)
Voice VLAN: none
Administrative private-vlan host-association: none
Administrative private-vlan mapping: none
Administrative private-vlan trunk native VLAN: none
Administrative private-vlan trunk encapsulation: dot1q
Administrative private-vlan trunk normal VLANs: none
Administrative private-vlan trunk private VLANs: none
Operational private-vlan: none
Trunking VLANs Enabled: ALL
Pruning VLANs Enabled: 6-1001
Capture Mode Disabled
Capture VLANs Allowed: ALL
```

A. Switch A is pruning all VLANs except for VLAN 1.

B. The switches are on incompatible links.

C. Switch B has an inactive native VLAN.

D. Both switches have a native VLAN mismatch.

54. What significance does VTP VLAN pruning provide?

A. VLAN pruning removes VLANs from the databases of other switches that they are not configured on.

B. VLAN pruning removes VLAN traffic from other switches that are not configured for the respective VLAN.

C. VLAN pruning automatically changes the allowed VLANs on all interfaces.

D. All of the above.

55. Which command enables VTP pruning?

A. `Switch(config)#vtp mode pruning`

B. `Switch(config)#vtp pruning`

C. `Switch(config)#vtp vlan pruning`

D. `Switch(config-vlan)#enable pruning`

56. When enabling VTP pruning, where does it need to be configured?

A. VTP pruning needs to be configured only on the VTP server.

B. VTP pruning needs to be configured only on the VTP client.

C. VTP pruning needs to be configured only on the VTP transparent.

D. VTP pruning needs to be configured on all VTP clients and the server.

57. You configure a new VLAN of 22 on Switch A. You have configured a few access links with the new VLAN and they work as normal. They do not forward traffic to ports configured in the same VLAN on Switch B. All other VLANs function fine between the switches. What is the problem? Refer to the following figure.

```
Current configuration : 202 bytes
!
interface FastEthernet0/32
 description Switch A to Switch B
 switchport trunk encapsulation dot1q
 switchport trunk native vlan 2
 switchport trunk allowed vlan 4,6,12,15
 switchport mode trunk
end
```

A. The native VLAN must be changed.

B. The VLAN is not allowed over the trunk.

C. The trunk encapsulation is wrong.

D. VTP is not set up on the remote switch.

58. Which command will turn off Dynamic Trunking Protocol (DTP) on an interface?

A. `no dtp`

B. `no switchport dtp enable`

C. `switchport dtp disable`

D. `switchport nonegotiate`

59. You are trunking Switch A and Switch B together. On Switch A you have the default of `switchport mode dynamic auto`. On Switch B, which command will you need to configure to allow trunking?

A. `switchport mode trunk`

B. `switchport mode dynamic trunk`

C. `switchport mode dynamic auto`

D. `switchport nonegotiate`

60. You are having an issue with a trunk between two switches. Examining the following figure, what can you conclude?

```
---------------------Switch A---------------------
SwitchA#show interfaces fastEthernet 0/2 trunk

Port        Mode         Encapsulation  Status      Native vlan
Fa0/2       Auto         802.1q         other       1

Port        Vlans allowed on trunk
Fa0/2       1-4,7,11,13-4094

Port        Vlans allowed and active in management domain
Fa0/2       1

Port        Vlans in spanning tree forwarding state and not pruned
Fa0/2       1
SwitchA#

---------------------Switch B---------------------
SwitchB#show interfaces fastEthernet 0/8 trunk

Port        Mode         Encapsulation  Status      Native vlan
Fa0/8       off          ISL            other       1

Port        Vlans allowed on trunk
Fa0/8       1-4,7,11,13-4094

Port        Vlans allowed and active in management domain
Fa0/8       1

Port        Vlans in spanning tree forwarding state and not pruned
Fa0/8       1
SwitchB#
```

A. The interfaces on both switches need to be set to trunk mode.

B. DTP is not running on Switch A.

C. All VLANs need to be allowed first.

D. There is a trunking protocol mismatch.

61. Which protocol is a Cisco proprietary protocol used for trunking switches?

A. ISL

B. 802.1Q

C. VTP

D. CDP

62. How does IEEE 802.1Q tag frames?

A. 802.1Q adds a 32-bit header to the frame with the VLAN tagging information.

B. 802.1Q adds a 32-bit header to the packet with the VLAN tagging information.

C. 802.1Q inserts a 32-bit field between the source MAC address and the type field.

D. 802.1Q inserts a 32-bit field between the destination MAC address and the type field.

63. Which commands will allow a trunk with another switch configured as mode
desirable auto?

A. `switchport trunk encapsulation dot1q`
`switchport mode trunk`

B. `switchport mode dynamic auto`
`switchport mode encapsulation dot1q`

    C. `switchport nonegotiate`

    D. `switchport encapsulation dot1q`

    `switchport mode trunk`

64. Which statement is correct about native VLANs?

    A. Any traffic tagged will be placed on the native VLAN.

    B. Any traffic that is not allowed over the trunk will be placed on the native VLAN.

    C. Any traffic not tagged will be placed on the native VLAN.

    D. Any traffic that is tagged with ISL on an 802.1Q trunk will be placed on the native VLAN.

65. You are setting up a switch. When you perform a `show run`, you notice that the VLANs are in the `running-config`. What could be concluded? Refer to the following figure.

```
Switch#sh run
Building configuration...

Current configuration : 1139 bytes
[output cut]
spanning-tree mode pvst
!
vlan 2
 name office
!
vlan 3
 name warehouse
!
vlan 4
 name showroom
!
interface FastEthernet0/1
[output cut]
```

    A. Nothing; the VLANs are normally stored in the `running-config`.

    B. The switch is set up with a VTP mode of client.

    C. The switch is set up with a VTP mode of server.

    D. The switch is set up with a VTP mode of transparent.

66. You have configured `switchport nonegotiate` on an interface with a default configuration. What effect will it have on the neighboring interface when the other switch is plugged in with its interface in default configuration?

    A. The switchport will transition to a trunk port.

    B. The switchport will remain an access port.

    C. The interface will remain shut down.

    D. The interface will enter an `err-disable` state.

67. Switch A has default configuration on its interface. You need to configure Switch A for VLAN 5. Which command will configure the interface to become a member of VLAN 5?

    A. `switchport mode access`

    `switchport access vlan 5`

    B. `switchport trunk`

    `switchport native vlan 5`

    C. `switchport access`

       `switchport access vlan 5`

    D. `switchport mode trunk`

       `switchport native vlan 5`

68. Switch A is configured with the command of `switchport mode dynamic desirable` on its interface. Which command would you need to configure on Switch B to create a trunk between them?

    A. `switchport mode dynamic auto`

    B. `switchport mode dynamic desirable`

    C. `switchport mode trunk`

    D. All of the above

69. Which statement is correct about the command `switchport mode dynamic auto`?

    A. The interface will become a trunk if requested on the neighboring port.

    B. The interface will become a trunk if the neighboring port is configured the same.

    C. The interface will remain an access link if the neighboring port is configured as a trunk.

    D. The interface will remain an access link if the native VLAN is changed.

70. Which command is similar to `show interfaces trunk` but will show greater detail?

    A. `show interfaces trunk detail`

    B. `show switchport`

    C. `show interfaces switchport`

    D. `show running-config`

71. On a switch you enter the commands `switchport mode access` and `switchport nonegotiate`. Which statement is true about the interface you've configured?

    A. The interface will become a trunk switchport if a switch is plugged in and DTP is turned on for the other switch.

    B. The interface will always remain an access switchport, regardless of whether another switch is plugged in.

    C. The interface will become a trunk switchport if a switch is plugged in and the other switch is set statically to a trunk switchport.

    D. The interface will become a trunk switchport if a non-Cisco switch is plugged in and statically configured as a trunk switchport.

72. You need to configure a trunk interface to support the protocol of 802.1Q. Which command will achieve this?

    A. `switchport mode trunk 802.1q`

    B. `switchport trunk encapsulation 802.1q`

    C. `switchport 802.1q`

    D. `switchport encapsulation trunk 802.1q`

73. You are trying to configure a trunk port on an interface for 802.1Q encapsulation. However, after entering the proper command, you receive the error % `Invalid input detected at '^' marker`. What is wrong?

    A. 802.1Q is not supported on the switch you are configuring this on.

    B. The interface will not allow configuration of 802.1Q.

    C. The switch only supports the ISL trunking protocol.

    D. The switch only supports the 802.1Q trunking protocol.

74. When a frame is not tagged with 802.1Q VLAN identifying information, what happens when it traverses a trunk port?

    A. The frame is dropped to the bit bucket.

    B. The frame is forwarded to the default VLAN.

    C. The frame is forwarded to the native VLAN.

    D. The frame is sent to the first VLAN ID configured on the trunk.

75. Which protocol is an open standard trunking protocol?

    A. ISL

    B. VTP

    C. 802.1Q

    D. 802.1X

76. You have several VLANs and need to route between them. You configure a trunk between your router and switch. What will you need to configure on the router to support each VLAN for routing?

    A. Virtual interface

    B. Switched virtual interface

    C. Subinterface

    D. VLAN database

77. How many bytes are used in an 802.1Q frame for tagging of VLANs?

    A. 2 bytes

    B. 4 bytes

    C. 8 bytes

    D. 16 bytes

78. What is the difference between a default VLAN and a native VLAN?

    A. A default VLAN is configured on all access ports of the switch from the factory.

    B. A native VLAN is configured on all access ports of the switch from the factory.

    C. A default VLAN is configured on all trunks for tagged frames.

    D. A native VLAN is configured on all trunks for tagged frames.

79. Which command will show you the native VLAN for only Fa0/15?

   A. `show running-config`

   B. `show interface fastethernet 0/15`

   C. `show interface fastethernet 0/15 switchport`

   D. `show switchport fastethernet 0/15`

80. You need to change the native VLAN for interface Fa0/23 from VLAN 1 to VLAN 999. Which command would you use?

   A. `switchport trunk native vlan 999`

   B. `native vlan 999`

   C. `switchport native vlan 999`

   D. `no switchport native vlan 1`

      `switchport native vlan 999`

81. When you change the native VLAN of a trunk from VLAN 1 to VLAN 999 and you receive the error `%CDP-4-NATIVE_VLAN_MISMATCH: Native VLAN mismatch -discovered....` What is the possible problem?

   A. CDP is not running on the other interface, causing a mismatch.

   B. The interface is the first to be changed.

   C. The interface is running ISL.

   D. The version of CDP is wrong on the other switch.

82. Switch A and Switch B have a trunk. On Switch A, the native VLAN is set to VLAN 10 on Switch B and the native VLAN is defaulted. What problems will occur?

   A. CDP will not function.

   B. VTP will not function.

   C. All broadcasts will be forwarded to Switch B.

   D. Any traffic not tagged on Switch B when traversing the trunk will be switched onto VLAN 10.

83. When you have a native VLAN mismatch on a configured trunk, which protocol will alert you to the issue?

   A. VTP

   B. CDP

   C. 802.1Q

   D. ISL

84. You are trying to change the native VLAN from VLAN 1 to VLAN 1002. You have configured both sides with `switchport native vlan 1002`. However, the native VLAN traffic keeps failing. What is wrong?

   A. The native VLAN must be VLAN 1.

   B. The native VLAN cannot be an extended VLAN.

   C. VLAN 1002 is not allowed for Ethernet traffic.

   D. The problem is not the native VLAN; everything is configured properly.

85. Which protocol is an IEEE standard that collects information from neighboring devices on their identity and capabilities?

A. CDP

B. LLDP

C. 802.1b

D. 802.1a

86. You want to turn off CDP on a switch. Which command would you enter?

A. cdp disable

B. no cdp enable

C. no cdp

D. no cdp run

87. How often are CDP frames sent out of the device by default?

A. Every 30 seconds

B. Every 60 seconds

C. Every 90 seconds

D. Every 180 seconds

88. Which Cisco proprietary protocol collects information from neighboring devices about their identity and capabilities?

A. 802.1ab

B. LLDP

C. CDP

D. 802.1a

89. What is the default value of the CDP holddown timer for CDP entries?

A. 30 seconds

B. 60 seconds

C. 90 seconds

D. 180 seconds

90. You want to turn off CDP on a single interface. Which command would you enter?

A. cdp disable

B. no cdp enable

C. no cdp

D. no cdp run

91. Which command gives information that's identical to the output of the show cdp neighbors detail command?

    A. sh cdp neighbors all

    B. sh cdp neighbors *

    C. sh cdp entries all

    D. sh cdp entry *

92. You have several non-Cisco IP phones and you want to allow automatic power adjustments on the Cisco Power over an Ethernet (PoE) switch. Which command will allow you to achieve this?

    A. Switch#lldp run

    B. Switch(config)#lldp run

    C. Switch(config)#lldp enable

    D. Switch#lldp enable

93. Which command will allow you to see LLDP devices connected to a switch?

    A. show lldp

    B. show lldp devices

    C. show lldp neighbor detail

    D. show cdp neighbor detail

94. What is the default LLDP advertisement interval?

    A. 30 seconds

    B. 60 seconds

    C. 90 seconds

    D. 120 seconds

95. You want to disable LLDP from sending advertisements on a single interface. Which command will you use?

    A. no lldp

    B. no lldp transmit

    C. no lldp receive

    D. no lldp enable

96. What is the default value of the LLDP holddown timer for entries?

    A. 30 seconds

    B. 60 seconds

    C. 90 seconds

    D. 120 seconds

97. The following figure shows the output of the CDP details. Which statement is correct about what is displayed?

```
SwitchB#sh cdp neighbors detail

Device ID: SwitchA
Entry address(es):
  IP address : 192.168.1.1
Platform: Cisco 3560, Capabilities:
Interface: GigabitEthernet0/2, Port ID (outgoing port): GigabitEthernet0/1
Holdtime: 162

Version :
Cisco IOS Software, C3560 Software (C3560-ADVIPSERVICESK9-M),
Version 12.2(37)SE1, RELEASE SOFTWARE (fc1)
Copyright (c) 1986-2007 by Cisco Systems, Inc.
Compiled Thu 05-Jul-07 22:22 by pt_team

advertisement version: 2
Duplex: full
```

A. The advertisement was seen 162 seconds ago.

B. Switch B interface Gi0/1 connects to Switch A.

C. Switch B interface Gi0/2 connects to Switch A.

D. The IP address of Switch B is 192.168.1.1.

98. You have a layer 2 connection to your ISP. You want to make sure you do not send information on the capabilities of your switch, but you don't want to affect the use of CDP. Which command will you configure?

A. cdp disable

B. no cdp

C. no cdp disable

D. no cdp enable

99. Which command will show the interfaces that CDP is advertising on?

A. show cdp

B. show cdp interface

C. show interface

D. show interface cdp

100. What is the maximum number of interfaces that can be aggregated with EtherChannel and PAgP?

A. 2

B. 8

C. 16

D. 4

101. Which is a true statement about EtherChannel?

   A. EtherChannel works with 802.1Q to block the redundant links.

   B. EtherChannel can aggregate multiple links with varying speed.

   C. EtherChannel can aggregate interfaces across multiple stand-alone switches.

   D. When configured, EtherChannel acts as a single layer 2 connection.

102. You have a switch with 2 gigabit interface ports and 48 Fast Ethernet ports and are using PAgP. What is the highest bandwidth you can achieve?

   A. 2 Gb/s

   B. 2.2 Gb/s

   C. 400 Mb/s

   D. 2.6 Gb/s

103. Which aggregation protocol is an IEEE standard?

   A. LACP

   B. 802.1Q

   C. PAgP

   D. 802.1X

104. You need to aggregate multiple connections between a VMware ESXi host and the switch. Which protocol will you choose?

   A. EtherChannel

   B. LACP

   C. Channel Group

   D. PAgP

105. What is the maximum number of interfaces that can be aggregated with EtherChannel and LACP?

   A. 2

   B. 8

   C. 16

   D. 4

106. Which mode forces the aggregation of links without the use of a control protocol?

   A. LACP off mode

   B. PAgP off mode

   C. On mode

   D. 802.3ad mode

107. Which is a correct statement about aggregating ports together?

    A. The term *EtherChannel* is a Cisco proprietary term for port channeling.

    B. PAgP can be used with non-Cisco products.

    C. LACP can only be used with other Cisco switches.

    D. PAgP can bundle several different links with varying speeds and duplexes together.

108. Which negotiation protocol is a Cisco-proprietary standard?

    A. LACP

    B. 802.1Q

    C. PAgP

    D. 802.1ab

109. How often does PAgP send messages to control the status of the links in the bundle?

    A. Every 30 seconds

    B. Every 60 seconds

    C. Every 90 seconds

    D. Every 120 seconds

110. You want to configure two switches so that LACP is used between the switches. Which mode should you use on both sides to force LACP?

    A. Active mode on both sides

    B. Passive mode on both sides

    C. Auto mode on both sides

    D. Desirable mode on both sides

111. What is the effect of configuring a port channel with one side set to passive mode and the other side set to active mode?

    A. The channel group will use PAgP.

    B. The channel group will not be formed.

    C. The channel group will use LACP.

    D. The channel group will use EtherChannel.

112. Which command is used to verify the negotiation protocol for a port channel?

    A. `show etherchannel`

    B. `show port-channel`

    C. `show interface`

    D. `show run`

113. What is the effect of configuring a port channel with one side set to passive mode and the other side set to passive mode?

   A. The channel group will use PAgP.

   B. The channel group will not be formed.

   C. The channel group will use LACP.

   D. An unconditional port channel will be formed.

114. What is the effect of configuring a port channel with one side set to on mode and the other side set to on mode?

   A. The channel group will use PAgP.

   B. The channel group will not be formed.

   C. The channel group will use LACP.

   D. An unconditional port channel will be formed.

115. What is the IEEE specification for Spanning Tree Protocol (STP)?

   A. 802.1X

   B. 802.1w

   C. 802.1D

   D. 802.1s

116. Which statement is correct about STP?

   A. STP runs on a central switch by creating a topology database.

   B. STP runs as a distributed process on each switch and creates a topology database.

   C. STP uses routing protocols to check for network loops.

   D. STP uses the MAC address table to check for switching loops.

117. How does STP detect and monitor loops in networks?

   A. STP detects and monitors BPDUs being received on multiple interfaces.

   B. STP detects and monitors normal traffic frames being received on multiple interfaces.

   C. STP detects and monitors CDP frames being received on multiple interfaces.

   D. STP detects and monitors access ports in the same VLAN.

118. What is the IEEE specification for Rapid Spanning Tree Protocol (RSTP)?

   A. 802.1X

   B. 802.1w

   C. 802.1D

   D. 802.1s

119. What is the link cost with respect to STP?

   A. Link cost is the latency of a frame traversing across the link.

   B. Link cost is the calculation of all the ports in the path to the root bridge.

   C. Link cost is the monetary cost to traverse a link.

   D. Link cost is a numeric value associated with the speed of a link.

120. What is the path cost with respect to RSTP?

    A. Path cost is the latency of a frame traversing across the link.

    B. Path cost is the calculation of all the ports in the path to the root bridge.

    C. Path cost is the monetary cost to traverse a link.

    D. Path cost is a numeric value associated with the speed of a link.

121. Which protocol is a Cisco proprietary enhancement for 802.1D that allows separate spanning-tree instances for each VLAN?

    A. IEEE 802.1w

    B. PVST+

    C. CST

    D. RSTP

122. Which protocol is a Cisco-proprietary enhancement for 802.1W that allows separate spanning-tree instances for each VLAN?

    A. Rapid PVST+

    B. PVST+

    C. CST

    D. RSTP+

123. Which statement is correct about the Common Spanning Tree (CST)?

    A. CST elects a root bridge for each VLAN.

    B. CST elects a single root bridge for the entire physical network.

    C. CST has an immediate convergence because it elects a single root bridge.

    D. CST is best implemented for really large networks because it scales efficiently.

124. Which statement is correct about RSTP?

    A. RSTP allows for multiple root bridges.

    B. RSTP is backward compatible with STP.

    C. RSTP has a convergence time of around 50 seconds.

    D. RSTP has five port states to which the interfaces could possibly transition.

125. How do switches participating in an STP network become aware of topology changes?

    A. The root bridge is responsible for sensing the change and sending topology change notification BPDUs.

    B. Each switch is responsible for sensing the change and sending topology change notification BPDUs.

    C. The root bridge polls each switch participating in STP for changes.

    D. The switches participating in STP poll the root bridge for changes.

126. Which of the following standards is an IEEE standard that replaces Rapid PVST+?

    A. 802.1X

    B. 802.1w

    C. 802.1D

    D. 802.1s

127. You have a network consisting of four switches, all configured with the same bridge priority. Which switch will be elected the root bridge?

    A. 0081.023a.b433

    B. 0011.03ae.d8aa

    C. 0041.0611.1112

    D. 0021.02fa.bdfc

128. What is the default STP mode all Cisco switches run?

    A. 802.1D

    B. 802.1w

    C. PVST+

    D. Rapid PVST+

129. Which option is a correct statement about alternate ports in RSTP?

    A. An alternate port receives BPDUs from another port on the same switch and, therefore can replace the designated port if it fails.

    B. An alternate port receives BPDUs from another switch and, therefore can replace the designated port if it fails.

    C. An alternate port is always placed in a forwarding state.

    D. An alternate port receives BPDUs from another switch and, therefore can replace the root port if it fails.

130. How is the root bridge in STP elected?

    A. The root bridge is the switch with the highest IP address and priority.

    B. The root bridge is the switch with the lowest IP address and priority.

    C. The root bridge is the switch with the lowest MAC address and priority.

    D. The root bridge is the switch with the highest MAC address and priority.

131. Why is a root bridge elected for STP to function properly?

    A. The root bridge is the logical center of the STP topology.

    B. The root bridge allows all forwarding decisions of frames.

    C. The root bridge calculates the port cost for the rest of the network.

    D. The root bridge calculates the fastest path for the rest of the network.

132. How does a switch calculate the bridge ID?

    A. The bridge ID is a 6-byte number containing a 2-byte bridge priority and a 4-byte IP address.

    B. The bridge ID is an 8-byte number containing a 4-byte bridge priority and a 4-byte IP address.

    C. The bridge ID is an 8-byte number containing a 2-byte bridge priority and a 6-byte MAC address.

    D. The bridge ID is a 10-byte number containing a 4-byte bridge priority and a 6-byte MAC address.

133. What is the definition of a designated port?

    A. A port that is determined to have the lowest cost and placed in a forwarding state for a network segment

    B. A port that is determined to have the highest cost and placed in a forwarding state for a network segment

    C. A port that is determined to have the lowest path cost to the root bridge and placed in a forwarding state for a network segment

    D. A port that is determined to have the highest path cost to the root bridge and placed in a blocking state for a network segment

134. Which is a correct statement about bridge port roles in STP?

    A. Every switch, excluding the root bridge, must have at least one root port.

    B. Every switch, including the root bridge, must have at least one designated port.

    C. Every switch, excluding the root bridge, must have at least one alternate port.

    D. Every switch, including the root bridge, must have at least one backup port.

135. What is the definition of an STP root port?

    A. A port that is determined to have the lowest cost to the network segment and placed in a forwarding state

    B. A port that is determined to have the highest cost to the network segment and placed in a forwarding state

    C. A port that is determined to have the lowest path cost to the root bridge and placed in a forwarding state for a network segment

    D. A port that is determined to have the highest path cost to the root bridge and placed in a blocking state for a network segment

136. What is the definition of an STP designated port?

    A. A port that is determined to have the lowest cost to the network segment and placed in a forwarding state

    B. A port that is determined to have the lowest path cost to the root bridge and placed in a forwarding state for a network segment

    C. A port that is determined to have the highest path cost to the root bridge and placed in a blocking state for a network segment

    D. A port that is determined to have the highest cost to the network segment and placed in a forwarding state

137. How is the bridge ID calculated for PVST+?

    A. The bridge ID is a 4-byte bridge priority, a 12-byte sys-id-ext, and a 6-byte MAC address.

    B. The bridge ID is a 4-byte bridge priority and sys-id-ext and a 6-byte MAC address.

    C. The bridge ID is a 4-bit bridge priority, a 12-bit sys-id-ext, and a 6-byte MAC address.

    D. The bridge ID is a 4-bit bridge priority, a 12-bit sys-id-ext, and an 8-byte IP address.

138. What is the default bridge priority for all STP switches?

    A. Bridge priority of 8,192

    B. Bridge priority of 16,384

    C. Bridge priority of 32,768

    D. Bridge priority of 65,526

139. Which is a correct statement about bridge port roles in STP?

    A. A designated port is always in a blocking state.

    B. Every switch, including the root bridge, must have at least one designated port.

    C. Every switch, excluding the root bridge, must have at least one nondesignated port.

    D. All ports on the root bridge are in a designated port state.

140. Which is a correct statement about backup ports in RSTP?

    A. A backup port receives BPDUs from another port on the same switch and, therefore can replace the designated port if it fails.

    B. A backup port receives BPDUs from another switch and, therefore can replace the designated port if it fails.

    C. A backup port is always placed in a forwarding state.

    D. A backup port receives BPDUs from another switch and, therefore can replace the root port if it fails.

141. What is the default wait time for STP convergence to complete?

    A. Convergence takes 60 seconds to complete.

    B. Convergence takes 5 seconds to complete.

    C. Convergence takes 30 seconds to complete.

    D. Convergence takes 50 seconds to complete.

142. When a computer is connected to an interface with STP enabled in default mode, which is the correct order of the port transitions?

    A. Listening, learning, blocking, forwarding

    B. Forwarding, listening, learning, blocking

    C. Blocking, listening, learning, forwarding

    D. Blocking, learning, listening, forwarding

143. Which statement describes an STP port that is placed into a blocking state?

    A. When a port is placed into a blocking state, it blocks all frames, including BPDUs.

    B. When a port is placed into a blocking state, it blocks redundant frames, excluding BPDUs.

    C. When a port is placed into a blocking state, it blocks all frames, excluding BPDUs.

    D. When a port is placed into a blocking state, it blocks redundant frames, including BPDUs.

144. When a computer is connected to an interface with RSTP enabled in default mode, which is the correct order of the port transitions?

    A. Discarding, learning, blocking, forwarding

    B. Discarding, listening, forwarding

    C. Blocking, listening, learning, forwarding

    D. Discarding, learning, forwarding

145. In RSTP, which port mode replaces the blocking and listening port states?

    A. Discarding

    B. Learning

    C. Forwarding

    D. Backup

146. Which new port state does RTSP have compared to STP?

    A. Learning

    B. Forwarding

    C. Blocking

    D. Discarding

147. You receive a call that when computers boot up, they display an error message stating they cannot reach a domain controller. However, after a few tries, the problem goes away, and the domain controller can be reached. Which command would you enter into the interface if you suspect spanning-tree convergence problems?

    A. `SwitchA(config-if)#no switchport spanning-tree`

    B. `SwitchA(config)#switchport spanning-tree portfast`

    C. `SwitchA(config)#spanning-tree portfast default`

    D. `SwitchA(config-if)#spanning-tree portfast`

148. On which types of ports should you configure PortFast mode?

    A. Trunk ports

    B. Access ports

    C. Voice ports

    D. Designated ports

149. What will the command `spanning-tree portfast default` entered in global configuration mode do?

A. Turn on PortFast mode for all ports

B. Turn on PortFast mode for all access ports only

C. Turn off Spanning Tree on all ports

D. Turn off Spanning Tree on all access ports only

150. What will happen if you plug a hub into two ports on the same switch configured with PortFast on all the interfaces?

A. You will create a temporary switching loop.

B. You will create a permanent switching loop.

C. Both ports will sense the switch and `err-disable`.

D. One of the links will disable via Spanning Tree.

151. Which feature will protect a switch immediately if it sees another switch's advertisement?

A. BPDU Guard

B. BPDU Detection

C. Loop Guard

D. UplinkFast

152. What is the transition of states when PortFast is configured?

A. Forwarding, listening, learning, blocking

B. Listening, forwarding, learning, blocking

C. Listening, learning, forwarding, blocking

D. Blocking, listening, learning, forwarding

153. Which command would you use to configure BPDU Guard on an interface?

A. `switchport mode bpduguard`

B. `switchport bpduguard enable`

C. `spanning-tree bpduguard enable`

D. `spanning-tree bpduguard`

154. After you configure an access switch on your network, you receive a call that the users have lost connectivity. You examine the trunk interface with the command `show interfaces Gi 0/1`. What might be the problem?

```
SwitchB#sh interfaces gigabitEthernet 0/1
GigabitEthernet0/1 is down, line protocol is down (err-disabled)
  Hardware is Lance, address is 0060.5c22.d319 (bia 0060.5c22.d319)
  BW 1000000 Kbit, DLY 1000 usec,
         reliability 255/255, txload 1/255, rxload 1/255
  Encapsulation ARPA, loopback not set
  Keepalive set (10 sec)
  Full-duplex, 1000Mb/s
  input flow-control is off, output flow-control is off
  ARP type: ARPA, ARP Timeout 04:00:00
  Last input 00:00:08, output 00:00:05, output hang never
  Last clearing of "show interface" counters never
  Input queue: 0/75/0/0 (size/max/drops/flushes); Total output drops: 0
  Queueing strategy: fifo
  output queue :0/40 (size/max)
  [output cut]
```

    A. A Spanning Tree loop has been detected.

    B. The switch uplink cable is bad.

    C. BPDU Guard was configured on a trunk.

    D. Flow control is turned off.

155. Which option is a best practice when configuring links on an access switch?

    A. Never configure Spanning-Tree PortFast mode on an access link.

    B. Always configure BPDU Guard along with PortFast.

    C. Always configure BPDU Guard on trunks.

    D. Always configure BPDU Guard along with UplinkFast.

156. Which command will show you if a port has been configured for PortFast mode?

    A. `show portfast`

    B. `show interface fa 0/1`

    C. `show spanning-tree`

    D. `show spanning-tree interface fa 0/1`

157. Which command would you use to remove BPDU Guard from an interface?

    A. `switchport bdpugaurd disable`

    B. `spanning-tree bpduguard enable`

    C. `no switchport bpduguard`

    D. `spanning-tree bpduguard disable`

158. You have BPDU Guard configured on an interface. What happens if a BPDU is advertised on the interface?

    A. The interface will become administratively disabled.

    B. The interface will become disabled.

    C. The interface will become err-disabled.

    D. A small switching loop will happen until convergence.

159. Which command will show you if BPDU Guard is enabled by default?

    A. `show interface gi 0/1`

    B. `show spanning-tree summary`

    C. `show spanning-tree vlan 2`

    D. `show spanning-tree`

160. You are configuring an edge switch and want to make sure someone does not connect another switch in accidentally. Which feature will you configure?

    A. PortFast

    B. UplinkFast

    C. BackboneFast

    D. BPDU Guard

161. You require a density of 100 wireless clients in a relatively small area. Which design would be optimal?

    A. Autonomous WAPs with a WLC

    B. Lightweight WAPs with a WLC

    C. Autonomous WAPs without a WLC

    D. Lightweight WAPs without a WLC

162. Which mode will allow a Cisco AP to detect interference of Bluetooth devices?

    A. BT mode

    B. Sniffing mode

    C. Analysis mode

    D. Monitoring mode

163. Which wireless mode allows for a network connection without a wireless infrastructure in place?

    A. BSS

    B. ESS

    C. IBSS

    D. DS

164. Which statement is correct about root and non-root wireless devices?

    A. Non-root devices can connect to other non-root devices.

    B. Non-root devices can connect to root devices.

    C. Root devices can connect to other root devices.

    D. Repeaters are considered root devices.

165. Which type of WAP can operate independently?

    A. Lightweight WAP

    B. WLC

    C. Mesh

    D. Autonomous WAP

166. You have three buildings that are separated by a number of public roads but have a relatively close proximity to each other. You need to network them together to a central point. Which type of wireless technology should you deploy?

    A. Point-to-point wireless bridge

    B. Mesh wireless network

    C. Point-to-multipoint wireless bridge

    D. Autonomous wireless network

167. What is the maximum length of an SSID?

  A. 16 characters

  B. 32 characters

  C. 48 characters

  D. 64 characters

168. A customer complains that their wireless network drops signal when they are performing inventory in the back of their warehouse. The customer wants to cover the small area for as little money as possible. What would you recommend?

  A. Wireless bridging

  B. Mesh wireless system

  C. Addition of a wireless LAN controller

  D. Wireless repeater

169. Which type of wireless access point (WAP) requires a wireless controller?

  A. Lightweight WAP

  B. BSS

  C. Bridges

  D. Autonomous WAP

170. You need to cover a large public area with high speed wireless coverage. Many of the areas are too far away from the wired switching equipment. What should you implement?

  A. Mesh wireless network

  B. Autonomous wireless network

  C. Point-to-multipoint wireless bridges

  D. Wireless repeaters

171. You are running a WLC for a WLAN. You want to allow for guests to be segmented to the guest VLAN. What is the simplest implementation you can configure on the WLC?

  A. Access control lists for one SSID

  B. Two SSIDs, one configured to the production VLAN and another configured to the guest VLAN

  C. Dynamic VLANs for the SSID

  D. Access control lists for two SSIDs

172. You need more bandwidth to your wireless controller from the router. Currently you have one Gigabit Ethernet connection in use and both your router and wireless controller have another available Gigabit Ethernet connection. What can you do to get more bandwidth?

  A. Nothing. Routers cannot aggregate bandwidth from multiple connections.

  B. Use RIP to balance the bandwidth.

  C. Bundle both Gigabit Ethernet connections in an EtherChannel.

  D. Use the wireless controller to perform inter-VLAN routing.

173. You are connecting a WLC to the network and anticipate requiring several different network segments for voice and data. Which type of port should you configure on the switch?

    A. Access port

    B. Trunk port

    C. Voice port

    D. Routed switchport

174. You are connecting a Cisco WLC to a non-Cisco switch and need to aggregate two ports between the two devices. Which type of link should you research on the non-Cisco device?

    A. LACP

    B. PAgP

    C. LAG

    D. PortChannel

175. How is traffic load-balanced from a WLC to a switch using LAG?

    A. Round-robin

    B. Hash-based

    C. First in, first out (FIFO)

    D. Spill and fill

176. What is the maximum number of ports you can bundle in a LAG between a WLC and a switch?

    A. 16

    B. 8

    C. 4

    D. 2

177. Your company has been contracted to implement a 802.11 wireless system for a small town. Which type of implementation is this considered?

    A. WMAN

    B. WPAN

    C. WLAN

    D. WWAN

178. You currently have a WLC with only two physical access ports. One port is used for guest network access and the other port is used for your business communications. You need to add several other networks to the WLC for your manufacturing and quality control departments. What is the simplest and best way to achieve this?

    A. Upgrade the WLC to accommodate more ports.

    B. Convert the current access ports to LAGs.

    C. Convert one of the current access ports to a trunk.

    D. Add a second WLC to accommodate the new departments.

179. What is the term for a small wireless network that does not extend past 30 feet?

   A. WPAN

   B. WLAN

   C. WMAN

   D. WWAN

180. You have been asked by your manager to configure a port for a new WAP to be installed for your WLC. How should you configure the port?

   A. Access port

   B. Wireless port

   C. Trunk port

   D. LAG port

181. Which application provides terminal emulation over a network?

   A. SNMP

   B. Telnet

   C. HTTP

   D. TFTP

182. You need to make a Telnet connection to a remote router from a router you are configuring. Which command will allow you to do this?

   A. `198.56.33.3`

   B. `connect 198.56.33.3`

   C. `remote 198.56.33.3`

   D. `vty 198.56.33.3`

183. Which port and protocol does TACACS+ use?

   A. UDP/69

   B. TCP/74

   C. UDP/47

   D. TCP/49

184. Which management access method should be configured on network devices for encryption of the session?

   A. RADIUS

   B. HTTP

   C. SSH

   D. SFTP

185. You need to deploy several network devices across your enterprise network. Which method will help you achieve the goal with the least amount of effort and provide a consolidated view?

  A. CLI

  B. SNMP

  C. SSH

  D. APIC

186. You are using several Catalyst 9000-M series switches in your network. Which technology will provide automatic firmware upgrade and configuration management?

  A. Cloud-based management

  B. TFTP

  C. SSH

  D. RADIUS

187. Which technology is used to facilitate encryption for the SSH protocol?

  A. Symmetrical encryption

  B. Code block ciphers

  C. At-rest encryption

  D. Asymmetrical encryption

188. When debugging a WAP, where is the debug information displayed by default?

  A. Console

  B. SSH

  C. Logging server

  D. Local storage

189. Which authentication system is an open standard originally proposed by the Internet Engineering Task Force (IETF)?

  A. RADIUS

  B. TACACS+

  C. Kerberos

  D. LDAP

190. Which management method can use Advanced Encryption Standard (AES) for encryption of user credentials and session data?

  A. SSH

  B. TACACS+

C. HTTPS

D. RADIUS

191. You are setting up an autonomous WAP for the first time. How must you connect to the device?

A. HTTPS

B. SSH

C. Console

D. Telnet

192. What is the connection speed for console access to Cisco equipment?

A. 19.2 kb/s

B. 9600 kb/s

C. 9600 baud

D. 19200 baud

193. What is the definition of a trust boundary in relation to QoS?

A. A trust boundary is where the QoS markings are first configured.

B. A trust boundary is where the QoS markings are stripped at the router.

C. A trust boundary is where the network begins to trust the QoS markings from devices.

D. A trust boundary is the separation of QoS queues based on their priority.

194. Which IEEE specification defines WLAN QoS for wireless data?

A. 802.11e

B. 802.11r

C. 802.1p

D. 802.11k

195. You are creating a WLAN in the GUI of the WLC. You need to make sure that only corporate hosts can connect to the newly formed WLAN. How can you achieve this?

A. Disable SSID broadcasting

B. Set a unique PSK

C. Use MAC filtering

D. Add an LDAP server

196. Which protocol should be enabled on a WLAN to allow a client device to download a list of neighboring WAPs?

   A. 802.11r

   B. 802.11e

   C. 802.11k

   D. 802.11ac

197. You are planning to implement wireless VoIP phones in your wireless network. Which QoS profile should you associate with the wireless network for the VoIP phones?

   A. Bronze

   B. Silver

   C. Gold

   D. Platinum

198. You were just notified by your maintenance department that they lost all wireless connectivity. Earlier, you had a contractor working on the WLC. You log into the WLC and click on the WLAN of MaintDept shown in the following figure. What can you do to correct the problem?

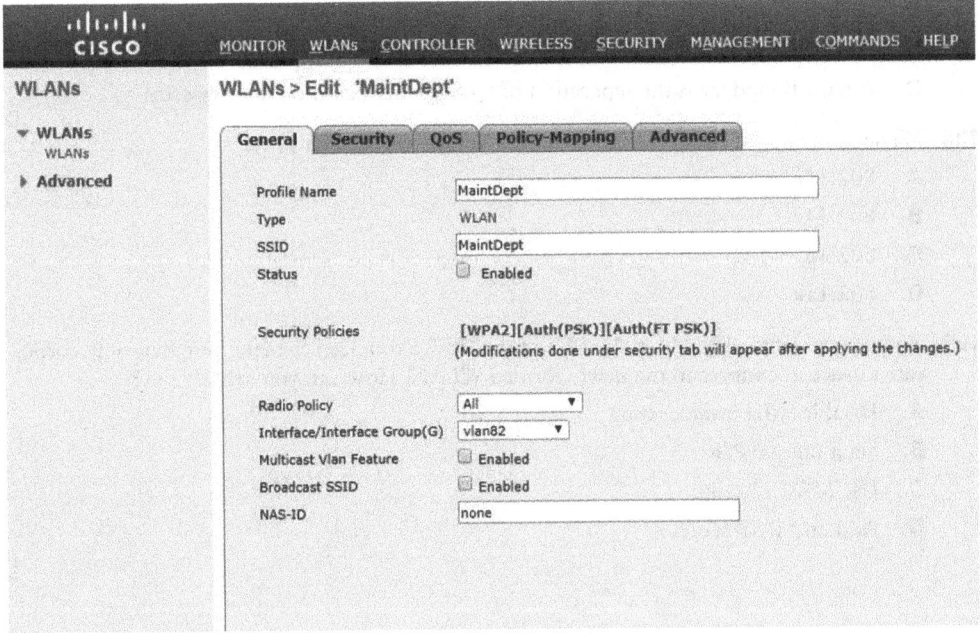

   A. Enable the status.

   B. Change the Radio Policy value.

   C. Enable the Multicast VLAN feature.

   D. Enable Broadcast SSID.

199. Which statement is true about the WLAN in the following figure?

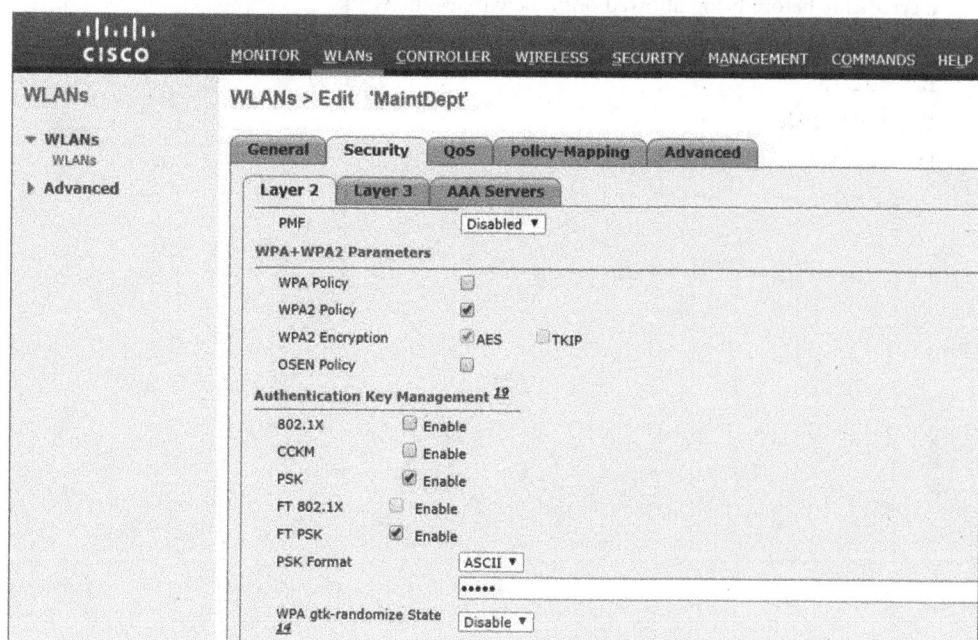

- **A.** WPA is enabled.
- **B.** WPA2 enterprise is enabled.
- **C.** WPA2 personal is enabled.
- **D.** 802.1X is enabled.

200. Which statement is correct about Flex Connect mode versus Local mode?
- **A.** Flex Connect mode creates a CAPWAP tunnel to the WLC to transport data.
- **B.** Local mode creates a CAPWAP tunnel to the WLC to transport data.
- **C.** Local mode allows for switching of VLANs at the WAP.
- **D.** Flex Connect mode allows for switching of VLANs at the WLC.

201. You need to set up a WLAN for connectivity to send and receive large files to roaming clients. The WLAN will exist with other WLAN traffic. Which QoS profile should the new WLAN be associated with?
- **A.** Bronze
- **B.** Gold
- **C.** Platinum
- **D.** Silver

202. Which type of security can be implemented on a WLAN that requires the host PC to present a certificate before being allowed onto the wireless network?

- **A.** MAC filtering
- **B.** 802.1X
- **C.** WPA2 PSK
- **D.** Fast Transitioning

Chapter 3

IP Connectivity (Domain 3)

THE CCNA EXAM TOPICS COVERED IN THIS PRACTICE TEST INCLUDE THE FOLLOWING:

✓ **3.0 IP Connectivity**

    3.1 Interpret the components of routing table

        3.1.a Routing protocol code

        3.1.b Prefix

        3.1.c Network mask

        3.1.d Next hop

        3.1.e Administrative distance

        3.1.f Metric

        3.1.g Gateway of last resort

    3.2 Determine how a router makes a forwarding decision by default

        3.2.a Longest prefix match

        3.2.b Administrative distance

        3.2.c Routing protocol metric

    3.3 Configure and verify IPv4 and IPv6 static routing

        3.3.a Default route

        3.3.b Network route

        3.3.c Host route

        3.3.d Floating static

    3.4 Configure and verify single area OSPFv2

        3.4.a Neighbor adjacencies

        3.4.b Point-to-point

3.4.c Broadcast (DR/BDR selection)

3.4.d Router ID

3.5 Describe the purpose, functions, and concepts of first hop redundancy protocol

1. Which is a reason for using a dynamic routing protocol?
   A. You have a network with only a few routers and subnets per branch.
   B. You have a network with only a few VLANs and one router.
   C. You have a network with a large number of VLANs and only one router.
   D. You have a network with a few subnets and many routers.

2. How are routers managed with interior gateway routing protocols?
   A. Routers are grouped into autonomous systems.
   B. Routing protocols are redistributed between ASs.
   C. All routers use the same interior routing protocol.
   D. All network IDs are advertised with the same autonomous system number.

3. What is the maximum hop count for RIP?
   A. 15 hops
   B. 100 hops
   C. 255 hops
   D. 16 hops

4. Which statement is true about RIPv2 advertisements?
   A. RIPv2 allows for neighborship through hello packets.
   B. RIPv2 broadcasts only updates on all active interfaces.
   C. RIPv2 multicasts the full routing table every 30 seconds.
   D. RIPv2 multicasts the full routing table every 60 seconds.

5. Which multicast address does RIPv2 use for advertising routes?
   A. 224.0.0.5
   B. 224.0.0.9
   C. 224.0.0.6
   D. 224.0.0.2

6. In the following figure, a packet from network 192.168.1.0/24 is destined for 192.168.4.0/24. The route the packet will take will be Router A to Router B, determined by RIPv2. However, the bandwidth is only 64 Kb/s. How can you force packets to travel over the 1.544 Mb/s links?

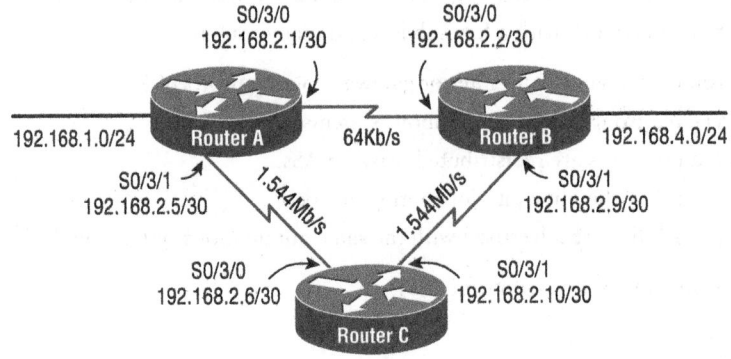

```
RouterA#sh ip route
[output cut]
    192.168.1.0/24 is variably subnetted, 2 subnets, 2 masks
C    192.168.1.0/24 is directly connected, GigabitEthernet0/0
L    192.168.1.1/32 is directly connected, GigabitEthernet0/0
    192.168.2.0/24 is variably subnetted, 5 subnets, 2 masks
C    192.168.2.0/30 is directly connected, Serial0/3/0
L    192.168.2.1/32 is directly connected, Serial0/3/0
C    192.168.2.4/30 is directly connected, Serial0/3/1
L    192.168.2.5/32 is directly connected, Serial0/3/1
R    192.168.2.8/30 [120/1] via 192.168.2.6, 00:00:25, Serial0/3/1
R    192.168.4.0/24 [120/1] via 192.168.2.2, 00:00:22, Serial0/3/0
RouterA#
```

A. RouterA(config-router)#passive interface serial 0/3/0
    RouterB(config-router)#passive interface serial 0/3/0

B. RouterA(config)#ip route 192.168.4.0 255.255.255.0 serial 0/3/1
    RouterB(config)#ip route 192.168.1.0 255.255.255.0 serial 0/3/1

C. RouterA(config-router)#cost 2 serial 0/3/0
    RouterB(config-router)#cost 2 serial 0/3/0

D. RouterA(config-if)#metric 2 serial 0/3/0
    RouterB(config-if)#metric 2 serial 0/3/0

7. Which routing protocol will not contain a topology table of the network?

    A. EIGRP

    B. RIP

    C. OSPF

    D. BGP

8. Which routing loop avoidance method is used by routers to prevent routing updates from exiting an interface in which they have been learned?

   A. Routing to infinity

   B. Route poisoning

   C. Holddowns

   D. Split horizon

9. You are examining a routing table and see a route marked with S*. Which type of route is this?

   A. Static route

   B. Static default route

   C. Dynamic route

   D. OSPF route

10. You are examining a routing table and see the entry in the following figure. What does the 4 in the underlined number represent?

```
R 172.16.2.0 [120/4] via 1.1.1.13, 00:13:24, FastEthernet0/1
```

   A. It represents the administrative distance.

   B. It represents the protocol.

   C. It represents the metric.

   D. It represents the position in the routing table.

11. Which command will allow you to verify routes line by line in a subset of the general route statement?

   A. `show ip route 160.45.23.0 255.255.255.0 longer-prefixes`

   B. `show ip route 160.45.23.0 255.255.255.0`

   C. `show ip route bgp`

   D. `show ip route`

12. Examining the `show ip route` statement in the figure, which will be the next hop for a destination address of 192.168.1.5?

```
Router#show ip route
[output cut]
192.168.1.0/24 is subnetted, 1 subnets
C 192.168.1.0/24 is directly connected, serial 0/0
O 192.168.1.0/24 [110/421356] via 172.16.1.200, 00:00:33, Ethernet0
R 192.168.1.0/24 [90/2] via 172.16.1.100, 00:00:16, Ethernet0
```

   A. The gateway 172.16.1.200

   B. The exit interface Serial 0/0

   C. The gateway 172.16.1.100

   D. The exit interface Ethernet0

13. Which route statement is configured when an IP address of 203.80.53.22/19 is configured on an interface?

    A. `S 203.80.16.0/19 is directly connected, Serial 0/0/0`

    B. `S 203.80.32.0/19 is directly connected, Serial 0/0/0`

    C. `S 203.80.48.0/19 is directly connected, Serial 0/0/0`

    D. `S 203.80.53.22/19 is directly connected, Serial 0/0/0`

14. In the following figure, what does the top line of the output represent?

```
Router#sh ip route
[output cut]
 10.0.0.0/8 is variably subnetted, 3 subnets, 2 masks
C 10.10.0.0/16 is directly connected, serial0/2/0
L 10.10.1.1/32 is directly connected, serial0/2/0
S 10.20.0.0/16 [1/0] via 192.168.4.2
[output cut]
```

    A. The 10.0.0.0/8 is a route in the routing table.

    B. The 10.0.0.0/8 is a summarization of the routes in the table.

    C. The 10.0.0.0/8 is the router's network address.

    D. The 10.0.0.0/8 has been populated from another router.

15. You are examining a routing table and see the entry in the following figure. What does the underlined number represent?

```
R 172.16.2.0 [120/4] via 1.1.1.13, 00:13:24, FastEthernet0/1
```

    A. The number represents the current time.

    B. The number represents the delay in microseconds of the connection.

    C. The number represents the time the route has been in the routing table.

    D. The number represents the time the interface has been up.

16. In the following figure is a copy of the running-config. What is the next hop for a destination address of 192.168.4.85?

```
Router#show run
!
[output cut]
ip route 0.0.0.0 0.0.0.0 Serial0/2/0
ip route 192.168.4.0 255.255.255.0 Serial0/0/1
ip route 192.168.5.0 255.255.255.0 192.168.4.2
ip route 10.20.0.0 255.255.0.0 192.168.4.2
ip route 192.168.0.0 255.255.0.0 198.22.34.3
```

    A. Interface Serial 0/2/0

    B. IP address 192.168.4.2

    C. Interface Serial 0/0/1

    D. IP address 198.22.34.3

17. Using the following figure, if traffic enters Router A for a destination address of 198.44.4.7, what must be configured to allow routing to the host?

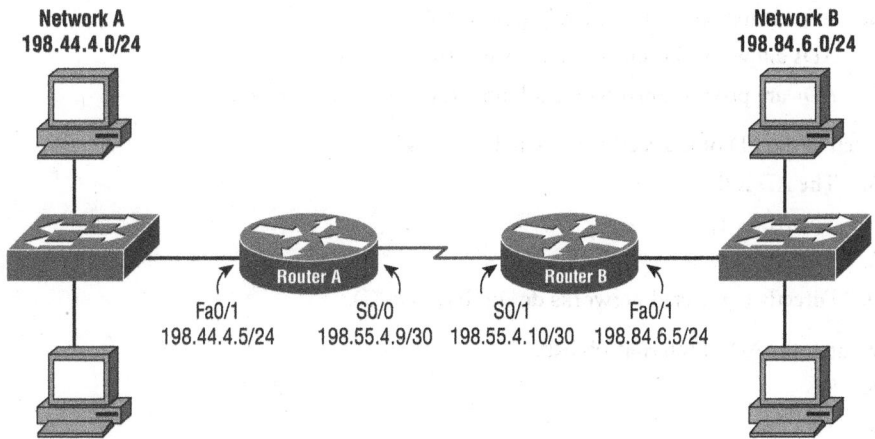

Network A
198.44.4.0/24

Network B
198.84.6.0/24

Router A

Router B

Fa0/1
198.44.4.5/24

S0/0
198.55.4.9/30

S0/1
198.55.4.10/30

Fa0/1
198.84.6.5/24

  A. `ip route 198.44.4.0 255.255.255.0 198.44.4.5`

  B. `ip route 198.44.4.0 255.255.255.0 fast 0/1`

  C. `ip route 198.44.4.0/24 fast 0/1`

  D. Nothing needs to be done.

18. You need to create a route for 205.34.54.85/29 with the next hop being 205.34.55.2. Which command would create this route?

  A. `ip route 205.34.54.85/24 205.34.55.2`

  B. `ip route 205.34.54.85 255.255.255.248 205.34.55.2`

  C. `ip route 205.34.54.85 255.255.255.240 205.34.55.2`

  D. `ip route 205.34.55.2 255.255.255.248 205.34.54.85`

19. When a static route is made, what is the default AD?

  A. AD of 1

  B. AD of 0

  C. AD of 2

  D. AD of 255

20. What is the AD of RIP?

  A. AD of 90

  B. AD of 100

  C. AD of 110

  D. AD of 120

21. Why are administrative distances (ADs) used with routing tables?

   A. ADs define protocol standards.

   B. ADs define reliability of routing protocols.

   C. ADs allow for the shortest distance between routes.

   D. ADs are programmed by the administrator for path selection.

22. What is the AD of a directly connected network?

   A. The AD is 0.

   B. The AD is 1.

   C. The AD is 5.

   D. Directly connected networks do not have an AD.

23. What is the AD of internal EIGRP?

   A. 90

   B. 100

   C. 110

   D. 120

24. What is the definition of administrative distance (AD)?

   A. The AD is a metric that routing protocols use to select the best route.

   B. The AD is a value assigned by network administrators for route selection.

   C. The AD is a rating of trust when multiple routes exist to the same destination.

   D. The AD is a value associated with the cost to the destination.

25. Which can be configured so that EIGRP can calculate the best route based on throughput?

   A. Bandwidth

   B. Delay

   C. Reliability

   D. Load

26. You perform a `show ip route` on the router and see several routes with an AD of 90. Which routing protocol has generated these route statements?

   A. IGRP

   B. OSPF

   C. EIGRP

   D. RIP

27. Which statement is true when there are multiple route statements from different routing protocols for the same destination network?

   A. The route from the protocol with the highest AD is chosen.

   B. The route chosen has the lowest metric.

   C. The route from the protocol with the lowest AD is chosen.

   D. The route chosen has the highest metric.

28. You have a network with varied bandwidths and need to choose a dynamic routing protocol. Which would you choose for optimal performance?

   A. RIPv1

   B. RIPv2

   C. EIGRP

   D. BGP

29. What is the Cisco metric for OSPF?

   A. 10^8 / bandwidth

   B. Delay, bandwidth, reliability, load

   C. K metrics

   D. Bandwidth

30. You enter a `show ip route` command and see the following line. What does the `[110/1]` identify?

   `O     192.168.3.0/24 [110/1] via 192.168.10.6, 00:58:55, Serial0/3/1`

   A. AD of 110 and a 100 Mb/s link

   B. AD of 110 and a 10 Mb/s link

   C. AD of 1 and a 110 Mb/s link

   D. AD of 110 and a 1 Gb/s link

31. What type of route is the destination of 0.0.0.0/0?

   A. Local route

   B. Dynamic route

   C. Default route

   D. Loopback route

32. What role does ICMP take in the routing of a packet?

   A. ICMP populates the routing table.

   B. ICMP is used when routes are not reachable.

   C. ICMP maintains the routing table.

   D. ICMP performs continuous diagnosis of the network paths.

33. How is a route selected when the route table contains overlapping destination prefixes?

   A. The route with the lowest cost is selected.

   B. The route with the longest matching prefix is selected.

   C. The route with the highest AD is selected.

   D. The route with the lowest AD is selected.

34. You are examining a router and discover that there is a static default route configured for a next hop of 192.168.1.2. You also notice that there is a default route being populated from RIP for a next hop of 192.168.2.2. Which default route will be selected?

A. The route with the lowest AD

B. The route with the highest AD

C. The route with the lowest metric

D. The route being populated from RIP

35. Which is true of a host route in the routing table?

A. The host route is the route a packet will take if no other route matches in the routing table.

B. The routing table creates host routers for the destination hosts it discovers.

C. A host route is a specific route with a netmask of /32 for a specific host.

D. The host route is populated from HSRP.

36. Which element of a routing table will identify where the route was learned from?

A. Prefix and network mask

B. Routing protocol code

C. Metric

D. Next hop

37. Which criteria are routing decisions based on?

A. Source IP

B. Destination IP address

C. TTL

D. Destination MAC address

38. Which type of routing requires network administrator intervention?

A. Link-state routing

B. Distance-vector routing

C. Static routing

D. Dynamic routing

39. Which is a correct statement about the subnet mask?

A. The subnet mask is used by the host to determine the destination network.

B. The subnet mask is used in routing to determine the destination network.

C. The router uses its subnet mask when routing a packet.

D. The destination computer checks the subnet mask on the packet to verify that it's intended for that computer.

40. What protocol does the router or host use to find a MAC address for a destination IP address when it determines that the IP address is on the local network?

    A. IGMP

    B. RARP

    C. ARP

    D. ICMP

41. When a host sends a packet destined for an address on a remote network, what happens?

    A. The destination IP address is changed to the router's IP address.

    B. The destination MAC address is changed to the destination host's MAC address.

    C. The destination MAC address is changed to the router's MAC address.

    D. The source IP address is changed to the router's IP address.

42. Which statement describes correctly what happens when a packet moves through a router?

    A. The destination IP address is changed to the original destination.

    B. The packet's TTL is decremented.

    C. The source MAC address is changed to the original source MAC address.

    D. All of the above.

43. When a packet is determined to be on the local network, what happens?

    A. The destination IP address is changed to the router IP address.

    B. The destination MAC address is changed to the destination host's MAC address.

    C. The destination MAC address is changed to the router's MAC address.

    D. The source IP address is changed to the router's IP address.

44. How does the sending host know if the destination is local or remote with respect to its immediate network?

    A. The host compares the IP address to its internal routing table.

    B. The host performs ANDing on its subnet mask and the destination IP address, comparing the result to its own network address.

    C. The host performs ANDing on the destination subnet mask and the destination IP address, comparing the result to its own network address.

    D. The IP address is verified to be local to its network via ICMP.

45. What is the current method Cisco routers use for packet forwarding?

    A. Process switching

    B. Fast switching

    C. Intelligent packet forwarding

    D. Cisco Express Forwarding

46. What is the process called at layer 2 when a packet hops from router to router and eventually to the host?

    A. IP routing

    B. Frame rewrite

    C. Packet hopping

    D. Packet switching

47. When a host sends an ARP request packet out, what is the destination address of the frame?

    A. The router's MAC address

    B. The host's MAC address

    C. The MAC address, in the form of a broadcast

    D. The MAC address, in the form of a multicast

48. What does every network device use to limit the number of ARP packets?

    A. ARP cache

    B. IP multicasting

    C. Frame casting

    D. IP cache

49. Which statement describes what happens when a packet enters a router?

    A. The router accepts all incoming frames regardless of their destination MAC address.

    B. The router decapsulates the packet and inspects the destination IP address.

    C. Routers do not need to decapsulate packets to inspect the destination IP address.

    D. Routers make routing decisions first by examining the source MAC address.

50. Which command will display the router's ARP cache?

    A. `show arp`

    B. `show arp table`

    C. `show arp cache`

    D. `show ip arp`

51. What is the default time an entry will live in the ARP cache?

    A. 180 seconds

    B. 240 seconds

    C. 300 seconds

    D. 600 seconds

52. Which type of routing allows for routers to share their routes with other routers in the network?

    A. Default routing

    B. Stub routing

    C. Static routing

    D. Dynamic routing

53. Which statement describes what happens during the routing process?

   A. As a packet travels through the routers, the TTL of the packet will increase by one.

   B. When a route to the destination network is found, the router will attach the destination MAC address of the next-hop router to the packet.

   C. When a packet travels through the router, the transport information will be checked for the destination network.

   D. When a route to the destination network is found, the router will attach the destination IP address for the next hop to the packet.

54. Which protocol allows for testing and connectivity of a route?

   A. IGMP

   B. RARP

   C. ARP

   D. ICMP

55. Which routing protocol is a distance-vector routing protocol?

   A. OSPF

   B. RIP

   C. EIGRP

   D. BGP

56. When an IP packet reaches a router for which it has no further route, what happens?

   A. The router will discard the packet without notification.

   B. The router will change the TTL of the packet to 0.

   C. The router will send the packet back to the originating host.

   D. The router will send back a destination unreachable message.

57. Which statement accurately describes asynchronous routing?

   A. Packets are routed out one interface but come back on a different interface.

   B. Packets transmitted within a series of routers and never reach the destination.

   C. Packets reach the expiry TTL before reaching the destination network.

   D. Packets are routed via an inefficient path.

58. Which routing protocol is a link-state routing protocol?

   A. OSPF

   B. RIP

   C. EIGRP

   D. IGRP

59. Where are dynamic routes stored in a router?

   A. RAM

   B. Flash

   C. Startup configuration

   D. Running configuration

60. Which is a correct statement about SVI inter-VLAN routing (IVR)?

    A. Latency is low with SVI IVR because of ASICs.

    B. Latency is high with SVI inter-VLAN routing because of resource use.

    C. SVI inter-VLAN routing is a cheaper alternative to ROAS.

    D. Bandwidth is limited compared to ROAS.

61. Which is a disadvantage of using ROAS?

    A. The lack of ISL support for VLANs.

    B. The number of VLANs you can route is tied to the number of physical ports.

    C. Scalability of ROAS for the number of VLANs.

    D. The lack of dynamic routing protocol support.

62. Which is a correct statement about IVR?

    A. Each VLAN requires a unique IP network.

    B. IVR reduces the number of broadcast domains.

    C. It does not support ACLs.

    D. IVR restricts the use of subnetting.

63. What is the method of using a single router interface to route between VLANs called?

    A. Interface routing

    B. ROAS routing

    C. SVI routing

    D. Bridge routing

64. What is a disadvantage of routing between VLANs on a router's interface?

    A. Routers do not handle large amounts of traffic very well.

    B. When using ROAS, bandwidth problems are encountered.

    C. Security cannot be implemented with ROAS.

    D. Broadcast traffic is increased.

65. What is the method of routing between VLANs on a layer 3 switch?

    A. Interface routing

    B. ROAS routing

    C. SVI routing

    D. Bridge routing

66. Which routing technique requires no administrator intervention when a route goes down?

    A. Dynamic routing

    B. Directly connected routes

    C. Default routing

    D. Static routing

67. Which routing technique requires increased time for configuration as networks grow?

    A. RIP routing

    B. OSPF routing

    C. Static routing

    D. Default routing

68. Which routing technique requires the lowest amount of router RAM consumption?

    A. RIP routing

    B. OSPF routing

    C. Static routing

    D. Default routing

69. Which dynamic routing protocol has the lowest overhead?

    A. BGP

    B. OSPF

    C. RIP

    D. EIGRP

70. Which is an advantage of dynamic routing protocols?

    A. Resiliency when routes become unavailable

    B. Lower router RAM usage

    C. Lower router CPU usage

    D. Less bandwidth usage

71. Which routing protocol broadcasts updates for routes?

    A. RIP

    B. OSPF

    C. EIGRP

    D. BGP

72. What is an advantage of dynamic routing protocols?

    A. Centralized routing tables

    B. Optimized route selection

    C. Ease of configuration

    D. Lower bandwidth utilization

73. Which routing protocol has a maximum of 255 hops?

    A. RIP

    B. OSPF

    C. EIGRP

    D. BGP

74. Which protocol is considered a hybrid protocol?

   A. RIP

   B. OSPF

   C. EIGRP

   D. BGP

75. What is a characteristic of distance-vector protocols?

   A. They track the status of routes learned.

   B. They re-advertise routes learned.

   C. Each router keeps its own topology database.

   D. Each router checks the routes it learns.

76. Which type of network are distance-vector protocols best suited for?

   A. Networks containing fewer than 255 routes

   B. Networks containing fewer than 15 routers

   C. Networks containing more than 15 routers

   D. Networks containing more than 255 routers

77. Which problem could arise from use of a distance-vector routing protocol?

   A. Routing loops

   B. Router incompatibility

   C. Complexity of configuration

   D. Default route advertisement

78. Which dynamic routing protocol uses the diffusing update algorithm as its routing algorithm?

   A. RIP

   B. EIGRP

   C. OSPF

   D. BGP

79. Which is a disadvantage of distance-vector routing protocols?

   A. Router incompatibility for RIP

   B. Slow convergence of routing tables

   C. Resource usage of CPU and RAM

   D. The complexity of RIP design

80. Which dynamic routing protocol uses the Bellman–Ford routing algorithm?

   A. RIP

   B. EIGRP

   C. OSPF

   D. BGP

81. Which is a design concept used to stop routing loops with distance-vector dynamic routing protocols?

   A. Use of a topology database

   B. Use of holddown timers

   C. Use of anti-flapping ACLs

   D. Use of counting-to-infinity conditions

82. Which is an exterior gateway routing protocol?

   A. RIPv1

   B. OSPF

   C. EIGRP

   D. BGP

83. Which protocol is a Cisco-proprietary interior gateway protocol?

   A. RIPv1

   B. OSPF

   C. EIGRP

   D. BGP

84. Which statement is correct about interior gateway protocols (IGPs) vs. exterior gateway protocols (EGPs)?

   A. IGPs are used to exchange information between autonomous systems.

   B. EGPs are used to exchange information between routers within an autonomous system.

   C. IGPs are used to exchange information between routers within an autonomous system.

   D. EGPs are used in the core of an internal network.

85. Which statement is correct about IGPs?

   A. IGPs require a small number of resources, such as CPU and RAM.

   B. IGPs function within an administrative domain.

   C. An EGP is an example of an IGP.

   D. IGPs use autonomous system numbers (ASNs) that have been assigned by ARIN.

86. Why would you need to use an EGP?

   A. You need to connect your company to the Internet.

   B. You have been delegated a large number of IP addresses.

   C. You want to achieve fast routing to the Internet.

   D. You are dual-homed with two different ISPs.

87. When RIP is configured on a router, what must be configured to allow for classless routing?

   A. `Router(config)#ip classless`

   B. `Router(config)#router rip v2`

   C. `Router(config-router)#ip classless`

   D. `Router(config-router)#version 2`

88. You need to configure the advertisement of the network 192.168.1.0/24 for RIPv2. Which command will achieve this?

  A. `network 192.168.1.0`

  B. `network 192.168.1.0 0.0.0.255`

  C. `network 192.168.1.0/24`

  D. `network 192.168.1.0 255.255.255.0`

89. What is the entry for the IP address in the routing table called in IOS 15 code when an interface is configured?

  A. IP address route

  B. Local route

  C. Dynamic route

  D. Static route

90. Which metric does RIPv2 use to calculate routes?

  A. Delay

  B. Bandwidth

  C. Hop count

  D. Bandwidth and delay

91. Which command will allow you to inspect RIPv2 calculations for routes discovered?

  A. `show ip protocols rip`

  B. `show ip rip database`

  C. `show ip interface`

  D. `show ip rip topology`

92. Which command would allow you to see the next hop information for CEF?

  A. `show cef`

  B. `show ip cef`

  C. `show cef nop`

  D. `show cef route`

93. Which component of a network transmission changes during the routing process?

  A. Destination MAC address

  B. Destination IP address

  C. Source IP address

  D. Internal routes

94. What will a router do if a matching route is not present in the router table?

  A. Flood the packet to all active interfaces.

  B. Multicast the packet to other routers.

  C. Drop the packet.

  D. Send the original packet back to the source.

95. By default, which type of routing is used automatically on a router?

  A. Default routing

  B. Dynamic routes

  C. Static routes

  D. Connected routes

96. Which command would set the IPv6 default route for a router to interface s0/0?

  A. `ip route 0.0.0.0/0 s0/0`

  B. `ipv6 route 0.0.0.0/0 s0/0`

  C. `ipv6 unicast-route ::0/0 s0/0`

  D. `ipv6 route ::0/0 s0/0`

97. Which dynamic routing protocol(s) can be used with IPv6?

  A. RIPng

  B. OSPFv3

  C. EIGRPv6

  D. All of the above

98. You need to see all routes in the routing table for only IPv6. Which command will achieve this?

  A. `show route`

  B. `show ip route`

  C. `show ipv6 route`

  D. `show route ipv6`

99. What is the relevance of the default gateway address on a host that is transmitting to a destination for the first time?

  A. The destination IP address is replaced with the default gateway when the destination is remote.

  B. The host sends the default gateway packets that are deemed remote via a broadcast.

  C. The host sends an ARP packet for the default gateway when the destination is remote.

  D. The host creates a dedicated connection with the default gateway for remote traffic.

100. Which command will display the router's routing table?

  A. `show ip route`

  B. `show route`

  C. `show route table`

  D. `show routes`

101. Which protocol is used by TCP/IP to help facilitate the routing of packets?

  A. IGMP

  B. RARP

  C. ARP

  D. ICMP

102. What uses ICMP to directly check the status of a router?

    A. SNMP traps

    B. Notifications

    C. `ping`

    D. ARP

103. You have just used the `ping` command for a distant router. You received back five exclamation marks. What do these mean?

    A. The distant router is not responding.

    B. The distant router has a high response time.

    C. The distant router is responding.

    D. The distant router has a low response time.

104. You need to create a route for a network of 192.168.4.0/24 through the gateway of serial 0/1 on a Cisco 2621 router. Which is the proper command?

    A. `ip route 192.168.4.0/24 serial 0/1`

    B. `ip route 192.168.4.0 255.255.255.0 serial 0/1`

    C. `ip route 192.168.4.0/24 interface serial 0/1`

    D. `ip route Router(config-rtr)#192.168.4.0/24 serial 0/1`

105. You type into the router `ip default-gateway 192.168.11.2`. Why will traffic not route out the default gateway?

    A. The `ip default-network` needs to be used in conjunction with `ip default-gateway 192.168.11.2`.

    B. The command is only used for the management plane of the router itself.

    C. The command is used for dynamic routing only.

    D. The specified gateway is wrong.

106. In the following figure, which route statement needs to be configured on Router A to allow routing to Network B?

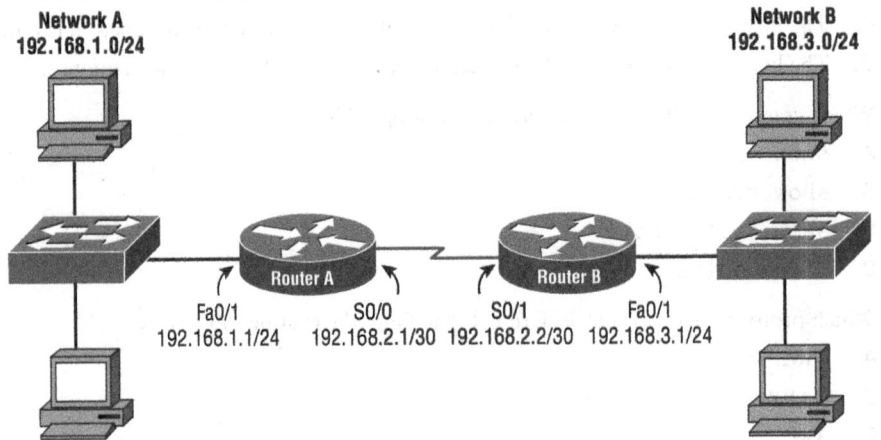

A. `ip route 192.168.3.0 255.255.255.0 serial 0/1`

B. `ip route 192.168.3.0 255.255.255.0 192.168.2.1`

C. `ip route 192.168.3.0 255.255.255.0 192.168.2.2`

D. `ip route 192.168.3.0 255.255.255.0 192.168.3.1`

107. When you configure an IP address on a router interface, what happens to the routing table?

A. The router creates a /32 route for the IP address.

B. The router creates a summary address for the network.

C. The router creates a routing update if dynamic routing is configured.

D. All of the above.

108. You want to verify the IP addresses configured on the router. Which command will you use?

A. `show ip`

B. `show ip interfaces brief`

C. `show interfaces`

D. `show ip brief`

109. You configure a brand-new IP address on a new router's interface. However, when you look at the routing table, it does not show up. You see a link light on the interface. What is wrong?

A. The interface is administratively shut down.

B. The interface speed is incorrect.

C. The interface bandwidth is not set.

D. The route will not show up until you save the config.

110. What is a benefit of static routing?

A. Adding networks is an easy task for network administrators.

B. It is suited for large networks because changes will not disturb routing.

C. It reduces bandwidth used by router-to-router communications.

D. It allows for configuration by any network admin in the network.

111. Where are static routes stored?

A. RAM

B. Flash

C. Startup configuration

D. Routing database

112. You want to route 192.168.1.0/24, 192.168.2.0/24 to a destination address of 198.43.23.2. How can you accomplish this with one route statement so that other networks are not affected?

   A. `ip route 192.168.0.0 255.255.0.0 198.43.23.2`

   B. `ip route 192.168.0.0 255.255.255.0 198.43.23.2`

   C. `ip route 192.168.0.0 255.255.240.0 198.43.23.2`

   D. `ip route 192.168.0.0 255.255.0.240 198.43.23.2`

113. Why would you create a second route statement to the same network using a different AD and different interface?

   A. If the first one fails to route to the destination, the second route will succeed.

   B. If the first interface goes down, the second route will become active.

   C. If there is a high amount of traffic on the first interface, the second route will become active.

   D. If there is a routing loop on the first interface, the second will overcome the loop.

114. Which route statement is configured when an IP address of 208.43.34.17/29 is configured on an interface?

   A. `S 208.43.34.17/32 is directly connected, Serial 0/0/0`

   B. `S 208.43.34.24/29 is directly connected, Serial 0/0/0`

   C. `S 208.43.34.8/29 is directly connected, Serial 0/0/0`

   D. `S 208.43.34.17/29 is directly connected, Serial 0/0/0`

115. In the following figure, which network is routable?

```
Router#sh ip route
[output cut]
   172.16.0.0/16 is variably subnetted, 2 subnets, 2 masks
C 172.16.0.0/16 is directly connected, Serial0/0/0
L 172.16.1.1/32 is directly connected, Serial0/0/0
   192.168.1.0/24 is variably subnetted, 2
C 192.168.1.0/24 is directly connected, Serial0/0/1
L 192.168.1.1/32 is directly connected, Serial0/0/1
S 192.168.4.0/24 is directly connected, Serial0/0/1
S 192.168.5.0/24 [1/0] via 192.168.4.2
   198.23.24.0/24 is variably subnetted, 2 subnets, 2 masks
C 198.23.24.0/24 is directly connected, Serial0/1/1
L 198.23.24.1/32 is directly connected, Serial0/1/1
```

   A. The 172.30.0/16 network

   B. The 192.168.128.0/24 network

   C. The 192.168.0.0/16 network

   D. The 192.168.4.0/24 network

116. In the following figure, what must be configured on Router B to allow routing to Network A?

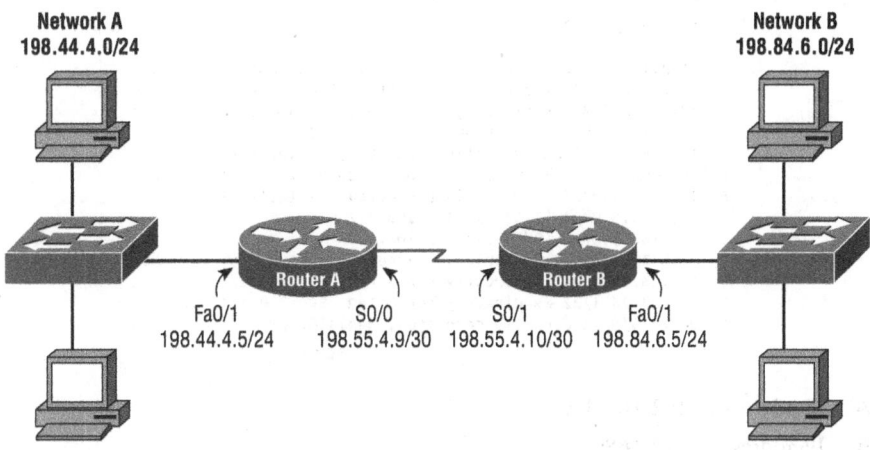

Network A
198.44.4.0/24

Network B
198.84.6.0/24

Router A   Router B

FaO/1   SO/0   SO/1   FaO/1
198.44.4.5/24   198.55.4.9/30   198.55.4.10/30   198.84.6.5/24

- **A.** `ip route 198.44.4.0/24 198.55.4.9`
- **B.** `ip route 198.44.4.0 255.255.255.0 198.55.4.10`
- **C.** `ip route 198.44.4.0 255.255.255.0 Serial 0/0`
- **D.** `ip route 198.44.4.0 255.255.255.0 Serial 0/1`

117. Which route statement is displayed when an IP address of 194.22.34.54/28 is configured on an interface?

- **A.** `S 194.22.34.48/28 is directly connected, Serial 0/0/0`
- **B.** `S 194.22.34.64/28 is directly connected, Serial 0/0/0`
- **C.** `S 194.22.34.54/28 is directly connected, Serial 0/0/0`
- **D.** `S 194.22.34.32/28 is directly connected, Serial 0/0/0`

118. Which command will create a default route through Serial 0/0 for IPv6?

- **A.** `ip route 0.0.0.0 0.0.0.0 serial 0/0`
- **B.** `ipv6 route 0.0.0.0 0.0.0.0 serial 0/0`
- **C.** `ipv6 route ::/0 serial 0/0`
- **D.** `ip route ::/0 serial 0/0`

119. Which command would configure the route for an IPv6 network of FC00:0:0:1 with the exit interface of serial 0/0/0?

- **A.** `ip route fc00:0:0:1 serial 0/0/0`
- **B.** `ipv6 route fc00:0:0:1/64 serial 0/0/0`
- **C.** `ip route fc00:0:0:1/64 serial 0/0`
- **D.** `ipv6 route fc00:0:0:1 serial 0/0/0`

120. In the following figure, which interface or IP address will a packet be routed to with a destination address of 192.168.5.6?

```
Router#sh ip route
[output cut]
     172.16.0.0/16 is variably subnetted, 2 subnets, 2 masks
C    172.16.0.0/16 is directly connected, Serial0/0/0
L    172.16.1.1/32 is directly connected, Serial0/0/0
     192.168.1.0/24 is variably subnetted, 2
C    192.168.1.0/24 is directly connected, Serial0/0/1
L    192.168.1.1/32 is directly connected, Serial0/0/1
S    192.168.4.0/24 is directly connected, Serial0/0/1
S    192.168.5.0/24 [1/0] via 192.168.4.2
S    192.168.5.0/24 [5/0] via 192.168.4.5
     198.23.24.0/24 is variably subnetted, 2 subnets, 2 masks
C    198.23.24.0/24 is directly connected, Serial0/1/1
L    198.23.24.1/32 is directly connected, Serial0/1/1
S*   0.0.0.0/0 is directly connected, Serial0/2/0
```

A. IP address of 192.168.4.2

B. IP address of 192.168.4.5

C. Interface Serial 0/0/1

D. Interface Serial 0/2/0

121. What is the purpose of issuing the command `no switchport` on a layer 3 switch?

A. It configures an SVI.

B. It configures an access port.

C. It configures a trunk port.

D. It configures a port as a routed interface.

122. You need to configure a router that has three interfaces to route five VLANs. What is the best way to accomplish this task?

A. Purchase another router with additional interfaces.

B. Configure the router as a ROAS.

C. Purchase a new router with five interfaces.

D. Configure a dynamic routing protocol.

123. Which command do you need to enter on a switch to allow routing between VLANs?

A. `routing`

B. `ip router`

C. `ip routing`

D. `ip route`

124. When routing between VLANs with a router's interface, which trunking protocol is always supported?

A. 802.1x

B. 802.1Q

C. ISL

D. VTP

125. Which command would configure the interface on the ROAS configuration as the native VLAN?

- **A.** `Router(config-subif)#switchport native vlan 2`
- **B.** `Router(config-if)#interface gi 0/1.2 native`
- **C.** `Router(config-subif)#native vlan 2`
- **D.** `Router(config-subif)#encapsulation dot1q 2 native`

126. Which commands would you use to configure an IP address on a Switched Virtual Interface (SVI)?

- **A.** `Switch(config)#interface vlan 10`
     `Switch(config-if)#ip address 192.168.10.1 255.255.255.0`
     `Switch(config-if)#no shutdown`
- **B.** `Switch(config)#interface vlan 10`
     `Switch(config-if)#ip address 192.168.10.1/24`
- **C.** `Switch(config)#interface vlan 10`
     `Switch(config-if)#ip address 192.168.10.1/24`
     `Switch(config-if)#no shutdown`
- **D.** `Switch(config)#vlan 10`
     `Switch(config-vlan)#ip address 192.168.10.1 255.255.255.0`
     `Switch(config-vlan)#no shutdown`

127. When configuring ROAS, which mode must be configured for the switchport on the switch?

- **A.** Trunk mode
- **B.** Access mode
- **C.** Routed mode
- **D.** Switched mode

128. When configuring the subinterfaces on a router for ROAS, what is a best practice when naming the subinterface?

- **A.** Always name the subinterface the same as the VLAN name.
- **B.** Always name the subinterface the same as the VLAN number.
- **C.** Always name the subinterface the same as the default gateway address.
- **D.** Always name the subinterface the same as the switch's interface number.

129. Which command enables the routers to direct the frames tagged for a particular VLAN to the subinterface?

- **A.** `Router(config-if)#interface gi 0/1.5`
- **B.** `Router(config-subif)#vlan 5`
- **C.** `Router(config-subif)#encapsulation dot1q 5`
- **D.** `Router(config-subif)#switchport access vlan 5`

130. Which command must be entered on 2960-XR switches to enable IP routing?

    A. `ip lanbase`

    B. `sdm prefer lanbase-routing`

    C. `sdm lanbase-routing`

    D. `sdm routing`

131. You want to verify the configured SVI VLAN interfaces. Which command will show you the configured IP addresses on each of the SVI VLAN interfaces?

    A. `show ip interface brief`

    B. `show interfaces status`

    C. `show svi`

    D. `show switchports ip`

132. You enter the command `ip address 192.168.2.0 255.255.255.0` on interface VLAN 2. When you enter the command, you receive a "Bad mask /24 for address" error. What is the problem?

    A. The subnet mask is incorrect.

    B. The subnet of 192.168.2.0 cannot be used for this interface.

    C. The IP address is invalid.

    D. The VLAN has not been configured yet.

133. You have purchased a layer 3 switch with the LAN Base feature. When you enter `ip routing` in global configuration mode, you receive an "Invalid input detected" error. What is the problem?

    A. There are no IP addresses configured on the switch.

    B. The SDM of LAN Base routing has not been enabled.

    C. There is not enough memory for routing tables.

    D. The IP Base feature is required.

134. You have a 3560 switch that supports layer 3 routing. You need to configure a physical interface to route a subnet. Which command needs to be used?

    A. `switchport routed`

    B. `no ip-routing`

    C. `no switchport`

    D. `ip address 192.168.2.1 255.255.255.0`

135. Which command will allow you to examine a switch's port to see if it is routed or switched?

    A. `show interface gi 0/2 switchport`

    B. `show interface gi 0/2 state`

    C. `show switchport interface gi 0/2`

    D. `show status interface gi 0/2`

136. You need to configure ROAS on a router's interface to route VLAN 5 with ISL. Which command will specify the encapsulation and achieve this?

    A. `Router(config-if)#encapsulation 5`

    B. `Router(config-if)#encapsulation isl 5`

    C. `Router(config-subif)#switchport encapsulation isl 5`

    D. `Router(config-subif)#encapsulation isl 5`

137. You have just configured a new VLAN and have configured the SVI with an IP address and `no shutdown` command on the interface. However, when you perform a `show ip route`, it does not show a valid directly connected route for the SVI. What is the problem?

    A. The VLAN is in a shutdown state.

    B. No interfaces have been configured with the new VLAN yet.

    C. The `show ip route` command will not display SVI directly connected routes.

    D. No dynamic routing protocols have been configured.

138. Which of the following is a correct statement about ROAS?

    A. Using a ROAS is a highly efficient alternative to routed SVIs.

    B. Using a ROAS is a cheaper alternative to inter-VLAN routing (IVR) on a switch.

    C. A ROAS can only be used with 802.1Q.

    D. A ROAS is limited to a maximum of 16 routes.

139. Before configuring ROAS, which command should be entered in the interface connecting to the switch?

    A. `ip routing`

    B. `no ip address`

    C. `ip encapsulation dot1q`

    D. `sdm routing`

140. You have configured a ROAS and set up the switch to connect to the router. However, you cannot route between VLANs. Which command would you use on the switch to verify operations?

    A. `show ip route`

    B. `show interface status`

    C. `show interface trunk`

    D. `show switchport`

141. When configuring a router in a ROAS configuration, which command will enable the interface to accept frames tagged for VLAN 10?

    A. `Switch(config-subif)#encapsulation vlan 10 dot1q`

    B. `Switch(config-if)#interface Fa 0/0.10`

    C. `Switch(config-subif)#encapsulation dot1q 10`

    D. `Switch(config-subif)#ip address 192.168.10.1 255.255.255.0`

142. Which statement is correct about ARP in relation to ROAS?

    A. Each physical interface has a unique MAC address, which responds to ARP requests.

    B. Each subinterface has a unique MAC address, which responds to ARP requests.

    C. Each IP address has a unique MAC address, which responds to ARP requests.

    D. All of the above.

143. Which statement is correct about implementing ROAS?

    A. Each IP address is configured on the subinterface as the gateway for the VLAN.

    B. The main interface must be configured with the summary IP address for all VLANs.

    C. You must configure at least one native VLAN.

    D. All of the above.

144. Which routing technique is a type of static routing?

    A. OSPF routing

    B. EIGRP routing

    C. Default routing

    D. RIP routing

145. Which is an advantage of using static routing?

    A. There is less administrative overhead.

    B. It is extremely secure.

    C. It can create resiliency in a network.

    D. It is extremely scalable without issues.

146. Which routing technique has the lowest bandwidth overhead?

    A. RIP routing

    B. OSPF routing

    C. EIGRP routing

    D. Static routing

147. Which type of routing technique allows for route summarization to be computed automatically by routers?

    A. Dynamic routing

    B. Directly connected routes

    C. Default routing

    D. Static routing

148. Which routing technique requires administrator intervention when a route goes down?

    A. Dynamic routing

    B. Directly connected routes

    C. Default routing

    D. Static routing

149. You have several routes configured on a router. Which command will show only the static routes?

- **A.** show static routes
- **B.** show ip static routes
- **C.** show ip routes static
- **D.** show ip routes

150. On interface Serial 0/1, you type `ipv6 address 2000:db8:4400:2300::1234/64`. Which statement is true?

- **A.** The router will calculate a network ID of 2000:0db8::.
- **B.** The IPv6 address of 2000:0db8:4400:2300:1234:0000:0000:0000/128 will be assigned to Serial 0/0.
- **C.** The router will calculate a network ID of 2000:0db8:4400:2300::/64 for Serial 0/0.
- **D.** The router will calculate a network ID of 2000:db8:4400:2300:0000/64 for Serial 0/0.

151. When you check the IPv6 addresses configured on the interfaces, you find two IPv6 addresses: One address is a 2001:db8::/64 address, and the other is an ff80::/64 address. However, you do not see a route statement for the ff80::/64 address in the routing table. Why?

- **A.** Multicast addresses do not get added to the routing tables.
- **B.** Link-local addresses do not get added to the routing tables.
- **C.** Only one route statement can be in the routing table at a time for an interface.
- **D.** Broadcast addresses do not get added to the routing tables.

152. In the following figure, RIP is running on all of the routers. On Router A, you want to make sure that if Router B fails, a backup route is used through Router C to Network B. Which statement will achieve this?

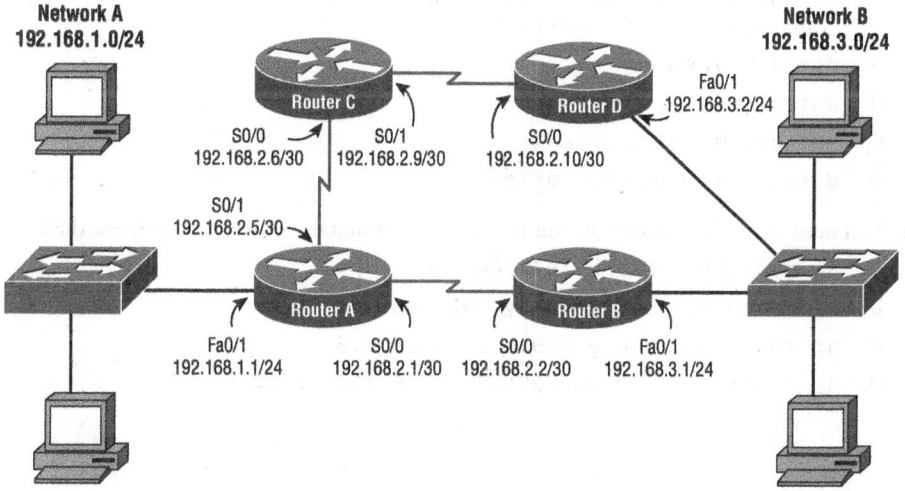

    A. `ip route 192.168.2.8 255.255.255.252 192.168.2.6`

    B. `ip route 192.168.3.0 255.255.255.0 192.168.2.6 220`

    C. `ip route 192.168.3.0 255.255.255.0 192.168.2.6 90`

    D. `ip route 192.168.3.0 255.255.255.0 192.168.2.10`

153. In the following figure, which command on Router B will allow hosts on Network B to reach the Internet?

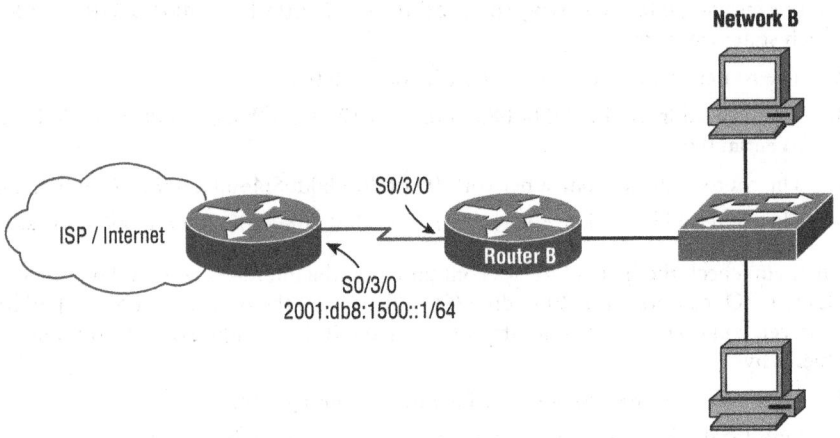

    A. `RouterB(config-if)#ipv6 address default`

    B. `RouterB(config)#ip route ::/0 serial 0/3/0`

    C. `RouterB(config-if)#ipv6 address autoconfig default`

    D. `RouterB(config-if)#ipv6 address slaac`

154. You have RIPv2 configured on an Internet-facing router. Which command will propagate the default route to all other RIPv2 routers?

    A. `network 0.0.0.0`

    B. `default-route advertise`

    C. `network 0.0.0.0 default`

    D. `default-information originate`

155. You need to implement default routing. Which command will help you achieve this?

    A. `ip default-network 192.168.2.6`

    B. `ip route default-gateway 192.168.2.6`

    C. `ip route 0.0.0.0 0.0.0.0 192.168.2.6`

    D. `ip route 0.0.0.0 255.255.255.255 192.168.2.6`

156. You ping a distant router in your network and find that the TTL returned in 252. What can you conclude?

    A. The ping took 252 milliseconds.

    B. The ping has a delay of 252 milliseconds.

    C. The ping moved through 252 routers.

    D. The ping moved through 3 routers.

157. Which command would you use so that you can view only the RIP route entries in the route table?

    A. `show ip rip`

    B. `show ip route`

    C. `show ip rip route`

    D. `show ip route rip`

158. Which protocol is a true link-state protocol?

    A. RIP

    B. OSPF

    C. EIGRP

    D. BGP

159. Which dynamic routing protocol uses the Dijkstra routing algorithm?

    A. RIP

    B. EIGRP

    C. OSPF

    D. BGP

160. Why don't link-state protocols suffer from routing loops as distance-vector protocols do?

    A. Link-state protocols require routers to maintain their own topology database of the network.

    B. Link-state protocols share the topology database among all routers.

    C. Link-state protocols allow routers to maintain a link-state database of all routers.

    D. Link-state protocols use multiple routes to the same destination.

161. What is an advantage of a link-state dynamic routing protocol?

    A. The only metric needed is hop count.

    B. Link-state dynamic routing protocols support CIDR and VLSM.

    C. OSPF requires only a small amount of resources such as CPU and RAM.

    D. Link-state dynamic routing protocols use triggered updates for recalculation of routing tables.

162. What type of network is best suited for a link-state routing protocol such as OSPF?

    A. Extremely small networks of three routers

    B. Networks with routers that have a limited amount of RAM and CPU

    C. Large hierarchical networks like global networks

    D. Networks within organizations with limited training of network admins

163. Which is an example of an interior gateway protocol that is nonproprietary?

    A. EGP

    B. OSPF

    C. EIGRP

    D. BGP

164. You have several sites, each with a different administrative unit, in your company. Which routing protocol should you choose?

    A. BGP

    B. OSPF

    C. RIPv2

    D. EGP

165. Which area must be present when using the OSPF routing protocol with multiple areas?

    A. Area 0

    B. Area 1

    C. Area 10

    D. Area 4

166. In the following figure, what is Router A called in OSPF terminology?

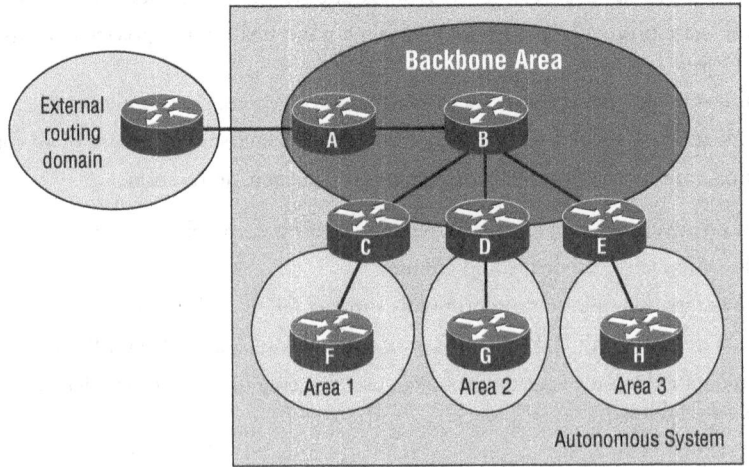

   A. Area border router

   B. Autonomous system router

   C. Autonomous system boundary router

   D. Area backup router

167. Which multicast address is used by OSPF for neighbor discovery?

   A. 224.0.0.9

   B. 224.0.0.5

   C. 224.0.0.6

   D. 224.0.0.7

168. In the following figure, what are Routers C, D, and E called in OSPF terminology?

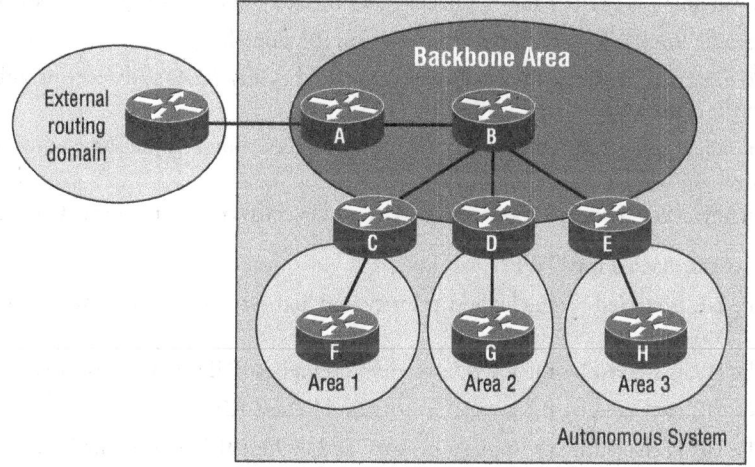

   A. Area border routers

   B. Autonomous system routers

   C. Autonomous system boundary routers

   D. Area backup routers

169. Which statement is true about OSPF?

   A. OSPF is a distance-vector protocol.

   B. OSPF performs default auto-summarization.

   C. OSPF broadcasts changes to the routing tables.

   D. OSPF updates are event triggered.

170. How do Cisco routers determine their router ID (RID)?

    A. The lowest IP address configured on the loopback interfaces

    B. The highest IP address configured on the router

    C. The lowest IP address configured on the router

    D. The highest MAC address configured on the router

171. What is the definition of an OSPF link?

    A. Two routers participating in OSPF routing

    B. Two routers that share the same area ID

    C. A routed interface added to the OSPF process

    D. Two routers that share the same AS number

172. Which statement is correct about adjacency with OSPF on a broadcast network (LAN)?

    A. An adjacency is formed between routers on the same link.

    B. An adjacency is formed between the designated router (DR) and every neighbor router on the same area.

    C. An adjacency is formed between the DR and every router in the same autonomous system.

    D. An adjacency is formed between the DR and every router in the same OSPF area.

173. How is a DR elected for OSPF?

    A. The DR is elected by the highest priority and highest RID in the same autonomous system.

    B. The DR is elected by the lowest priority and highest RID in the same area.

    C. The DR is elected by the lowest priority and lowest RID.

    D. The DR is elected by the highest priority and highest RID in the same area.

174. In which database can you see all of the routers discovered in the OSPF network in which hello packets were sent and acknowledged?

    A. The routing table database

    B. The neighborship database

    C. The topological database

    D. The link-state database

175. Which is a correct statement about OSPF?

    A. OSPF uses autonomous systems for scalability.

    B. OSPF uses process IDs for scalability.

    C. OSPF uses areas for scalability.

    D. OSPF uses RID for scalability.

176. Which is an example of a broadcast (multi-access) network?

- **A.** An X.25 network
- **B.** Frame Relay
- **C.** ATM network
- **D.** A LAN

177. Which multicast address is used by OSPF for communication between the DR and adjacencies formed?

- **A.** 224.0.0.9
- **B.** 224.0.0.5
- **C.** 224.0.0.6
- **D.** 224.0.0.7

178. What does the command `router ospf 20` configure?

- **A.** An OSPF router process ID of 20
- **B.** An OSPF router area of 20
- **C.** An OSPF router autonomous system of 20
- **D.** An OSPF cost of 20

179. Which command will verify the bandwidth of an interface participating in OSPF?

- **A.** `show ospf`
- **B.** `show interface`
- **C.** `show running-config`
- **D.** `show ospf interface`

180. Which command will tune the cost of the OSPF metrics for integration with non-Cisco routers to participate in OSPF?

- **A.** `Router(config-if)#ip cost 20000`
- **B.** `Router(config)#ip ospf cost 20000`
- **C.** `Router(config)#ip cost 20000`
- **D.** `Router(config-if)#ip ospf cost 20000`

181. Which command will configure a network of 192.168.1.0/24 for OSPF area 0?

- **A.** `router ospf 0`
  `network 192.168.1.0 0.0.0.255`
- **B.** `ospf 0`
  `network 192.168.1.0 0.0.0.255`
- **C.** `router ospf 0`
  `network 192.168.1.0 255.255.255.0`
- **D.** `router ospf 1`
  `network 192.168.1.0 0.0.0.255 area 0`

182. What is the default number of equal-cost routes for OSPF on Cisco routers?

   A. 4 routes

   B. 8 routes

   C. 16 routes

   D. 32 routes

183. You want to advertise a network of 131.40.32.0/27 with OSPF. Which wildcard mask will you need to use?

   A. 255.255.224.0

   B. 0.0.32.255

   C. 0.0.0.31

   D. 0.0.224.255

184. Which command will allow changing the number of equal-cost routes for OSPF?

   A. `Router(config)#ospf equal-cost 10`

   B. `Router(config-router)#ospf equal-cost 10`

   C. `Router(config)#ospf maximum-paths 10`

   D. `Router(config-router)#maximum-paths 10`

185. What is the maximum number of equal-cost routes that can be configured for OSPF on Cisco routers?

   A. 4 routes

   B. 8 routes

   C. 16 routes

   D. 32 routes

186. Which command will allow you to verify the router's RID for OSPF?

   A. `show ip ospf`

   B. `show ip interface`

   C. `show ip ospf rid`

   D. `show ip ospf neighbor`

187. You want to advertise a network of 192.168.1.16/28 with OSPF. Which wildcard mask will you need to use?

   A. 0.0.0.16

   B. 255.255.255.240

   C. 0.0.0.15

   D. 0.0.0.240

188. Which command will allow you to verify if a remote router has formed an adjacency with the current router?

　A. `show ip ospf neighbor`

　B. `show router adjacency`

　C. `show ip ospf`

　D. `show ip ospf router`

189. What is the default OSPF hello interval in which hello packets are sent out on a broadcast (multi-access) network?

　A. 5 seconds

　B. 10 seconds

　C. 30 seconds

　D. 60 seconds

190. You are running OSPF on a router. One of the interfaces, Gi0/1, connects to your ISP. You want to make sure you do not forward any OSPF packets to your ISP. How can you achieve this?

　A. `Router(config-if)#passive-interface`

　B. `Router(config-router)#passive-interface gigabitethernet 0/1`

　C. `Router(config)#passive-interface gigabitethernet 0/1`

　D. `Router(config-if)#passive-interface default`

191. Which command will allow you to verify the interfaces that hello packets are being sent out for OSPF?

　A. `show interfaces`

　B. `show ip routes`

　C. `show ip ospf interface`

　D. `show ip ospf brief`

192. Which command will statically set the RID for OSPF and override all others?

　A. `Router(config)#interface fa 0/1`
　　 `Router(config-if)#ip address 192.168.1.5 255.255.255.0`

　B. `Router(config)#interface loopback 0`
　　 `Router(config-if)#ip address 192.168.1.5 255.255.255.0`

　C. `Router(config-router)#rid 192.168.1.5`

　D. `Router(config-router)#router-id 192.168.1.5`

193. Which command(s) will only allow interface Gi0/2 to send hello packets for OSPF?

    A. `active-interface gigabitethernet 0/2`

    B. `passive-interface default`
       `active-interface gigabitethernet 0/2`

    C. `passive-interface default`
       `no passive-interface gigabitethernet 0/2`

    D. `passive-interface gigabitethernet 0/2`

194. After changing the router's RID for OSPF, which command needs to be entered?

    A. `Router#clear ip ospf`

    B. `Router(config-router)#shutdown`
       `Router(config-router)#no shutdown`

    C. `Router(config-router)#clear ip ospf`

    D. `Router#clear ospf`

195. Which statement about OSPF area border routers is correct?

    A. ABRs sit between an autonomous system and OSPF.

    B. ABRs exchange Type 1 link-state advertisements between areas.

    C. ABRs exchange Type 2 link-state advertisements between areas.

    D. ABRs exchange Type 3 link-state advertisements between areas.

196. In the following figure, you have two areas that you want OSPF to advertise routes for. Which command(s) will achieve this?

    A. `network 128.24.0.0/22 area 0`
       `network 128.24.0.0/22 area 1`

    B. `network 128.24.0.0 0.0.252.255 area 0`
       `network 128.24.0.0 0.0.252.255 area 1`

    C. `network 128.24.0.0 0.0.254.255 area 0`
       `network 128.24.0.0 255.254.255 area 1`

    D. `network 128.24.0.0 0.0.255.255`

197. Which command will allow you to see the summary of OSPF link-state advertisements?

   A. `show ip ospf database`

   B. `show ip ospf states`

   C. `show ip ospf neighbors`

   D. `show ip ospf topology`

198. You have configured OSPF on Router B. The network command entered was `network 197.234.3.0 0.0.0.63 area 0`. You find out that one of the interfaces is not partici-pating in OSPF. Which interface is not participating? Refer to the following figure.

```
RouterB#show ip interface brief
Interface          IP-Address     OK?   Method Status                   Protocol
Gigabitethernet0/0 197.234.3.65   YES   manual up                       up
Gigabitethernet0/1 unassigned     YES   unset  administratively down    down
Gigabitethernet0/2 unassigned     YES   unset  administratively down    down
Serial0/3/0        unassigned     YES   manual up                       up
Serial0/3/0.1      197.234.3.17   YES   manual up                       up
Serial0/3/0.2      197.234.3.33   YES   manual up                       up
Serial0/3/0.3      197.234.3.49   YES   manual up                       up
RouterB#
```

   A. Interface Serial 0/3/0

   B. Interface Serial 0/3/0.1

   C. Interface Serial 0/3/0.2

   D. Interface GigabitEthernet 0/0

199. Two routers, called Router A and Router B, are configured in the same area and share a common LAN. However, they cannot form an adjacency. What could the problem be?

   A. There is a static route configured between the two routers.

   B. Router A is configured with multiple area IDs.

   C. Router A is configured with a hello timer of 30.

   D. Router B is configured with a hello timer of 10.

200. Which is a direct benefit of a hierarchical OSPF design?

   A. Fast convergence

   B. Reduction of configuration complexity

   C. Increased bandwidth

   D. Better security

201. In the following figure, which router is the DR?

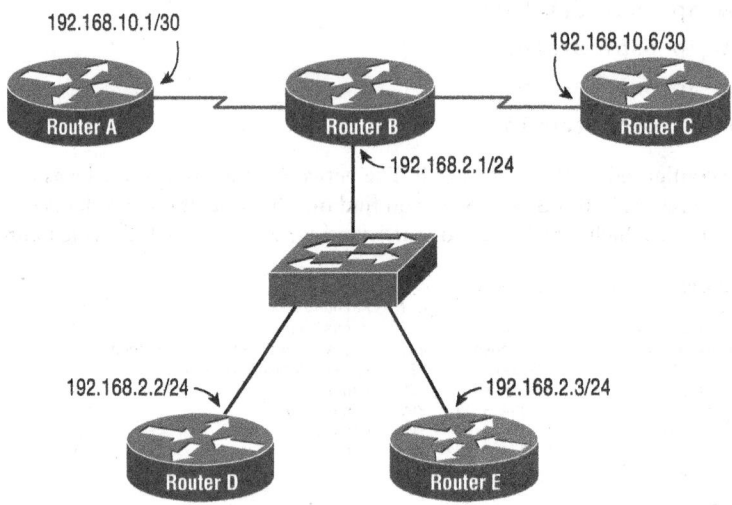

```
RouterB#sh ip ospf neighbor

Neighbor ID      Pri   State           Dead Time    Address        Interface
192.168.10.1      0    FULL/ -         00:00:30     192.168.10.1   Serial0/3/0
192.168.10.6      0    FULL/ -         00:00:36     192.168.10.6   Serial0/3/1
192.168.2.2       1    FULL/DROTHER    00:00:34     192.168.2.2    GigabitEthernet0/0
192.168.2.3       1    FULL/BDR        00:00:30     192.168.2.3    GigabitEthernet0/0
RouterB#
```

A. Router C

B. Router B

C. Router D

D. Router E

202. In the following figure, what is Router B called in this hierarchy?

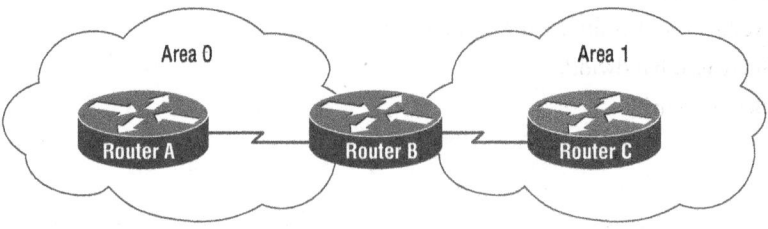

A. ASBR

B. ABR

C. DR

D. BDR

203. You have configured a router with the following command. However, when you enter show
ip routes you do not see any routes for OSPF. What is the problem?

```
Router(config)#router ospf 255
Router(config-router)#network 10.0.0.0 0.0.0.0 area 255
```

A. The process ID is incorrect.

B. The area number is incorrect.

C. The subnet mask is incorrect.

D. The network ID is incorrect.

204. In the following figure, Router A and Router B will not form an adjacency. What is the
cause of the problem?

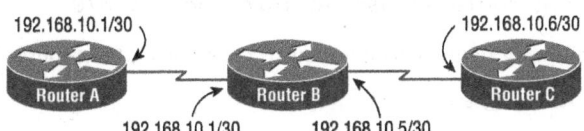

192.168.10.1/30   192.168.10.6/30

Router A   Router B   Router C

192.168.10.1/30   192.168.10.5/30

```
RouterA#show ip ospf interface
Serial0/3/0 is up, line protocol is up
  Internet address is 192.168.10.1/30, Area 0
  Process ID 1, Router ID 192.168.10.1, Network Type POINT-TO-POINT, Cost: 64
  Transmit Delay is 1 sec, State POINT-TO-POINT, Priority 0
  No designated router on this network
  No backup designated router on this network
  Timer intervals configured, Hello 30, Dead 40, Wait 40, Retransmit 5
     Hello due in 00:00:03
  Index 2/2, flood queue length 0
  Next 0x0(0)/0x0(0)
[output cut]
```

```
RouterB#show ip ospf interface
Serial0/3/0 is up, line protocol is up
  Internet address is 192.168.10.2/30, Area 0
  Process ID 23, Router ID 192.168.10.5, Network Type POINT-TO-POINT, Cost: 64
  Transmit Delay is 1 sec, State POINT-TO-POINT, Priority 0
  No designated router on this network
  No backup designated router on this network
  Timer intervals configured, Hello 10, Dead 40, Wait 40, Retransmit 5
     Hello due in 00:00:08
  Index 2/2, flood queue length 0
  Next 0x0(0)/0x0(0)
[output cut]
```

A. The hello and dead timers do not match.

B. The link is a point-to-point connection.

C. The process IDs do not match.

D. The area IP addresses do not match.

205. Which state in the neighbor table indicates that the router has successfully downloaded the
LSA information from a neighboring router?

A. FULL state

B. EXSTART state

C. INIT state

D. EXCHANGE state

206. In the following figure, which is a correct statement about the neighbor ID of 192.168.2.2?

```
RouterB#sh ip ospf neighbor

Neighbor ID    Pri  State      Dead Time  Address       Interface
192.168.10.1    0   FULL/ -    00:00:30   192.168.10.1  Serial0/3/0
192.168.10.6    0   FULL/ -    00:00:36   192.168.10.6  Serial0/3/1
192.168.2.2     1   2WAY/      00:00:34   192.168.2.2   GigabitEthernet0/0
192.168.2.3     1   FULL/BDR   00:00:30   192.168.2.3   GigabitEthernet0/0
RouterB#
```

A. The neighbor is having a problem forming an adjacency.

B. The neighbor's OSPF process is recalculating cost.

C. This router's OSPF process is recalculating cost.

D. Both routers have formed an adjacency.

207. You have two links that enter the same OSPF router with the same bandwidth. You want to prefer one route over the other yet allow the second as a backup route. Which command would you use to achieve this?

A. `Router(config-router)#ip ospf priority 25`

B. `Router(config-if)#ip ospf route primary`

C. `Router(config-if)#ip ospf cost 25`

D. `Router(config-router)#passive interface gi 0/0`

208. Referring to the following figure, which is a correct statement about router ID 192.168.2.2?

```
RouterB#sh ip ospf neighbor

Neighbor ID    Pri  State          Dead Time  Address       Interface
192.168.10.1   0    FULL/ -        00:00:30   192.168.10.1  Serial0/3/0
192.168.10.6   0    FULL/ -        00:00:36   192.168.10.6  Serial0/3/1
192.168.2.2    1    FULL/DROTHER   00:00:34   192.168.2.2   GigabitEthernet0/0
192.168.2.3    1    FULL/BDR       00:00:30   192.168.2.3   GigabitEthernet0/0
RouterB#
```

A. It is in the process of forming an adjacency.

B. It is the designated router.

C. It is not participating in this OSPF area.

D. It will only form an adjacency with the DR or BDR.

209. Refer to the following figure. You want to make Router D the DR. Which command will assure that it becomes the DR?

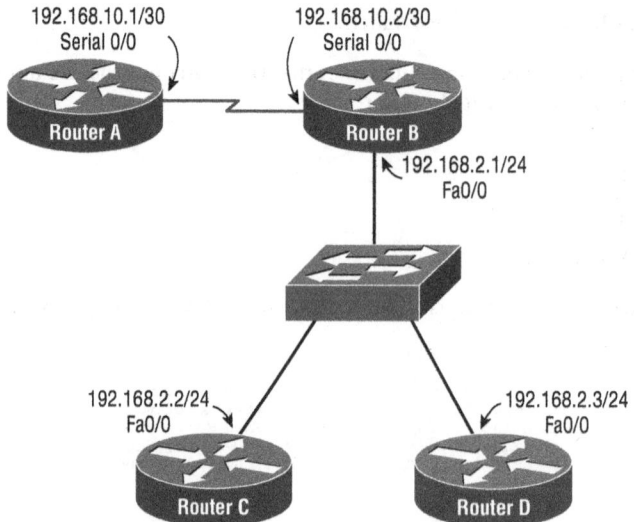

    A. `ospf priority`

    B. `ip ospf priority 10`

    C. `ip address 192.168.5.2 255.255.255.0`

    D. `ip ospf cost 15`

210. Which command will display the DR for a LAN?

    A. `show ip ospf neighbor`

    B. `show ip ospf database`

    C. `show ip ospf dr`

    D. `show ip ospf interface`

211. In the following figure, Router A will not form an adjacency with Router B. What is the problem?

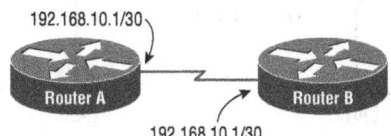

192.168.10.1/30

192.168.10.1/30

```
RouterA#show ip ospf interface                                    RouterB#show ip ospf interface
Serial0/3/0 is up, line protocol is up                            Serial0/3/0 is up, line protocol is up
  Internet address is 192.168.10.1/30, Area 0                       Internet address is 192.168.10.2/30, Area 1
  Process ID 1, Router ID 192.168.10.1, Network Type POINT-TO-POINT, Cost: 64   Process ID 23, Router ID 192.168.10.5, Network Type POINT-TO-POINT, Cost: 64
  Transmit Delay is 1 sec, State POINT-TO-POINT, Priority 0          Transmit Delay is 1 sec, State POINT-TO-POINT, Priority 0
  No designated router on this network                              No designated router on this network
  No backup designated router on this network                      No backup designated router on this network
  Timer intervals configured, Hello 10, Dead 40, Wait 40, Retransmit 5   Timer intervals configured, Hello 10, Dead 40, Wait 40, Retransmit 5
      Hello due in 00:00:03                                             Hello due in 00:00:08
  Index 2/2, flood queue length 0                                  Index 2/2, flood queue length 0
  Next 0x0(0)/0x0(0)                                               Next 0x0(0)/0x0(0)
[output cut]                                                       [output cut]
```

    A. The hello and dead timers do not match.

    B. There is no designated router on the network.

    C. The process IDs do not match.

    D. The area IDs do not match.

212. In the following figure, you have one OSPF area and want to populate the default route to all routers in the OSPF area. Which command would you use?

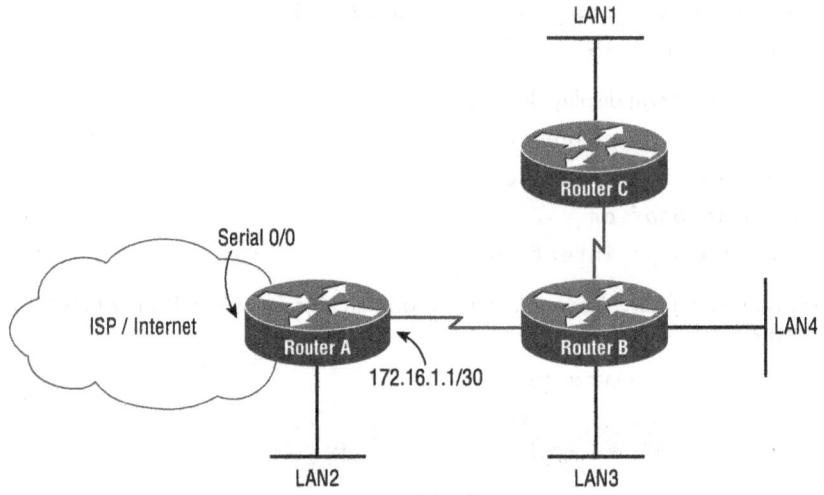

- **A.** `ip route 0.0.0.0 0.0.0.0 serial 0/0`
- **B.** `default-route originate`
- **C.** `default-information originate`
- **D.** `network 0.0.0.0 0.0.0.0 area 0`

213. Which command will set the bandwidth of an interface to 2.048 Mb/s?
- **A.** `bandwidth 2048`
- **B.** `bandwidth 2048000000`
- **C.** `bandwidth 2.048`
- **D.** `bandwidth 2048000`

214. Which command would you use to make sure Router A never becomes a DR?
- **A.** `no ospf designated`
- **B.** `no ospf designated`
- **C.** `passive interface gi 0/0`
- **D.** `ip ospf priority 0`

215. Which command will configure a loopback interface with an address of 192.168.1.2/24?
- **A.** `interface loopback 0`
  `ip address 192.168.1.2/24`
- **B.** `interface loopback 0`
  `ip address 192.168.1.2 255.255.255.0`

    C. `interface loopback`
        `ip address 192.168.1.2/24`

    D. `interface loopback`
        `ip address 192.168.1.2 255.255.255.0`

216. Which is a correct statement about support for OSPF on an MPLS network?

    A. The provider edge (PE) routers can only host area 0.

    B. The customer edge (CE) routers can only host area 0.

    C. The customer edge (CE) routers must use GRE for OSPF.

    D. Both the customer edge (CE) routers and the provider edge (PE) routers can participate in area 0.

217. What is the default priority for Open Shortest Path First (OSPF) routers?

    A. 1

    B. 100

    C. 255

    D. 32,768

218. You have changed the router's priority for OSPF to make the router the DR, but the router has not become a DR. What must be done to force the election?

    A. You must use the `shutdown` and `no shutdown` commands on the interface with the highest IP address.

    B. In global configuration mode, you must enter the command `ospf election force`.

    C. In privileged exec mode, you must enter the command `clear ip ospf process x`.

    D. In privileged exec mode on the DR, you must enter the command `clear ip ospf process x`.

219. Two routers, called Router A and Router B, are configured in the same area on Frame Relay. However, they cannot form an adjacency. What could the problem be?

    A. The two routers do not have the same hello timer of 30 seconds.

    B. Router A is configured with multiple area IDs.

    C. Router A is configured with a hello timer of 10.

    D. Router B is configured with a hello timer of 10.

220. What is the AD for OSPF?

    A. 90

    B. 110

    C. 120

    D. 200

221. Which protocol is an IEEE standard that is supported openly as a first hop redundancy protocol (FHRP)?

    A. Proxy ARP

    B. VRRP

    C. GLBP

    D. HSRP

222. In the MAC address 0000.0c07.ac0a, what is the well-known Hot Standby Router Protocol (HSRP) ID?

    A. 0000.0c

    B. 0c07

    C. 0a

    D. 07.ac

223. Which protocol is a Cisco-proprietary protocol for load-balancing routers?

    A. Proxy ARP

    B. VRRP

    C. GLBP

    D. HSRP

224. In the MAC address 0000.0c07.ac01, what is the HSRPv1 group number?

    A. 0000.0c

    B. 0c07

    C. 01

    D. 07.ac

225. What is the default priority of HSRP?

    A. 100

    B. 110

    C. 200

    D. 10

226. What is the maximum number of HSRPv1 groups that can be created?

    A. 8

    B. 16

    C. 255

    D. 256

227. Which port and protocol are used by HSRP for communications?

    A. UDP/1935

    B. UDP/1985

    C. UDP/1895

    D. UCP/3222

228. Which statement is correct about HSRP?

    A. All routers in an HSRP group are active.

    B. Only one router in an HSRP group can be active.

    C. The virtual router sends hello packets to the HSRP group.

    D. HSRP allows for per-packet load balancing.

229. What type of communication is used between HSRP members?

    A. Unicast

    B. Broadcast

    C. Multicast

    D. Layer 2 flooding

230. When a host sends an outgoing packet to an HSRP group, which router provides the destination address for the default gateway?

    A. Virtual router

    B. Active router

    C. Standby router

    D. Monitor router

231. Which timer must expire for a standby router in an HSRP group to become the active router?

    A. Hello timer

    B. Standby timer

    C. Hold timer

    D. Virtual timer

232. Which port and protocol are used by Gateway Load Balancing Protocol (GLBP) for communications?

    A. UDP/1935

    B. UDP/1985

    C. UDP/1895

    D. UDP/3222

233. Which is a difference between HSRPv1 and HSRPv2?

    A. HSRPv2 does not use hello packets.

    B. HSRPv1 uses broadcasts, and HSRPv2 uses multicasts.

    C. HSRPv1 supports IPv6.

    D. HSRPv2 uses milliseconds.

234. Which statement is correct about GLBP?

    A. The active router is responsible for responding to clients with the virtual router's MAC address.

    B. The active virtual gateway will respond with a MAC address of the active router.

    C. The active virtual gateway will respond with a MAC address of an active virtual forwarder.

    D. The virtual router is responsible for responding to tracking requests.

235. Which router is elected to become the GLBP active virtual gateway?

    A. The router with the lowest priority

    B. The router with the highest priority

    C. The router with the lowest priority and lowest IP address

    D. The router with the highest priority and highest IP address

236. How many active virtual forwarders are supported per the GLBP group?

    A. 2

    B. 4

    C. 16

    D. 1,024

237. Which command will allow Router B to always become the active router for HSRP?

    A. `standby 1 priority 150`

    B. `standby 1 priority 70`

    C. `hsrp 1 priority 150`

    D. `hsrp 1 priority 90`

238. What is the maximum number of HSRPv2 groups that can be created?

    A. 255

    B. 256

    C. 1,024

    D. 4,096

239. Your company is running an FHRP. You notice that the MAC address of the default gateway is 0000.0c9f.f123. Which FHRP is being employed?

    A. HSRPv1

    B. GLBP

    C. HSRPv2

    D. VRRP

240. What is the definition of preemption for HSRP?

    A. It allows the protocol to effectively load-balance per packet.

    B. It watches an upstream interface and fails over when the interface goes down.

    C. It ignores the priorities of the routers and elects an active router by highest IP address.

    D. When a standby router comes online, it allows for a reelection of the active router.

241. Which is a method of configuring HSRP so that traffic is not directed to one router?

    A. Configure version 2 for all HSRP groups.

    B. Configure an HSRP group per VLAN and alternate the priority above 100.

    C. Configure PPPoE on the router interfaces.

    D. Configure all routers in the HSRP as active routers.

242. Which command will allow you to verify the state of the current router for HSRP?

    A. `show hsrp`

    B. `show ip standby`

    C. `show standby`

    D. `show ip hsrp`

243. You have just changed the priority on Router A to 150, and it has not become the active router. All other routers have the default priority. What is wrong?

    A. The default priority is 150.

    B. The hold timer is set too high and needs to timeout.

    C. The HSRP group is not set for preemption.

    D. Router A's IP address is too low.

244. Which command will allow you to enable preemption for HSRP?

    A. `Router(config)#standby 1 preemption`

    B. `Router(config-if)#standby 1 preemption`

    C. `Router(config-if)#hsrp 1 preempt`

    D. `Router(config-if)#standby 1 preempt`

245. Which command will configure VRRP on an interface with an IP address of 10.1.2.3?

    A. `vrrp 1 10.1.2.3 gi 0/0`

    B. `vrrp 1 ip 10.1.2.3`

    C. `vrrp 1 10.1.2.3`

    D. `standby 1 10.1.2.3`

    E. `standby 1 vrrp`

246. Refer to the following figure. You are running HSRP on Router A and Router B. You intermittently have ISP outages. What command should you configure to alert HSRP to the outage?

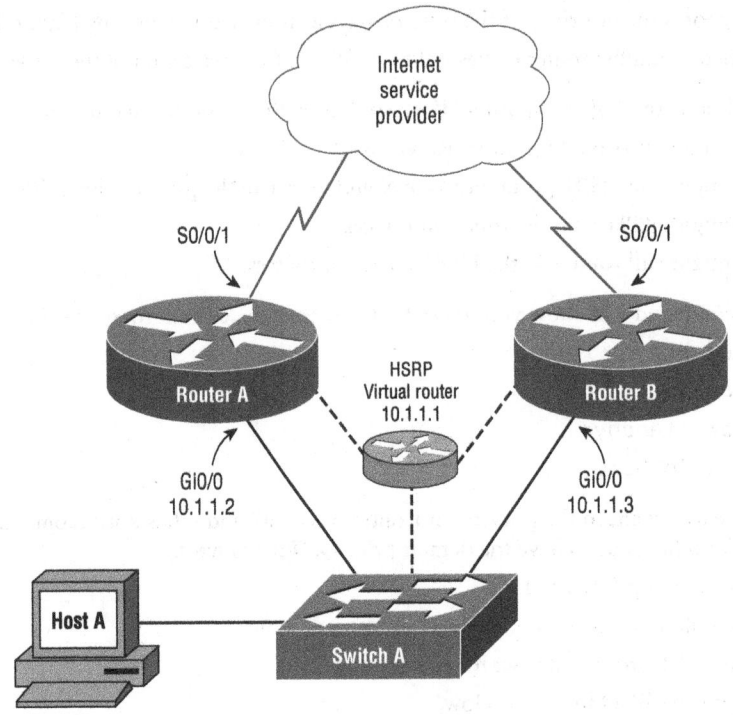

A. RouterA(config-if)#standby 1 interface tracking serial 0/0/1
    RouterB(config-if)#standby 1 interface tracking serial 0/0/1

B. RouterA(config-if)#standby 1 tracking serial 0/0/1
    RouterB(config-if)#standby 1 tracking serial 0/0/1

C. RouterA(config-if)#standby 1 track serial 0/0/1
    RouterB(config-if)#standby 1 track serial 0/0/1

D. RouterA(config-if)#interface serial 0/0/1
    RouterA(config-if)#standby 1 interface tracking
    RouterA(config-if)#interface serial 0/0/1
    RouterB(config-if)#standby 1 interface tracking

247. Which command will allow you to see real-time diagnostics of HSRP?

A. show ip hsrp

B. debug ip hsrp

C. debug standby

D. debug ip standby

248. Which statement is correct about GLBP?

  A. GLBP allows for per-host load balancing.

  B. The active virtual gateway will respond with a MAC address of the active router.

  C. GLBP allows for per-subnet load balancing.

  D. The virtual router is responsible for responding to tracking requests.

249. Which command will allow you to set the hello and hold timers for HSRPv2 to a hello of 200 milliseconds and a hold of 700 milliseconds?

  A. `standby 1 timers msec 200 msec 700`

  B. `standby 1 timers 200 msec 700 msec`

  C. `standby 1 timers 700 msec 200 msec`

  D. `standby 1 timers msec 700 msec 200`

250. You have four routers configured with HSRP. Four routers—Router A, Router B, Router C, and Router D—are configured with the default priority. You change the priority of Router A to 80, Router B to 100, Router C to 140, and Router D is unchanged. Which router will become the active router?

  A. Router A will become the active router.

  B. Router B will become the active router.

  C. Router C will become the active router.

  D. Router D will become the active router.

Chapter 4

IP Services (Domain 4)

THE CCNA EXAM TOPICS COVERED IN THIS PRACTICE TEST INCLUDE THE FOLLOWING:

✓ **4.0 IP Services**

  4.1 Configure and verify inside source NAT using static and pools

  4.2 Configure and verify NTP operating in a client and server mode

  4.3 Explain the role of DHCP and DNS within the network

  4.4 Explain the function of SNMP in network operations

  4.5 Describe the use of syslog features including facilities and severity levels

  4.6 Configure and verify DHCP client and relay

  4.7 Explain the forwarding per-hop behavior (PHB) for QoS such as classification, marking, queuing, congestion, policing, and shaping

  4.8 Configure network devices for remote access using SSH

  4.9 Describe the capabilities and function of TFTP/FTP in the network

1. Which method will allow you to use RFC 1918 addresses for Internet requests?

    A. CIDR

    B. Classful addressing

    C. NAT

    D. VPN

2. In the following figure, what is the inside local IP address?

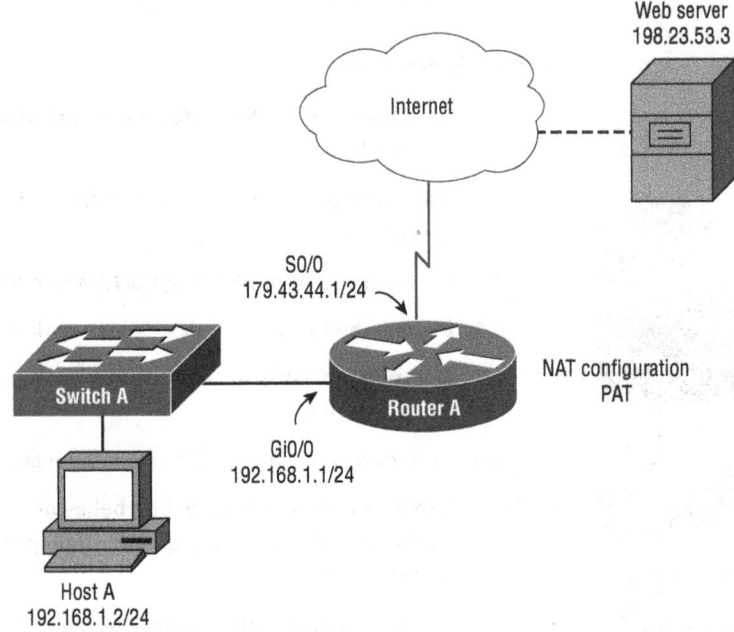

    A. 192.168.1.2 Host A

    B. 192.168.1.1 Router A Gi0/0

    C. 179.43.44.1 Router A S0/0

    D. 198.23.53.3 web server

3. In the following figure, what is the inside global IP address?

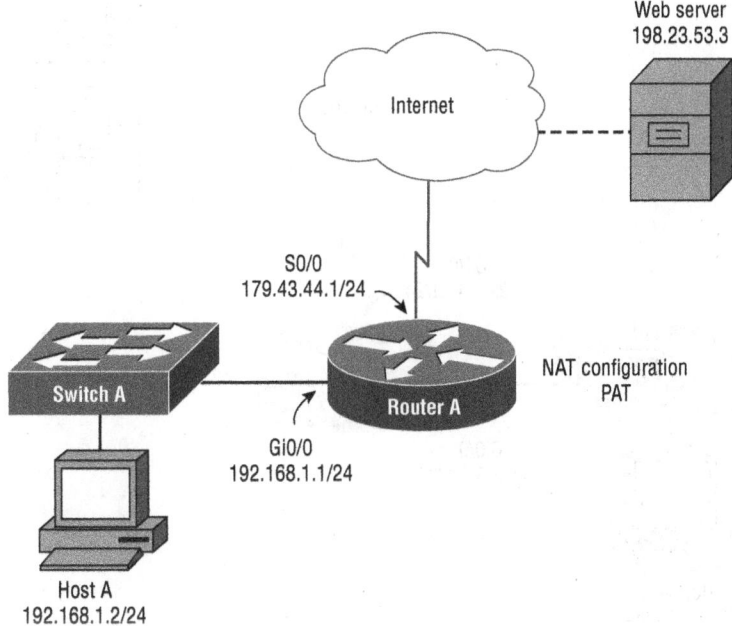

A. 192.168.1.2 Host A

B. 192.168.1.1 Router A Gi0/0

C. 179.43.44.1 Router A S0/0

D. 198.23.53.3 web server

4. In the following figure, what is the outside global IP address?

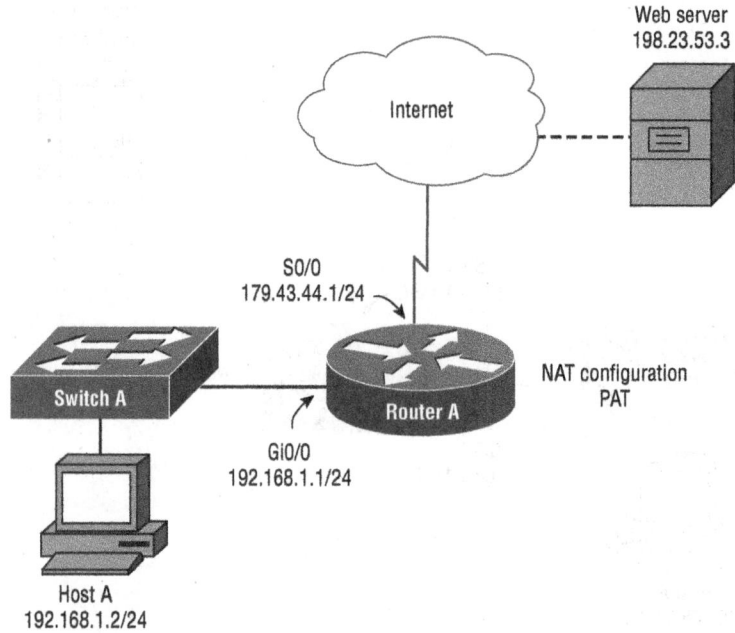

- **A.** 192.168.1.2 Host A
- **B.** 192.168.1.1 Router A Gi0/0
- **C.** 179.43.44.1 Router A S0/0
- **D.** 198.23.53.3 web server

5. Which command will allow you to view the NAT translations active on the router?
- **A.** show ip nat translations
- **B.** show nat translations
- **C.** debug ip nat translations
- **D.** show translations nat

6. Which command will display an overview of the current number of active NAT translations on the router, as well as other overview information?
- **A.** show ip nat translations
- **B.** show ip nat summary
- **C.** show ip nat status
- **D.** show ip nat statistics

7. In the following figure, which command will configure static NAT for the internal web server?

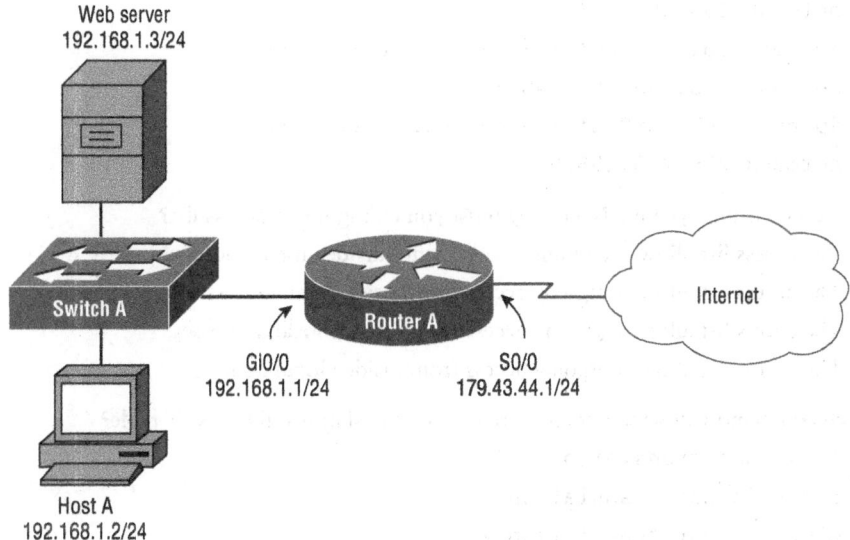

A. `ip nat inside source static 192.168.1.3 179.43.44.1`

B. `nat source static 192.168.1.3 179.43.44.1`

C. `ip nat static 192.168.1.3 179.43.44.1`

D. `ip nat source static 192.168.1.3 179.43.44.1`

8. In the following figure, the enterprise owns the address block of 179.43.44.0/28. Which command will create a NAT pool for dynamic NAT?

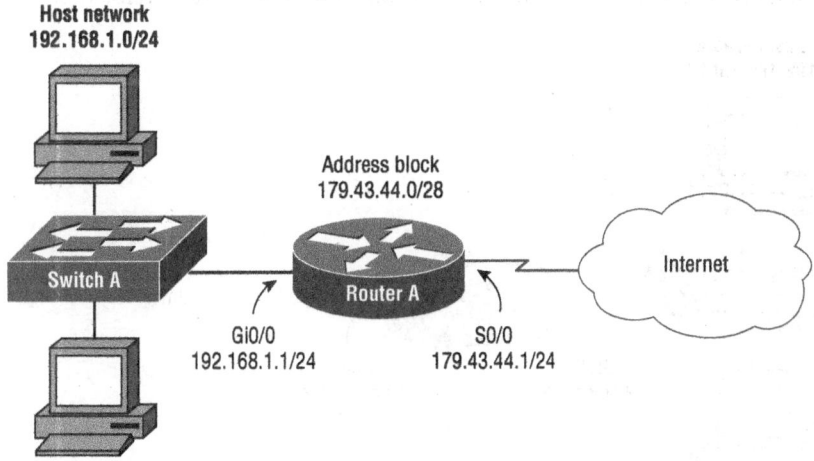

    A. `ip nat pool EntPool 179.43.44.0/28`

    B. `ip pool EntPool 179.43.44.2 179.43.44.15`
       `netmask 255.255.255.0`

    C. `ip nat pool EntPool 179.43.44.1 179.43.44.15`
       `netmask 255.255.255.240`

    D. `ip nat pool EntPool 179.43.44.2 179.43.44.15`
       `netmask 255.255.255.0`

9. When configuring dynamic NAT, why must you configure an access list?

    A. The access list allows incoming access from outside global addresses.

    B. The access list allows outgoing access from inside local addresses.

    C. The access list allows outgoing access from outside local addresses.

    D. The access list allows outgoing access from inside global addresses.

10. Which command will wipe out all current NAT translations in the NAT table?

    A. `no ip nat translation`

    B. `clear ip nat translation`

    C. `clear ip nat translation *`

    D. `clear ip nat`

11. Which command will allow you to see real-time network address translations?

    A. `show ip translations`

    B. `debug ip nat`

    C. `debug ip translations`

    D. `show ip nat`

12. In the following figure, which commands will configure Port Address Translation?

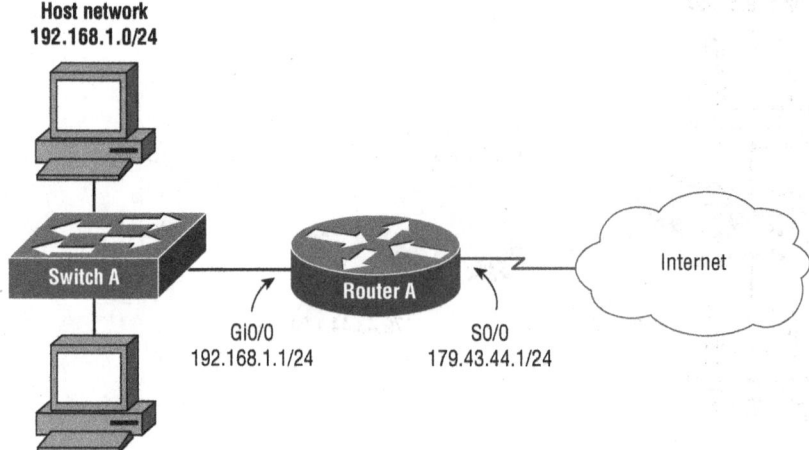

   A. access-list 1 permit 192.168.1.0 0.0.0.255
       ip nat pool EntPool 179.43.44.1 179.43.44.1
       ip nat inside source list 1 pool EntPool

   B. ip nat pool EntPool 179.43.44.1 179.43.44.1
       netmask 255.255.255.0
       ip nat source pool EntPool

   C. access-list 1 permit 192.168.1.0 0.0.0.255
       ip nat pool EntPool 179.43.44.1 179.43.44.1
       netmask 255.255.255.0
       ip nat inside source list 1 pool EntPool overload

   D. access-list 1 permit 192.168.1.0 0.0.0.255
       ip nat pool EntPool 179.43.44.1 179.43.44.1
       netmask 255.255.255.0
       ip nat inside source list 1 pool EntPool

13. Which command will allow your router to synchronize with a time source of 129.6.15.28?

   A. Router(config)#ntp server 129.6.15.28

   B. Router#ntp server 129.6.15.28

   C. Router(config)#ntp client 129.6.15.28

   D. Router#ntp client 129.6.15.28

14. Which command configures the router or switch to trust its internal time clock?

   A. ntp server

   B. ntp master

   C. ntp clock source

   D. ntp trusted

15. Which command will allow you to see if the router or switch is using NTP?

   A. show clock detail

   B. show ntp

   C. show time

   D. show time source

16. Which command will allow you to view the time details from a configured server?

   A. show clock detail

   B. show ntp detail

   C. show ntp associations detail

   D. show ntp skew

17. Which protocol and port does NTP use for time synchronization by default?

  A. TCP/161

  B. TCP/123

  C. UDP/69

  D. UDP/123

18. Which command will help you diagnose if the router or switch is getting an answer back from an NTP server?

  A. show ntp

  B. show ip ntp

  C. debug ntp packets

  D. debug ntp messages

19. Which is a best practice for setting up NTP?

  A. Always configure the time source to a DNS address.

  B. Configure all devices to a public NTP server.

  C. Configure all devices to different NTP servers for redundancy.

  D. Configure all devices as master servers.

20. Which command will allow you to view the time drift observed by NTP?

  A. show ntp

  B. show ip ntp status

  C. show ntp status

  D. debug ntp drift

21. Which command sets the time zone of a router for Pacific Standard Time?

  A. clock timezone pacific

  B. clock timezone pst -8 0

  C. timezone pacific

  D. timezone pst -8

22. You are configuring NTP on your switch. You want to configure the switch so if any interface fails, NTP will still be available. Which type of interface should you use? Choose the best answer.

  A. Tunnel interface

  B. NTP interface

  C. Loopback interface

  D. Switched Virtual Interface (SVI)

23. Which command will configure NTP to use the internal loopback interface?

   A. `ntp source loopback 0`

   B. `ntp loopback 0`

   C. `ntp master loopback 0`

   D. `ntp clock loopback 0`

24. Which command will set the router's internal clock to 2:24 a.m., August 1, 2024?

   A. `Router(config)#clock set 2:24:00 1 august 2024`

   B. `Router#clock set 2:24:00 1 august 2024`

   C. `Router(config)#clock set 2:24:00 august 1 2024`

   D. `Router#clock 2:24:00 1 august 2024`

25. Which statement is correct about reverse lookups?

   A. A reverse lookup is when the request needs to be reversed to another DNS server.

   B. A reverse lookup is the resolution of an IP address to FQDN.

   C. A reverse lookup is when the DNS queried can answer the request without asking another DNS server.

   D. A reverse lookup is the resolution of an FQDN to an IP address.

26. Which record type is used for an IPv4 address mapping to FQDN for DNS queries?

   A. The A record

   B. The CName record

   C. The PTR record

   D. The AAAA record

27. What gets appended to hostname queries for DNS resolution?

   A. The DNS domain name

   B. The DNS zone

   C. The host header

   D. The hostname PTR record

28. Which is the most secure method of name resolution for routers and switches?

   A. DNS

   B. PTR records

   C. Static hostname entries

   D. LLMNR

29. Which type of DNS record holds the IPv4 IP address for a hostname?

   A. The A record

   B. The CName record

   C. The PTR record

   D. The AAAA record

30. What limits the amount of time that a DNS entry is available in the DNS cache?

    A. An A record

    B. TTL

    C. SOA

    D. Default of 5 minutes

31. Which message is sent from the DHCP client to the DHCP server to confirm the offer of an IP address?

    A. Acknowledgment

    B. Discover

    C. Offer

    D. Request

32. What form of communication does a DHCP client use to initially acquire an IP address?

    A. Layer 3 broadcast

    B. Layer 3 multicast

    C. Layer 3 802.1Q

    D. Layer 3 unicast

33. At what point of the lease time will the client ask for a renewal of the IP address from the DHCP server?

    A. One-quarter of the lease

    B. One-half of the lease

    C. Seven-eighths of the lease

    D. End of the lease

34. Which statement is correct about the DHCP process?

    A. The DHCP server is responsible for maintaining the life cycle of an IP address.

    B. DHCP uses multicasting between the client and server.

    C. The DHCP client is responsible for maintaining the life cycle of an IP address.

    D. The DHCP lease is negotiated between client and server.

35. Which transport protocol does DHCP use?

    A. UDP

    B. ICMP

    C. TCP

    D. RARP

36. What happens when a router or switch detects a duplicate IP address for a DHCP process?

    A. The IP address is still served to the client.

    B. The IP address is removed from the DHCP pool.

    C. The DHCP server will halt.

    D. The DHCP will serve the IP address in the future.

37. Which version of SNMP offers authentication and encryption?

    A. SNMP version 1

    B. SNMP version 2e

    C. SNMP version 2c

    D. SNMP version 3

38. What is the database of variables that SNMP uses to allow for collection of data?

    A. Object identifiers (OIDs)

    B. Management information base (MIB)

    C. SNMP agent

    D. SNMP community string

39. What is the component that an SNMP agent sends information to?

    A. Syslog

    B. Network management station

    C. Object identifier

    D. Management information base

40. What type of SNMP message is sent to a network management station when an interface goes down?

    A. Get-request message

    B. Get-response message

    C. Set-request message

    D. Trap message

41. Which of the following is a hierarchical set of variables that make up the management information base?

    A. Object identifiers (OIDs)

    B. The SNMP community string

    C. The SNMP agent

    D. SNMP messages

42. What is the difference between trap messages and inform messages for SNMP?

    A. Trap messages are always encrypted.

    B. Inform messages do not use acknowledgments.

    C. Trap messages always use acknowledgments.

    D. Inform messages always use acknowledgments.

43. Which security method does SNMP version 2c employ?

    A. Encryption

    B. User authentication

    C. Community strings

    D. Message integrity

44. Which of the following can be used in conjunction with an SNMP agent configuration for added security?

- **A.** Encrypted communities
- **B.** Access control lists
- **C.** SNMP callback security
- **D.** SHA-256

45. Which command(s) will configure SNMPv2c to trap messages to a network management station in the event of component failure?

- **A.** `snmp-server 192.168.1.5 version 2c C0mmun1ty`
  `snmp-server enable traps`
- **B.** `snmp-server host 192.168.1.5 version 2c`
  `snmp-server enable traps`
- **C.** `snmp-server host 192.168.1.5 version 2c C0mmun1ty`
  `snmp-server enable traps`
- **D.** `snmp contact trap 192.168.1.5 version 2c`

46. Which protocol and port number does SNMP use for trap and inform messages to the NMS?

- **A.** UDP/161
- **B.** TCP/162
- **C.** UDP/162
- **D.** UDP/514

47. Which command will allow you to verify the network management station that is configured to receive trap notifications?

- **A.** `show snmp`
- **B.** `show snmp community`
- **C.** `show snmp host`
- **D.** `show snmp notifications`

48. When you configure SNMPv3 for a restricted OID, what is the first step?

- **A.** Configuring a group
- **B.** Configuring a view
- **C.** Configuring a user
- **D.** Configuring a community

49. Which protocol and port number does syslog use?

- **A.** UDP/161
- **B.** TCP/162
- **C.** UDP/162
- **D.** UDP/514

50. Which command will configure the severity level of syslog events that will be sent to the syslog server for debugging?

- **A.** `syslog debugging`
- **B.** `logging debugging`
- **C.** `logging trap debugging`
- **D.** `log-level debugging`

51. Which command will send all warnings to the syslog server?

- **A.** `logging server 4`
- **B.** `logging trap 4`
- **C.** `logging trap 5`
- **D.** `logging server 5`

52. Which command will send logging with time stamps rather than sequence numbers?

- **A.** `logging timestamps log datetime`
- **B.** `logging timestamps datetime`
- **C.** `service datetime timestamps`
- **D.** `service timestamps log datetime`

53. Which command will limit console logging to the severity level of alerts?

- **A.** `Router(config)#logging console 0`
- **B.** `Router(config-line)#logging level 0`
- **C.** `Router(config)#logging console 7`
- **D.** `Router(config-line)#logging level 7`

54. Which command will configure logging stored in RAM to include only logs with a severity level of emergencies and alerts?

- **A.** `logging buffered 1`
- **B.** `logging 1`
- **C.** `logging buffered 2`
- **D.** `logging 2`

55. Which command will allow you to see the commands you previously entered?

- **A.** `show commands`
- **B.** `show log`
- **C.** `show history`
- **D.** `show buffer`

56. What severity is being logged to in the following figure?

```
RouterD#
%LINEPROTO-5-UPDOWN: Line protocol on Interface GigabitEthernet0/0, changed state to down
%LINEPROTO-5-UPDOWN: Line protocol on Interface GigabitEthernet0/0, changed state to up
```

A. Informational (6)

B. Notifications (5)

C. Warnings (4)

D. Debugging (7)

57. You need to check the current CPU utilization on a router. Which command will achieve this?

A. `show cpu`

B. `show cpu-stats`

C. `show processes`

D. `show environment cpu`

58. Which command will direct logging to the internal log space?

A. `logging buffered`

B. `logging internal`

C. `logging ram`

D. `logging console`

59. What is the default destination to which Cisco devices send syslog messages?

A. Broadcasts to a syslog server

B. Console

C. TTY

D. NVRAM

60. What is the default level for syslog facility logging?

A. Notification (5)

B. Informational (6)

C. Warning (4)

D. Debugging (7)

61. Which command will allow you to verify the active DHCP server that has assigned an IP address to the router?

A. `show dhcp lease`

B. `show ip dhcp lease`

C. `show ip lease`

D. `show ip interface`

62. Which statement is true about the Offer packet of DHCP?

A. The layer 3 destination is a unicast to the DHCP client.

B. The layer 2 destination is the MAC address of the DHCP client.

C. The layer 2 source is the MAC address of the server.

D. The layer 3 source is a link-local address of the client.

63. Which command will configure a DHCP relay agent on an interface to the DHCP server of 10.10.1.101?

A. `Router(config)#ip dhcp server 10.10.1.101`

B. `Router(config-if)#ip dhcp server 10.10.1.101`

C. `Router(config-if)#ip relay-agent 10.10.1.101`

D. `Router(config-if)#ip helper-address 10.10.1.101`

64. Which DHCP field helps a DHCP server decide which scope to serve to the DHCP relay agent?

A. CIADDR

B. GIADDR

C. SIADDR

D. CHADDR

65. In the following figure, what is required on the network to allow Host A to receive an IP address from the existing DHCP server?

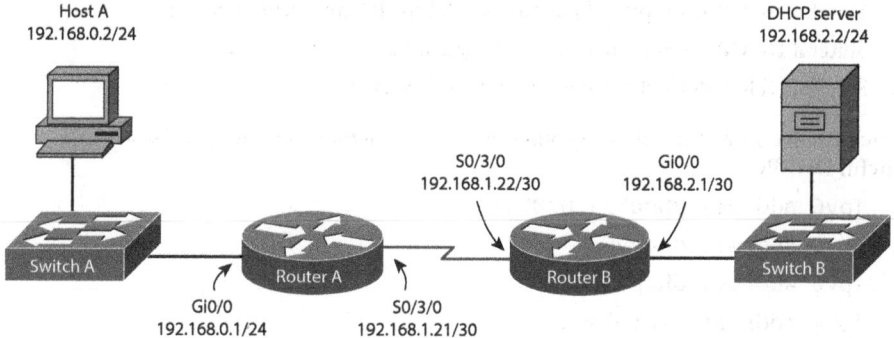

A. A second DHCP server on the Host A network

B. A DHCP relay agent on Router B interface Gi0/0

C. A DHCP relay agent on Switch A

D. A DHCP relay agent on Router A interface Gi0/0

66. Which command will allow you to diagnose DHCP relay agent messages on a router or switch?

A. `debug dhcp`

B. `show ip dhcp detail`

C. `debug ip dhcp server packet`

D. `debug ip dhcp`

67. What is DHCPv6 used for when a network is configured for Stateless Address Autoconfiguration (SLAAC)?

   A. Stateful configuration of clients for IPv6 addressing

   B. Configuration of clients with the IPv6 network IDs

   C. Configuration of clients with IPv6 options

   D. Stateless configuration of clients for IPv6 addressing

68. The DHCP server in the network went down. What happens to clients that have obtained IP addresses from the DHCP server?

   A. They lose their IP address immediately.

   B. They lose their IP address after one-half of their lease has expired.

   C. They lose their IP address after seven-eighths of their lease has expired.

   D. They lose their IP address after their entire lease has expired.

69. Which statement is correct about stateful DHCPv6?

   A. Stateful DHCPv6 supplies the network ID and host ID.

   B. Stateful DHCPv6 supplies the network ID, host ID, and default router.

   C. Stateful DHCPv6 communicates via broadcasts.

   D. Stateful DHCPv6 works in conjunction with SLAAC.

70. Which command will configure a router interface to obtain its IP address via a stateful DHCPv6?

   A. `ipv6 address dhcp gi 0/0`

   B. `ipv6 address dhcpv6`

   C. `ipv6 address dhcp`

   D. `ipv6 address stateless`

71. What happens if you delete a current lease on the DHCP server?

   A. The server will contact the client to immediately relinquish the IP address.

   B. The client will immediately renew its lease for the current IP address.

   C. The server will offer the IP address to another node, which will cause a duplicate address.

   D. The server will offer the IP address to another node, at which time the original client will relinquish the IP address.

72. What happens at the client when the lease for an IP address reaches seven-eighths of the lease cycle?

   A. The DHCP client will perform a DHCP rebinding.

   B. Nothing. The DHCP client will retain the lease.

   C. The DHCP client will renew its lease.

   D. The DHCP client will relinquish the use of the IP address.

73. How do routers classify traffic for QoS?

    A. Access control lists

    B. Layer 2 ASICs

    C. Route tables

    D. Frame filters

74. Which measurement describes the variation of consecutive packet time from source to destination?

    A. Bandwidth

    B. Delay

    C. Jitter

    D. Loss

75. Which is a true statement about the Class of Service field?

    A. The Class of Service field is a layer 3 field.

    B. The Class of Service field is only present in 802.1Q frames.

    C. The Class of Service field is present from end to end of a transmission.

    D. The Class of Service field is 6 bits.

76. What is the measurement of packets discarded due to congestion of queues?

    A. Bandwidth

    B. Delay

    C. Jitter

    D. Loss

77. Which DSCP marking has the highest priority?

    A. DSCP AF 43

    B. DSCP EF 46

    C. DSCP AF 11

    D. DSCP AF 00

78. What is the recommended maximum delay VoIP traffic should not exceed?

    A. 10 ms

    B. 90 ms

    C. 150 ms

    D. 300 ms

79. Which QoS queue has priority over all other queues in the scheduler?

    A. CBWFQ

    B. LLQ

    C. FIFO

    D. CIR

80. Which method helps combat queue starvation for QoS queuing?

    A. LLQ

    B. Policing

    C. CBWFQ

    D. FIFO

81. Which statement is correct about shaping of traffic for QoS?

    A. Shaping holds packets in the queue over the configured bit rate to cause delay.

    B. Shaping drops packets over the configured bit rate to cause loss.

    C. Shaping holds packets in the queue over the configured bit rate to cause jitter.

    D. Shaping slows packets in the queue over the configured bit rate to adhere to the speed.

82. Which QoS method uses a round-robin scheduler for packet queuing?

    A. LLQ

    B. FIFO

    C. CBWFQ

    D. PQ

83. Which statement is correct about policing of traffic for QoS?

    A. Policing holds packets in the queue over the configured bit rate to cause delay.

    B. Policing drops packets over the configured bit rate to cause loss.

    C. Policing holds packets in the queue over the configured bit rate to cause jitter.

    D. Policing slows packets in the queue over the configured bit rate to adhere to the bit rate.

84. Why should QoS policing be implemented?

    A. To help police LAN applications

    B. To maintain a contracted CIR

    C. To help police WAN applications

    D. To maintain a contracted burst rate

85. How do congestion avoidance tools help to prevent tail drop?

    A. When the queue depth is full, a percentage of TCP packets are dropped.

    B. When the queue depth is empty, a percentage of TCP packets are dropped.

    C. When the queue depth is below the minimum threshold, a percentage of TCP packets are dropped.

    D. When the queue depth is above the minimum threshold, a percentage of TCP packets are dropped.

86. If a traffic is marked with AF31 and another traffic pattern is marked with AF41, which statement explains the traffic markings?

A. AF31 marked traffic has a better queue than AF41 marked traffic.

B. AF41 marked traffic has a better queue than AF31 marked traffic.

C. Both AF31 and AF41 marked traffic have an equal queue.

D. During high congestion, AF41 queues will be dropped and AF31 queues won't.

87. What is required before generating the encryption keys for SSH on a router or switch?

A. Setting the time and date

B. Setting the hostname and domain name

C. Setting the key strength

D. Setting the key repository

88. Which command will enable SSH version 2 for logins?

A. `Router(config)#ip ssh version 2`

B. `Router(config-line)#version 2`

C. `Router(config-ssh)#version 2`

D. `Router(config)#ssh version 2`

89. Which command will configure the router or switch to allow SSH as a protocol for management with a fallback of Telnet?

A. `Switch(config)#login ssh telnet`

B. `Switch(config-line)#login ssh telnet`

C. `Switch(config-line)#transport ssh telnet`

D. `Switch(config)#transport ssh telnet`

90. Why should Telnet be replaced with SSH?

A. Telnet has weak encryption.

B. SSH allows for file copy.

C. SSH makes it easier to create ACLs for access.

D. SSH is encrypted.

91. You have created the SSH encryption keys, but you cannot enable SSH version 2. What is the problem?

A. The time and date need to be corrected.

B. The key strength needs to be 768 bits or higher.

C. The DNS server is not configured.

D. There is no host record for the switch or router.

92. Which command will configure a local user for SSH access?

    A. `username user1 password Password20!`

    B. `account user1`

        `password Password20!`

    C. `user user1 Password20!`

    D. `user-account user1 password Password20!`

93. Which command will generate the encryption keys for SSH?

    A. `Router(config)#generate crypto key rsa`

    B. `Router(config)#crypto key generate rsa`

    C. `Router(config)#crypto generate key rsa`

    D. `Router#crypto key generate rsa`

94. You want to turn on local authentication so that a user must supply a username and password when managing the switch. You have created the username and password combinations on the switch. Which command will direct SSH and Telnet to use this authentication model?

    A. `Switch(config)#new aaa model`

    B. `Switch(config)#local authentication`

    C. `Switch(config-line)#local authentication`

    D. `Switch(config-line)#login local`

95. Which banner will be displayed first when a user connects to a Cisco device via SSH?

    A. MOTD banner

    B. Login banner

    C. Exec banner

    D. Incoming banner

96. Which command will restore configuration to the running-config for a device from a server?

    A. `archive tftp: running-config`

    B. `restore tftp://192.168.1.2 running-config`

    C. `copy tftp: running-config`

    D. `copy server: running-config`

97. Which command will begin the upgrade of an IOS from a TFTP server?

    A. `copy tftp flash`

    B. `copy tftp ios`

    C. `copy tftp nvram`

    D. `upgrade tftp flash`

98. Which command will allow you to boot a router from a TFTP server for the image of c2900-universalk9-mz.SPA.151-4.M4.bin on the TFTP server of 192.168.1.2?

    A. `Router#boot tftp://192.168.1.2`

    B. `Router(config)#boot tftp://192.168.1.2`

    C. `c2900-universalk9-mz.SPA.151-4.M4.bin`

    D. `Router(config)#boot system tftp://192.168.1.2`

    E. `c2900-universalk9-mz.SPA.151-4.M4.bin`

    F. `Router(config)#boot system`

    G. `c2900-universalk9-mz.SPA.151-4.M4.bin tftp://192.168.1.2`

99. You're upgrading the flash memory on a 2900 router with a brand-new flash card. What needs to be done to restore the IOS?

    A. The new flash memory will have a mini-IOS installed. You will need to upgrade it from the mini-IOS.

    B. The router will boot into the ROMMON, and from there you will need to TFTP download the IOS.

    C. Nothing needs to be done because the IOS is not storage on the flash memory card.

    D. Format the flash card with the FAT operating system and copy the IOS image to the card.

100. Which command(s) are required before you can use an FTP server for backing up configuration? Assume that the username is USER and the password is USERPASS.

    A. `ip ftp username USER password USERPASS`

    B. `ftp USER password USERPASS`

    C. `ip ftp username USER`

        `ip ftp password USERPASS`

    D. `username USER password USERPASS`

Chapter 5

Security Fundamentals (Domain 5)

THE CCNA EXAM TOPICS COVERED IN THIS PRACTICE TEST INCLUDE THE FOLLOWING:

✓ **5.0 Security Fundamentals**

    5.1 Define key security concepts (threats, vulnerabilities, exploits, and mitigation techniques)

    5.2 Describe security program elements (user awareness, training, and physical access control)

    5.3 Configure and verify device access control using local passwords

    5.4 Describe security password policy elements, such as management, complexity, and password alternatives (multifactor authentication, certificates, and biometrics)

    5.5 Describe IPsec remote access and site-to-site VPNs

    5.6 Configure and verify access control lists

    5.7 Configure and verify Layer 2 security features (DHCP snooping, dynamic ARP inspection, and port security)

    5.8 Compare authentication, authorization, and accounting concepts

    5.9 Describe wireless security protocols (WPA, WPA2, and WPA3)

    5.10 Configure and verify WLAN within the GUI using WPA2 PSK

1. Which term describes the outside of the corporate firewall?

    A. DMZ

    B. Perimeter

    C. Internal

    D. Trusted

2. Which term describes the area accessible to the Internet yet protected by the corporate firewall?

    A. DMZ

    B. Perimeter

    C. Internal

    D. Trusted

3. Which type of device can prevent an intrusion on your network?

    A. Honeypots

    B. IDS

    C. IPS

    D. HIDS

4. When dealing with firewalls, the term *trusted network* is used to describe what?

    A. Internal network

    B. The Internet

    C. The DMZ

    D. A network with SSL

5. Which is a common attack method used to overwhelm services with traffic from multiple Internet sources?

    A. Denial of service

    B. Distributed denial of service

    C. IP address spoofing

    D. Session hijacking

6. Which type of device can detect an intrusion on your network?

    A. Honeypots

    B. IDS

    C. IPS

    D. HIDS

7. Which method can be used to stop ping sweep scans?

    A. Deploying host intrusion detection systems

    B. Deploying network intrusion detection systems

    C. Blocking RFC 1918 addresses at the perimeter

    D. Blocking ICMP echo requests and echo replies at the perimeter

8. Which appliance can be used to mitigate denial-of-service attacks?

   A. Honeypots

   B. IDS

   C. IPS

   D. HIDS

9. Which is a common attack method used to attempt to gain access to a system using a false identity?

   A. Denial of service

   B. Distributed denial of service

   C. IP address spoofing

   D. Malware

10. Which method would prevent tampering of data in transit?

   A. Access control lists (ACLs)

   B. Spoofing mitigation

   C. SSL

   D. Encryption of the data

11. A rogue wireless access point (WAP) is created with the same SSID as the corporate SSID. The attacker has employees connect to the SSID and watches the information as it's relayed to the original SSID. What type of attack is described here?

   A. Smurf attack

   B. Compromised key attack

   C. Sniffer attack

   D. On-path attack

12. What can you use to protect against spoofing of internal IP addresses on the perimeter of your network?

   A. ACLs

   B. Intrusion detection systems

   C. SSL

   D. Host intrusion detection systems

13. Which is a requirement for the use of DHCP snooping to protect a device?

   A. The device is on a layer 2 switch port on the same VLAN.

   B. The DHCP server is running on the layer 2 switch.

   C. The device is on a layer 3 routed port on the same VLAN.

   D. Configuration of a dedicated IP address for monitoring DHCP transactions.

14. What attack vector can be used for an on-path attack?

   A. DHCP

   B. DNS

   C. Wireless

   D. All of the above

15. Which attack can be used on a native VLAN?

   A. Double tagging

   B. VLAN traversal

   C. Trunk popping

   D. Denial of service

16. Which command is used to configure the port of a switch as trusted for DHCP snooping?

   A. `ip dhcp snooping trust`

   B. `dhcp snooping trust`

   C. `ip dhcp snooping trust interface gi 2/3`

   D. `ip dhcp trust`

17. Why should you always change the native VLAN?

   A. The native VLAN contains frames from all VLANs.

   B. The native VLAN is configured on all switches for logging.

   C. The native VLAN is the default on all switchports.

   D. The native VLAN provides no encryption.

18. What can protect users from a phishing attack that is sent via email?

   A. Training

   B. Antimalware software

   C. Antivirus software

   D. Certificates

19. Your company provides medical data to doctors from a worldwide database. Because of the sensitive nature of the data, it's imperative that authentication be established on each session and be valid only for that session. Which of the following authentication methods provides credentials that are valid only during a specific period of time?

   A. Token

   B. Certificate

   C. Smartcard

   D. License

20. A user has brought an email to your attention that is not from his bank, but it looks like their bank's website when they click on the link. What is this most likely?

A. Spam

B. Password cracking

C. Phishing

D. Worm

21. What type of filters can be placed over a monitor to prevent the data on the screen from being readable when viewed from the side?

A. Security

B. Privacy

C. Degaussing

D. Tempered

22. Which form of social engineering is nothing more than looking over someone's shoulder while they enter or view sensitive information?

A. Shoulder surfing

B. Phishing

C. Tailgating

D. Whaling

23. Several office-level users have administrative privileges on the network. Which of the following is the easiest to implement to immediately add security to the network?

A. Biometric authentication

B. Hardware tokens

C. Active Directory

D. Least privilege

24. You need to protect your users from Trojans, viruses, and phishing emails. What should you implement?

A. Multifactor authentication

B. Software firewalls

C. Antimalware software

D. Antivirus software

25. What is a method for stopping tailgating?

A. User authentication

B. Access control vestibules

C. Strong passwords

D. Change SSIDs

26. Which command will configure the enable password for a router or switch?

   A. `password enable Password20!`

   B. `enable Password20!`

   C. `enable secret Password20!`

   D. `secret enable Password20!`

27. You need to set the login password for Telnet. Which command will you type first?

   A. `interface vlan 1`

   B. `line console 1`

   C. `line aux 1`

   D. `line vty 0 5`

28. You have set the enable password using `enable password Password20!`. However, when you try to get to a privileged exec prompt, the router states you are using an incorrect password. What is the problem?

   A. You originally entered the wrong password.

   B. The enable secret password is set to something else.

   C. The password Password20! contains a special character.

   D. The password is too long and has been truncated.

29. Which command(s) will set a password and require login for a line?

   A. `set password Password20!`
      `request login`

   B. `password Password20!`
      `login password`

   C. `password Password20!`
      `login`

   D. `login password Password20!`

30. You Telnet to a switch and receive the error `Password required, but none set.[Connection to 192.168.1.1 closed by foreign host]`. What is the problem?

   A. The enable secret is not set.

   B. The enable password is not set.

   C. The line login password is not set.

   D. The line is administratively down.

31. What is required before generating the encryption keys for SSH on a router or switch?

   A. Setting the time and date

   B. Setting the hostname and domain name

   C. Setting the key strength

   D. Setting the key repository

32. Which command will enable SSH version 2 for logins?

- **A.** `Router(config)#ip ssh version 2`
- **B.** `Router(config-line)#version 2`
- **C.** `Router(config-ssh)#version 2`
- **D.** `Router(config)#ssh version 2`

33. Which command will configure the router or switch to allow SSH as a protocol for management with a fallback of Telnet?

- **A.** `Switch(config)#login ssh telnet`
- **B.** `Switch(config-line)#login ssh telnet`
- **C.** `Switch(config-line)#transport ssh telnet`
- **D.** `Switch(config)#transport ssh telnet`

34. Why should Telnet be replaced with SSH?

- **A.** Telnet has weak encryption.
- **B.** SSH allows for file copy.
- **C.** SSH makes it easier to create ACLs for access.
- **D.** SSH is encrypted.

35. Which command will create and apply an access list to secure router or switch management?

- **A.** `Switch(config)#access-list 1 permit host 192.168.1.5`
  `Switch(config)#interface vlan 1`
  `Switch(config-if)#ip access-group 1 in`
- **B.** `Switch(config)#access-list 1 permit host 192.168.1.5`
  `Switch(config)#line vty 0 5`
  `Switch(config-line)#ip access-group 1 in`
- **C.** `Switch(config)#access-list 1 permit host 192.168.1.5`
  `Switch(config)#line vty 0 5`
  `Switch(config-line)#ip access-class 1 in`
- **D.** `Switch(config)#access-list 1 permit host 192.168.1.5`
  `Switch(config)#ip access-group 1 in`

36. You have created the SSH encryption keys, but you cannot enable SSH version 2. What is the problem?

- **A.** The time and date need to be corrected.
- **B.** The key strength needs to be 768 bits or higher.
- **C.** The DNS server is not configured.
- **D.** There is no host record for the switch or router.

37. Which command will configure a local user for SSH access?

    A. `username user1 password Password20!`

    B. `account user1`

        `password Password20!`

    C. `user user1 Password20!`

    D. `user-account user1 password Password20!`

38. You configured the password for Telnet access, but when you perform a `show running-configuration`, the password shows in clear text. Which command should be run?

    A. `password encryption`

    B. `service password-encryption`

    C. `service encryption`

    D. `password-encryption service`

39. Which command will generate the encryption keys for SSH?

    A. `Router(config)#generate crypto key rsa`

    B. `Router(config)#crypto key generate rsa`

    C. `Router(config)#crypto generate key rsa`

    D. `Router#crypto key generate rsa`

40. Which command will disable auto-disconnect for idle privileged exec sessions?

    A. `Switch(config-line)#exec-timeout 0 0`

    B. `Switch(config)#exec-timeout 0`

    C. `Switch(config-line)#timeout 0 0`

    D. `Switch(config-line)#no exec-timeout`

41. In the following figure, you have listed all management sessions on the switch. On which line are you connected?

```
Switch#show users
Line      User    Host(s)     Idle       Location
0 con 0   admin               00:00:20
1 vty 0   admin   10.30.2.3   00:00:00   10.30.2.3
2 vty 1   admin   10.30.2.4   00:00:00   10.30.2.4
3 vty 2   admin   10.30.2.5   00:00:00   10.30.2.5
```

    A. Console 0

    B. VTY 0

    C. VTY 1

    D. VTY 2

42. You want to turn on local authentication so a user must supply a username and password when managing the switch. You have created the username and password combinations on the switch. Which command will direct SSH and Telnet to use this authentication model?

A. `Switch(config)#new aaa model`

B. `Switch(config)#local authentication`

C. `Switch(config-line)#local authentication`

D. `Switch(config-line)#login local`

43. During a recent external security audit, it was determined that your enable password should be secured with SHA-256 scrypt. Which command will change the password strength on the switches and routers?

A. `enable secret 9`

B. `service password-encryption scrypt`

C. `enable secret algorithm-type scrypt`

D. `enable algorithm-type scrypt secret Password20!`

44. What is the default encryption method for passwords when you configure a line password?

A. MD5

B. SHA-128

C. SHA-256

D. Clear text

45. You need to change the default idle time before disconnection of privileged exec mode for network administrators. Which command will change it to 30 minutes?

A. `Switch(config)#exec-timeout 30 0`

B. `Switch(config-line)#exec-timeout 30 0`

C. `Switch(config-line)#exec-timeout 0 30`

D. `Switch(config-line)#timeout 30 0`

46. You need to disconnect a network admin from the switch or router. Which command would you use?

A. `no enable secret`

B. `no line vty 2`

C. `disconnect line vty 2`

D. `clear line vty 2`

47. Which banner can deliver a message only to authenticated users regardless of connection type?

A. MOTD banner

B. Login banner

C. Exec banner

D. Incoming banner

48. Which technology will give selective access to the network based on authentication?

    A. 802.1Q

    B. ACLs

    C. 802.1X

    D. Firewall

49. What is the end device that sends credentials for 802.1X called?

    A. Authenticator

    B. Supplicant

    C. AAA server

    D. RADIUS server

50. What is the switch called in an 802.1X configuration?

    A. Authenticator

    B. Supplicant

    C. AAA server

    D. RADIUS server

51. What protocol does the supplicant communicate to the authenticator for 802.1X?

    A. 802.1X EAP

    B. UDP

    C. TCP

    D. IP

52. Which protocol is used by 802.1X for supplicant to authenticator and authenticator to authentication server?

    A. 802.1X authentication headers

    B. IPsec

    C. EAP

    D. RADIUS

53. Which device is the supplicant during the 802.1X authentication process?

    A. The device requesting access

    B. The server that is providing authentication

    C. The device that is controlling access via 802.1X

    D. The device connecting the layer 3 network

54. A smartcard is an example of which type of authentication?

    A. Single-factor authentication

    B. RADIUS authentication

    C. Multifactor authentication

    D. Active Directory authentication

55. You believe a user's account has been compromised via a password attack. What should have been enforced to prevent this? (Choose the best answer.)

A. Password complexity

B. Password expiration

C. Phishing protection

D. Time restrictions

56. Which statement is correct about Generic Routing Encapsulation (GRE) tunnels?

A. GRE uses IPsec security.

B. GRE uses a protocol of 57.

C. GRE provides per-packet authentication.

D. GRE provides packet-in-packet encapsulation.

57. Which tunnel protocol is a Cisco-proprietary protocol?

A. GRE

B. PPP

C. IPsec

D. SSL

58. Which layer 3 protocol does GRE use?

A. Protocol 4

B. Protocol 43

C. Protocol 47

D. Protocol 57

59. In the following figure, you are configuring a GRE tunnel. What is wrong with this configuration?

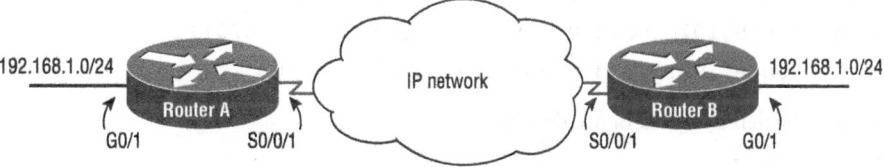

```
Router A#show run
interface serial0/0/1
  ip address 198.34.54.2 255.255.255.0
!
interface tunnel0
  ip address 192.168.2.1 255.255.255.0
  tunnel mode gre ip
  tunnel source serial0/0/1
  tunnel destination 198.44.34.5
interface GigbitEthernet 0/1
  ip address 192.168.2.1
!
[Output Cut]
```

```
Router B#show run
interface serial0/0/1
  ip address 198.44.34.5 255.255.255.0
!
interface tunnel0
  ip address 192.168.2.2 255.255.255.0
  tunnel mode gre ip
  tunnel source serial0/0/1
  tunnel destination 198.34.54.2
interface GigbitEthernet 0/1
  ip address 192.168.2.1
!
[Output Cut]
```

    A. Nothing is wrong with the configuration.

    B. The destination on Router A of the tunnel is incorrect.

    C. The network is unrouteable.

    D. The serial interfaces are on different networks.

60. In the following figure, you are configuring a GRE tunnel and need to configure a route statement on Router A. Which is the correct route statement?

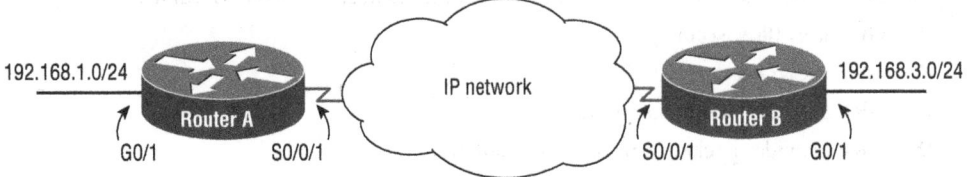

```
Router A#show run                               Router B#show run
interface serial0/0/1                           interface serial0/0/1
  ip address 198.34.54.2 255.255.255.0            ip address 198.44.34.5 255.255.255.0
!                                               !
interface tunnel0                               interface tunnel0
  ip address 192.168.2.1 255.255.255.0            ip address 192.168.2.2 255.255.255.0
  tunnel mode gre ip                              tunnel mode gre ip
  tunnel source serial0/0/1                       tunnel source serial0/0/1
  tunnel destination 198.44.34.5                  tunnel destination 198.34.54.2
interface GigbitEthernet 0/1                    interface GigbitEthernet 0/1
  ip address 192.168.2.1                          ip address 192.168.2.1
!                                               !
[Output Cut]                                    [Output Cut]
```

    A. `ip route 192.168.3.0 255.255.255.0 tunnel 0`

    B. `ip route 192.168.2.0 255.255.255.0 tunnel 0`

    C. `ip route 192.168.3.0 255.255.255.0 serial 0/0/1`

    D. `ip route 192.168.3.0 255.255.255.0 192.168.2.2`

61. What is the default MTU of a GRE tunnel?

    A. MTU 1476

    B. MTU 1492

    C. MTU 1500

    D. MTU 1528

62. Which command will help you verify the source and destination of a GRE tunnel?

    A. `show ip tunnel 0`

    B. `show interface tunnel 0`

    C. `show ip gre`

    D. `show ip route`

63. In the following figure, if you do a `traceroute` on Router A to a destination of 192.168.3.50, how many hops will show?

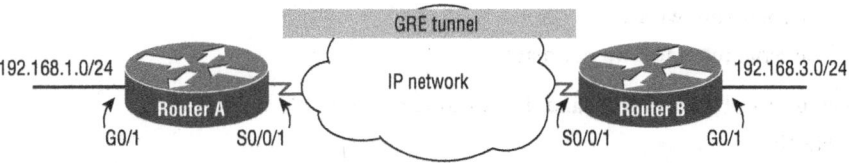

```
Router A#show run
interface serial0/0/1
 ip address 198.34.54.2 255.255.255.0
 !
 interface tunnel0
 ip address 192.168.2.1 255.255.255.252
 tunnel mode gre ip
 tunnel source serial0/0/1
 tunnel destination 198.44.34.5
 interface GigbitEthernet 0/1
 ip address 192.168.2.1
 !
 ip route 192.168.3.0 255.255.255.0 192.168.2.2
 [Output Cut]
```

```
Router B#show run
interface serial0/0/1
 ip address 198.44.34.5 255.255.255.0
 !
 interface tunnel0
 ip address 192.168.2.2 255.255.255.252
 tunnel mode gre ip
 tunnel source serial0/0/1
 tunnel destination 198.34.54.2
 interface GigbitEthernet 0/1
 ip address 192.168.2.1
 !
 ip route 192.168.1.0 255.255.255.0 192.168.2.1
 [Output Cut]
```

A. One hop

B. Two hops

C. Four hops

D. Zero hops

64. Refer to the following figure. You are configuring a GRE tunnel. However, you cannot ping from Router A to 192.168.3.1. What is the problem?

```
Router A#show run
interface serial0/0/1
 ip address 198.34.54.45 255.255.255.0
 !
 interface tunnel1
 ip address 192.168.2.45 255.255.255.252
 tunnel mode gre ip
 tunnel source serial0/0/1
 tunnel destination 198.44.34.5
 interface GigbitEthernet 0/1
 ip address 192.168.2.1
 !
 ip route 192.168.3.0 255.255.255.0 198.44.34.5
 [Output Cut]
```

```
Router B#show run
interface serial0/0/2
 ip address 198.44.34.5 255.255.255.0
 !
 interface tunnel0
 ip address 192.168.2.46 255.255.255.252
 tunnel mode gre ip
 tunnel source serial0/0/2
 tunnel destination 198.34.54.2
 interface GigbitEthernet 0/1
 ip address 192.168.2.1
 !
 ip route 192.168.1.0 255.255.255.0 198.34.54.45
 [Output Cut]
```

    A.   The tunnel numbers do not match.

    B.   The destination on Router A of the tunnel is incorrect.

    C.   The routes are wrong.

    D.   The serial interfaces do not match.

65. Which protocol helps resolve and direct traffic for DMVPN connections?

    A.   HSRP

    B.   NHRP

    C.   ARP

    D.   GRE

66. Refer to the following figure. You have configured a point-to-point dedicated line between two locations. However, you cannot ping between the two routers. What is the problem?

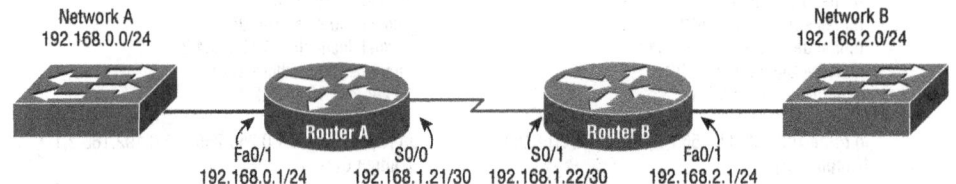

```
RouterA#show interfaces serial 0/0
Serial0/0 is up, line protocol is down (disabled)
  Hardware is HD64570
  Internet address is 192.168.1.21/30
  MTU 1500 bytes, BW 1544 Kbit, DLY 20000 usec,
    reliability 255/255, txload 1/255, rxload 1/255
  Encapsulation HDLC, loopback not set, keepalive set (10 sec)
[Output Cut]
RouterA#
```

```
RouterB#show interfaces serial 0/1
Serial0/1 is up, line protocol is down (disabled)
  Hardware is HD64570
  Internet address is 192.168.1.22/30
  MTU 1500 bytes, BW 1544 Kbit, DLY 20000 usec,
    reliability 255/255, txload 1/255, rxload 1/255
  Encapsulation PPP, loopback not set, keepalive set (10 sec)
[Output Cut]
RouterB#
```

    A.   The interface is administratively shut down.

    B.   There is a wiring problem.

    C.   There is a protocol mismatch.

    D.   There is an IP address mismatch.

67. DMVPN is an example of which topology?

    A.   Point-to-point

    B.   Hub-and-spoke

    C.   Full-mesh

    D.   Dual-homed

68. Which benefit of using a secure VPN allows verification that a packet was not tampered with in transit?

   A. Authentication

   B. Data integrity

   C. Anti-replay

   D. Confidentiality

69. Which Cisco technology is often used to create VPN tunnels between sites?

   A. Catalyst switches

   B. Cisco routers

   C. Cisco FTD

   D. Policy-based routing

70. You have several remote workers who enter patient information and require a high level of security. Which technology would best suit the connectivity for these workers?

   A. GRE tunnels

   B. Wireless WAN

   C. Client SSL/VPN

   D. Site-to-site VPN

71. Which protocol does IPsec use to encrypt data packets?

   A. AH

   B. ESP

   C. IKE

   D. ISAKMP

72. What is a benefit of site-to-site IPsec VPNs?

   A. Lower bandwidth requirements

   B. Lower latency

   C. Scalability

   D. Support for multicast

73. What is the range of a standard access list?

   A. 1 to 99

   B. 1 to 100

   C. 100 to 199

   D. 100 to 200

74. Which statement is correct about a standard ACL?

   A. Conditions can be based on only the destination address.

   B. Conditions can be based on only the source address and source port.

   C. Conditions can be based on only the source address.

   D. Conditions can be based on the source or destination address and source or destination port.

75. What is the range of an extended access list?

   A. 1 to 99

   B. 1 to 100

   C. 100 to 199

   D. 100 to 200

76. What is at the end of every ACL?

   A. `permit any any`

   B. `deny any any`

   C. `log all`

   D. End of ACL marker

77. Which statement is correct about an ACL?

   A. Packets are compared sequentially against each line in an access list, and the last matching condition is the action taken.

   B. Packets are compared sequentially against each line in an access list until a match is made.

   C. Packets are compared, and if no matching rule exists, they are allowed.

   D. At the end of the ACL, there is an implicit allow.

78. What is an advantage of using a standard ACL?

   A. More secure

   B. Less processing overhead

   C. More specific rules

   D. Blocking of applications

79. What is the expanded range of a standard access list?

   A. 1000 to 1999

   B. 1100 to 1299

   C. 1300 to 1999

   D. 2000 to 2699

80. You need to filter traffic for the 172.16.0.0/12 network. Which wildcard mask would you use?

    A. 255.240.0.0

    B. 0.0.240.255

    C. 0.15.255.255

    D. 255.3.0.0

81. Which command would configure an ACL to block traffic coming from 192.168.1.0/24?

    A. `ip access-list 20 192.168.1.0 0.0.0.255`

    B. `ip access-list 100 192.168.1.0 0.0.0.255`

    C. `ip access-list 1 192.168.1.0/24`

    D. `ip access-list 2 192.168.1.0 255.255.255.0`

82. If you configure a rule with the address of 0.0.0.0 and wildcard mask of 255.255.255.255, what are you doing?

    A. Defining the broadcast address

    B. Defining no addresses

    C. Defining the network address

    D. Defining all addresses

83. Which statement is correct about applying ACLs to an interface?

    A. An ACL can be applied in only one direction.

    B. An ACL can be applied only to a single protocol.

    C. A port can only have a single ACL applied.

    D. All of the above.

84. You need to filter an application. Which type of access list will you use to complete the task?

    A. Standard

    B. Extended

    C. Dynamic

    D. Expanded

85. What is the expanded range of an extended access list?

    A. 1000 to 1999

    B. 1100 to 1299

    C. 1300 to 1999

    D. 2000 to 2699

86. You need to filter traffic for the 192.168.1.0/25 network. Which wildcard mask would you use?

   A. 255.255.255.128

   B. 0.0.0.128

   C. 0.0.0.127

   D. 0.0.0.63

87. Which type of ACL allows for removing a single entry without removing the entire ACL?

   A. Standard

   B. Dynamic

   C. Extended

   D. Named

88. Which type of ACL allows you to open a port only after someone has successfully logged into the router?

   A. Standard

   B. Dynamic

   C. Extended

   D. Named

89. Which statement configures a standard access list?

   A. `access-list 20 deny 172.16.0.0 0.255.255.255`

   B. `access-list 180 permit udp any 172.16.0.0 0.255.255.255 eq 161`

   C. `access-list 130 permit permit ip any any`

   D. `access-list 150 deny any 172.16.0.0 0.255.255.255`

90. Which statement can be used in lieu of `access-list 5 permit 192.168.1.5 0.0.0.0`?

   A. `access-list 5 permit 192.168.1.5`

   B. `access-list 5 permit 192.168.1.5/24`

   C. `access-list 5 permit host 192.168.1.5`

   D. `access-list 5 permit 192.168.1.0 0.0.0.255`

91. Referring to the following figure, you need to block traffic from the host 192.168.2.6 to the HR web application server but allow it to get to all other servers and the Internet. Which command(s) will achieve this?

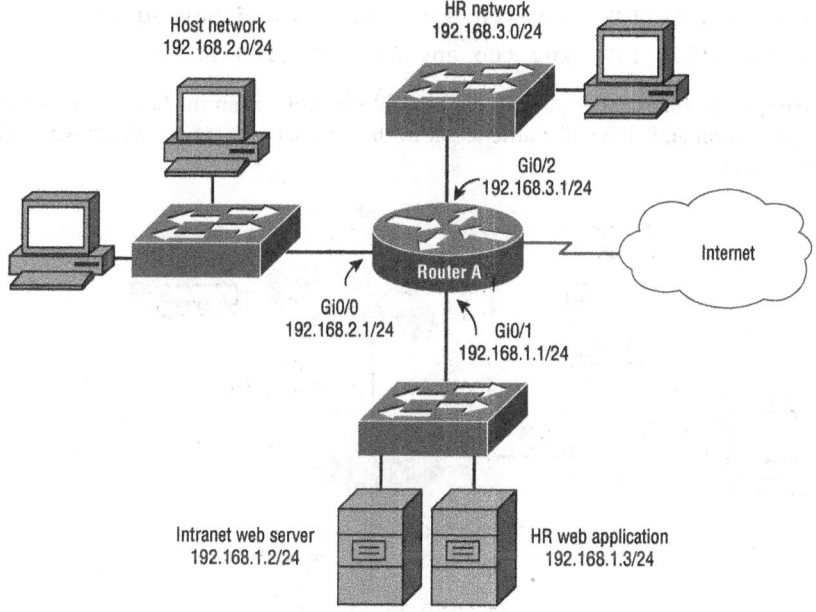

A. `access-list 101 deny tcp host 192.168.2.6 host 192.168.1.3 eq 80`
   `access-list 101 permit any any`

B. `access-list 101 deny tcp host 192.168.2.6 host 192.168.1.3 eq 80`
   `access-list 101 permit ip any any`

C. `access-list 101 deny host 192.168.2.6 host 192.168.1.3 eq 80`
   `access-list 101 permit any any`

D. `access-list 101 deny tcp host 192.168.2.6 host 192.168.1.3 eq 80`
   `access-list 101 permit ip any any eq 80`

92. Which type of access list limits you to describing traffic by source address?
   A. Extended
   B. Named
   C. Dynamic
   D. Standard

93. Which statement will block traffic for a server of 192.168.1.5 for SSH?

    A. `access-list 90 deny ip host 192.168.1.5 eq 22`

    B. `access-list 90 deny tcp any host 192.168.1.5 eq 22`

    C. `access-list 199 deny tcp host 192.168.1.5 any eq 23`

    D. `access-list 199 deny tcp any host 192.168.1.5 eq 22`

94. Referring to the following figure, you need to block traffic from the host network to the HR web application and allow all traffic to get to the intranet web server. Which type of ACL would you use?

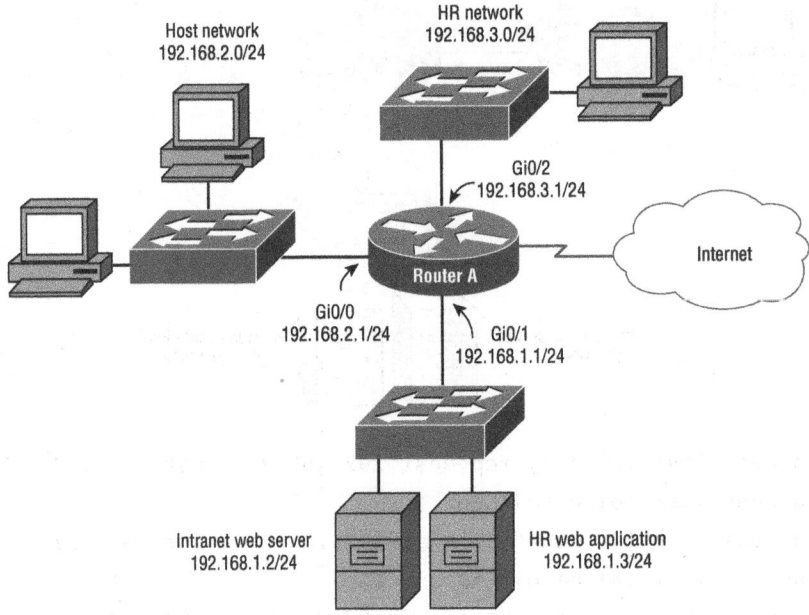

    A. Standard

    B. Dynamic

    C. Extended

    D. Expanded

95. Which statement configures a valid access list?

    A. `access-list 99 deny tcp host 192.168.2.7 eq 443`

    B. `access-list 189 deny any host 192.168.1.5 eq 22`

    C. `access-list 143 permit tcp host 192.168.8.3 eq 80 any`

    D. `access-list 153 permit any host 192.168.4.5 eq 22`

96. You want to apply an access list of 198 to an interface to filter traffic into the interface. Which command will achieve this?

   A. `ip access-list 198 in fast 0/1`

   B. `ip access-list 198 in`

   C. `ip access-class 198 in`

   D. `ip access-group 198 in`

97. Referring to the following figure, you want to block the host network from accessing the HR network. Which commands will place the access list on the proper interface to make it effective?

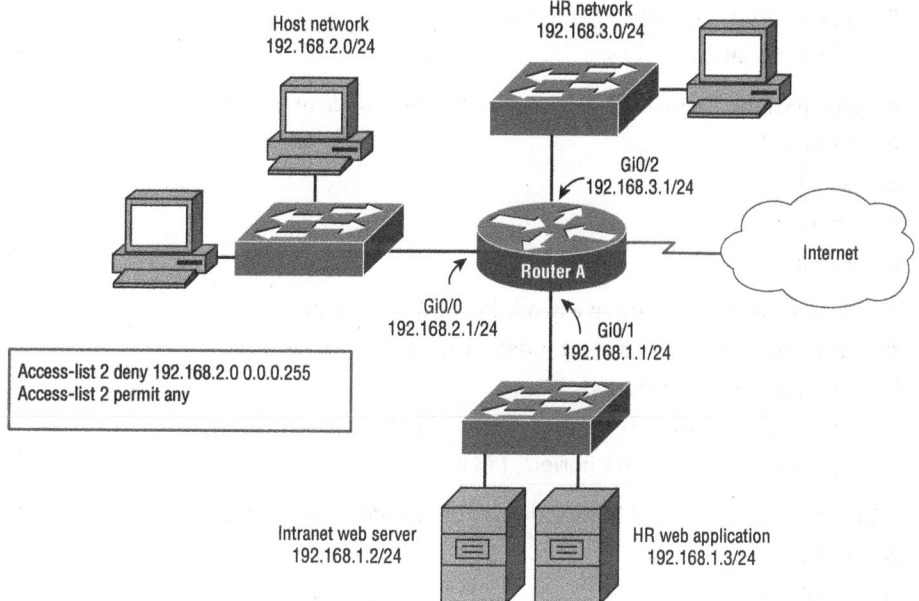

   A. `interface gi 0/0`
   `ip access-group 2 in`

   B. `interface gi 0/0`
   `ip access-group 2 out`

   C. `interface gi 0/2`
   `ip access-group 2 in`

   D. `interface gi 0/2`
   `ip access-group 2 out`

98. Which command will allow you to see the output in the following figure with the line numbers?

```
[Output Cut]
Extended IP access list named_list
    10 permit ip any any
    20 permin tcp host 192.168.1.6 host 192.168.2.3 eq 23
    30 permit udp any host 192.168.2.3 eq 123

Switch#
```

   A. `show access-list named_list`

   B. `show ip access-list named_list`

   C. `show running-configuration`

   D. `show ip access-list`

99. Which type of ACL should be placed closest to the source of traffic?

   A. Extended

   B. Standard

   C. Dynamic

   D. Expanded

100. Which command will create an extended named access list?

   A. `access-list 101 allow host 192.168.1.5 any`

   B. `ip access-list named_list`

   C. `ip access-list extended named_list`

   D. `ip access-list 101 named_list`

101. Which type of ACL should be placed closest to the destination of traffic?

   A. Extended

   B. Standard

   C. Dynamic

   D. Expanded

102. Which command should you start with when trying to diagnose port security issues?

   A. `show port-security`

   B. `show mac address-table`

   C. `show interface`

   D. `show security`

103. You have configured an access port for a remote office computer. The office has no IT persons on site. You want to stop workers from plugging in a WAP and exposing your company's internal network. Which feature should you configure?

   A. Dynamic VLANs

   B. Port security

   C. ACLs

   D. VLAN pruning

104. Which method can restrict a user from plugging a wireless access point into a corporate network?

    A. Access control lists

    B. Port security

    C. Wired Equivalent Privacy

    D. Static MAC addresses

105. What does port security use to block unauthorized access?

    A. Source MAC addresses

    B. Destination MAC addresses

    C. Source IP addresses

    D. Destination IP addresses

106. Which command will enable port security?

    A. `Switch(config)#switchport port-security`

    B. `Switch(config)#port-security enable`

    C. `Switch(config-if)#switchport port-security`

    D. `Switch(config-if)#port-security enable`

107. If port security is enabled on an interface, what is the maximum number of MAC addresses allowed by default?

    A. 1 MAC address

    B. 2 MAC addresses

    C. 0 MAC addresses

    D. 10 MAC addresses

108. Which layer of the OSI model does port security use for securing a port?

    A. Layer 0

    B. Layer 1

    C. Layer 2

    D. Layer 3

109. Why would a network admin choose to configure port security on an interface?

    A. To allow or disallow VLANs

    B. To allow or disallow IP addresses

    C. To prevent unauthorized access by MAC address

    D. To prevent unauthorized access by users

110. Which statement is correct about port security?

    A. Port security works best in mobile environments.

    B. Port security requires a higher amount of memory.

    C. Port security works best in static environments.

    D. Port security always results in admin intervention to reset the port.

111. When configuring port security on a port that contains a VoIP phone with a voice VLAN and a computer connected to the phone, how many MAC addresses must you allow?

    A. 1 MAC address

    B. 2 MAC addresses

    C. 0 MAC addresses

    D. 10 MAC addresses

112. What is the default action of port security on the interface when the maximum number of MAC addresses is exceeded?

    A. Administrative shutdown

    B. Err-disabled shutdown

    C. Restricted access without logging

    D. Restricted access with logging

113. You are configuring a port for port security and receive the error `Command rejected: FastEthernet0/1 is a dynamic port`. Which commands will help you configure the port?

    A. `no switchport dynamic`
        `switchport port-security`

    B. `switchport mode access`
        `switchport port-security`

    C. `switchport mode access`
        `switchport nonnegotiate`
        `switchport port-security`

    D. `switchport mode access`
        `no dynamic`
        `switchport port-security`

114. Which command will allow you to configure two MAC addresses for port security?

    A. `switchport maximum 2`

    B. `switchport port-security maximum 2`

    C. `port-security maximum 2`

    D. `switchport port-security limit 2`

115. Which command will limit devices via port security without disabling the port and logging the restricted device?

    A. `switchport port-security violation shutdown`

    B. `switchport port-security restrict`

    C. `switchport port-security violation protect`

    D. `switchport port-security violation restrict`

116. Which command will allow you to inspect the status of a port that has been configured for port security?

    A. `show running-configuration`

    B. `show port-security interface gi 2/13`

    C. `show port-security details interface gi 2/13`

    D. `show port-security gi 2/13`

117. Which command will limit devices via port security and send an SNMP trap notification?

    A. `switchport port-security violation shutdown`

    B. `switchport port-security restrict`

    C. `switchport port-security violation protect`

    D. `switchport port-security violation restrict`

118. Which command will limit devices via port security without disabling the port and not provide logging for a security violation counter?

    A. `switchport port-security violation shutdown`

    B. `switchport port-security restrict`

    C. `switchport port-security violation protect`

    D. `switchport port-security violation restrict`

119. Which command will allow you to see logged security violations for port security?

    A. `show violations`

    B. `show port-security violations`

    C. `show port-security`

    D. `show psec violations`

120. You have been tasked to secure ports with port security. You need to make sure that only the computers installed can access the network. The computers are installed already. Which type of configuration for port security would require the least amount of administration?

    A. Static port security

    B. Dynamic port security

    C. Sticky port security

    D. Time limit port security

121. Refer to the following figure. You received a call that a port is no longer active. The port has port security configured on it. What is the problem?

```
SwitchA#show interfaces fastEthernet 0/1
FastEthernet 0/1 is down, line protocol is down (err-disabled)
  Hardware is Lance, address is 0002.17ac.a601 (bia 0002.17ac.a601)
  MTU 1500 bytes, BW 100000 kbit, DLY 1000 usec,
       reliability 255/255, txload 1/255, rxload 1/255
  Encapsulation ARPA, loopback not set
  Keepalive set (10 sec)
  Half-duplex, 100Mb/sec
  input flow-control is off, output flow-control is off
  ARP tpye: ARPA, ARP Timeout 04:00:00
  [Output Cut]
```

    A. The port has been administratively shut down.

    B. The port has an access violation on it.

    C. The port has bad wiring.

    D. The port on the switch is configured as a trunk.

122. Which command will allow the first MAC address learned on the port to be allowed to only pass traffic on the port via port security?

    A. `switchport port-security mac-address sticky`

    B. `switchport port-security mac-address dynamic`

    C. `switchport port-security mac-address static`

    D. `switchport port-security mac-address learn`

123. Refer to the following figure. You receive a call that a port on the switch is not working. You determine that a port-security violation has been experienced. Once the violation has been remediated, how will you reset the port so that it functions again?

```
SwitchA#show interfaces fastEthernet 0/1
FastEthernet 0/1 is down, line protocol is down (err-disabled)
  Hardware is Lance, address is 0002.17ac.a601 (bia 0002.17ac.a601)
  MTU 1500 bytes, BW 100000 kbit, DLY 1000 usec,
        reliability 255/255, txload 1/255, rxload 1/255
  Encapsulation ARPA, loopback not set
  Keepalive set (10 sec)
  Half-duplex, 100Mb/sec
  input flow-control is off, output flow-control is off
  ARP tpye: ARPA, ARP Timeout 04:00:00
  [Output Cut]
```

    A. `no port-security`

    B. `no shutdown`

    C. `no switchport port-security`

    D. `shutdown`
       `no shutdown`

124. Which command will configure the port with only the MAC address you want to allow via port security?

    A. `switchport port-security mac-address sticky`

    B. `switchport port-security mac-address 0334.56f3.e4e4`

    C. `switchport port-security mac-address static 0334.56f3.e4e4`

    D. `switchport port-security static 0334.56f3.e4e4`

125. Which command is used to see the output in the following figure?

Secure Port	MaxSecureAddr	CurrentAddr (Count)	SecurityViolation (Count)	Security Action (Count)
G12/1	1	1	0	Restrict
G12/2	1	1	0	Restrict
G12/3	1	1	0	Restrict
G12/4	1	1	0	Restrict
G12/5	1	1	0	Restrict
G12/6	1	1	0	Restrict
G12/7	1	1	0	Restrict
G12/8	1	1	0	Restrict
G12/9	1	1	0	Restrict
G12/10	1	1	0	Restrict
G12/11	1	1	0	Restrict
G12/12	1	1	0	Restrict
G12/13	1	1	0	Restrict
G12/14	1	1	0	Restrict

A. show port-security details

B. show mac address-table secure

C. show port-security address

D. show port-security

126. Which command will allow you to globally reset all ports with an err-disable state with minimal disruption?

A. Switch#clear err-disable

B. Switch#clear switchport port-security

C. Switch#clear port-security violation

D. Switch(config)#errdisable recovery cause psecure_violation

127. You need to verify the sticky MAC addresses learned on a port on the switch. Which command will allow you to verify the addresses learned?

A. show running-config

B. show port-security

C. show port-security details

D. show port-security status

128. Which server will centralize authentication for all Cisco routers and switches?

A. Active Directory server

B. AAA server

C. 802.1X server

D. Terminal server

129. Which protocol and port does RADIUS authentication use?

A. UDP/1845

B. UDP/1645

C. TCP/1645

D. UDP/1911

130. Which is an authentication protocol for AAA servers to secure Telnet authentication?

A. 802.1X

B. TACACS+

C. AD

D. EAP

131. Which command will configure the router to use a TACACS+ server and a backup of local for authentication of logins?

A. aaa authentication login default group tacacs+ local

B. authentication login group tacacs+ local

C. aaa-authentication login default tacacs+ local

D. aaa authentication login tacacs+ local

132. You configured the AAA authentication for login to default local but forgot to create a local AAA user. What will happen when you log out?

    A. The enable secret will work.

    B. The console will still be available.

    C. The router will lock you out.

    D. Nothing, since a username and password have not been set.

133. You were routinely looking at logs and found that a security incident occurred. Which type of incident detection is described?

    A. Passive

    B. Active

    C. Proactive

    D. Auditing

134. A RADIUS server is an example of which type of server?

    A. DNS

    B. Email

    C. Proxy

    D. Authentication

135. Matilda is interested in securing her SOHO wireless network. What should she do to be assured that only her devices can join her wireless network?

    A. Disable WPA2

    B. Enable MAC filtering

    C. Enable port security

    D. Disable SSID broadcasts

136. Which is a requirement of WPA2-Enterprise?

    A. Creation of a PSK

    B. Certificate infrastructure

    C. 192-bit key strength

    D. 802.11ac

137. Which mechanism in WPA prevents the altering and replay of data packets?

    A. TKIP

    B. MIC

    C. AES

    D. CRC

138. Which security mode does WPA3-Enterprise use that offers the highest level of security?

    A. 64-bit

    B. 128-bit

    C. 192-bit

    D. 256-bit

139. Which statement is correct about WPA?

    A. WPA was released at the same time as WEP.

    B. WPA was released as a fix for poor coverage.

    C. WPA was released as a fix for poor encryption.

    D. The Wi-Fi Alliance wanted to rebrand WEP with WPA.

140. Which feature does 802.11i add to the WPA security protocol?

    A. The use of certificates

    B. Frame-level encryption

    C. Pre-shared keys

    D. CRC checking

141. Which mode of encryption does 802.11i (WPA2) introduce?

    A. RC4

    B. MD5

    C. AES-CCMP

    D. SHA1

142. Which feature was introduced with WPA3 to enhance security?

    A. Certificate support

    B. Per-frame encryption

    C. SAE authentication

    D. TKIP

143. When configuring WPA2-Enterprise mode on a wireless LAN controller, what must be configured?

    A. NTP server

    B. RADIUS server

    C. PSK

    D. Captive portal

144. When configuring WPA2, you want to ensure that it does not fall back to the older WPA specification. What parameter should you disable?

    A. 802.1X

    B. AES

    C. TKIP

    D. MAC filtering

145. What is the mechanism that allows for authentication using a symmetrical key with WPA2?

    A. PSK

    B. AES

    C. Certificates

    D. TKIP

146. After configuring a WLAN, your users complain they do not see the SSID. What could be wrong?

    A. SSID beaconing is enabled.

    B. Multicast support is disabled.

    C. Radio Policy is configured to all.

    D. Status is disabled.

147. How many preshared keys can be configured for a specific WPA2 WLAN?

    A. One PSK (one hex or one ASCII)

    B. Two PSKs (one hex and one ASCII)

    C. Four PSKs (two hex and two ASCII)

    D. Unlimited number of PSKs

148. You are configuring a WPA2 WLAN. Which security configuration should you use for the highest level of security?

    A. WPA-AES

    B. WPA2-TKIP

    C. WPA2-RC4

    D. WPA2-AES

149. You are setting up a wireless network for a client. Their requirements are to minimize the infrastructure and support the highest security. Which wireless encryption standard should be configured to satisfy the requirements?

    A. WPA-Enterprise

    B. WPA2-Personal

    C. WPA3-Enterprise

    D. WPA-Personal

150. Which protocol will restrict you from achieving high throughput rates?

    A. AES

    B. TKIP

    C. CCMP

    D. PSK

Chapter

6

Automation and Programmability (Domain 6)

THE CCNA EXAM TOPICS COVERED IN THIS PRACTICE TEST INCLUDE THE FOLLOWING:

✓ **6.0   Automation and Programmability**

  6.1   Explain how automation impacts network management

  6.2   Compare traditional networks with controller-based networking

  6.3   Describe controller-based and software defined architectures (overlay, underlay, and fabric)

    6.3.a Separation of control plane and data plane

    6.3.b North-bound and southbound APIs

  6.4   Explain AI (generative and predictive) and machine learning in network operations

  6.5   Describe characteristics of REST-based APIs (authentication types, CRUD, HTTP verbs, and data encoding)

  6.6   Recognize the capabilities of configuration management mechanisms, such as Ansible and Terraform

  6.7   Recognize components of JSON encoded data

1. Which is a reason to automate a process for the configuration of several routers?

 A. To increase the possibility for misconfiguration

 B. To create an outcome that can be reproduced

 C. To decrease problems from the new configuration

 D. To allow you to do less work

2. You need to configure a new static route on the existing 20 routers. Which is the best way to do this?

 A. Copy and paste scripts built in Notepad++ into each router.

 B. Copy and paste scripts built in Microsoft Excel into each router.

 C. Create a Python script to configure each router.

 D. Work with a partner so both of you can double-check each other's work and cut the time in half.

3. Which is the number one motivating factor to use network automation?

 A. Reduce the number of changes to be made

 B. Reduce the complications that arise from changes

 C. Reduce the human error factor

 D. Reduce the planning time for the changes

4. What is the term used to describe the framework responsible for assisting in network automation?

 A. NetOps

 B. DevOps

 C. SysOps

 D. SecOps

5. Which management methodology is commonly used by developers for network automation?

 A. Lean and Agile

 B. Waterfall

 C. Kanban

 D. Scrum

6. After you release a network automation script to production, which step should be completed?

 A. Testing

 B. Building

 C. Planning

 D. Monitoring

7. Which element of YAML defines a key-value pair?

   A. Definition

   B. Mapping

   C. Lists

   D. Keys

8. How can you identify that a file is a YAML file?

   A. The file begins with three dashes.

   B. The file begins with a hashbang preprocessor.

   C. The contents are contained between curly brackets.

   D. The contents are contained between square brackets.

9. Which structured data format closely resembles HTML?

   A. YAML

   B. JSON

   C. CSV

   D. XML

10. Which data format is structured by white space?

    A. YAML

    B. JSON

    C. XML

    D. CSV

11. You are creating a network automation script to configure a network device. What should you research to identify what can be controlled with your script?

    A. User interface layout

    B. API reference

    C. Source code of the device

    D. Data storage of the device

12. You are developing a network automation script that retrieves information. Which interface can you implement that will act similar to an API?

    A. CLI

    B. SNMP

    C. Syslog

    D. SSH

13. Which protocol was created as a replacement for SNMP?

    A. NETCONF

    B. Syslog

    C. REST

    D. SSH

14. Which protocol uses the YANG data model?

    A. NETCONF

    B. REST

    C. SNMP

    D. YAML

15. Which protocol uses an HTTPS transport to configure and retrieve details programmatically?

    A. NETCONF

    B. RESTCONF

    C. SNMP

    D. Syslog

16. Which is a benefit of controller-based networking?

    A. Increased security

    B. Decreased problems

    C. Increased throughput

    D. Increased complexity

17. Which statement is correct about controller-based networking?

    A. Controller-based networking is always in the form of hardware appliances.

    B. Controller-based networking has a logically centralized control plane.

    C. Controller-based networking has a logically centralized data plane.

    D. Controller-based networking uses ASICs to centrally switch frames.

18. Which term is used with controller-based networking that combines multiple sites to act as one single network?

    A. SDN

    B. SD-WAN

    C. SD-LAN

    D. VPN

19. Which is a potential disadvantage with controller-based networking?

    A. Scalability

    B. Security

    C. Maturity

    D. Centralized provisioning

20. Which elements can be controlled with an SDN controller for an SDN-enabled switch?

    A. CPU utilization

    B. Memory utilization

    C. QoS

    D. Forwarding of traffic

21. Which statement is correct about SDN switches?

    A. All data is centrally switched at the SDN controller.

    B. All SDN switches are stateless with respect to configuration.

    C. All SDN switches are stateful with respect to configuration.

    D. All data flowing through the switch is stateless.

22. Which technology allows for the central remote monitoring of network switches and routers?

    A. SNMP

    B. Syslog

    C. SDN

    D. CDP

23. What is the SNMP component that aggregates all SNMP messages and polled metrics?

    A. Trap

    B. SNMP agent

    C. Syslog server

    D. NMS

24. Which method for configuration is used with Cisco Prime Infrastructure?

    A. SNMP

    B. CAPWAP

    C. LWAPP

    D. RESTCONF

25. Which type of architecture is used with controller-based networks?

    A. Three tier

    B. Spine/Leaf

    C. Collapsed core

    D. SAN fabric

26. Which is a correct statement about Spine/Leaf architecture?

    A. The Leaf switches connect to other Leaf switches.

    B. There is only one Spine switch per network.

    C. Spine switches provide access to hosts.

    D. The Leaf switches never connect to other Leaf switches, only Spine switches.

27. What is the flow of traffic in a Spine/Leaf network?

    A. Leaf to Spine to Leaf

    B. Leaf to Leaf to Spine

    C. Spine to Leaf to Spine

    D. Leaf to Leaf

28. Which current Cisco SDN solution is data center focused?

    A. Cisco APIC-EM

    B. OpenDaylight

    C. Cisco SD-WAN

    D. Cisco ACI

29. Your company has an application they need remote office/branch office employees to directly access. Which Cisco SDN solution should you implement?

    A. Cisco APIC-EM

    B. Cisco SD-WAN

    C. Cisco Prime Infrastructure

    D. OpenDaylight

30. What is the name of the networking model that incorporates a distribution layer?

    A. Spine/Leaf

    B. Campus

    C. CLOS

    D. SDN

31. Which statement is correct about the SDN controller?

    A. The SDN controller configures the management plane of network devices.

    B. The SDN controller monitors data plane traffic.

    C. The SDN controller replaces the control plane of the SDN device.

    D. The SDN controller complements the control plane of the SDN device.

32. Which platform is Cisco's SDN controller offering for enterprise connectivity?

    A. APIC-EM

    B. OpenSDN

    C. OpenStack

    D. OpenDaylight

33. Which network plane is used for Spanning Tree Protocol (STP)?

    A. Data plane

    B. Control plane

    C. Management plane

    D. Switch plane

34. Which network plane is used by syslog for delivering messages from the router or switch?

A. Data plane

B. Control plane

C. Management plane

D. Switch plane

35. When a network packet is routed in a router, which network plane is facilitating the traffic?

A. Data plane

B. Control plane

C. Management plane

D. Switch plane

36. On which network plane would a routing protocol perform?

A. Data plane

B. Control plane

C. Management plane

D. Routing plane

37. On which SDN plane does CDP function?

A. Data plane

B. Control plane

C. Network plane

D. Management plane

38. Which is used for communication directly to the SDN devices in the network?

A. The northbound interface (NBI)

B. The southbound interface (SBI)

C. The core of the controller

D. Applications hosted on the controller

39. What is an application program interface (API)?

A. An API is a program that allows for data transfer.

B. An API is a programming language for network programmability.

C. An API is a programming interface or standard allowing one program to communicate with another program.

D. An API allows for programs to be virtualized.

40. When an application communicates with an SDN controller, which mechanism does it use to communicate?

A. The southbound interface (SBI)

B. The core of the controller

C. The northbound interface (NBI)

D. Simple Network Management Protocol (SNMP)

41. Which networking plane is responsible for routing of packets to specific destinations?

  A. Control plane

  B. Data plane

  C. Management plane

  D. Routing plane

42. What is the maximum hop count of fabric switching?

  A. 1 hop

  B. 3 hops

  C. 4 hops

  D. 5 hops

43. Which component of an SDN is where the MTU is set?

  A. Overlay

  B. Tunnel

  C. Leaf

  D. Underlay

44. You are connecting to a router and configuring ACLs through the web interface. Which plane are you affecting?

  A. Management plane

  B. Configuration plane

  C. Data plane

  D. Control plane

45. Which WAN technology uses the overlay to connect remote offices?

  A. DMVPN

  B. VXLAN

  C. VLAN

  D. ECMP

46. Which protocol allows for the tunneling of layer 2 traffic over a layer 3 network?

  A. ECMP

  B. DMVPN

  C. VXLAN

  D. EIGRP

47. Which is a protocol used on the management plane?

  A. SNMP

  B. CDP

  C. ICMP

  D. VTP

48. Which next-hop packet forwarding protocol is used with SDN switching networks?

   A. ECMP

   B. OSPF

   C. MPLS

   D. CLOS

49. Which product is a replacement for APIC-EM?

   A. OpenFlow

   B. Cisco Prime Infrastructure

   C. Cisco DNA Center

   D. Cisco SD-WAN

50. Which protocol is not used by the DNA discovery process for reading the inventory of a network device?

   A. SSH

   B. HTTPS

   C. NETCONF

   D. OpenFlow

51. Which term describes the technology that can display reasoning?

   A. Machine learning

   B. Artificial intelligence

   C. Data analytics

   D. All of the above

52. Which term is used to describe pattern recognition?

   A. Machine learning

   B. Artificial intelligence

   C. Data analytics

   D. All of the above

53. Which model of artificial intelligence uses historical data to forecast future outcomes?

   A. Predictive

   B. Generative

   C. Anomaly detection

   D. Root cause analysis

54. What type of artificial intelligence is ChatGPT?

   A. Machine learning

   B. Predictive

   C. Generative AI

   D. Generative pretrained transformer

55. Which learning model uses trial and error to fine-tune the outcome?

    A. Supervised

    B. Unsupervised

    C. Reinforcement

    D. Controlled

56. Which Cisco technology uses machine language to automate provisioning of network devices?

    A. Cisco Meraki

    B. Cisco Thousand Eyes

    C. Cisco Secure Network Analytics

    D. Cisco AppDynamics

57. Which model of artificial intelligence method uses data models and reasoning to develop new models and develop insight into a problem?

    A. Predictive

    B. Generative

    C. Anomaly detection

    D. Root cause analysis

58. Which learning model uses unlabeled dataset to train the artificial intelligence model?

    A. Supervised

    B. Unsupervised

    C. Reinforcement

    D. Controlled

59. Which item will appear on the Cisco Catalyst Center that will suggest changes for performance?

    A. System-generated insights

    B. Proactive exploration

    C. AI/ML

    D. Analytics

60. Which protocol is normally used with REST APIs?

    A. SNMP

    B. HTTP

    C. SNTP

    D. SOAP

61. You are writing a script to pull information from the Cisco DNA Center via the REST-based API. How do you authenticate so you can communicate with the Cisco DNA Center API?

A. Pass the username and password in every request.

B. Send a POST to the API for an authentication token.

C. Send a GET to the API for an authentication token.

D. Create a public private key pair for the Cisco DNA Center appliance.

62. What is the CRUD framework used for?

A. Memory cleanup

B. Replacement for REST-based APIs

C. Data encoding

D. Data actions

63. Which type of authentication is used for REST-based token requests to the Cisco DNA Center?

A. Basic

B. AD integrated

C. SSL

D. Pass-through

64. After you obtain an authentication token, how do you apply it to subsequent actions?

A. Add it as a variable named X-Auth-Token in the script.

B. Place it in the header of the request as an X-Auth-Token element.

C. Pass the token in the URI of subsequent requests.

D. Perform a POST for the authentication token within 10 seconds of the subsequent request.

65. Which encoding method is used to transmit the username and password to obtain the X-Auth-Token?

A. SSL

B. AAA

C. Base64

D. Basic

66. You are creating a script to directly configure a Cisco switch using the YANG data model. Which network API will you use to perform this task?

A. OpenFlow

B. RESTCONF

C. SNMP

D. REST-based API

67. Which is a RESTCONF content type that is used with a RESTCONF request?

    A. `application/yang-data+json`

    B. `application/json`

    C. `data/json`

    D. `data/yaml`

68. You've initiated a REST-based API call to an SDN controller and received a 500 status code. What will most likely fix the problem?

    A. Format your response correctly.

    B. Authenticate to the device first.

    C. Nothing; this code means OK.

    D. Restart the REST-based service.

69. On which interface would you most likely use a RESTCONF request?

    A. Northbound interface

    B. Eastbound interface

    C. Westbound interface

    D. Southbound interface

70. How is a status code passed to the client after a REST-based request has been processed?

    A. HTTP header

    B. HTTP body

    C. Script variable

    D. Script data object

71. You have received a return status code of 201 from an SDN controller after executing an API request via REST. Which CRUD action have you executed, judging by the status code?

    A. POST

    B. GET

    C. PATCH

    D. DELETE

72. Which character signifies the starting point for a series of request query parameters in a URI string?

    A. Backslash

    B. Forward slash

    C. Question mark

    D. Ampersand

73. In a REST API, which HTTP action verb is used to insert or create a data item?

A. GET

B. UPDATE

C. POST

D. PUT

74. You just sent a request to the SDN controller, and after a little while, the result code came back as a 504 status code. What most likely happened?

A. The command is missing parameters.

B. The command has timed out.

C. The command is restricted.

D. The service is down.

75. Which function does Ansible perform in the network?

A. Network management station

B. Configuration management

C. Software-defined networking

D. Centralized logging

76. Which configuration management tool uses YAML to store configuration?

A. Ansible

B. Cisco DNA Center

C. Chef

D. Puppet

77. Which component in an Ansible setup defines the connection information so that Ansible can perform configuration management?

A. Playbook

B. Settings

C. Inventory

D. Modules

78. Which configuration management tool does not require an agent to apply changes to a Linux-based server?

A. Ansible

B. Puppet

C. Chef

D. Cisco DNA Center

79. What is the overarching used by Terraform to deploy cloud infrastructure?

    A. IaC

    B. DSC

    C. API

    D. REST

80. What language is Terraform configuration files written in?

    A. Python

    B. PowerShell

    C. HCL

    D. CLI

81. Which Terraform block would add functionality for a particular third-party cloud or software vendor?

    A. resource

    B. plan

    C. provider

    D. vendor

82. Which environment variable is checked to determine the location of the Ansible settings file?

    A. ANSIBLE_SETTINGS

    B. ANSIBLE_CONFIG

    C. ansible_connection

    D. /etc/ansible/hosts

83. Which command will give detailed information on modules in Ansible?

    A. man

    B. cat

    C. ad-hoc

    D. ansible-doc

84. Which Ansible tool will allow you to try commands against a host without making a Playbook?

    A. Knife interface

    B. ansible_playbook command

    C. Ad hoc interface

    D. Ansible Tower

85. Which command will prepare the workspace for Terraform?

    A. terraform plan

    B. terraform validate

    C. terraform init

    D. terraform apply

86. Which Terraform block would you specify a URL for a device or application?

   A. resource

   B. plan

   C. provider

   D. vendor

87. Which tool will allow for central management and RBAC and is supported by Red Hat?

   A. Ansible Tower

   B. Chef

   C. Puppet

   D. Ansible

88. Which configuration management utility allows for easy configuration of Cisco network devices?

   A. Ansible

   B. Puppet

   C. Chef

   D. Python

89. Which Cisco product is often used in conjunction with Terraform to create infrastructure for public and private clouds?

   A. Meraki

   B. Catalyst Center

   C. ACI

   D. Intersight

90. Which is a correct statement about configuration management?

   A. IaaS helps maintain configuration over the life cycle of the host.

   B. Configuration management prevents drift with NTP.

   C. IaC solutions prevent drift with Idempotence.

   D. Configuration management software requires per-host licensing.

91. Which configuration management utility is the easiest to set up?

   A. Chef

   B. Puppet

   C. Ansible

   D. Cisco DNA Center

92. Which format must a custom Ansible module be written in?

   A. YAML

   B. CSV

   C. JSON

   D. XML

93. What is at the beginning of every JSON that helps you identify the format?

A. Three dashes

B. A square bracket

C. A double quote

D. A curly bracket

94. In the following example, looking at the square brackets. What can be concluded?

```
{
  "name": "RouterA",
  "interfaces": [
    {
      "intName": "s1",
      "ipAddress": "209.166.183.1"
    },
    {
      "intName": "e1",
      "ipAddress": "172.16.1.1"
    }
  ]
}
```

A. The value that follows the square bracket is the value you are looking for.

B. There are several key-value pairs for the key you need.

C. The value is after the matching square bracket.

D. The value is unknown.

95. What is wrong with this JSON data?

```
{
    "interface": "Fa0/1",
    "bandwidth": "100mb",
    "status": "up",
    "address": {
        "ipaddress": "192.168.1.5",
        "subnetmask": "255.255.255.0",
        "default gateway": "192.168.1.1",
}
```

A. The interface of Fa0/1 is capitalized.

B. The address should have a square bracket.

C. There is a missing curly bracket.

D. Nothing is wrong.

96. Which is an advantage in using JSON over a CSV file?

    A. Values can be used that contain spaces.

    B. There are multiple values for a particular key.

    C. The files can be read line by line for every value.

    D. Hierarchical structure allows for programmability.

97. When you request information via a REST-based API, what format is the response in?

    A. JSON

    B. XML

    C. CSV

    D. YAML

98. Which statement best represents the following JSON data from an interface?

```
{
    "ipaddress": "192.168.1.2",
    "subnet_mask": "255.255.255.0",
    "defaultgw": "192.168.1.1",
    "routes": [
      {
        "route": "10.0.0.0/8 via 192.168.1.10"
        "route": "0.0.0.0/0 via 192.168.1.1"
      }
    ]
}
```

    A. The interface data is incorrect because it is missing a comma after the routes.

    B. The interface data is incorrect because it is missing a set of curly brackets around the first and second route.

    C. The interface data is incorrect because it contains an illegal underscore character.

    D. Nothing is wrong with the JSON data.

99. Which statement best represents the following JSON data?

```
{
    "ipaddress": [
      "192.168.1.2",
      [
        "192.168.1.4"
      ]
    ],
    "subnet_mask": "255.255.255.0",
    "defaultgw": "192.168.1.1"
}
```

A. The interface data is incorrect because it is missing a comma after `defaultgw`.

B. The interface data is incorrect because it is missing a subnet mask for the second IP address.

C. The interface data is incorrect because it contains an illegal underscore character.

D. Nothing is wrong with the data.

100. Which statement best represents the following JSON data?

```
{
  "interface": {
  "ipaddress": [
    "192.168.1.2",
    [
      "192.168.1.4"
    ]
  "subnet_mask": [
    "255.255.255.0",
    [
      "255.255.255.0"
    ]
  ],
  "defaultgw": "192.168.1.1"
}
}
```

A. The interface data is incorrect because it is missing a comma after `defaultgw`.

B. The interface data is incorrect because it is missing a closing square bracket after the list of IP addresses.

C. The interface data is incorrect because it contains an illegal underscore character.

D. Nothing is wrong with the JSON data.

Chapter 7

Practice Exam 1

THE CCNA EXAM TOPICS COVERED IN THIS PRACTICE TEST INCLUDE THE FOLLOWING:

- ✓ 1.0 Network Fundamentals
- ✓ 2.0 Network Access
- ✓ 3.0 IP Connectivity
- ✓ 4.0 IP Services
- ✓ 5.0 Security Fundamentals
- ✓ 6.0 Automation and Programmability

1. Which device acts like a multiport repeater?
   A. Firewall
   B. Hub
   C. Router
   D. Switch

2. Which benefit does a switch provide to a LAN?
   A. Breaks up broadcast domains
   B. Breaks up collision domains
   C. Forces full-duplex on all ports
   D. Allows for a fast uplink port

3. When a firewall matches a URI, it is operating at which layer?
   A. Layer 7
   B. Layer 5
   C. Layer 4
   D. Layer 3

4. Which topology does an autonomous WAP use?
   A. Star topology
   B. Full-mesh topology
   C. Partial-mesh topology
   D. Hybrid topology

5. Which is the default encapsulation on a serial connection for Cisco?
   A. MPLS
   B. HDLC
   C. PPP
   D. PPPoE

6. You are connecting a Cisco router to a leased line serial connection. The other side of the connection has non-Cisco equipment. Which protocol should you choose for compatibility?
   A. HDLC
   B. PPP
   C. PPPoE
   D. X.25

7. What is the term used to describe the telephone company's switching office?
   A. Demarcation point
   B. Network edge
   C. Central office
   D. Main data frame

8. What is the term that defines the access point for the service provider's services?

    A. Demarcation point

    B. Point of presence

    C. Customer edge

    D. Network edge

9. You have several VMs in a public cloud. What is a benefit of creating NTP VNF in the public cloud for the VMs?

    A. Better time synchronization

    B. Better response time from the VMs

    C. Lower bandwidth utilization from your premises

    D. Ability to overcome different time zones

10. When deciding to move DNS into the cloud for an application on the public cloud, what is the primary decision factor?

    A. Bandwidth

    B. Response time

    C. Proper DNS resolution

    D. The cloud provider's requirements

11. Which protocol is connectionless and contains no flow control?

    A. IP

    B. TCP

    C. UDP

    D. ICMP

12. You plug a laptop into a network jack. When you examine the IP address, you see 10.23.2.3, which was not originally configured when you checked prior to plugging it in. What can you conclude?

    A. The network jack is not working.

    B. Your laptop has a static IP address configured.

    C. The network is configured properly.

    D. The DHCP server is down.

13. Which network does the IP address 192.168.4.38/27 belong to?

    A. 192.168.4.8/27 network

    B. 192.168.4.16/27 network

    C. 192.168.4.32/27 network

    D. 192.168.4.64/27 network

14. What are stateless DHCPv6 servers used for?

    A. Configuring the default gateway

    B. Configuring the IPv6 address

    C. Configuring the IPv6 prefix length

    D. Configuring the DNS server address

15. Which mechanism in IPv6 allows for SLAAC to avoid duplicating an IPv6 address?

    A. NDP (NS/NA)

    B. DAD (NS/NA)

    C. SLAAC (RS/RA)

    D. ARPv6 (NS/NA)

16. Which term best describes the IPv6 address of 2202:0ff8:0002:2344:3533:8eff:fe22:ae4c?

    A. Multicast address

    B. EUI-64 address

    C. Anycast address

    D. Link-local address

17. If a switch uses the store and forward method of switching and receives a frame in which its CRC is invalid, what will happen?

    A. The switch will re-create the frame with a new CRC and correct the missing information.

    B. The switch will drop the frame and wait for retransmission of a new frame.

    C. The switch will send back a frame for retransmission of the frame.

    D. The switch will store the frame until a new frame with a matching CRC is received.

18. What is the issue with the network in the following figure?

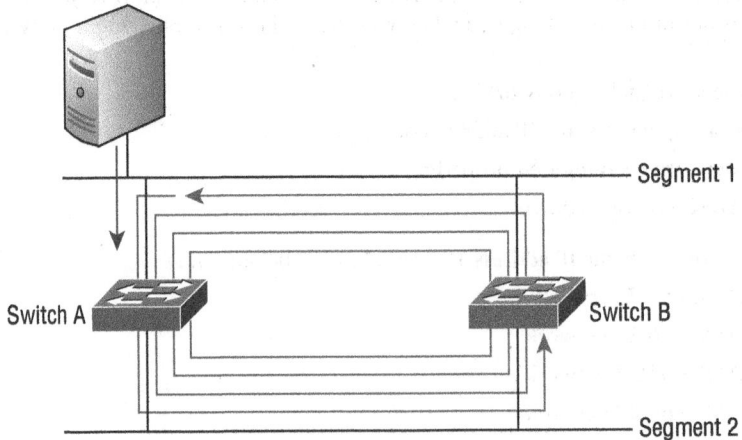

A. STP is not configured and a broadcast storm is occurring.

B. MAC table thrashing has occurred.

C. STP is not configured and duplication of unicast frames is occurring.

D. An STP loop has occurred.

19. Which command will show the number of entries in a MAC address table?

A. `show mac address-table`

B. `show mac address-table count`

C. `show mac count`

D. `show cam count`

20. When a switch receives a frame, what does it use to make a forwarding decision?

A. Destination MAC address in the frame

B. Source MAC address in the frame

C. Source IP address in the frame

D. Destination IP address in the frame

21. From the following figure, what can you conclude about the computer with the MAC address of 0002.160a.4c37?

```
                  Mac Address Table
-------------------------------------------------

vlan    Mac Address      Type      Ports
----    -------------    -------   -----
   1    0001.63c8.0a19   DYNAMIC   Gig0/1
   1    0002.160a.4c37   DYNAMIC   Gig0/1
   1    0010.1193.acbb   DYNAMIC   Fa0/1
   2    0001.63c8.0a19   DYNAMIC   Gig0/1
   3    0001.63c8.0a19   DYNAMIC   Gig0/1
   4    0001.63c8.0a19   DYNAMIC   Gig0/1
   5    0001.63c8.0a19   DYNAMIC   Gig0/1
  12    0001.63c8.0a19   DYNAMIC   Gig0/1
```

A. The computer is the only device on port Gi0/1.

B. The computer is on a hub connected to port Gi0/1.

C. The computer is connected to another switch.

D. The computer's MAC address has aged out of the table.

22. Which type of switchport strips all VLAN information from the frame before it egresses the interface on the switch?

A. Trunk port

B. Access port

C. Voice port

D. DTP port

23. Which is a correct statement about the output in the following figure?

```
Switch#show interface trunk
Port     Mode        Encapsulation    Status       Native vlan
Gi0/1    auto        n-802.1q         trunking     1
[output cut]
```

    A. The default native VLAN has been changed.

    B. The encapsulation has been negotiated.

    C. The switch is sending DTP frames.

    D. The adjacent switch is also set to auto for DTP.

24. You have a switch with several hundred interfaces. You only want to see the running-config for one interface, Gi3/45. Which command will allow you to see the running-config for only Gi3/45?

    A. `show interface gi 3/45`

    B. `show running-config | include 3/45`

    C. `show running-config interface gi 3/45`

    D. `show running gi 3/45`

25. Which command will display the serial number of the switch?

    A. `show version`

    B. `show serial`

    C. `show board`

    D. `show controller`

26. You have a rather large configuration on a switch. You want to see the running-config, but only after port gi4/45. Which command will achieve this?

    A. `show running-config begin 4/45`

    B. `show filter running-config 4/45`

    C. `show running-config interface gi 4/45`

    D. `show running-config | begin 4/45`

27. You have neighboring equipment on the switch that is running LLDP. Which command(s) will allow you to see the neighboring equipment's management IP addresses?

    A. `Switch(config)#enable lldp`
       `Switch(config)#exit`
       `Switch#show lldp neighbors detail`

    B. `Switch(config)#lldp run`
       `Switch(config)#exit`
       `Switch#show lldp neighbors detail`

C. `Switch#show lldp neighbors detail`

D. `Switch(config)#enable lldp`

`Switch(config)#exit`

`Switch#show lldp neighbors *`

28. You are mapping a network with the use of CDP. On the entry of cs-main.ntw, what is the connection of Gig 0/1 used for in the following figure?

```
es-switch2#show cdp neighbors
[output Cut]
Device ID        Local Intrfce    Holdtme    Capability   Platform    Port ID
cs-main.ntw      Gig 0/1          138            R S C    WS-C3560X   Gig 0/40
es-layer2.ntw    Gig 0/2          178              S I    WS-C3560X   Gig 1/1
es-switch3.ntw   Gig 0/3          178              S I    WS-C3560X   Gig 1/2
es-switch2#
```

A. The Gig 0/1 interface on es-switch2

B. The Gig 0/1 interface on cs-main.ntw

C. The Gig 0/1 interface on es-layer2.ntw

D. The Gig 0/1 interface on es-switch3.ntw

29. You check the status of the EtherChannel configured on the switch with the `show etherchannel` command. What can be concluded from the output? Refer to the following figure.

```
SwitchA#sh etherchannel
                                      Channel-group listing:
                                      --------------------

Group: 1
---------
Group state = L2
Ports: 2 Maxports = 8
Port-channels: 1 Max Port-channels = 1
Protocol:    -
SwitchA#
```

A. The EtherChannel is configured with PAgP.

B. The EtherChannel is configured with LACP.

C. The EtherChannel is configured with no control protocol.

D. The EtherChannel is configured as an access port.

30. You are configuring an EtherChannel between two switches. You check your configuration on the first switch and are ready to configure the second switch. What mode do you need to configure on the other switch? Refer to the following figure.

```
SwitchA#sh run
Building configuration...
[output cut]
!
interface Port-channel 1
!
[output cut]
interface GigabitEthernet0/1
 channel-group 1 mode auto
!
interface GigabitEthernet0/2
 channel-group 1 mode auto
[output cut]
```

    A. `channel-group 1 mode auto`

    B. `channel-group 1 mode desirable`

    C. `channel-group 1 mode active`

    D. `channel-group 1 mode passive`

31. You are configuring an EtherChannel between two switches for trunking. The EtherChannel will not form. You check your configuration on the first switch. What is the problem on the other switch? Refer to the following figure.

```
SwitchA#sh run
Building configuration...
[output cut]
!
interface Port-channel 1
!
[output cut]
interface GigabitEthernet0/1
 channel-group 1 mode passive
!
interface GigabitEthernet0/2
 channel-group 1 mode passive
[output cut]
```

    A. The other switch is configured as an access link.

    B. The other switch has CDP turned off.

    C. The other switch is configured for active mode.

    D. The other switch is configured for passive mode.

32. In the following figure, Rapid Spanning Tree Protocol (RSTP) is configured. Which interfaces will become the root ports?

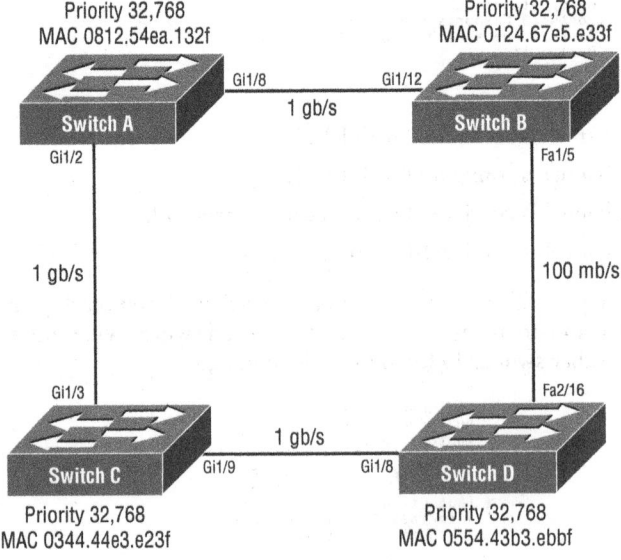

- **A.** Switch B interface Fa1/5 and Gi1/12
- **B.** Switch A interface Gi1/8 and Switch D interface Fa2/16
- **C.** Switch A interface Gi1/8, Switch D interface Fa2/16, and Switch C interface Gi1/3
- **D.** Switch A interface Gi1/2 and Switch D interface Gi1/8

33. When you're using 802.1w, which switchport state will always forward traffic?

- **A.** Disabled
- **B.** Backup
- **C.** Designated
- **D.** Alternate

34. You want to quickly configure an edge switch so all access ports are in PortFast mode. Which command will achieve this?

- **A.** `spanning-tree portfast default`
- **B.** `switchport spanning-tree portfast`
- **C.** `spanning-tree portfast enable`
- **D.** `spanning-tree portfast`

35. Which AP mode allows for RF analysis of the 802.11ac radio spectrum?

- **A.** Monitor mode
- **B.** Analysis mode
- **C.** FlexConnect mode
- **D.** Local mode

36. You have a small area in a warehouse in which you need wired connectivity to the network. However, wiring cannot be run easily, but there is a direct line of sight for wireless. Which AP feature can be used to connect the area?

- **A.** Wireless mesh
- **B.** LightWeight mode
- **C.** Local mode
- **D.** WorkGroup Bridge

37. You need to configure a link aggregation group for a Cisco wireless controller. What should be configured on the EtherChannel to establish a link?

- **A.** Auto mode
- **B.** On mode
- **C.** Desirable mode
- **D.** Passive mode

38. Which is a benefit of using TACACS+?

   A. It is an open standard.

   B. It sends the passwords of users in clear text.

   C. It supports authenticating a user to a subset of commands.

   D. It supports authenticating a user to a length of time.

39. Why should you always provide a second method of local when setting up AAA remote authentication with a router or switch?

   A. To allow for a backdoor.

   B. To provide a backup if the TACACS+ server is down or unreachable.

   C. The local second method is required.

   D. All of the above.

40. You want all guests to register for wireless Internet access before granting them access. What should you implement?

   A. Captive portal

   B. AAA server

   C. ESS

   D. RRM

41. When an IP address is configured on the router's interface, what happens in the route table?

   A. A route entry is created for the network attached to the IP address on the interface.

   B. A route entry is created for the IP address attached to the interface.

   C. Dynamic routing protocols update all other routers.

   D. All of the above.

42. In the following figure, which interface or IP address will a packet be routed to for a destination address of 192.168.4.56?

```
Router#sh ip route
[output cut]
     172.16.0.0/16 is variably subnetted, 2 subnets, 2 masks
C    172.16.0.0/16 is directly connected, Serial0/0/0
L    172.16.1.1/32 is directly connected, Serial0/0/0
     192.168.1.0/24 is variably subnetted, 2
C    192.168.1.0/24 is directly connected, Serial0/0/1
L    192.168.1.1/32 is directly connected, Serial0/0/1
S    192.168.4.0/24 is directly connected, Serial0/0/1
S    192.168.5.0/24 [1/0] via 192.168.4.2
S    192.168.5.0/24 [5/0] via 192.168.4.5
     198.23.24.0/24 is variably subnetted, 2 subnets, 2 masks
C    198.23.24.0/24 is directly connected, Serial0/1/1
L    198.23.24.1/32 is directly connected, Serial0/1/1
S*   0.0.0.0/0 is directly connected, Serial0/2/0
```

   A. Interface Serial 0/0/1

   B. Interface Serial 0/0/0

   C. IP gateway of 192.168.4.1

   D. Interface Serial 0/2/0

43. In the following figure, which interface or IP address will the packet with a destination of 198.23.34.2 be routed to?

```
Router#sh ip route
[output cut]
      172.16.0.0/16 is variably subnetted, 2 subnets, 2 masks
C  172.16.0.0/16 is directly connected, Serial0/0/0
L  172.16.1.1/32 is directly connected, Serial0/0/0
      192.168.1.0/24 is variably subnetted, 2
C  192.168.1.0/24 is directly connected, Serial0/0/1
L  192.168.1.1/32 is directly connected, Serial0/0/1
S  192.168.4.0/24 is directly connected, Serial0/0/1
S  192.168.5.0/24 [1/0] via 192.168.4.2
S  192.168.5.0/24 [5/0] via 192.168.4.5
      198.23.24.0/24 is variably subnetted, 2 subnets, 2 masks
C  198.23.24.0/24 is directly connected, Serial0/1/1
L  198.23.24.1/32 is directly connected, Serial0/1/1
S* 0.0.0.0/0 is directly connected, Serial0/2/0
```

A. Interface Serial 0/1/1

B. Interface Serial 0/0/1

C. Interface Serial 0/2/0

D. There is no suitable route.

44. What is the administrative distance of OSPF?

A. 90

B. 100

C. 110

D. 120

45. Which command will allow you to see the next advertisement interval for RIPv2?

A. show ip protocols

B. show ip rip database

C. show ip rip

D. show ip interface

46. Which command will allow you to inspect RIPv2 advertisements?

A. show ip protocols

B. debug rip

C. show ip rip

D. debug ip rip

47. You need to advertise the routes 192.168.1.0/24, 192.168.2.0/24, and 192.168.3.0/24. Assuming RIPv2 is configured, which configuration will achieve this?

A. network 192.168.0.0

B. network 192.168.1.0

    network 192.168.2.0

    network 192.168.3.0

C. network 192.168.0.0/16

D. network 192.168.0.0 0.0.255.255

48. You have RIPv2 configured on an Internet-facing router. Which command will suppress RIPv2 advertisements on the interface link?

  A. `Router(config-if)#ip rip passive-interface`

  B. `Router(config-if)#rip passive-interface`

  C. `Router(config-router)#passive-interface serial 0/0`

  D. `Router(config-if)#ip rip suppress-advertisement`

49. Which is a problem with using RIPv2 in a network?

  A. Complex configuration

  B. Slow convergence

  C. The use of broadcasts

  D. Routing support for classless networks

50. Which technique is used to stop routing loops with RIPv2?

  A. Split horizons

  B. Advertisement intervals

  C. Zoning

  D. Invalid timers

51. Which algorithm does RIPv2 use to calculate routes?

  A. Shortest Path First

  B. Dijkstra

  C. Bellman–Ford

  D. DUAL

52. Which command will need to be configured for support of discontinuous networks?

  A. `Router(config-router)#network discontiguous`

  B. `Router(config)#network discontiguous`

  C. `Router(config)#no auto-summary`

  D. `Router(config-router)#no auto-summary`

53. Which command configures RIPv2 on a router and advertises a network of 192.168.20.0/24?

  A. `ip router ripv2`
     `network 192.168.20.0`

  B. `router rip`
     `version 2`
     `network 192.168.20.0`

  C. `router rip`
     `version 2`
     `network 192.168.20.0 0.0.0.255`

   D. `ip router rip`
   `version 2`
   `network 192.168.20.0 0.0.0.255`

54. Which routing technique is best suited for small networks in which the administrator wants control of routing?

   A. OSPF routing

   B. EIGRP routing

   C. Static routing

   D. RIP routing

55. Which command will allow you to verify the IPv6 addresses configured on a router?

   A. `show ipv6`

   B. `show ip interfaces brief`

   C. `show ipv6 interfaces brief`

   D. `show ipv6 brief`

56. Which command will show you the IPv6 routes in the route table?

   A. `show ipv6 route`

   B. `show ip route`

   C. `show ipv6 route summary`

   D. `show ipv6 route brief`

57. In the following figure, which route statement will need to be added to the routers to allow routing between the networks?

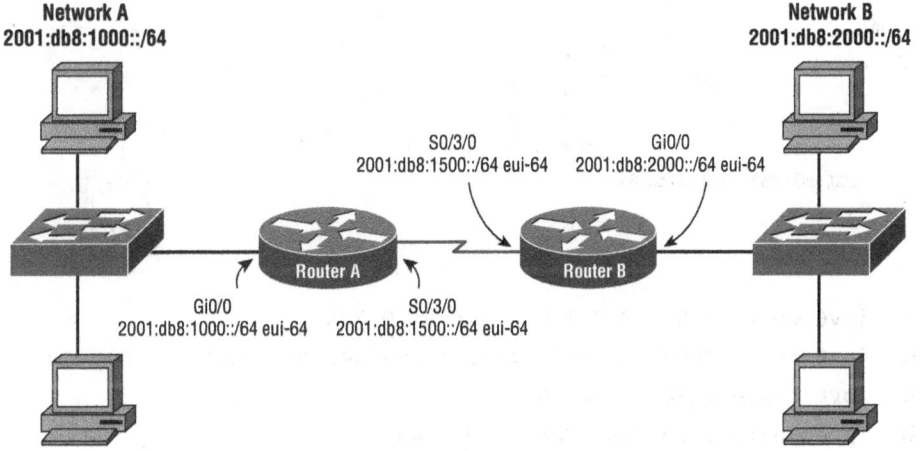

A. RouterA(config)#ip route 2001:db8:1000/64 serial 0/3/0

RouterB(config)#ip route 2001:db8:2000/64 serial 0/3/0

B. RouterA(config)#ip route 2001:db8:2000::/64 serial 0/3/0

RouterB(config)#ip route 2001:db8:1000::/64 serial 0/3/0

C. RouterA(config)#ipv6 route 2001:db8:2000::/64 serial 0/3/0

RouterB(config)#ipv6 route 2001:db8:1000::/64 serial 0/3/0

D. RouterA(config)#ipv6 route 2001:db8:2000::/64
2001:db8:1500::/64 eui-64

RouterB(config)#ipv6 route 2001:db8:1000::/64
2001:db8:1500::/64 eui-64

58. Which command will only show you all of the directly connected routes for IPv6?

A. show ipv6 interface summary

B. show ipv6 route connected

C. show ipv6 interface brief

D. show ipv6 summary

59. In the following figure, you need to configure Router B so that hosts on Network B can reach the Internet. Which statement on Router B will allow hosts to reach the Internet?

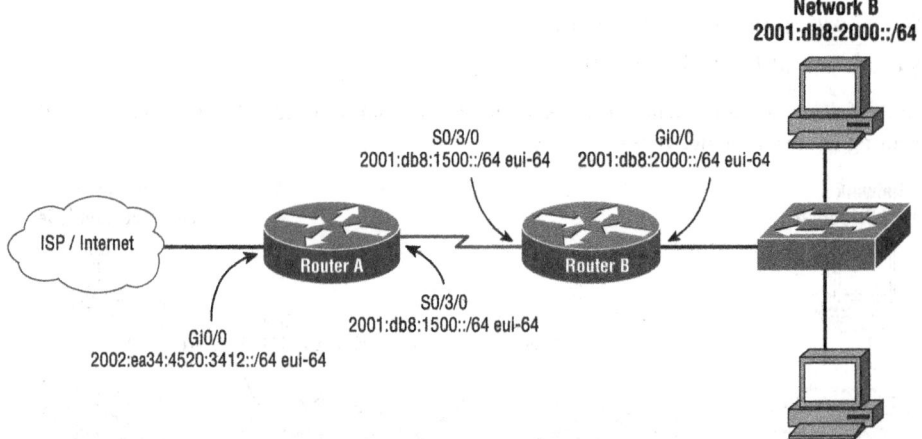

A. ipv6 route 0.0.0.0 0.0.0.0 serial 0/3/0

B. ipv6 route 2002:ea34:4520:3412::/64 serial 0/3/0

C. ipv6 route ::/0 serial 0/3/0

D. ipv6 route ::/0 2001:db8:1500::/64 eui

60. In the following figure, which route statement will need to be added to the routers to allow routing between the networks?

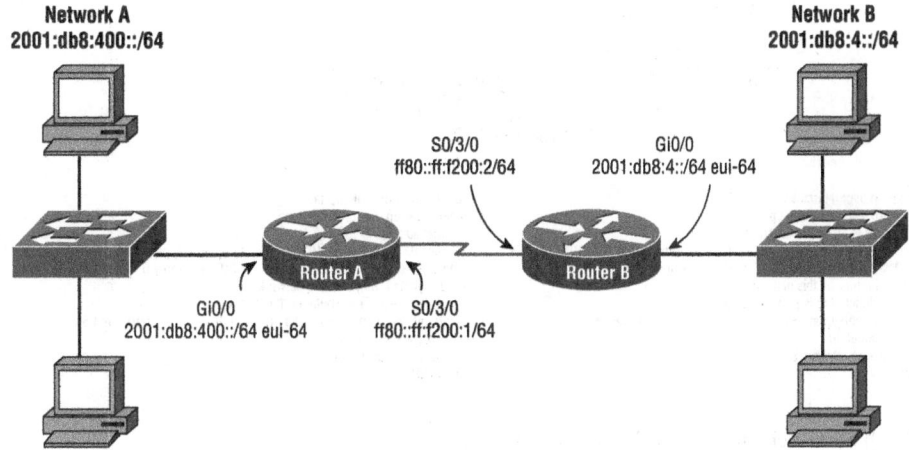

Network A
2001:db8:400::/64

Network B
2001:db8:4::/64

S0/3/0
ff80::ff:f200:2/64

Gi0/0
2001:db8:4::/64 eui-64

Router A

Router B

Gi0/0
2001:db8:400::/64 eui-64

S0/3/0
ff80::ff:f200:1/64

- **A.** RouterA(config)#ip route 2001:db8:4/64 ff80::ff:f200:2
  RouterB(config)#ip route 2001:db8:400/64 ff80::ff:f200:1
- **B.** RouterA(config)#ip route 2001:db8:400::/64 serial 0/3/0
  RouterB(config)#ip route 2001:db8:4::/64 serial 0/3/0
- **C.** RouterA(config)#ipv6 route 2001:db8:400::/64 serial 0/3/0
  RouterB(config)#ipv6 route 2001:db8:4::/64 serial 0/3/0
- **D.** RouterA(config)#ipv6 route 2001:db8:4/64 ff80::ff:f200:2
  RouterB(config)#ipv6 route 2001:db8:400/64 ff80::ff:f200:1

61. Which command will allow you to check basic connectivity at layer 3?
- **A.** show ip route
- **B.** ping 192.168.4.1
- **C.** pathping 192.168.4.1
- **D.** ip ping 192.168.4.1

62. Which command will allow you to see the path on which a packet gets routed to its destination?
- **A.** show ip route
- **B.** tracert 192.168.7.56
- **C.** pathping 192.168.7.56
- **D.** traceroute 192.168.7.56

63. In the following figure, Router A will not form an adjacency with Router B. What is the problem?

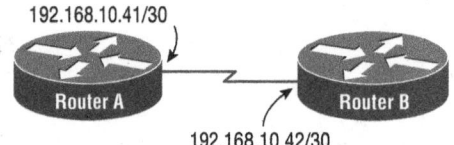

192.168.10.41/30

Router A

Router B

192.168.10.42/30

```
RouterA#show ip ospf interface
Serial0/3/0 is up, line protocol is up
  Internet address is 192.168.10.41/30, Area 0
  Process ID 1, Router ID 192.168.10.41, Network Type POINT-TO-POINT, Cost: 64
  Transmit Delay is 1 sec, State POINT-TO-POINT, Priority 0
  No designated router on this network
  No backup designated router on this network
  Timer intervals configured, Hello 10, Dead 40, Wait 40, Retransmit 5
  oob-resync timeout 40
  No Hellos (Passive interface)
[output cut]
```

```
RouterB#show ip ospf interface
Serial0/3/0 is up, line protocol is up
  Internet address is 192.168.10.42/30, Area 0
  Process ID 23, Router ID 192.168.10.42, Network Type POINT-TO-POINT, Cost: 64
  Transmit Delay is 1 sec, State POINT-TO-POINT, Priority 0
  No designated router on this network
  No backup designated router on this network
  Timer intervals configured, Hello 10, Dead 40, Wait 40, Retransmit 5
  oob-resync timeout 40
  No Hellos (Passive interface)
[output cut]
```

    A. The routers are not in the same network.

    B. The routers have mismatched process IDs.

    C. The routers have passive interfaces.

    D. The hello/dead interval is wrong for serial links.

64. Which command will allow you to see the networks the current router is advertising for OSPF?

    A. `show ip protocols`

    B. `show ip ospf`

    C. `show ip ospf database`

    D. `show ip ospf neighbors`

65. A client has an IP address of 192.168.1.5/24 and a default gateway of 192.168.1.1. HSRP is in use in the network. Which type of router is the default gateway?

    A. Active router

    B. Standby router

    C. Virtual router

    D. Support router

66. Which of the following is an advantage to using Port Address Translation?

    A. Lower levels of jitter

    B. Lower levels of packet loss

    C. Flexibility of Internet connections

    D. Lower memory usage than other NAT types

67. Which command would you configure on the private network interface for NAT?

   A. `Router(config-if)#ip nat outside`

   B. `Router(config)#ip nat inside gi0/0`

   C. `Router(config-if)#ip nat private`

   D. `Router(config-if)#ip nat inside`

68. Why is time synchronization important for routers and switches?

   A. It is important for serialized communication frame alignment.

   B. It is important for quality of service queuing.

   C. It is important for logging accuracy.

   D. It helps delivery of packets via timed queues.

69. Which statement describes FQDNs?

   A. A DNS server always processes the entire FQDN.

   B. FQDNs are always registered with a registrar.

   C. FQDNs are significant from left to right, starting with a period for the root.

   D. FQDNs are significant from right to left, starting with a period for the root.

70. Which protocol and port number does SNMP use for polling from the NMS?

   A. UDP/161

   B. TCP/162

   C. UDP/162

   D. UDP/514

71. Which command will allow you to verify the syslog server set for logging and the logging level set?

   A. `show logging`

   B. `show syslog`

   C. `show log-server`

   D. `show ip logging`

72. Which command will allow you to verify the IP addresses assigned to a router's interface?

   A. `show ip dhcp bindings`

   B. `show ip interface`

   C. `show ip lease`

   D. `show ip dhcp lease`

73. Where should QoS marking be performed?

   A. Closest to the source of the traffic

   B. Closest to the Internet router

   C. On every device in the network

   D. On the core router in the network

74. Which is a correct statement about device trust boundary for QoS?

    A. The trust boundary should always be an asset IT controls.

    B. The switch should always be set as the trust boundary.

    C. Only routers can create trust boundaries.

    D. Only IP phones can become trust boundaries.

75. Which command needs to be configured to enable the Secure Copy Protocol (SCP)?

    A. `ip ssh server enable`

    B. `ip scp server enable`

    C. `service scp enable`

    D. `service scp-server`

76. What is the attack in which DTP is exploited by a malicious user?

    A. Native VLAN

    B. VLAN hopping

    C. VLAN traversal

    D. Trunk popping

77. Which layer 2 protocol has built-in security for WAN connections?

    A. HDLC

    B. PPP

    C. IPsec

    D. Metro Ethernet

78. Chelsea is worried about the threat of malware on the network. She wants to install software that will detect worms and Trojan horses on every workstation. Which type of software should she install?

    A. Malware

    B. Antivirus

    C. Software firewalls

    D. Spyware

79. Which command will configure the login banner to read "CCNA Routing and Switching"?

    A. `Router(config)#login banner CCNA Routing and Switching`

    B. `Router(config)#banner login CCNA Routing and Switching`

    C. `Router(config)#banner login ^CCNA Routing and Switching^`

    D. `Router(config-line)#banner login ^CCNA Routing and Switching^`

80. You have configured a message of the day (MOTD) banner, but it only shows up after you have logged into the router. What is the problem?

    A. You are connecting via SSH.

    B. You are connecting via Telnet.

    C. You are connecting via the console.

    D. You do not have an enable password set.

81. Which mechanism is used to authenticate EAP-TLS during the 802.1x authentication process?

    A. MD5

    B. Certificates

    C. SSH

    D. Passwords

82. You have been asked to recommend a private WAN technology. All of the remote offices have varied physical connectivity paths. Which private WAN technology should you recommend?

    A. MPLS

    B. Metro Ethernet

    C. PPPoE

    D. GRE tunnels

83. Which protocol does IPsec use to check integrity of data packets?

    A. AH

    B. ESP

    C. IKE

    D. ISAKMP

84. If a router has two interfaces and you only use IPv4, how many ACLs can be configured on the router's interfaces?

    A. One

    B. Two

    C. Four

    D. Eight

85. Which command will achieve the same goal as the command `access-list 2 permit host 192.168.2.3`?

    A. `access-list 2 permit 192.168.2.3 255.255.255.255`

    B. `access-list 2 permit 192.168.2.3 0.0.0.0`

    C. `ip access-list 2 permit host 192.168.2.3`

    D. `access-list 2 permit 192.168.2.3`

86. You have just configured DHCP snooping. Which ports should be trusted?

   A. Ports connecting to clients

   B. Ports connecting to web servers

   C. Ports connecting to other switches

   D. Ports connecting to the DNS server

87. Which is a correct statement about how DHCP snooping works?

   A. Untrusted ports allow Discover and Offer messages to be switched.

   B. Untrusted ports drop Discover and Offer messages.

   C. Untrusted ports drop Offer and Acknowledgment messages.

   D. Untrusted ports allow Offer and Acknowledgment messages to be switched.

88. Which command will configure the RADIUS server 192.168.1.5 with a secret of aaaauth?

   A. `radius host 192.168.1.5 key aaaauth`

   B. `radius-server host 192.168.1.5 key aaaauth`

   C. `radius-server 192.168.1.5 key aaaauth`

   D. `radius-server host 192.168.1.5 secret aaaauth`

89. Which protocol was released to fix WEP?

   A. WPA

   B. WPA2

   C. WPA3

   D. RC4-TKIP

90. You are configuring a WLAN and you need to use WPA PSK, but you also need to restrict access to certain devices. What should you implement to achieve this goal?

   A. Captive portal

   B. RADIUS

   C. MAC filtering

   D. Disable broadcast SSID

91. An employee has left, and you are required to change the password of 50 routers. What is the quickest way to complete this task?

   A. Creating a script with Python

   B. Creating a script with JSON

   C. Applying a YAML template to the routers

   D. Applying a JSON template to the routers

92. Which is a negative outcome from automating a configuration change across the enterprise?

   A. Increased odds of typographical errors

   B. Increased odds of configuration conflicts

   C. Increased time spent building configurations

   D. Decreased time spent building configurations

93. You have been given the task of mapping a network. You have several routers and switches that are interconnected. Which Cisco tool will help you map the network?

   A. CDP

   B. Running configuration

   C. OSPF neighbor table

   D. EIGRP neighbor table

94. Which protocol is used with the southbound interface in the SDN controller?

   A. Python

   B. OpenFlow

   C. REST

   D. JSON

95. On which layer does the fabric of a software-defined network switch packets?

   A. Layer 2

   B. Layer 3

   C. Layer 6

   D. Layer 7

96. Where inside of the Cisco DNA Center can you configure the upgrade of IOS for network devices?

   A. Provision

   B. Design

   C. Policy

   D. Assurance

97. You are testing a POST function on a REST-based API and a 401 status code was returned. What does that mean?

   A. The POST was accepted.

   B. The POST was redirected to another URI.

   C. The POST was unauthorized.

   D. The POST was not in the right format.

98. Which configuration management mechanism uses Python and YAML as a configuration language?

   A. DSC

   B. Chef

   C. Puppet

   D. Ansible

99. Which is a requirement for using Ansible for configuration management?

    A. Internet access

    B. Root SSH

    C. Unrestricted firewall

    D. Ruby

100. Which command is used to output JSON from the execution of a command on a Cisco router or switch?

    A. `show interface status | json-pretty native`

    B. `json interface status`

    C. `show interface status | json`

    D. `show interface status json`

Chapter 8

Practice Exam 2

THE CCNA EXAM TOPICS COVERED IN THIS PRACTICE TEST INCLUDE THE FOLLOWING:

- ✓ 1.0 Network Fundamentals
- ✓ 2.0 Network Access
- ✓ 3.0 IP Connectivity
- ✓ 4.0 IP Services
- ✓ 5.0 Security Fundamentals
- ✓ 6.0 Automation and Programmability

1. Which device will create broadcast domains and raise effective bandwidth?
    A. Firewall
    B. Hub
    C. Router
    D. Switch

2. Which devices create collision domains, raising effective bandwidth?
    A. Firewalls
    B. Hubs
    C. Routers
    D. Switches

3. In which zone should an email server be located?
    A. Inside zone
    B. Outside zone
    C. DNS zone
    D. DMZ

4. If you had limited cable access for the distribution switches, which topology would you need to plan for?
    A. Star topology
    B. Full-mesh topology
    C. Partial-mesh topology
    D. Hybrid topology

5. Which subprotocol inside of the PPP suite is responsible for tagging layer 3 protocols so that multiple protocols can be used over a PPP connection?
    A. MPLS
    B. NCP
    C. LCP
    D. PCP

6. Which command will configure PPP on a serial interface?
    A. `encapsulation ppp`
    B. `protocol ppp`
    C. `ppp enable`
    D. `ppp protocol`

7. What device connects the remote office DSL modem to the telco's PSTN and the Internet?
    A. DSL access multiplier
    B. DSL concentrator

    C. 5ESS switch

    D. Digital cross-connect system

8. When purchasing a Metro Ethernet connection, which option is generally tied to the monthly recurring cost of the connection?

    A. IP addresses used to support the service

    B. Routing protocols used to support the service

    C. The committed information rate on the EVC

    D. The use of QoS

9. Which cloud service is likely to be used for software development?

    A. SaaS

    B. IaaS

    C. PaaS

    D. DRaaS

10. You are running several web servers in a cloud with a server load balancer. As demand increases, you add web servers. According to the NIST standard of cloud computing, which feature can you use to increase your compute capability for demand?

    A. Resource pooling

    B. Measured services

    C. Broad network access

    D. Rapid elasticity

11. Which flags are used during the three-way handshake process for TCP?

    A. FIN and ACK

    B. SYN and ACK

    C. SYN and FIN

    D. SYN and RDY

12. Which network is part of the summary route of 172.16.32.0/21?

    A. 172.16.64.0/24

    B. 172.16.48.0/24

    C. 172.16.40.0/24

    D. 172.16.38.0/24

13. Which classification of IP address does 225.34.5.4 belong to?

    A. Class A

    B. Class B

    C. Class C

    D. Class D

14. What is the process of stateful DHCPv6 for IPv6?

    A. Discover, Offer, Request, Acknowledge

    B. Solicit, Advertise, Request, Reply

    C. Neighbor Solicitation, Neighbor Advertisement

    D. Router Solicitation, Router Advertisement

15. When SLAAC is performed on an IPv6 host, which process happens first?

    A. A Router Solicitation message is sent from the client.

    B. A Router Advertisement message is sent from the router.

    C. A link-local address is auto-configured on the client.

    D. DAD is performed on the IPv6 address.

16. In IPv6, the solicited-node multicast message is used for what?

    A. Discovery of the gateway

    B. Discovery of the network ID

    C. Resolution of the MAC address for an IPv6 address

    D. Capability discovery of neighboring devices

17. The following figure is an Ethernet frame. What is field A in the figure?

7-byte preamble	SFD	Field A	Field B	Field C	Field D	Field E

    A. Source MAC address

    B. Destination MAC address

    C. Type field

    D. Frame Checking Sequence (FCS)

18. In the following figure, what is field C used for?

7-byte preamble	SFD	Field A	Field B	Field C	Field D	Field E

    A. The destination MAC address

    B. The next upper-layer protocol to send the information to

    C. The beginning of data, also called the start frame delimiter

    D. The cyclical redundancy checksum value

19. Which command would you use to reset the MAC address table for learned MAC addresses in a switch?

    A. `reset mac address-table`

    B. `clear mac-address-table dynamic`

    C. `clear mac-address-table`

    D. `clear mac table`

20. You need to see all of the MAC addresses associated with a single interface. Which command would you use?

    A. `Switch>show mac address-table interfaces fast 0/1`

    B. `Switch>show address-table interfaces fast 0/1`

    C. `Switch#show mac interfaces fast 0/1`

    D. `Switch#show address-table fast 0/1`

21. Which statement is correct about the following figure?

```
Switch#show monitor session 1 detail
Session 1
---------
Type                  : Local Session
Description           : -
Source Ports          :
    RX Only           : None
    TX Only           : None
    Both              : Fa0/1
Source VLANs          :
    RX Only           : None
    TX Only           : None
    Both              : 2
Source RSPAN VLAN     : None
Destination Ports     : Fa0/2
    Encapsulation     : Native
        Ingress       : Disabled
Filter VLANs          : None
Dest RSPAN VLAN       : None
```

    A. The source interface is Fa0/1 with a destination interface of Fa0/2.

    B. The source interface is Fa0/2 with a destination interface of Fa0/1.

    C. The source interface is Fa0/1 with a destination interface of Fa0/2 via VLAN 2.

    D. The source interface is Fa0/1 and VLAN 2 with a destination interface of Fa0/2.

22. When VLANs are configured in global configuration mode, where are the VLANs stored by default?

    A. In the running configuration or RAM

    B. In the startup configuration or NVRAM

    C. In the `vlan.dat` file on the flash

    D. In the `vlan.dat` file on the NVRAM

23. Which command will allow you to configure interfaces Gi1/1 to Gi1/12?

 A. `interface gigabitethernet range 1/1 - 12`

 B. `interface range gigabitethernet 1/1 - 12`

 C. `interface range gigabitethernet 1/1 1/12`

 D. `interface range gigabitethernet range 1/1,12`

24. You have VLAN 10 and VLAN 11 configured on a trunk switchport as allowed. What will happen if you enter the command `switchport trunk allowed vlan 12` on the trunk interface?

 A. VLAN 12 will be added to the existing allowed VLAN list.

 B. VLANs 1 through 12 will be added to the allowed VLAN list.

 C. The native VLAN will be switched to VLAN 12.

 D. Only VLAN 12 will be on the allowed VLAN list.

25. Which protocol assists in synchronizing a VLAN database across multiple Cisco switches?

 A. NTP

 B. IGMP

 C. ISL

 D. VTP

26. In the following figure, interface Gi 1/1 on both switches is configured as a trunk, between the switches. Which statement is correct about the following figure?

```
SwitchA#show interfaces status

Port     Name Status    Vlan     Duplex  Speed Type
Gi1/1    Switch B       trunk    full    auto 10/100/1000-TX
Gi1/2    Computer A     23       auto    auto 10/100/1000-TX
Gi1/3    Computer B     23       auto    auto 10/100/1000-TX
Gi1/4    Computer C     23       a-full  a-10 10/100/1000-Tx
[output Cut]

SwitchB#show interfaces status

Port     Name Status    Vlan     Duplex  SpeedType
Gi1/1    Switch A       trunk    a-half  auto 10/100/1000-TX
Gi1/2    Computer D 41  auto     auto    10/100/1000-TX
Gi1/3    Computer E 41  auto     auto    10/100/1000-TX
Gi1/4    Computer F 41  a-full   a-10    10/100/1000-TX
[output Cut]
```

 A. The interface Gi1/1, which is connecting the switches, has a wiring fault.

 B. The interface Gi1/1 is operating nominally.

 C. The interface Gi1/1, which is connecting the switches, has the wrong duplex configured.

 D. The two switches have a VLAN mismatch.

27. You are examining the output of the command `show cdp neighbors detail`. One of the devices has the capability of S and R. What does this mean?

 A. The device has source route bridge capability.

 B. The device has switch capability.

    C. The device has router capability.

    D. The device has switch and router capability.

28. Your network is connected in a star topology. You are assessing a network upgrade. Which command will help you determine the version of IOS on the switches and routers in your network with the least amount of effort?

    A. `show version`

    B. `show running-config`

    C. `show cdp neighbors detail`

    D. `show lldp neighbors`

29. You have just configured the adjacent side of an EtherChannel from the console and receive the message in the following figure. What is the problem?

```
%PM-4-ERR_DISABLE: channel-misconfig error detected on Gig0/1, putting Gig0/1 in err-disable state
%LINK-5-CHANGED: Interface GigabitEthernet0/1, changed state to down
%LINEPROTO-5-UPDOWN: Line protocol on Interface GigabitEthernet0/1, changed state to down
%LINEPROTO-5-UPDOWN: Line protocol on Interface Port-channel 1, changed state to down
%PM-4-ERR_DISABLE: channel-misconfig error detected on Gig0/2, putting Gig0/2 in err-disable state
%LINK-5-CHANGED: Interface GigabitEthernet0/2, changed state to down
%LINEPROTO-5-UPDOWN: Line protocol on Interface GigabitEthernet0/2, changed state to down
```

    A. One of the switches is configured with on mode and the other with desirable mode.

    B. One of the switches is configured with auto mode and the other with desirable mode.

    C. One of the switches is configured with active mode and the other with active mode.

    D. One of the switches is configured with passive mode and the other with passive mode.

30. You have configured the command `channel-group 1 mode active` on a range of interfaces that will participate in an EtherChannel. Which pseudo interface is created for overall management of the EtherChannel?

    A. `ether-channel 1`

    B. `port-group 1`

    C. `port-channel 1`

    D. `channel-group 1`

31. You are configuring a channel group for two interfaces. You configure the command `channel-group 1 mode passive`. What must be configured on the other switch to use LACP?

    A. The other switch must be configured with `channel-group 1 mode active`.

    B. The other switch must be configured with `channel-group 1 mode desirable`.

    C. The other switch must be configured with `channel-group 1 mode on`.

    D. The other switch must be configured with `channel-group 1 mode auto`.

32. When you connect a device to a switch, the device takes a minute before it is reachable via its IP address. What should be configured to fix this issue so that you can get immediate access to the device?

    A. Turn off auto-negotiation on the interface.

    B. Configure PortFast mode for Spanning Tree.

    C. Configure BPDU Guard mode for Spanning Tree.

    D. Turn off port security.

33. You enter the show spanning-tree vlan 100 command on a switch. The output shows that all ports on the switch are in designated mode. What can be determined from this?

    A. This switch is connected to a root bridge.

    B. This switch is the root bridge.

    C. This switch is not participating in STP.

    D. This switch is a backup root bridge.

34. You have BPDU Guard configured on an interface. You receive a call that the interface is down. You perform a show interface gi 0/1 only to find that the port is in an err-disabled state. What caused the err-disabled state?

    A. A neighboring switch recalculated its STP.

    B. The endpoint device connected to the interface sent a BPDU.

    C. The endpoint device was disconnected for a long period of time.

    D. The interface is transitioning between an up and down state rapidly, called interface flapping.

35. Which AP mode requires all traffic to be centrally switched at the WLC?

    A. Monitor mode

    B. Local mode

    C. FlexConnect mode

    D. Central mode

36. Which AP mode supports location-based services but will not serve clients?

    A. FlexConnect mode

    B. Monitor mode

    C. Local mode

    D. Locate mode

37. You have configured a LAG consisting of two links for your wireless LAN controller (WLC). What will happen if one of the links fails?

    A. Both links will enter into an err-disabled mode.

    B. The traffic on the failed link will be migrated to the active link.

    C. Both links will enter into an administratively disabled mode.

    D. Only half of the traffic will be sent over the active link.

38. Which protocol will encrypt the entire packet from the switch or router to the AAA server?

   A. 802.1X

   B. IPsec

   C. RADIUS

   D. TACACS+

39. Which copy method will encrypt the IOS over the network during an upgrade?

   A. HTTP

   B. TFTP

   C. FTP

   D. SCP

40. When you configure a WLAN, what is the default QoS configured for the WLAN?

   A. Gold

   B. Silver

   C. Bronze

   D. Platinum

41. You configure Router A in the following figure with a route statement to get to Network B. However, you cannot ping a host on Network B. What is the problem?

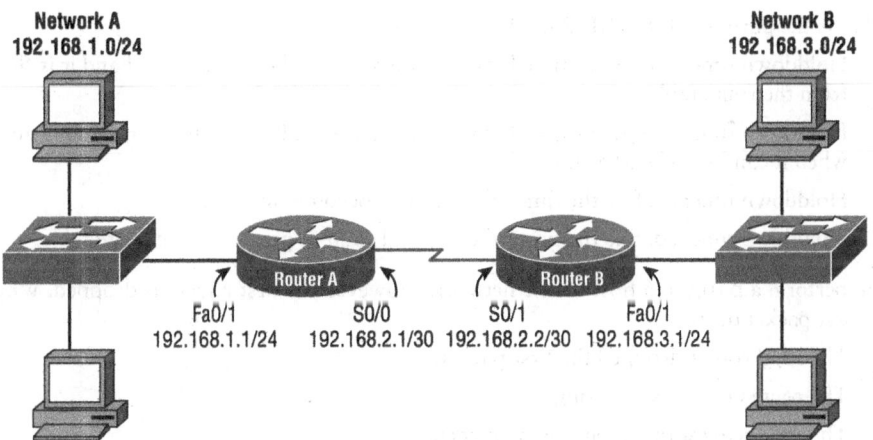

   A. You must issue the `ip routing` command.

   B. The host on Network B is misconfigured.

   C. The host on Network A is misconfigured.

   D. You must enter a network route on Router B for Network A.

42. A router has three routes to the same network: one route from RIP with a metric of 4, another from OSPF with a metric of 3053092, and another from EIGRP with a metric of 4039043. Which of the three routes will be used for the routing decision?

    A. EIGRP

    B. OSPF

    C. RIP

    D. All of the above

43. Why can a route have a destination of an interface rather than an IP address?

    A. Serial interfaces are point-to-point connections.

    B. The router on the other side of an interface routes all traffic discovered.

    C. Routing tables cause the destination address to change.

    D. All of the above.

44. Which command will configure a static route with an administrative distance higher than RIP?

    A. `ip route 192.168.2.0 255.255.255.0 192.168.4.1 110`

    B. `ip route 192.168.2.0 255.255.255.0 192.168.4.1 130`

    C. `ip route 110 192.168.2.0 255.255.255.0 192.168.4.1`

    D. `ip route 130 192.168.2.0 255.255.255.0 192.168.4.1`

45. What is the purpose of the RIPv2 holddown timer?

    A. Holddown timers allow for time between when a route becomes invalid and it is flushed from the route table.

    B. Holddown timers allow for time between when a route has become unreachable and when it can be updated again.

    C. Holddown timers define the time when a route becomes invalid.

    D. Holddown timers define the time when a valid route is present in the route table.

46. You perform a `ping` to a host on the network. However, the first packet is dropped. Why did the first packet drop?

    A. The local router dropped the first packet.

    B. The route table was updating.

    C. The ARP request timed out the ping packet.

    D. The remote router dropped the first packet.

47. You are configuring RIP for a network and you need to advertise the network. Which command will advertise the route for 203.244.234.0/24?

    A. `network 203.244.234.0`

    B. `network 203.244.234.0 255.255.255.0`

    C. `network 203.244.234.0 0.0.0.255`

    D. `network 203.244.234.0/24`

48. In the following figure, what type of routing is being used?

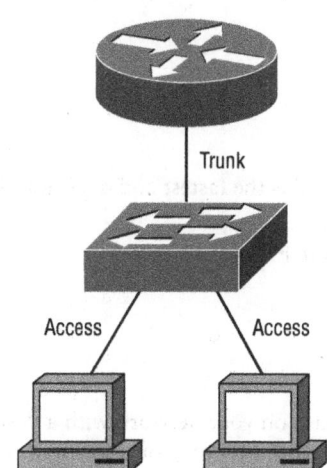

Trunk

Access   Access

VLAN 2   VLAN 3

A. Default routing

B. SVI routing

C. ROAS routing

D. Stub routing

49. Which command must be enabled on a switch to enable routing between switched virtual interfaces for VLAN routing?

A. `ip route svi`

B. `feature svi routing`

C. `svi routing`

D. `ip routing`

50. In the following figure, why do the first and third ARP entries have a dash for their age?

```
Switch#show ip arp
Protocol  Address      Age(min)  Hardware Addr   Type  Interface
Internet  172.16.10.1  -         00d0.565d.05ac  ARPA  Ethernet1
Internet  172.16.10.2  6         0030.9492.ee55  ARPA  Ethernet1
Internet  172.16.20.1  -         00d0.565d.05ab  ARPA  Ethernet0
```

A. The entries are static ARP entries.

B. The entries have just been added to the ARP table.

C. The entries belong to the physical interfaces of the router.

D. The entries have less than 1 minute before they expire.

51. Which field in the IP header is used to prevent a packet from endlessly routing?

    A. Checksum

    B. Flags

    C. TTL

    D. Header length

52. Which packet forwarding method is the fastest and does not directly use the central processing unit (CPU)?

    A. Cisco Express Forwarding (CEF)

    B. Process switching

    C. Fast switching

    D. Expedited forwarding

53. You see a number of IPv6 packets on your network with a destination address of ff02::a. What can be concluded about what is running on your network?

    A. Routing Information Protocol Next Generation (RIPng) is running on the network.

    B. Open Shortest Path First version 3 (OSPFv3) is running on the network.

    C. Enhanced Interior Gateway Routing Protocol (EIGRP) for IPv6 is running on the network.

    D. Stateless Address Autoconfiguration (SLAAC) is running on the network.

54. You ping from a router to another router and receive back ! ! ! ! !. What does this mean?

    A. All packets have been dropped.

    B. All packets are successfully acknowledged.

    C. There is congestion in the path.

    D. The packets were received, but after the ICMP timeout.

55. You want to ping a router on your network from interface Serial 0/0 and not the path in the route table. How can you achieve this?

    A. This cannot be done; packets cannot disregard the route table.

    B. Enter the interface from the global configuration mode, and ping the remote router.

    C. Enter `extended ping`, and specify the exit interface.

    D. Configure a temporary route for the router exit interface.

56. You perform a `traceroute` to a destination network and receive back several lines of output. On the end of each line are three parameters such as `1 192.168.1.1 20 msec 34 msec 67 msec`. What do they mean?

    A. They are the three response times of each ICMP request.

    B. They are the minimum, maximum, and average of the ICMP query.

    C. They are the minimum, average, and maximum of the ICMP query.

    D. They are the maximum, average, and minimum of the ICMP query.

57. Which key sequence will cause a break during a network command such as `ping` or `traceroute`?

   A. Ctrl+C

   B. Ctrl+4

   C. Ctrl+Shift+6

   D. Ctrl+Shift+1

58. In the following figure, Host A suddenly cannot communicate with Host B. Using the `ping` command, which device will you ping first to diagnose the problem?

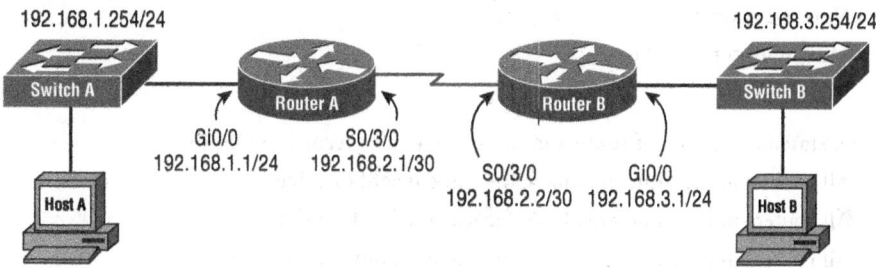

192.168.1.254/24

192.168.3.254/24

Switch A

Router A

Router B

Switch B

Gi0/0   S0/3/0
192.168.1.1/24   192.168.2.1/30   S0/3/0   Gi0/0
                                192.168.2.2/30   192.168.3.1/24

Host A

Host B

   A. Switch A

   B. Router A

   C. Router B

   D. Switch B

59. Which command can you use to verify that a ping packet is exiting the interface you expect it to exit, which in this example is Gi0/1 with an IP address of 192.168.3.5?

   A. `ping 192.168.3.5 Gi 0/1`

   B. `ping Gi 0/1 192.168.3.5`

   C. `debug ip packet`

   D. `debug ip ping`

60. Which is a correct statement about the following figure?

```
Tracing the route to 192.168.3.1

  1   192.168.10.2    10 msec   1 msec   0 msec
  2   192.168.10.6     2 msec   2 msec   3 msec
  3                *        *        *
  4   192.168.20.3     2 msec   3 msec   3 msec
RouterA#
```

   A. The third hop is down.

   B. The third hop is not responding to ICMP requests.

   C. The `traceroute` never completed.

   D. The third hop is unavailable and packets have been rerouted.

61. Which additional feature is available when using an extended ping?

    A. Larger datagram size

    B. Larger repeat counts

    C. Changing the timeout

    D. Source interface or IP address

62. You want to perform a `traceroute` with more than three ICMP packets using an extended traceroute. Which attribute will you change to allow for multiple ICMP packets?

    A. Probe count

    B. Numeric display

    C. Maximum time to live

    D. Packet type

63. Which statement is true of routers in the same area in regard to OSPF?

    A. All routers in the same area have the same neighbor table.

    B. All routers in the same area have the same hello/dead timers.

    C. All routers in the same area have the same topology table.

    D. All routers in the same area have the same process IDs.

64. Which OSPF packets contain link-state and routing information?

    A. Hello packets

    B. LSA packets

    C. LSAck packets

    D. Dead packets

65. What option should be configured along with interface tracking that will allow the original router to regain its active status once a failed link is repaired?

    A. Interface tracking resets

    B. Failback option

    C. Preempt option

    D. Priority tracking

66. Which is a disadvantage of using NAT?

    A. Creates switching path delays

    B. Introduces security weaknesses

    C. Requires address renumbering

    D. Increases bandwidth utilization

67. Which type of NAT is used for one-to-one mapping between local and global addresses?

    A. Dynamic NAT

    B. Static NAT

   C. NAT Overloading

   D. Symmetric NAT

68. Which protocol helps synchronize time for routers and switches?

   A. SNMP

   B. NTP

   C. Syslog

   D. ICMP

69. Which protocol and port number does DNS use for direct queries?

   A. UDP/53

   B. TCP/53

   C. UDP/55

   D. UDP/68

70. Which version of SNMP supports the Inform SNMP message?

   A. SNMP version 1

   B. SNMP version v2

   C. SNMP version 2c

   D. SNMP version 3

71. Which command will configure all event logs to be sent to a syslog server?

   A. `logging server 192.168.1.6`

   B. `logging 192.168.1.6`

   C. `logging host 192.168.1.6`

   D. `syslog server 192.168.1.6`

72. Which command will configure a router to use DHCP for IP address assignment?

   A. `RouterA(config)#ip address dhcp`

   B. `RouterA(config-if)#ip address auto`

   C. `RouterA(config-if)#ip address dhcp`

   D. `RouterA(config)#ip address auto`

73. Which measurement describes the time a packet takes from source to destination?

   A. Bandwidth

   B. Delay

   C. Jitter

   D. Loss

74. Which layer 3 protocol is used for marking packets with QoS?

   A. DSCP

   B. 802.1Q

   C. CoS

   D. QoE

75. You have enabled the SCP server on a switch, but when you try to log in it returns "access denied." Which command must you configure to allow access to the SCP server if your username was *scpadmin* and your password was *Sybex*?

   A. `ip scp user scpadmin password Sybex`

   B. `username scpadmin password Sybex`

   C. `username scpadmin privilege-level 15 password Sybex`

   D. `ip scp user scpadmin privilege-level 15 password Sybex`

76. In a basic VLAN hopping attack, which switch feature do attackers take advantage of?

   A. An open Telnet connection

   B. Automatic encapsulation negotiation

   C. Forwarding of broadcasts

   D. The default automatic trunking configuration

77. Which security mitigation technique can be used to stop a MAC address flooding attack?

   A. ACLs

   B. NAT

   C. Port security

   D. VLAN access control lists (VACLs)

78. Which of the following is a recommended physical security method?

   A. Locking doors

   B. Installing antivirus software

   C. Enabling firewalls

   D. Applying directory-level permissions

79. You are connected to the console of a switch. As you are configuring the switch, console logging is disrupting your commands and making it hard to configure the switch properly. Which command will allow the console message to still appear but not disrupt what you are typing?

   A. `Switch#no logging inline`

   B. `Switch(config)#logging synchronous`

   C. `Switch(config-line)#logging synchronous`

   D. `Switch#logging synchronous`

80. You have a router that you configured with a password, but you have forgotten the password. You have a copy of a recent configuration, and the password line reads as `password 7 06074352EFF6`. How can you access the router?

A. You must call the Cisco Technical Assistance Center to reverse the password.

B. You need to enter the password **06074352EFF6**.

C. Log into another router and type **decrypt-password 06074352EFF6** in privileged exec mode.

D. Perform a password recovery on the router.

81. Which port must be open to the RADIUS or AAA server for authentication from the authenticator?

A. UDP/49

B. UDP/1821

C. UDP/1812

D. UDP/1813

82. What is a consideration that can restrict GRE tunnel creation?

A. The tunnel interface number

B. ACLs on the firewall

C. Speed of the tunnel

D. Number of hops between the source and destination

83. Which WAN protocol does not support multicast packets?

A. GRE

B. IPsec

C. PPP

D. MPLS

84. Which command will configure an access list that will deny Telnet access from the 192.168.2.0/24 network and allow all other traffic?

A. `access-list 101 deny tcp 192.168.2.0 0.0.0.255 any eq 23`
`access-list 101 permit ip any any`

B. `access-list 101 deny 192.168.2.0 0.0.0.255 eq 23`
`access-list 101 permit ip any any`

C. `access-list 101 block tcp 192.168.2.0 0.0.0.255 any eq 23`
`access-list 101 permit ip any any`

D. `access-list 101 deny 192.168.2.0 0.0.0.255 any eq 23`
`access-list 101 permit any any`

85. You need to make a modification to a rule in a standard conventional access list. How can you achieve this?

    A.   Enter the ACL editor and change the entry.

    B.   Remove the entire ACL and add it back with the modification.

    C.   Remove the line number and add the new line number back with the modification.

    D.   Remove the entry with the no command and add it back.

86. Which command is used to view the DHCP snooping database?

    A.   `show dhcp binding`

    B.   `show ip dhcp binding`

    C.   `show ip dhcp snooping database`

    D.   `show ip dhcp snooping binding`

87. Refer to the following figure. What will happen when a computer with a different MAC address connects to the interface?

```
switch(config)#int fa0/6
switch(config-if)#switchport port-security
switch(config-if)#switchport port-security mac-address sticky 00e4.6a51.8dd9
```

    A.   The computer will not be allowed to communicate, but the port will remain up.

    B.   The computer will be allowed to communicate.

    C.   The computer will not be allowed to communicate and the port will enter an err-disabled state.

    D.   The computer will be allowed to communicate and the access will be logged.

88. Which authentication method will allow an authenticated user to access only certain commands on a router or switch?

    A.   TACACS+

    B.   AAA

    C.   RADIUS

    D.   802.1X

89. You need to implement a wireless authentication system that provides encryption and authentication of user accounts. Which technology would you deploy?

    A.   WPA2-PSK

    B.   WPA2-EAP

    C.   WPA2-LEAP

    D.   WPA3-PSK

90. When configuring a WLAN with WPA2 PSK using the GUI of a wireless LAN controller, which parameter policy should be configured for the highest security?

    A.   802.1X

    B.   WPA2 Policy-AES

    C. WPA Policy

    D. PSK

91. Which is the most important aspect to understand when automating changes across an enterprise?

    A. How to automate the change

    B. The effect of the change

    C. The topology of the network

    D. The connections between the devices

92. Which is a popular scripting language used to automate changes that also allows for easy readability of the script?

    A. C++

    B. Python

    C. C#

    D. JSON

93. Which tool allows you to manage all of your Cisco device licensing needs through a single user interface?

    A. Cisco SMARTnet

    B. Cisco License Manager

    C. Cisco Network Assistant

    D. Cisco Prime Infrastructure

94. Which is a protocol found on the overlay of an SDN?

    A. VXLAN

    B. OSPF

    C. OpenFlow

    D. JSON

95. Which is commonly used with the northbound interface of an SDN controller?

    A. CLOS

    B. OpenFlow

    C. Python

    D. NETCONF

96. You need to configure some default servers for DNS, AAA, and NTP for device provisioning. Which section in Cisco DNA Center will allow you to configure these defaults?

    A. Design

    B. Discovery

    C. Provision

    D. Platform

97. Which REST-based HTTP verb is used to update or replace data via the API?

    A. POST

    B. GET

    C. UPDATE

    D. PUT

98. You just finished creating a script that will interface with Cisco DNA Center via the REST-based API. When you run the script, you receive a 400 status code. What is wrong?

    A. Nothing; it is okay.

    B. Forbidden request.

    C. Bad request.

    D. Internal server error.

99. Which programming language is used for creating a Chef recipe to apply configuration management?

    A. Ruby

    B. Python

    C. PowerShell

    D. YAML

100. Which statement best describes how the JSON file format starts and ends?

    A. A JSON file starts with double quotes and ends with double quotes.

    B. A JSON file starts with single quotes and ends with single quotes.

    C. A JSON file starts with square brackets and ends with square brackets.

    D. A JSON file starts with curly brackets and ends with curly brackets.

Appendix

Answers to Review Questions

Chapter 1: Network Fundamentals (Domain 1)

1. **A.** In the figure, only one broadcast domain exists because a PC on the left hub can send an ARP request and the PC on the right hub can hear it. If you wanted to create multiple broadcast domains, you would need to create VLANs and route them. Two, three, and seven broadcast domains could be achieved by creating additional VLANs and a router-on-a-stick configuration with the router between the VLANs.

2. **C.** In the figure, there are three collision domains present. Keep in mind that a collision domain is a network segment in which a collision can occur and the colliding frame is created. A switch will create collision segmentation as seen in the figure. There is one giant broadcast domain, but this is not going to affect collisions. You could argue that only two collision domains exist on both of the hubs. However, you would assume that the router and switch were configured full-duplex, avoiding collisions. So, it should always be assumed that half-duplex communications is in operation, because it is possible. Seven collision domains is a wrong answer.

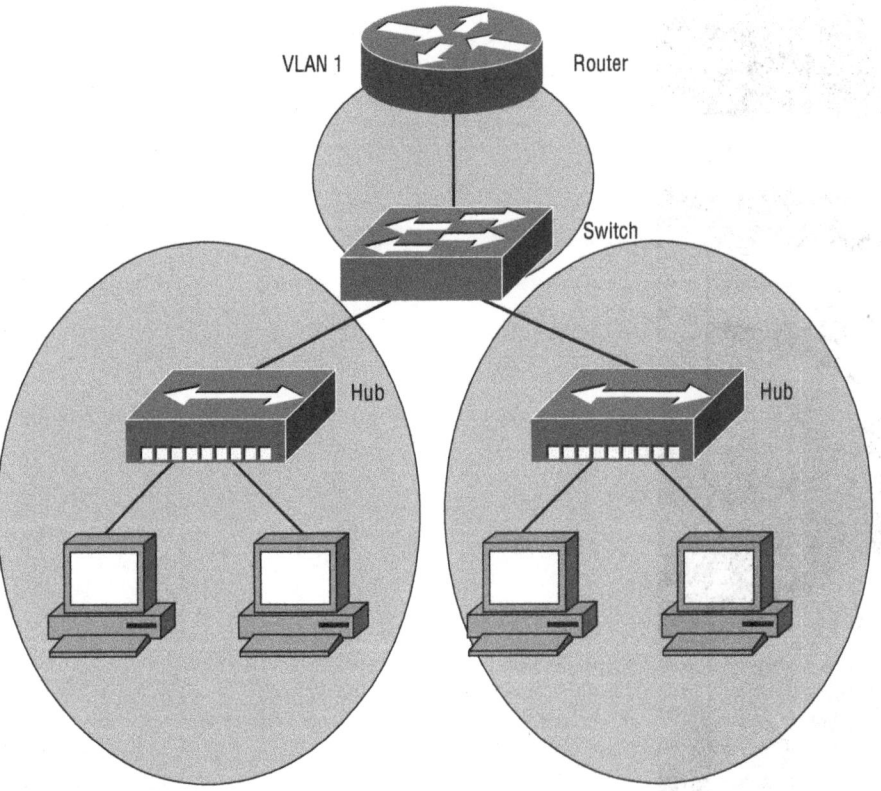

VLAN 1   Router   Switch   Hub   Hub

3. **A.** A collision domain is defined as a group of computers that can potentially have a frame collision. Adding switches that can negotiate full-duplex and forward/filter fixes these issues. The potential of receiving broadcast frames can increase the number of collisions. But

broadcasts do not create collision domains (consider that unicast messages can also cause collisions). It is more common to see computers in collision domains set to 10 Mb/s half-duplex, not full-duplex.

4. A. Currently, all of the computers are within one giant collision domain. Replacing the hub with a switch will create four separate potential collision domains. Switches create microsegmentation, which increases the number of collision domains and increases bandwidth. The number of collision domains would only decrease if you swapped a switch for a hub, thus creating one collision domain. The number of broadcast domains would be unaffected using either a switch or a hub unless a router was used for routing between VLANs.

5. C. In the figure, there are two broadcast domains, VLAN 1 and VLAN 2. In each of the broadcast domains there exists a single collision domain, along with the collision domain between the switch and router. Therefore, three collision domains exist with two broadcast domains. One collision domain with one broadcast domain would only be true if the switch was replaced with a hub and VLANs were not used. Two collision domains with one broadcast domain would only be true if the hubs were directly connected together and VLAN routing was not in use. Seven collision domains existing with two broadcast domains would only be true if the hubs were swapped out for switches.

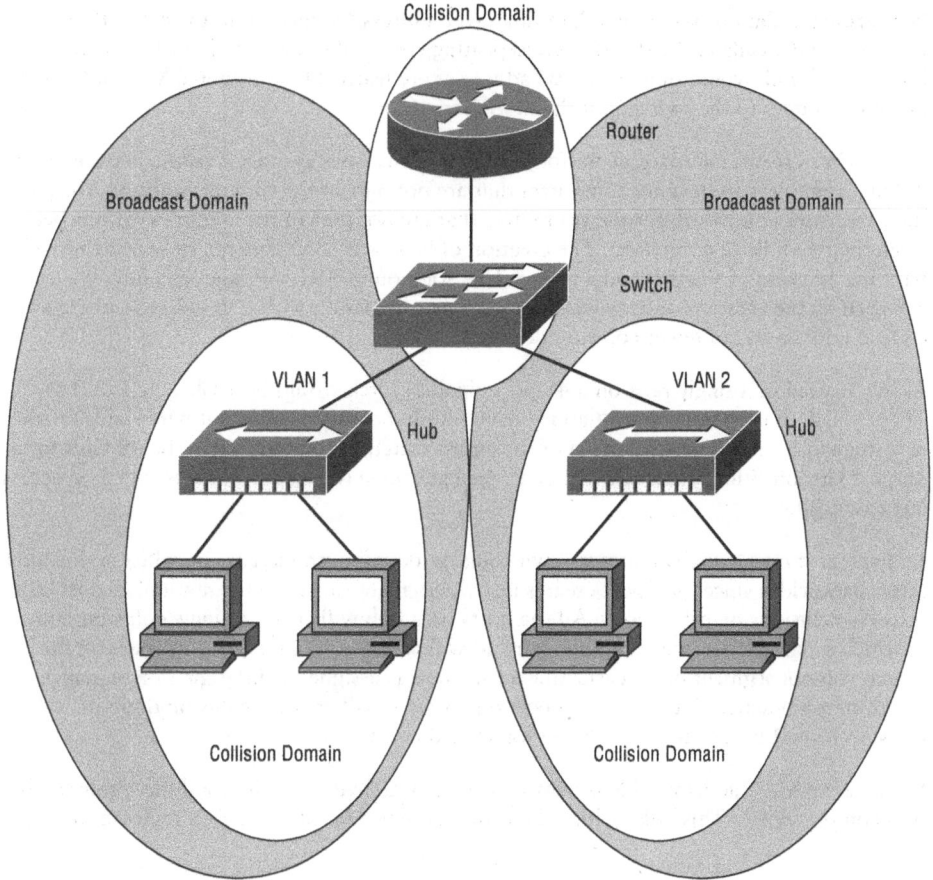

6. B. The End of Row (EoR) switch acts as a distribution switch for the Top of Rack (ToR) switches. A ToR switch will sit at the top of the rack and create an access method for all the equipment in the rack. *Core switch* is a term used for the aggregation and core switching functions of all the distribution switches. *Virtual switch* is a term used for switching inside of a hypervisor, in which software switching occurs.

7. A. Switches allow for low latency because frames are forwarded with ASIC hardware-based switching and have low cost. Software switching is only used by legacy bridges and virtual switches. Software switching can actually create latency. Using a switch lowers the cost (latency); it does not raise the cost.

8. A. The replacement of hubs with switches increases collision domains and effectively increases bandwidth. The replacement of switches with hubs can decrease the number of collision domains, creating a much larger collision domain. The replacement of hubs with switches has no effect on broadcast domains. Broadcast domains would only be affected if a router was introduced.

9. D. The switch learns MAC addresses based upon incoming ports and examination of the source MAC address. It will build a MAC address table for future lookups. It then determines forwarding interfaces based on the destination MAC address contained in the frame. Forwarding of data is based on a data-link layer address "burned" into the network interface card (NIC) called a MAC address. Repeating electrical signals to all ports describes how a dumb hub would operate. MAC addresses are learned by the source MAC address on incoming frames to the switch, not the destination frames.

10. D. A switch creates microsegmentation, which in turns isolates unicast traffic between two talking computers from other computers that are not part of the communications. This, in turn, increases bandwidth for the computers that are not part of the communications between the two talking computers. The creation of broadcast domains can only be achieved with the addition of VLANs and a router. The isolation of ARP messages can only be achieved by the creation of broadcast domains. Segmentation with a switch will create more collision domains, not fewer collision domains.

11. A. Wire speed of a single port on a 48-port gigabit switch would be 1 Gb/s, or 1,000 Mb/s. Theoretically, a port can transmit and receive simultaneously 1 Gb/s, but wire speed refers to a single direction. The wire speed of the entire switch (backplane) could be 48 Gb/s for a 48-port Gigabit Ethernet switch, although the backplane is usually oversubscribed on access layer switching.

12. C. Each port on a switch creates its own collision domain. An increase in collision domains raises bandwidth since each port creates its own segment (micro-segmentation) and isolates possible collisions on other ports. All the ports on a hub will create a single collision domain, in which a signal from one computer can and will collide with another. Each port on the switch will not segment broadcasts unless each port is assigned a different VLAN, which is not common practice. Although each port on a switch will create a collision domain, it does not stop layer 2 broadcasts from being forwarded to all ports.

13. B. Since the MAC address table is empty on Switch A, Switch A will flood the frame to all ports on the switch. This will include the router attached to interface Fa0/3. However, a router does not perform forward/filter decisions, so the frame will not be flooded any further on Router A. Switch A will forward the frame to all ports, but the router will not forward the frame onto the segment where Switch B is located. Switch B will never see the frame from Switch A because Router A segments the two networks.

14. C. The demilitarized zone (DMZ) is where Internet-facing servers/services are placed. The outside zone is where the public Internet connection is connected and it is the least trusted. The enterprise network zone is considered the inside zone. The inside zone is considered to be the highest trusted network because it is the internal network that you control.

15. B. Firewalls should always be placed at key security boundaries, which can be the Internet and your internal network. However, proper placement is not exclusive to the boundaries of the Internet and internal networks. For example, it could be placed between two internal networks, such as R&D and guest networks. The demilitarized zone (DMZ) is a segment of a firewall where Internet-facing services are placed. Firewalls are normally not placed only between the DMZ and the Internet because most networks have an internal network.

16. B. Firewalls are not commonly deployed to provide protection from internal attacks on internal resources. They are designed to protect networks from external attacks or attacks emanating from the outside or directed toward the Internet. Firewalls normally provide stateful packet inspection. Firewalls can also control application traffic by port number and higher-layer attributes.

17. A. All physical access to a firewall should be controlled tightly so that it is not tampered with, which could allow external threats to enter the network. This control should include vendors and approved administrators. Physical access to the firewall is a security principle and therefore not a consideration for the management of a firewall. All firewall policies should be documented as a part of the firewall management process. Firewall logs should be regularly monitored for suspicious activity as part of the firewall management process. Firewalls can allow or deny traffic by default; this is a consideration when managing a firewall.

18. C. Firewalls keep track of the TCP conversation before and after the three-way handshake. This is done so that an attack on the TCP/UDP flow is not executed; in addition, denial-of-service (DoS) attacks can be thwarted, such as a SYN flood. *Zone state* is terminology that is used with firewalls; therefore, it is an incorrect answer. Firewalls do not protect by keeping statistics or accounting information for the state of packets. Firewalls do not transition between defense states.

19. A. ASAs allow for zones to be created and the connections applied to the zones. This methodology allows for security rules to be applied uniformly to the outside zone. There is no such thing as an ISP zone. You can apply an ACL to the zone but not directly to the interface. Each connection can be managed by a group once it is added to the same zone.

20. B. Servers should be placed in the DMZ so they can access both the inside zone and the outside zone. This will allow a server, such as a web server, to allow client access from the web (outside). Rules could also be applied so that the server (e.g., a database server) could allow access to data from within the internal network (inside). Placing the servers into the DMZ will give you the flexibility to apply rules for external access on the Internet and rules for internal access on the internal network.

21. C. An intrusion detection system (IDS) will detect unauthorized access. However, it will not prevent unauthorized access. It is a form of audit control in a network. A firewall will protect your network from attack by placing rules on connections as to how people can connect as well as which traffic can pass. An intrusion protection system (IPS) will detect the presence of an intrusion and alert an administrator. A honeypot will attract a malicious user so their tactics can be observed. It performs this function by diverting the malicious user from production systems to the honeypot, which is a sacrificial system.

22. C. When more than one WAP covers the same SSID, it is called an extended service set (ESS). A wireless LAN (WLAN) controller coordinates the cell or coverage area so the same SSID is on two different channels. A broadcast domain is one single layer 3 broadcast network in which layer 3 broadcasts will traverse. A basic service set (BSS) is used when a WAP covers a single SSID, such as wireless in your home. A wireless mesh is used when an Ethernet cable cannot be run to each WAP. The WAPs will use one frequency to connect to each other for the backhaul of the data while using another frequency to serve clients.

23. D. Control and Provisioning of Wireless Access Points (CAPWAP) is a protocol that's responsible for provisioning of LWAPs and forwarding data to the wireless LAN controller. The Spanning Tree Protocol (STP) is used to stop switching loops when redundant connections in a LAN are present. Bridge Protocol Data Units (BPDUs) are frames used by STP to define the root bridge and learn the switching topology for a network. Orthogonal Frequency Division Multiplexing (OFDM) is a wireless modulation method introduced with 802.11a.

24. C. The wireless LAN controller (WLC) is responsible for centralized authentication of users and/or computers on a wireless network. When a wireless device is roaming, the WLC is responsible for maintaining the authentication between access points. A basic service set (BSS) is normally served by a single WAP for a single SSID. An extended service is used when two or more WAPs provide coverage for one or more SSIDs. The service set ID (SSID) is a friendly name beaconed to wireless clients so the client can be configured to associate and/or authenticate.

25. B. The requirement for multiple protocols is a compelling reason to use MPLS. The protocols moving across MPLS nodes are irrelevant to the technology. This is because layer 3 information is not examined to route packets. The use of MPLS can be configured to support multicast packets, but this is not a primary driver in selecting MPLS. The use of MPLS does not give you any higher bandwidth than you would have with any other technology. MPLS supports encryption, just as any other WAN technology supports encryption.

26. D. A service-level agreement (SLA) is a contracted agreement between the Internet service provider (ISP) and the customer. This agreement defines the level of service. SLAs are based on uptime, quality of service, bandwidth, and any other stipulations the customer might deem necessary. Uptime is usually the most important when shopping for a provider. SLAs are not exclusive to ISPs and their customers; anywhere there is a service that requires uptime, an SLA can be found.

27. A. Centralized authentication of clients is a valid reason to implement a WLC. Although a WLC makes it easier to implement multiple SSIDs and VLANs, this task can be performed with autonomous WAPs, each performing its own authentication. The use of autonomous

WAPs negates the reasons you would use a WLC because each WAP would be independently managed and no coordination would exist between the autonomous WAPs. The use of multiple SSIDs can be achieved with an autonomous WAP without a WLC. Multiple VLANs can also be used with an autonomous WAP without a WLC.

28. D. A wireless LAN controller (WLC) keeps track of which LWAP a client has associated it with and centrally forwards the packets to the LWAP that's appropriate for a client to access while roaming. A single SSID by itself will not support seamless roaming between access points. A single service set such as a basic service set will not support seamless roaming of wireless clients. 802.11ac is a wireless modulation specification and by itself does not support the seamless roaming of clients.

29. B. When WAPs are introduced to the wireless LAN controller, the WLC is responsible for synchronizing the WAPs to a standardized IOS. This allows for uniform support and features of the wireless system and is dependent on the model of WAP. WLCs can allow for autonomous WAPs to coexist; however, a WLC's main purpose is to manage lightweight access points. WLCs can be configured to work with Connected Mobile Experiences (CMX) for user triangulation, but a WLC cannot provide this service by itself. A WLC will manage the frequencies and channels for wireless clients, but using a WLC will not allow you to use all the wireless frequencies and channels.

30. D. Only switching between campus (distribution) switches should be performed at the core layer. Nothing should be done to slow down forwarding of traffic, such as using ACLs, supporting clients, or routing between VLANs. Routing of data should be performed at the distribution layer of the Cisco three-tier model. Supporting clients should be done at the access layer of the Cisco three-tier model. The configuration of access should be performed at the distribution layer of the Cisco three-tier model.

31. A. A star topology has a centralized switch connecting all of the devices outward like a star. A full-mesh topology allows for a decentralized switching design, where any link failure will not affect switching. A partial-mesh topology is normally performed between the layers of core, distribution, and access to allow for a single link failure while maintaining switching services. A hybrid topology is where several different topologies are employed, such as star and mesh.

32. B. Increased redundancy of connections is a direct benefit of a full- mesh topology. Although bandwidth will increase because of multiple paths, additional dynamic routing protocols will need to be implemented to achieve this. A full-mesh topology will not decrease the switch count and can even require more switching equipment because of the number of connections. When a full-mesh topology is employed, it increases complexity, but this is not considered a benefit.

33. C. The hybrid topology is most often seen at the access layer. The devices are connected in a star topology and the access layer switches are partially meshed to the distribution layer switches. The distribution layer is normally connected with a full mesh topology. *Routing layer* is not terminology used to describe one of the three layers in the Cisco three-tier design model.

34. B. Distribution layer switches are fully meshed for redundancy. The number of links can be calculated with the formula of $N(N - 1)$. So if you had four distribution switches, the ports required for a full mesh would be $4(4 - 1) = 4 \times 3 = 12$ ports among the four switches. The formula of $N(N - 1) / 2$ would give you the number of links (connected ports): $4(4 - 1) / 2 = 4 \times 3 / 2 = 6$ links. The core layer is normally implemented with a star topology. The access layer is normally implemented with a partial mesh topology or hybrid topology. *Routing layer* is not a valid term in the Cisco three-tier design model.

35. A. Core layer switches are commonly set up in a star topology. This is because core layer switches connect multiple campuses via distribution layer switches. The distribution layer is normally implemented with a full mesh topology. The access layer is normally implemented with a hybrid topology. *Routing layer* is not a valid term in the Cisco three-tier design model.

36. A. The collapsed core layer switch uses a star topology connecting outward to the access layer switches. This design is often found in small enterprise and single campus design. The full-mesh topology is normally found at the distribution layer in the Cisco three-tier design model. The partial-mesh or hybrid topology is often found at the access layer in the Cisco three-tier design.

37. C. The two-tier, or collapsed core, model contains only the distribution and access layer switches. The three-tier design model contains the core, distribution, and access layer switches. The core and distribution layer switches are found in the upper two layers of the Cisco three-tier design model. There is no such thing as the Internet layer in any of the design models.

38. A. Based on the layout of your network, the collapsed core model is the most appropriate model to design. If at a later time other campuses are joined to the network, the core layer can be added. The three-tier model is better situated for a network with multiple campuses. *DOD model* is a term used when referring to the layers of the OSI model in a macro model. *Access model* is not a term used with switching and routing design.

39. C. The collapsed core design model is best suited for small enterprises. It can later be expanded out to a three-tier model as an enterprise grows in size. It has no effect on bandwidth if designed right. The collapsed core design does not and should not bottleneck bandwidth.

40. B. Access layer switches connect to users and are edge network devices. The distribution layer connects other switches for redundancy. The core layer connects campuses together. Both the distribution layer and the core layer can connect the Internet to the network.

41. A. Distribution layer switches connect to access layer switches and core switches to provide redundancy. Access layer switches connect to users and are edge network devices. The core layer connects campuses together. Both the distribution layer and the core layer can connect the Internet to the network.

42. C. Core layer switches connect campuses together via the distribution layer switches. Distribution layer switches connect to access layer switches and core switches to provide redundancy. Access layer switches connect to users and are edge network devices. Both the distribution layer and the core layer can connect the Internet to the network.

43. B. Based on the layout of your network, the three-tier model is the most appropriate model to design. Since there are four campuses, the core layer is recommended for connectivity between the campuses. The collapsed core model is best suited to a single campus. *DoD model* is a term used when referring to the layers of the OSI model in a macro model. *Access model* is not a term used with switching and routing design.

44. B. The distribution layer is where redistribution of routing protocols should be performed. It should never be performed at the core or access layer. The core layer is where basic routing and switching is performed without slowing down any of the backbone communications. The access layer is where clients and end-user devices are supplied with network connectivity, allowing them to "access" the network. *Routing layer* is not terminology used to describe one of the three layers in the Cisco three-tier design model.

45. C. The access layer is where collision domains should be created. This is called network segmentation. The core layer is where basic routing and switching is performed without slowing down any of the backbone communications. The distribution layer is where redistribution of routing protocols should be performed. *Routing layer* is not terminology used to describe one of the three layers in the Cisco three-tier design model.

46. B. The distribution layer is a partial-mesh topology. Links between the distribution switches and core switches are multihomed to each device for redundancy. Also, the links between the distribution switches and access switches are multihomed to each device for redundancy. Although this might seem to be a full-mesh topology, the distribution switches are not connected to each other. A full-mesh topology can often be found between the distribution and core layers. The core layer uses a star topology in a collapsed core design to connect lower layer switches. The ring topology is a legacy LAN topology and is often used in WAN communications.

47. A. The E-Tree services of Metro Ethernet allow for a root to be established to serve the remote sites or leaf endpoints. The root can communicate to the leaf endpoints and the leaf endpoints can communicate to the root. However, the leaf endpoints cannot communicate with each other. Wireless WAN provides connectivity by using a star topology. E-Line and E-LAN provide services in a point-to-point or point-to-multipoint topology.

48. B. The most common hub-and-spoke WAN design is the way an Internet service provider (ISP) is connected to its customers. The Internet connection is centrally located in a common physical location of the Internet provider called the point of presence or meet-me room. All lines connect out from this point in a hub-and-spoke design. Connections for an enterprise spread over a metropolitan area can connect in a number of different topologies, depending on what is available. Connections between two or more corporate locations are often a point-to-point or point-to-multipoint topology. An internal connection inside of a service provider's network can be made a number of ways using several different topologies.

49. C. The Cisco Dynamic Multipoint Virtual Private Network (DMVPN) is always configured in a hub-and-spoke topology. The central router creates a multiport GRE connection between all of the branch routers. IPsec uses a point-to-point topology for connectivity. MPLS and Metro Ethernet use a point-to-point or point-to-multipoint topology for connectivity.

50. C. The Link Control Protocol (LCP) provides the authentication phase of a PPP connection. Multiprotocol Label Switching (MPLS) is a WAN connectivity protocol and connection method. The Network Control Protocol (NCP) allows for multiple upper-layer protocols to be used with PPP. There is no protocol called ACP; therefore, it is an invalid answer.

51. B. The High-Level Data Link Control (HDLC) protocol is used as the encapsulation method for serial links. This protocol is the open standard HDLC compared to the native Cisco proprietary version. The Point-to-Point Protocol over Ethernet (PPPoE) is widely used with digital subscriber lines (DSLs) and WiMax wireless services. Multiprotocol Label Switching is a WAN connectivity method. X.25 is a legacy WAN protocol used to transmit data.

52. C. The Challenge Handshake Authentication Protocol (CHAP) works by sending a random number called the challenge. This challenge is received by the authenticating router and used to hash the password. The password is transferred to the challenging router and authenticates the authenticating router. The Password Authentication Protocol transmits the username and password in clear text. There is no protocol called PSAP; therefore, it is an invalid answer. The Lightweight Directory Access Protocol is a protocol used to look up data, and it is used primarily with Active Directory. It does not provide encryption by itself but can be used with SSL/TLS to provide encryption.

53. C. The Link Control Protocol (LCP) provides the facility for multilink connections. Multiprotocol Label Switching (MPLS) is a WAN connectivity protocol and connection method. The Network Control Protocol (NCP) allows for multiple upper-layer protocols to be used with PPP. There is no protocol called ACP; therefore, it is an invalid answer.

54. A. MultiLink PPP simplifies layer 3 configuration. It does this by bundling the connections together at layer 2. It provides a pseudo-interface representing the individual interface where all layer 3 configuration is applied. You can use routing protocols with MLPPP, and in larger networks, it is recommended and required. MLPPP should be used with authentication protocols to authenticate the incoming connections. The MLPPP protocol does not provide end-to-end encryption.

55. A. The pseudo interface must be created first with the command `interface multilink 1`. Then the encapsulation must be set to PPP with `encapsulation ppp`. The `ppp multilink` command configures the ability to use multilink for the encapsulation of PPP. Then the IP address is configured. Last, the `ppp multilink group 1` command associates the interface multilink 1 with the multilink group to be used for bundling. All of the other options are incorrect.

56. B. The first step is to set the username of RouterB to use for authentication via `username RouterB password cisco`. Then enter the interface, in this case using the `interface serial 0/1/0` command, and configure authentication with the command ppp `authentication chap pap`. All of the other options are incorrect.

57. D. The `LCP closed` line states that the LCP process has not completed. This could be due to numerous reasons, such as conflicting options or authentication failure. When the LCP process has completed, it will be in an "open" state when reviewing the interface. The router does not need to have an IP address configured since this is a layer 2 communication process. If the serial line was disconnected, the interface would show as down with a line protocol of down.

58. B. Asymmetrical Digital Subscriber Line (ADSL) connectivity typically uses PPPoE to authenticate subscribers. The subscriber's credentials are often relayed to a RADIUS server for subscription checks. Metro Ethernet is a WAN connectivity method and not a protocol that is used with ADSL. PPP does not need to be configured for use over an ADSL connection, but the authentication portion of PPPoE must be configured. MPLS is a WAN connectivity method and not a protocol that is used with ADSL.

59. A. Amazon Web Services (AWS) and Microsoft Azure are examples of public cloud providers. Private clouds are internally created, and hybrid clouds are a combination of services between your private cloud and the public cloud. Private clouds are purchased and maintained by a private entity and not available for public use, usually on your internal network. Hybrid clouds are a mixture of private and public clouds, usually where your infrastructure exists partially in the public cloud and partially in your private cloud. There is no such thing as dynamic cloud providers since all cloud providers must have a level of elasticity for their clients.

60. B. If you were looking to create a fault-tolerant colocation site as a cloud provider, you would be searching for an infrastructure-as-a-service (IaaS) provider. This would allow you to install your own operation system and applications. A platform-as-a-service (PaaS) solution is similar to running applications in the cloud, where the platform supports some level of programming language, such as Python, Ruby, or Visual Basic. Software-as-a-service (SaaS) is probably the most common, since services such as email, contract management, and many others are hosted by SaaS providers. Backup-as-a-service (BaaS) is popular today because it can allow for the long-term storage of data offline after a backup has completed.

61. C. Automated billing is not a NIST criterion for cloud computing. It is essential for the cloud computing vendor but is not relevant if you are hosting your own private cloud. The five NIST criteria for cloud computing are on-demand self-service, broad network access, resource pooling, rapid elasticity, and measured service.

62. C. When an internal IT department hosts the virtualization for a company, they are hosting a private cloud. A public cloud is virtualization infrastructure that is open to the public. An elastic cloud is a cloud that has elasticity. Rapid elasticity is one of the five characteristics that NIST defines as a characteristic of cloud computing. *Internal cloud* is not a term that describes virtualization; therefore, it is an invalid answer.

63. B. A cloud services catalog satisfies the self-service aspect of cloud computing. It does this by listing all of the available virtual machines (VMs) that can be created in the cloud environment, such as web servers, application servers, databases, and so on. The cloud services catalog does not define the capabilities for the cloud, since the capabilities could be much more expansive than the cloud services catalog. The cloud services catalog does not define the available VMs currently running in the cloud. The cloud services catalog also does not define the drivers for VMs in the cloud; this would be the agent or services file required for VMs running in the cloud.

64. C. A hosted medical records service is an example of the SaaS, or software-as-a-service, model. The customer cannot choose variables such as vCPU or RAM. The cloud provider is responsible for the delivery of the software, maintenance of the OS, and maintenance of the hardware. An example of platform-as-a-service (PaaS) would be Google App Engine or Microsoft Azure, where code could be executed on a virtual stack of equipment (programming platform). An example of infrastructure-as-a-service (IaaS) is Amazon Web Services (AWS) Elastic Compute (EC2), where a VM can be started up with virtual network services with only a credit card and you are billed periodically. An example of backup-as-a-service (BaaS) is Microsoft Azure cloud backup or Google Drive, just to name a couple.

65. **A.** A hosted service that allows you to develop upon it is an example of the platform-as-a-service (PaaS) model. The cloud provider is responsible for the delivery of APIs that developers can use to create programs. An example of infrastructure-as-a-service (IaaS) is Amazon Web Services (AWS), where a VM can be started up with virtual network services with only a credit card and you are billed periodically. An example of software-as-a-service (SaaS) is your email provider or a customer relation management (CRM) company such as Salesforce. An example of backup-as-a-service is Microsoft Azure cloud backup or Google Drive, just to name a couple.

66. **C.** An intercloud exchange is a service that connects multiple public clouds through a common private WAN connection. This allows a network engineer to configure the private WAN once and be able to transition between the public clouds on the service side without reconfiguration of the private WAN. A Multiprotocol Label Switching (MPLS) VPN is a VPN connection that is built over an MPLS network (private connection). An Internet VPN is a VPN connection that is built over the public Internet (public connection). A private wide area network (WAN) is one or more network connections between your facilities using public WAN connectivity methods.

67. **A.** Internal bandwidth usage is not a consideration after conversion to an SaaS application. External bandwidth and Internet connectivity should be considered since internal users will access the application through the Internet. Location of the users should also be a deciding factor in moving to an SaaS model.

68. **C.** You will need a virtual router to route between the two different networks. This type of service is called a virtual network function, or VNF. A virtual switch is built into just about every virtualization platform, since layer 2 communications are normally required. A virtual firewall is a piece of software that allows you to protect your virtualization infrastructure, just like their hardware counterparts. Another IP scheme at the provider could help, but a router would still be required for connectivity.

69. **C.** Network Time Protocol (NTP) is a standardized protocol for network time synchronization. Domain Name System (DNS) is a service that is used to translate a qualified domain name (FQDN) to an IP address. The rsync utility is a Linux/Unix utility used to synchronize (copy) a number of files to a remote system. A virtual private network (VPN) is a private encrypted tunnel that is normally created over a public Internet connection.

70. **B.** You would use a crossover cable because a switch is a data communications equipment (DCE) Ethernet device. When connecting a DCE Ethernet device to another DCE Ethernet device, you would need to cross the connection with a crossover cable. Newer switches have medium dependent interface-crossover (MDI-X) capabilities to detect the need for a crossover cable and will automatically switch the cable over if a straight-through cable is used. A straight-through cable is used to connect a DCE Ethernet device such as a switch to data terminal equipment (DTE) such as a host. A rolled cable is used for serial communication between a router or switch and a modem or serial adapter for configuration. A shielded cable has either a metal webbed shield or foil shield to filter out electrical magnetic interference (EMI).

71. B. Multimode fiber can be either 50 microns or 62.5 microns at its core. The maximum distance for a 50-micron fiber is 550 meters utilizing the 1000Base-LX specification. Unshielded twisted pair (UTP) is used in copper Ethernet cabling of hosts and network equipment. Single-mode fiber-optic cable is around 7 microns thick and is used for long-distance communications. Shielded twisted pair (STP) is used in industrial settings when there is the potential for electrical magnetic interference (EMI).

72. C. Although operation of computers connected to a switch uses a straight-through cable, management via the console port requires a rollover cable and an EIA/TIA 232 adapter. A straight-through cable is used to connect a data communications equipment (DCE) Ethernet device such as a switch to data terminal equipment (DTE) such as a host. You would use a crossover cable when connecting a DCE Ethernet device to another DCE Ethernet device; you would need to cross the connection with a crossover cable. Newer switches have medium dependent interface-crossover (MDI-X) capabilities to detect the need for a crossover cable and will automatically switch the cable over if a straight-through cable is used. A shielded cable has either a metal webbed shield or foil shield to filter out electrical magnetic interference (EMI).

73. C. 10GBase-CX is commonly used in data centers. It is referred to by its nickname of Twinax. It is a fixed, balanced coaxial pair that can be run up to 25 meters. 10GBase-T is usually category 6 cable that is nominally run up to 55 meters in length to achieve 10 Gb/s speeds. 40GBase-T is usually category 8 cable that is nominally run up to 30 meters to provide 40 Gb/s speeds. 100GBase-TX is not a valid specification for Ethernet connectivity. 100Base-TX is standard 100 Mb/s connectivity that supports full-duplex communications.

74. C. Cat5e can support up to 1 Gb/s via the 1000Base-T specification. Since 10Base-T, 100Base-T, and 1000Base-T can be run up to 100 meters in length, it allows for interchangeability with speeds. It was very common when Cat5e came out 20 years ago for installers to future-proof wiring installations with it. 10 Gb/s requires Category 6 or 6a cable to operate at speeds of 10 Gb/s. All other answers are incorrect.

75. D. Crossover cables are wired with the 568B specification on one side, and on the other side, the 568A specification is used. This change in wiring delivers the TX pair on pins 3 and 6 to the RX pair on pins 1 and 2. Straight-through cables are wired with the 568B specification on both sides.

76. C. The figure shows an example of a debug of outgoing packets, and therefore, the configuration problem is on this router. This router's username must match the adjacent router's hostname and both passwords must match. PAP is already configured on this router, as seen in the figure. PPP is also already configured on this router, as seen in the figure. This local router will not verify the remote username matches on the adjacent router; the adjacent router will verify when this router transmits its locally configured username and password.

77. B. The provider edge (PE) router is responsible for adding the MPLS label to a packet. The customer edge (CE) router is passed the MPLS packet with the label stripped off. The customer premise switch is the customer's local switching device and has no relation to MPLS. The term *label switch router (LSR)* is used to describe the internal switching of the MPLS network.

78. D. The demarc, or demarcation point, is the end of the provider's responsibility for the connection and the point where the customer's responsibility begins. This point is often a physical location where the provider can test their connection and hand off the service to the customer. Customer premises equipment (CPE) is the router or ancillary equipment used to facilitate the connection to the wide area network (WAN). The central office (CO) is a physical location where all of the customer connections on the local loop meet up and WAN services are delivered. The CO is also sometimes referred to as the point of presence (POP).

79. C. The speed of a DS1 connection is 1.544 Mb/s; it is also referred to as a T1 connection. The speed of a European DS1 called an E1 is 2.048 Mb/s. The speed of DS3 line is 44.736 Mb/s, and this line is also referred to as a T3. The speed of an optical carrier (OC-12) WAN connection is 622.08 Mb/s.

80. C. When you're checking for speed and/or duplex issues, the `show interface status` command will detail all of the ports with their negotiated speed and duplex. The commands `show speed`, `show duplex`, and `show diagnostics` are incorrect.

81. C. Although cabling could create an issue similar to this, it would not disable the interface. The most probable cause is that there is a duplex mismatch since there are a large number of late collisions. The most probable scenario is that the far end is set to half-duplex and the interface is set to full-duplex, or the opposite might also be true. The interface is not shut down because the figure would state that the interface was administratively disabled. There is no evidence in the figure that the interface has negotiated at half-duplex. The figure also shows no evidence that the cable is shorted on the interface.

82. A. The interface has been administratively down, which means that the interface has been placed into a shutdown state. To resolve the problem, a `no shutdown` command must be configured on the interface. There is no evidence in the figure that the interface has negotiated at half-duplex. The figure does not show any evidence that the duplex is mismatched on the interface, because the interface states it is administratively disabled. The figure also shows no evidence that the cable is shorted on the interface.

83. C. In order to clear the counters for a single interface, you would use the command `clear counters interface fast 0/1`. After it's entered, you will need to confirm clearing of the counters. Then you can monitor the solution provided on the interface. The commands `reset counters interface fast 0/1`, `clear interface fast 0/1`, and `clear statistics interface fast 0/1` are incorrect.

84. D. The counters on this interface are all nominal, but the interface and line protocol are down/down. This most likely suggests that the cable is disconnected. If the interface was shut down, it would state in the figure that the interface was administratively shut down. There is no evidence in the figure that the interface is negotiated at half-duplex. The interface is not operating nominally because it is in a down state.

85. A. It is recommended to set all servers and networking hardware statically for speed and duplex. If a network interface flaps (transitions between up and down), auto-negotiation of speed and duplex will be performed again, which could create a service outage. Changing the VLAN to another VLAN will not have any effect on interface resets and disconnects. Changing the switchport mode to a trunk is only applicable if the other side of the link is another switch that is configured as a trunk. Setting the switchport to auto-negotiate will turn on the Dynamic Trunking Protocol (DTP) and allow the switchport to become a trunk if plugged into another switch with DTP.

86. D. The txload and rxload counters are extremely high. This depicts that the interface is not fast enough for the data being transferred. The speed and duplex currently are 10 Mb/s and full-duplex. However, the interface on the switch is capable of 100 Mb/s. It is recommended to upgrade the node's NIC. Although there are no major problems with the interface, the counters depict congestion on the interface. The figure shows no evidence that the interface is auto-negotiating speed and duplex. Although there are a large number of broadcasts, this is not a problem compared to the load on the interface.

87. A. The commands to set the port back to auto-negotiation are `speed auto` and `duplex auto`. You can also negate the command with `no speed` and `no duplex` commands. Both methods will set auto-negotiation back on the port. The commands `speed autonegotiate`, `duplex autonegotiate`, `switchport autonegotiate`, and `interface autonegotiate` are incorrect.

88. B. Cisco switches can auto-detect speed, so the speed sensed will be 100 Mb/s. However, if the switch cannot detect the speed, then it will fall back to 10 Mb/s. Duplex is decided upon by bandwidth when IEEE auto-negotiation is turned off. If the speed is 10 Mb/s or 100 Mb/s, then the duplex will be half-duplex; otherwise it will be full-duplex on 1000 Mb/s links.

89. B. Hubs do not participate in IEEE negotiation, and therefore the speed will be detected. However, since duplex cannot be negotiated, 10 Mb/s and 100 Mb/s connections will be half-duplex and 1000 Mb/s connections will be full-duplex. Therefore the switch interface will be set to 100 Mb/s half-duplex.

90. C. The `show interfaces status` command will display the port number, description, connected status, VLAN, duplex, speed, and type of interface. The commands `show run`, `show interfaces counters`, and `show counters interfaces` are incorrect.

91. A. The Transport layer is responsible for flow control via the TCP/IP protocols of TCP and UDP. The Network layer is responsible for logical addressing of network nodes. The Data Link layer is responsible for the framing of data and the physical addressing of local nodes. Although the Data Link layer can perform a type of flow control, the Transport layer is synonymous with flow control. The Session layer is responsible for the setup of the dialog between two hosts.

92. C. User Datagram Protocol (UDP) does not guarantee segments are delivered. Therefore, the programmer must account for segments that are never received or out of order. Sockets Layer (SSL) is a protocol used to encrypt a network transmission. Transmission allows for the network to automatically deal with lost segments because TCP guarantees segments are delivered. *Network management station (NMS)* is a term used with Simple Network Management Protocol (SNMP) to describe the collecting host for SNMP messages.

93. D. TCP is a connection-based protocol via the three-way handshake. It is not faster than UDP. However, it allows for the retransmission of lost segments because of sequences and acknowledgments. TCP does not allow or account for error correction, only the detection of errors and lost or missing segments.

94. A. The sender allocates a port dynamically above 1024 and associates it with the request through a process called a handle. This way, if a web browser creates three requests for three different web pages, the pages are loaded to their respective windows. The receiver will respond back to the requesting port dynamically allocated to the request (over 1024); these ports are also known as ephemeral ports. Dynamic allocation is always over 1024, not below 1024, and it is always the responsibility of the sender, not the receiver.

95. D. The Simple Mail Transfer Protocol (SMTP) uses TCP port 25 to send mail. The Trivial File Transfer Protocol (TFTP) uses UDP/69 for communications. The Dynamic Host Configuration Protocol (DHCP) uses UDP/68 for communications. The Domain Name protocol uses UDP/53 for communications.

96. D. TCP guarantees delivery of segments with sequence and acknowledgment numbers. At the Transport layer, each segment is given a sequence number that is acknowledged by the receiver. The source and destination ports are used for the delivery of segments, but they do not guarantee delivery. TCP checksums are used to detect errors in segments but do not guarantee delivery. Window size is used to adjust buffer size on the sending and receiving hosts.

97. A. When a programmer decides to use UDP, it is normally because the programmer is sequencing and acknowledging datagrams already. The redundancy of acknowledgments at the Transport layer is not needed. Guaranteed delivery of segments is not a function of UDP. UDP does not provide windowing flow control because acknowledgment is not a function of UDP. A virtual circuit can only be created with a setup and teardown of communications, such as TCP offers.

98. B. When a daemon or server process starts, it binds to a port number on which to listen for a request. An example is a web server binding to the port number of TCP/80. A port is communicated in the header of TCP and UDP segments, but the header does not listen for requests or bind. MAC addresses are physical locations on a local area network (LAN) that are used to transmit framed data. Checksums are used to verify that data are not erroneously modified in transit.

99. A. The window size, which is a buffer, is established and agreed upon by the sender and receiver during the three-way handshake. Sliding windows does not allow for data of different lengths to be padded; it is used for fixed-length data segments. Port binding is used by TCP and UDP to indicate which upper-layer protocol (application) created the request. Routers only examine layer 3 information by default, so they can make decisive routing decisions.

100. C. DNS requests are usually small and do not require the overhead of sequence and acknowledgment of TCP. If a segment is dropped, the DNS protocol will ask again. Acknowledgment of data is not a function of UDP. Flow control is not a function of UDP since UDP does not offer flow control of data other than a stop/go action. UDP does not build temporary virtual circuits; this is a function of TCP.

101. A. A three-way handshake is required between sender and receiver before TCP can begin sending traffic. During this three-way handshake, the sender's window buffer size is synchronized with the receiver's window buffer size. Ports are not agreed upon; they are used for the addressing of traffic at the Transport layer. The sequencing and acknowledgment of segments is a function of the TCP protocol.

102. B. The IP address 172.23.23.2 is a Class B address. All of the other options are incorrect.

103. A. The default subnet mask of a Class A address is 255.0.0.0. The default subnet mask of a Class B address is 255.255.0.0. The default subnet mask of a Class C address is 255.255.255.0. The mask 255.255.255.255 is reserved to define a specific IP address and is not part of classful addressing.

104. C. The multicast range begins with 224 and ends with 239 in the first octet. Therefore, only the IP address 238.20.80.4 is correct. All of the other options are incorrect.

105. B. The IP address 135.20.255.255 is a Class B broadcast address. It is not a Class A address, nor is it the default gateway address. The default mask of a Class B address is 255.255.0.0.

106. B. The CIDR notation for 255.255.240.0 is /20. The first two subnets are 8 bits (8 × 2 = 16), and the 240 is 4 more bits (16 + 4 = 20). All of the other options are incorrect.

107. A. The mask you will need to use is 255.255.255.252. This will allow for two hosts per network for a total of 64 networks. The formula for solving for hosts is $2^x - 2$ is equal to or greater than 2 hosts, which in this case is $(2^2 - 2) = (4 - 2) = 2$. So 2 bits are used for the host side, leaving 6 bits for the subnet side. 6 bits + 24 bits (original subnet mask) = /30, or 255.255.255.252. All of the other options are incorrect.

108. D. The mask you will need to use is 255.255.255.224. This will allow for 30 hosts per network for a total of 8 networks. The formula for solving for hosts is $2^x - 2$ is equal to or greater than 22 hosts, which in this case is $(2^5 - 2) = (32 - 2) = 30$. So 5 bits are used for the host side, leaving 3 bits for the subnet side. 3 bits + 24 bits (original subnet mask) = /27, or 255.255.255.224. All of the other options are incorrect.

109. A. The valid IP address range for the 192.168.32.0/26 network is 192.168.32.1 to 192.168.32.62, 192.168.32.65 to 192.168.32.126 . . . . Therefore, 192.168.32.59 is within the valid IP range of 192.168.32.61/26. 192.168.32.63 is the broadcast address for the 192.168.32.0/26 network. 192.168.32.64 is the network ID for the 192.168.32.64/26 network. 192.168.32.72 is a valid IP address in the 192.168.32.64/26 network.

110. B. The subnet mask will be 255.255.240.0. Since you need to solve for the number of networks, the equation is as follows: 2^x is equal to or greater than 15 networks. $2^4 = 16$ completed the equation; the 4 bits represent the subnet side; you add the 4 bits to the 16 bits of the class B subnet mandated by the IETF. 16 + 4 = /20 = 255.255.240.0. All of the other options are incorrect.

111. C. The valid IP address range for 209.183.160.45/30 is 209.183.160.45–209.183.160.46. Both IP addresses are part of the 209.183.160.44/30 network. The IP address 209.183.160.47/30 is the broadcast address for the 209.182.160.44/30 network. The IP address 209.183.160.43/30 is the broadcast IP address for the 209.183.160.40/30 network.

112. C. The default gateway address for Computer A is 192.168.1.63. The IP address on the router (default gateway) is the broadcast address for the 192.168.1.0/26 network and cannot be used as that network's gateway. If you were to change Computer A's IP address, it would still not be able to communicate with Computer B because of the incorrect gateway address. Computer B's IP address and default gateway are fine, and both will function properly.

113. A. Computer A needs to have its IP address changed to align with the network that its gateway is in. Computer A is in the 192.168.1.32/27 network, while its gateway address is in the 192.168.1.0/27 network. Although changing the gateway address would work, the solution needs to be the one with the least amount of effort. Changing the gateway address, which is a valid IP address, would create more work for other clients. Computer B's IP address and default gateway are fine, and both will function properly.

114. B. The /21 subnet mask has subnets in multiples of 8. So the networks would be 131.50.8.0/21, 131.50.16.0/21, 131.50.24.0/21, 131.50.32.0/21, and 131.50.40.0/21. The IP address of 131.50.39.23/21 would belong to the 131.50.32.0/21 network with a valid range of 131.50.32.1 to 131.50.39.254. Therefore, the network 131.50.39.0/21 cannot be a network ID because it belongs to the 131.50.32.0/21 network. Both the 131.50.16.0/21 and 131.50.8.0/21 network IDs are outside of the range for the host used in this question.

115. D. The network for the computer with an IP address of 145.50.23.1/22 is 145.50.20.0/22. Its valid range is 145.50.20.1 to 145.50.23.254; the broadcast address for the range is 145.50.23.255. All of the other options are incorrect.

116. C. RFC 1918 defines three private address ranges, which are not routable on the Internet. Although RFC 1819, 1911, and 3030 are real requests for comments, they are all irrelevant to IP addressing.

117. A. The private IP address space was created to preserve the number of public IP addresses. Private IP addresses are nonroutable on the Internet, but this does not make them secure. Private IP addresses do not keep communications private, as their name implies. Private IP addresses are not publicly addressable for communications. Private IP addresses do not allow for an easier setup than public IP addresses.

118. D. Network Address Translation (NAT) is required to communicate over the Internet with private IP addresses. Although Internet routers are required for routing, by default they will not route private IP addresses to public IP addresses. An IPv4 tunnel or VPN tunnel is not required for communications on the Internet with private IP addresses.

119. A. The Class A private IP address range is defined as 10.0.0.0/8. The address range is 10.0.0.0 to 10.255.255.255. The network IDs 10.0.0.0/10 and 10.0.0.0/12 are wrong because the network mask is incorrect. The network ID 172.16.0.0/12 is the private IP address range for a Class B network.

120. C. The Class B private IP address range is defined as 172.16.0.0/12. The address range is 172.16.0.0 to 172.31.255.255. The network ID 10.0.0.0/8 defines a Class A private IP address range. Both the 10.0.0.0/12 and 10.0.0.0/10 network IDs are incorrect.

121. C. Although a Class C address has a classful subnet mask of 255.255.255.0, the private IP address range put aside for Class C address-es is 192.168.0.0 to 192.168.255.255, written in CIDR notation as 192.168.0.0/16. All of the other options are incorrect.

122. D. Any address in the range of 169.254.0.0/16 is a link-local address. It means that the computer has sensed that a network connection is present, but no DHCP is present. The network only allows local communications and no routing. Microsoft refers to this as an Automatic Private IP Addressing (APIPA) address. If the network jack was not working, then the computer would not sense a connection. Although it is possible to have a 169.254.0.0/16 address configured on the laptop, it is not probable because it is an automatic address. The conclusion that the network is configured properly is incorrect because there is no server or device serving DHCP.

123. D. 198.168.55.45 is a valid IPv4 public address. All of the other addresses are RFC 1918 compliant and thus nonroutable on the Internet.

124. A. The Internet Assigned Numbers Authority (IANA) is the governing body that distributes public IP addresses and registers them to ISPs. A request for comments (RFC) is an academic paper that is published to the Internet Advisory Board (IAB). The RFC is then voted on and can become a standard or informational or deemed a best current practice, just to name a few options. The Internet Engineering Task Force is a group of engineers that have helped form protocols used on networks as well as aspects of the Internet.

125. B. The Internet Group Messaging Protocol (IGMP) allows switches to join computers to the multicast group table. This allows the selective process of snooping to occur when a transmission is sent. Internet Control Message Protocol (ICMP) is used by IP utilities such as `traceroute` and `ping` for diagnostics and troubleshooting. Intelligent Platform Management Interface (IPMI) allows systems to be monitored and managed at the hardware level, independent of the CPU, memory, BIOS, and operating system. IPGRP is not a protocol that defines a standard, and therefore, it is an incorrect option.

126. B. IPv4 allows for 2^{32} = 4.3 billion addresses. However, only 3.7 billion are usable because of reservations and classful addressing. The current IPv4 address space is exhausted, and IPv6 allows for 2^{128} = 3.4 × 10^{38} addresses. IPv6 still requires NAT for backward compatibility with IPv4. Although IPv4 is slowly being replaced with IPv6, IPv4 is still dominant in networks and the Internet. IPv6 does not need to be subnetted like IPv4 by borrowing bits from the network mask; there are 16 bits dedicated for subnets.

127. C. An IPv6 address is 128 bits: 64 bits is the network ID, and 64 bits is the host ID. All of the other options are incorrect.

128. D. A 6to4 tunnel can be achieved between the routers. This encapsulates the IPv6 header in an IPv4 header so that it can be routed across the Internet. A dedicated leased line and Frame Relay are wide area network (WAN) connectivity methods. Dual stack means that a host or router will have both IPv4 and IPv6 configured, but it will not allow both facilities to communicate over the Internet.

129. D. In order to enable IPv6 on a router, you must globally configure the router with the command `ipv6 unicast-routing`. Although `ipv6 enable` will work, it will allow only link-local addressing. The commands `ipv6 address` and `ipv6 routing` are incorrect.

130.   D. When you configure routers, always use the rule of major/minor. The major protocol is `ipv6`, and the minor command is address. So the correct command is `ipv6`
`address 2001:0db8:85aa:0000:0000:8a2e:1343:1337/64`. The additional rule is to specify the network portion with a /64. The commands `ip address`
`2001:0db8:85aa:0000:0000: 8a2e:1343:1337`, `ipv6 address 2001:0db8:`
`85aa:0000:0000:8a2e:1343:1337`, and `ip address 2001:0db8:85aa:`
`0000:0000:8a2e:1343:1337/64` are incorrect.

131.   A. The first 4 bits of an IPv6 header contain the version number. In an IPv4 packet, this is
set to 0100, but in an IPv6 packet, this number is set to 0110. This allows for the host to
decide which stack to process the packet in. Flow labels in IPv6 explain to a router how to
handle packets and route them; they do not contain a version number. The source and destination addresses in IPv6 packets will be IPv6 addresses, but this is not how a dual-stack
machine decides which protocol to use.

132.   A. When you use a `show` command, always follow it with the major protocol and then the
parameters. The `show ipv6 interfaces brief` command would show all of the interfaces configured with an IPv6 address. The commands `show ip interfaces brief`,
`show interfaces status`, and `show ip addresses` are incorrect.

133.   D. You can remove leading 0s in the quartet, and you can condense four zeros
to one zero. However, you can use the :: to remove zeros only once. Therefore,
2001:db8:0000::8a2e::1337 and 2001:db8::8a2e::1337 are invalid notations. The address
2001:db8:::8a2e:0000:1337 contains three colons, and therefore, it is an invalid notation.

134.   C. Expanding out the IP of 2001::0456:0:ada4, you first expand the :0: to four zeros. Then
expand the remainder of the quartets to 0s to make a 32-digit (128-bit) number again. All
other options are incorrect.

135.   B. The first 48 bits of an IPv6 address are the global prefix; the next 16 bits are the subnet
portion of the IPv6 address. 48 bits + 16 bits = 64 bits for the network ID. 1234 is the site
ID, which is a portion of the network ID. 0023 is the first 16 bits of the interface ID. 8080 is
the second 16 bits of the interface ID.

136.   A. The network prefix is 2001:db8::/64. Expanded, it is written as
2001:0db8:0000:0000/64. However, the condensed version written in the answer is valid.
All of the other options are incorrect.

137.   C. The command to ping an IPv6 address is `ping ipv6`. The valid condensed address for
fc00:0000:0000:0000:0000:0000:0000:0004 is fc00::4. You cannot condense trailing zeros
such as fc00. You can only condense leading zeros. The command `ping` in options A and B
is incorrect; the proper command is `ping ipv6` for IPv6 addresses. Although the command
`ping ipv6` is correct, the IP address in option D is incorrect.

138.   A. A unicast address is a single valid IP address for direct communications purposes
between two hosts. A broadcast is a single address that is sent to a network of hosts. A
multicast address is a single address that is selectively sent to a multicast group of hosts. An
anycast address is a single IP address that is selectively routed to depending on the location
of the originating host.

139. B. DHCP uses a packet called a Discover packet. This packet is addressed to 255.255.255.255. Although ARP uses a broadcast, it is a layer 2 broadcast, not a layer 3 broadcast. IGMP is a layer 3 protocol that uses unicast to register members of a multicast group. SNMP is a layer 3 management protocol that uses unicasts for messaging.

140. B. A broadcast will forward a message to all computers in the same subnet. A unicast address is a single valid IP address for direct communications purposes between two hosts. A multicast address is a single address that is selectively sent to a multicast group of hosts. An anycast address is a single IP address that is selectively routed to depending on the location of the originating host.

141. B. The answer is 16,384 networks. You subtract 34 bits from 48 bits = 14 bits, then 2^{14} = 16,384. All of the other options are incorrect.

142. A. The Neighbor Discovery Protocol (NDP) uses Neighbor Solicitation (NS) and Neighbor Advertisement (NA) messages to look up an IP address from a MAC address through the use of multicast messages. Duplicate Address Detection (DAD) uses Neighbor and Neighbor Advertisement (NA) messages to check if another host has the same IPv6 address. Stateless Address Autoconfiguration (SLAAC) uses Router Solicitation (RS) and Router Advertisement (RA) to assign a network ID to a host. The ARP protocol is completely removed from IPv6; therefore, ARPv6 is not a valid option.

143. B. The global unicast address is defined as 2000::/3. This provides a valid range of 2000:: to 3fff::. An address with a network prefix of fe80::/10 is a link-local address. An address with a network prefix of fc00::/7 is a unique local unicast address. An address with a network prefix of ff00::/8 is a multicast address.

144. A. The first 23 bits are allotted to the ISP by the RIR for the region of the world for which the ISP is requesting the prefix. All of the other options are incorrect.

145. C. The unique local address is defined as fc00::/7. Unique local addresses have replaced site-local addresses as of 2004 and are nonroutable. The valid IPv6 range is fc00:: to fd00:: despite IANA reserving fc00::/7 as the fc00:: range. The range should not be used since the 8th bit is considered the "local bit" and is required to be a 1, as in, for example, 1111 1101 = fd. An address with a network prefix of fe80::/10 is a link-local address. An address with a network prefix of 2000::/3 is a unique local unicast address. An address with a network prefix of ff00::/8 is a multicast address.

146. A. IPv4 RFC 1918 addresses are defined as private non-routable IP addresses. In IPv6, link-local addresses are the equivalent to RFC 1918 addresses and are nonroutable. Global unicast addresses are similar to IPv4 public IP addresses. An EUI-64 address is the host interface portion of the IPv6 address when it is configured using the host's MAC address. Anycast addresses are IPv6 addresses that are applied to multiple hosts and routed to the hosts based on proximity; root DNS servers use anycast in this manner.

147. A. The link-local address is defined as fe80::/10. Any address starting with fe80 is nonroutable. A global unicast address is defined as 2000::/3. This provides a valid range of 2000:: to 3fff::. An address with a network prefix of fc00::/7 is a unique local unicast address. The network address of fd00 would be part of the fc00::/7 network range. An address with a network prefix of ff00::/8 is a multicast address.

148. D. Anycast is a way of allowing the same IP address on multiple machines in different geographical areas. The routing protocol is used to advertise in routing tables the closest IP by the use of metrics. Currently this is how DNS root servers work. A unicast address is a single valid IP address for direct communications purposes between two hosts. A broadcast will forward a message to all computers in the same subnet. A multicast address is a single address that is selectively sent to a multicast group of hosts.

149. D. The command to configure an anycast address on an interface would be `ipv6 address 2001:db8:1:1:1::12/128 anycast`. The /128 defines a single IP address to advertise in routing tables. The commands `ip address 2001:db8:1:1:1::12/64`, `ipv6 address 2001:db8:1:1:1::12/64 anycast`, and `ipv6 anycast address 2001:db8:1:1:1::12/128` are incorrect.

150. C. Multicast is used to allow computers to opt into a transmission. Examples of uses for multicast are video, routing protocols, and imaging of computers to name a few. A unicast address is a single valid IP address for direct communications purposes between two hosts. A broadcast will forward a message to all computers in the same subnet. A multicast address is a single address that is selectively sent to a multicast group of hosts. Anycast is a way of allowing the same IP address on multiple machines in different geographical areas. The routing protocol is used to advertise in routing tables the closest IP by the use of metrics.

151. D. The multicast address is defined as ff00::/8. Multicast addresses always start with ff. The link-local address is defined as fe80::/10. Any address starting with fe80 is nonroutable. A global unicast address is de-fined as 2000::/3. This provides a valid range of 2000:: to 3fff::. An address with a network prefix of fc00::/7 is a unique local unicast address. The network address fd00 would be part of the fc00::/7 network range.

152. A. When converting a MAC address to an EUI-64 host address, the first step is to split the MAC address into 6-byte sections of f42356 and 345623 and place fffe in between them, f423:56ff:fe34:5623. This gives you a 64-bit value composed of a 48-bit MAC address and a 16-bit filler. You must then invert (flip) the 7th bit. Example: f4 = 1111 0100 = flipped = 1111 0110 = f6. All of the other options are incorrect.

153. C. The EUI-64 address can always be found by looking at the last 64 bits. In between the last 64 bits of the address, you will always find fffe. For example, the last 64 bits of the address of 2001:db8:aa::f654:56ff:fe34:a633 are f654:56ff:fe34:a633. All other options are incorrect.

154. C. The command to set an EUI-64 address for the host portion of the IPv6 address on an interface is `ipv6 address 2001:db8:1234::/64 eui-64`. The commands `ip address eui-64 2001:db8:1234::/64`, `ip address 2001:db8:1234::/64 mac-address`, and `ipv6 address 2001:db8:1234::/64 mac` are incorrect.

155. C. The command `ipconfig /all` will help you verify the IP address, subnet mask, default gateway, and MAC address of your computer. The command `ipconfig` doesn't show the MAC address. The `ipconfig` command will give brief information about the interfaces on the Windows host. The command `ipstatus` is not a valid command. The command `hostname` will display the name of the Windows host.

156. A. The Windows command for tracing a route is `tracert`. The command `ping 198.78.34.2` will send ICMP packets to the destination host of 198.78.34.2 and report the round-trip time. The command `traceroute 198.78.34.2` is a Linux/Unix command for verifying the path on which a packet is routed. The command `route print` is used to view the routing table on a Windows host.

157. B. If the cache is cleared after the change has been made to DNS and you still get the same IP address, the reason is most likely that there is a host entry configured. The command `show running-config` will show you if there is an entry. The router is not likely to be configured to the wrong DNS server because the authoritative domain of `sybex.com` is used. The DNS administrator could have made an error, but it resolves correctly on your laptop. The domain name is not the problem because it resolves correctly on your laptop.

158. C. The command `nslookup routerb.sybex.com` will allow you to positively verify name resolution. The `ping` command should not be used because the failure of ICMP echo will make the command fail, giving you a false result. The `tracert` command is used for tracing the route a packet takes, and like `ping` it can give a false positive if the host is unreachable. The `dig` command is a great tool to use in place of `nslookup` for verifying DNS, but it is not installed on Windows by default.

159. B. The command `ipconfig /all` will display the generic information of IP, subnet mask, and gateway. It will also display the DHCP server that configured the client with an IP address. The standard `ipconfig` command will give you brief information, but not the DHCP server. The `ipconfig /showclassid` command will display the class information reported to the DHCP server. The `ipstatus` command is not a valid command, and therefore, it is not the correct answer.

160. C. The DHCP server is not configured properly. When a Windows client configures itself with an IP address of 169.254.x.x, it is using APIPA, or Automatic Private IP Addressing (link-local addressing). It is highly unlikely that anyone would configure an APIPA scope, since it is used in the absence of a DHCP server. It is also highly unlikely that you would configure a client with a static IP address in the APIPA range. DHCP servers cannot be configured for APIPA.

161. A. 802.11 uses a contention method of Carrier Sense Multiple Access/Collision Avoidance. 802.11 implements a Request-to-Send/Clear-to-Send mechanism that avoids collisions. Ethernet uses a contention method of Carrier Sense Multiple Access/Collision Detection. Both Direct-Sequence Spread Spectrum (DSSS) and Orthogonal Frequency Division Multiplexing (OFDM) are wireless modulations used to transmit data.

162. C. In the 2.4 GHz spectrum for 802.11, there are three nonoverlapping channels: 1, 6, and 11, each of which is 22 MHz wide. Although channel 14 technically is nonoverlapping, it is only allowed in Japan. All of the other options are incorrect.

163. D. The 802.11ac protocol will be least likely to overlap the wireless channels the tenants are using. The 802.11ac protocol uses the 5 GHz wireless frequency spectrum. The 5 GHz spectrum defines 24 nonoverlapping wireless channels. The 2.4 GHz spectrum defines 11 channels, but only 3 of them are nonoverlapping. Although 802.11n operates on 2.4 GHz and 5 GHz, 802.11ac only operates on 5 GHz. Therefore, 802.11ac will have the least likely overlap of current channels. 802.11b and 802.11g operate solely on the 2.4 GHz spectrum.

164. B. Wired Equivalent Privacy (WEP) uses either 40- or 104-bit encryption; it also uses a 24-bit initialization vector (IV) to randomize each session. The encryption and IV combined, WEP advertises encryption strength of 64-bit or 128-bit. All Protected Access (WPA) variants use a variety of other mechanisms, but they do not use initialization vectors.

165. D. WPA2 Enterprise does not use a preshared key (PSK) for authentication. In lieu of a PSK, WPA2 Enterprise uses certificates to authentication users. WPA, WPA2, and WEP use a preshared key for authentication.

166. C. The 5 GHz band for 802.11 a/n/ac has 24 nonoverlapping channels. The 2.4 GHz band for 802.11 b/g/n has only 3 nonoverlapping channels. If the clients are compatible with 802.11 a/n/ac, it is desirable to use 5 GHz. 2.4 GHz goes further than 5 GHz; therefore, 5 GHz should not be used when distance is a concern. 5 GHz will not allow more clients to join the wireless access point (WAP). There is the same amount of interference on both 2.4 GHz and 5 GHz.

167. B. The 2.4 GHz frequency spectrum is where Bluetooth operates, and the frequency is also shared with 802.11. 900 MHz is used by Zigbee, which is an Internet of Things (IoT) communication technology. 5 GHz is shared with some radar systems, mainly on the upper channels of the frequency spectrum.

168. A. The 802.11g wireless standard operates strictly on 2.4 GHz. The 802.11n wireless standard operates on both 2.4 GHz and 5 GHz. Both the 802.11a and 802.11ac wire-less standards operate on 5 GHz.

169. B. The hypervisor allows for multiple operating systems to share CPUs, RAM, network, and storage of a physical server. A physical server alone will not distribute resources over several operating systems. A virtual machine (VM) is what runs on top of the hypervisor. A virtual network is a resource that is shared on a hypervisor to the running virtual machines.

170. D. A virtual machine (VM) is an operating system that is running on hardware but is not directly attached to the hardware. It is decoupled from the hardware through the use of a hypervisor. The hypervisor creates an abstraction layer between the hardware and the operating system. An operating system that runs directly on hardware is not classified as a virtual machine since it monopolizes the hardware. An operating system that is running with dedicated hardware is not classified as a virtual machine because it has dedicated hardware. An operating system that is running on reduced hardware features is not classified as a VM because it still runs directly on the hardware.

171. A. The physical hardware (such as a server) used in virtualization is the host. The virtual machine (VM) runs on top of the hypervisor and allows for an operating system to be virtually installed. The hypervisor is installed on the host to allow multiple VMs to share the physical hardware. The guest is another name for virtual machines, since they are guests to the hardware via the hypervisor.

172. C. A virtual switch connects the virtual machine NIC to the physical network. The virtual network interface card (vNIC) is the virtualized network card presented to the virtual machine. A trunk is a mode for a switchport or virtual switch that allows multiple VLANs to be tagged over a single virtual or physical link. NX-OS is a Cisco operating system that runs on the line of Nexus data center switches.

173. B. A virtual firewall or virtual router is an example of a VNF. These devices are typically network functions that are found in internal networks such as firewalls and routers. These devices perform basic network functionality and run as virtual machines or virtual instances. A virtual switch is not considered a VNF because it is an elemental part of the hypervisor, used for communications. A database server and file server are not functions of a network; they are roles found on servers.

174. D. If you wanted to scale a web server out to several other web servers, you would use server load balancing as a service (SLBaaS) from your cloud provider. Adding resources such as vCPUs and vRAM is an example of scaling a server up, not out. Adding DNS will not offset or accommodate the additional load on the web servers.

175. D. When the Individual/Group (I/G) high order bit is set to 1, the frame is a broadcast or a multicast transmission. The OUI assigned by the IEEE is only partially responsible for MAC uniqueness. The vendor is responsible for the last 24 bits of a MAC address.

176. B. When you're diagnosing frame forwarding on a switch, the MAC address table needs to be inspected to see if the switch has learned the destination MAC address. You can use the command `show mac address-table` to inspect the MAC address table. The command `show route` is incorrect; it only displays layer 3 route decision information. The command `show mac table` is incorrect. The command `show interface` is also incorrect; it will not display information on how the switch will make forward/filter decisions.

177. B. The mechanism that switches use for loop avoidance is the Spanning Tree Protocol (STP). Port channels are used to aggregate bandwidth between two switches. *Ether channels* is a Cisco-centric term for port channels. Trunk is a switchport mode that allows multiple VLANs to traverse over a single link by tagging each frame with the respective VLAN.

178. D. When loop avoidance such as STP is not employed and loops exist, you will get duplicate unicast frames and broadcast storms. This will inevitably thrash the MAC address table and degrade bandwidth to nothing.

179. C. Store-and-forward mode is the default mode for mode edge switching equipment. Store-and-forward receives the frame, calculates the CRC, and then makes a forwarding decision. Cut-through mode allows the switch to make a forward/filter decision immediately after the destination MAC address is received. Frag-free mode inspects the first 64 bytes of an incoming frame, before a forward/filter decision is made. Fast switching is a method in which a caching table is created for MAC addresses received so that switching can be made faster.

180. B. Fragment-free mode reads the first 64 bytes and deems the frame intact and forwardable. This is because most collisions that would create frame fragments happen within the first 64 bytes of a frame. This method of switching is often found on SOHO switching equipment. Store-and-forward mode is the default mode for mode edge switching equipment.

Store-and-forward receives the frame, calculates the CRC, and then makes a forwarding decision. Cut-through mode allows the switch to make a forward/filter decision immediately after the destination MAC address is received. Fast switching is a method in which a caching table is created for MAC addresses received so that switching can be made faster.

181. D. The interface shows a high number of collisions. In a full-duplex network connection, there should be no collisions. This would suggest that the port on the switch or the NIC in the computer is set to half-duplex. Half-duplex causes collisions, which can degrade bandwidth by 40% to 60%. Upgrading the computer to 100 Mb/s will not solve the high collision rate; it will just allow more collisions to happen more quickly. You cannot conclude there is a wiring issue from the details of the interface. Although it is always possible a NIC is going bad, the NIC is still passing traffic, and there are not enough details in the output of the interface.

182. B. Switches learn MAC addresses by inspecting the frame's source MAC address on the incoming port. They then associate the source MAC address with the port it came in on. The destination MAC address is what the forward/filter decisions are based upon. Spanning Tree Protocol (STP) listens and learns Bridge Protocol Data Units (BPDUs) so it can detect loops or potential loops. Frame type learning is not a real concept; therefore, it is an invalid answer.

183. A. Computer A will no longer forward traffic because the static entry will override a dynamic entry. Computer A's frames will not be forwarded to port Fa0/4, only Fa0/1, because of the static entry. Computer B's frames will not be forwarded to all ports because computer B's MAC address will be learned on Fa0/1 along with the static entry.

184. C. Computer A's frames will be forwarded to its new port of Fa0/3 since the entries will be cleared out when the cables are disconnected and relearned. When Computer A is disconnected from Fa0/2, the MAC address entries for that port will be cleared from the table. Therefore, frames will no longer be forwarded to Fa0/2 on behalf of Computer A, only to Computer A's new port of Fa0/3. Frames are only forwarded to all active ports when the destination MAC address in a frame is not in the MAC address table.

185. C. The default MAC address aging time for dynamic entries is 300 seconds, or 5 minutes. All of the other options are incorrect.

186. C. The computer is connected to either another switch or another hub on Gi0/1 since there are multiple MAC address entries on Gi0/1. The computer is not likely directly connected because of the multiple entries for Gi0/1 unless it was acting as a bridge for other computers. The computer cannot be connected to Fa0/1 since an entry is not present for the computer. There is no evidence in the figure that there is a loop and the MAC address table is thrashed.

187. B. When a frame is received on an incoming port, both the incoming port and the source MAC address are added to the MAC address table and set with an aging timer. The destination MAC address in the incoming frame is used for forward/filter decisions only. The destination is never used to populate the table; the aging timer will only be updated when a frame is seen on the port and the source address is read. The source MAC address and the outgoing port number have no relationship.

188. C. MAC address aging time can be configured via the command `mac-address-table aging-time 400`. You can additionally specify a VLAN ID. The commands `set mac aging 400`, `mac aging-time 400 seconds`, and `mac address-aging 400` are incorrect.

189. A. Switches make forward/filter decisions based on the MAC address to port association in the MAC address table. Forward/filter decisions are layer 2 switching decisions and not layer 3 routing decisions; therefore, the routing table is irrelevant. A frame is only flooded to all active ports on a switch under two conditions; the destination MAC address is unknown or the MAC address table is full. Broadcasting for the MAC address is not a function of switching and is, therefore, an incorrect answer.

190. B. When a MAC address is unknown by the switch, the switch will forward the frame to all ports; this is also called flooding the frame. When the destination system acts upon it, the switch learns its MAC address through source MAC address learning. The uplink port will receive a copy of the flooded frame, but it will receive this copy along with all other active ports. Switches never drop frames unless the CRC for the frame is incorrect. The frame will never be forwarded to a broadcast MAC address of ffff.ffff.ffff unless that is the intended destination.

191. A. Since there is nothing in the current MAC address tables or either switch, the incoming frame on Switch A will be flooded to all ports. This will include the port connecting Switch B. Switch B in turn will flood the frame to all ports. However, nothing will respond on Switch B since the host is on Switch A. Although this is wasted traffic, it is minimal since it is only the initial communications. Switch A solely flooding traffic would happen under two specific conditions: Either the interface of Fa0/3 on Switch A was down or Switch B has an entry for the destination host. Neither of these conditions exists in the figure; therefore, both switches will flood the frame out all active ports. Switch A cannot switch the frame to Fa0/2 (Computer C) because the MAC address table is empty for that port.

192. A. Since there is nothing in the current MAC address tables or either switch, the incoming frame on Switch A will be flooded to all ports. This will include the port connecting Switch B. Switch B in turn will flood the frame to all ports. Switch A solely flooding traffic would happen under two specific conditions: the interface of Fa0/3 on Switch A was down or Switch B has an entry for the destination host. Neither of these conditions exists in the figure; therefore, both switches will flood the frame out all active ports. Both switches will flood the frame because both of their MAC address tables are empty. Switch B cannot switch the frame to Fa0/3 (Computer F) because the MAC address table is empty for that port.

193. C. The only time a frame is dropped is when the cyclic redundancy check (CRC) calculated against the frame's payload deems the frame corrupt. If the destination MAC address is not known, it will be flooded to all active ports on the switch, but it will not be dropped. If the source MAC address of the frame is unknown in the MAC address table, the source MAC address will be learned on the incoming port. If the destination MAC address exists in another switch's MAC address table, then it will either be forwarded to that switch or flooded to that switch if the current switch has an empty MAC address table for the entry.

194. A. The forward/filter function of a switch is used to look up the destination MAC address in a MAC address table and decide the egress interface for the frame. If the MAC address is not in the table, the frame is forwarded out all of the interfaces. When the client responds, its source MAC address will be recorded in the MAC address table for future lookup.

Address learning is performed when frames enter into the interface; the source address is written to the port it is observed on. Loop avoidance employs Spanning Tree Protocol (STP) to block redundant links to prevent loops. Frame flooding is a default action of the forward/filter process when a destination frame is unknown.

195. C. Computer A will create an ARP (broadcast) request. When that request is received on port Fa0/0, the switch will record Computer A's MAC address on Fa0/0. Then it will forward the message to all ports because the initial ARP packet/frame is a layer 2 broadcast. The switch will not directly communicate with Fa0/1 because the MAC address table is empty and the initial ARP packet/frame is a broadcast. The switch will only record Computer B's MAC address on port Fa0/1 when Computer B responds to the initial ARP packet/frame with a frame containing the source MAC address.

196. B. Since the MAC address table has the MAC address for Computer B, the switch will direct the frame to port Fa0/1 only. The switch will only forward the frame to all active ports if the MAC address table didn't contain the destination MAC address for Computer B. The switch will only record Computer A's MAC address on port Fa0/0 if the MAC address was not already populated in the table for that specific port. Likewise the switch will only record Computer B's MAC address on port Fa0/1 if the MAC address was not already populated in the table for that specific port.

197. B. The destination MAC address for broadcasts is always all fs, such as ffff.ffff.ffff. The source MAC address of the frame will be the specific MAC address of the host. The switch will broadcast the frame to all ports and not just the individual port the ARP request is trying to discover. The switch will not respond directly back with an ARP reply because switches do not process ARP requests; only routers can respond when configured as an ARP proxy, which is very rare.

198. C. When the destination MAC address is not in the MAC address table, the switch will flood the frame to all ports on the switch. When the computer or device responds, the switch will record the source MAC address with the port on which it sees the traffic. When the source MAC address is unknown by the switch, it is recorded in the MAC address table as previously described. When a multicast address is seen by the switch, it is selectively switched to specific ports. A MAC address is never set to 0000.0000.0000, as it is an invalid format for a MAC address.

199. C. MAC address tables, also called CAM tables, are always built and stored temporarily in RAM. When the switch is turned off or the clear command is issued, the table no longer exists. Flash is used to store the Internetwork Operating System (IOS) for the switch or router. The CPU registers, also called the configuration registers, explain to the switch how to boot. The nonvolatile random access memory (NVRAM) is where the configuration is stored; it is similar to flash and usually much smaller.

200. B. The command to see the MAC address table is show mac-address table. However, on some 4000 and 6500 series switches, the command show cam dynamic will perform the same function. The commands show mac, show cam table, and show mac table are incorrect.

201. D. The show interfaces status command will display the port number, connected status, VLAN, duplex, speed, and type of interface. The commands show ports, show counters interfaces, and show interfaces counters are incorrect.

Chapter 2: Network Access (Domain 2)

1. D. vlan.dat is the database for VLANs configured on a switch either manually or through VTP. It is persistent even if config.text (startup-configuration) is deleted. You must manually delete vlan.dat. Upgrading the IOS will not delete vlan.dat. Typing **erase startup-config**, confirming it, and reloading will not remove the current vlan.dat. Typing **clear vlan** will not remove the current vlan.dat.

2. A. The normal usable VLAN range for Cisco is 1 through 1001. VLANS 1002 to 1005 are reserved for Fiber-Distributed Data Interface (FDDI) and Token Ring and cannot be deleted. The extended VLAN range is 1006 to 4096 and is used for Ethernet VLANs only.

3. C. The flexibility of design for workgroups of clients, servers, services, etc. and the ongoing management of moving and adding people is a benefit of a routed VLAN enabled network. Migrating from a flat layer 2 network to a routed layer 3 network will not increase collision domains for increased bandwidth. When you add a layer 3 routed infrastructure to your flat layer 2 network, the network complexity of design and operation will increase. You will increase the number of broadcast domains for increased bandwidth when you add multiple routed VLANs.

4. C. The switchport is configured as a trunk, but since the computer was originally in VLAN 1 and the native VLAN of the interface is VLAN 1 by default, all traffic untagged was directed to the native VLAN. The command switchport nonegotiate will prevent the switchport from generating Dynamic Trunking Protocol (DTP) packets but will not prevent it from statically being assigned as a trunk link. The switchport will not form a trunk because the client is not configured to tag packets with 802.1q VLANs. Spanning-tree prevents switching loops and does not assist in tagging packets or directing data onto VLANs.

5. C. The extended VLAN range is VLAN 1006 to 4094. The normal usable VLAN range for Cisco is 1 through 1001. VLANS 1002 to 1005 are reserved for Fiber-Distributed Data Interface (FDDI) and Token Ring and cannot be deleted.

6. C. The command to delete VLAN 9 is no vlan 9 configured from a global configuration prompt. The command no vlan 9 configured from a VLAN prompt is incorrect. The commands delete vlan 9 and vlan 9 delete are incorrect.

7. D. Frames with MAC addresses that are not in the MAC address table are flooded only to the ports in the respective VLAN. Broadcast frames will not be sent outside of the VLAN they originate from because they cannot traverse a router. Unicast frames are not flooded to all ports in all VLANs; they are only flooded to all ports in the VLAN the frame has originated from. The ports that link switches together are usually trunk links so that multiple VLANs can traverse the connection.

8. D. The normal range of VLANs on a default Cisco switch is VLAN 1 to 1001. However, VLAN 1 cannot be modified, so option D is the correct answer. All other options are incorrect.

9. C. Static VLANs are VLANs that have been manually configured versus dynamic VLANs that are configured via a VLAN Membership Policy Server (VMPS). A node will not know which VLAN it is assigned to when it is statically set via the command `switchport access vlan 3`. Nodes use a VMPS if the VLAN is dynamically configured. Nodes are not assigned VLANs based on their MAC addresses when they are statically configured. All nodes are not necessarily in the same VLAN when static VLANs are being used.

10. D. The addition of another VLAN will increase the effective bandwidth by adding additional broadcast domains. A router is required to route between VLANs. However, it will not be required if you are logically partitioning the switch via VLANs. The switch will not necessarily increase the count of collision domains.

11. B. When adding VLANs, you immediately increase the number of broadcast domains. At the same time, you increase collision domains. If a switch had 12 ports and they all negotiated at 100 Mb/s half-duplex (one collision domain), when a VLAN is added you will automatically create two collision domains while adding an additional broadcast domain.

12. C. Dynamic VLANs are deprecated, but you may still see them in operations. A switch configured with dynamic VLANs checks a VLAN Management Policy Server (VMPS) when clients plug in. The VMPS has a list of MAC addresses to their respective VLANs. It is now recommended that dynamic VLAN installations are converted to 802.1x. The access port cannot be controlled with a VMPS based on user credentials. The access port is also not switched into the respective VLAN based on the computer's IP address, because the IP address is normally associated based on the VLAN. The access port cannot be switched into a respective VLAN based on ACLs since ACLs are used to restrict layer 3 traffic and not layer 2 traffic.

13. D. To verify a VLAN name change, you would use the command `show vlan id 3`. This would only show you the one VLAN configured in the database. The command `show vlans` is incorrect because the command is not plural; it is singular, `show vlan`. It will give you a complete listing of all VLANs. Performing a `show interface vlan 3` would not display the friendly name. The command `show run` will not display the VLAN database unless the switch is configured in transparent mode.

14. D. When the MTU is changed on the VLAN, it has little consequence to normal MTU communications. However, if you are going to utilize the new MTU for something like iSCSI, it must be supported end to end or it can actually decrease performance. All switching equipment between the two end devices must support jumbo frames. Clients will not autodetect the new MTU in IPv4 and use jumbo frames; the client normally must be configured to use the new MTU. Configuring the MTU can be difficult because you must make sure that all devices end to end support the new MTU.

15. C. When layer 3 (routed VLANs) is implemented, it allows for a more secure network with the use of ACLs applied to the VLAN interface. A single VLAN spanning multiple switches is a benefit of implementing VLANs and not routed VLANs. When you implement VLANs, you will increase the number of broadcast domains.

16. C. The correct command is `switchport access vlan 9`. This command entered into the interface configuration prompt for the respective interface will place that interface in

VLAN 9. When you're configuring an interface for a VLAN, only the VLAN number can be used; therefore, the commands `switchport vlan research` and `switchport access vlan research` are incorrect. The command `switchport vlan 9` is also incorrect.

17. A. The `switchport voice vlan 4` command will configure the interface to switch traffic with a CoS value of 5 (set by the phone) to the voice VLAN of 4. The commands `switchport vlan voice 4`, `switchport voip vlan 4`, and `switchport access vlan 4 voice` are incorrect.

18. A. All VLAN tagging is removed from the frame before it egresses an access port to the end device. Trunk ports carry the VLAN tagging from end to end. Voice ports tag packets only when the CoS value is modified from the default. Native ports are used when frames arrive on a trunk and do not contain any tagging information.

19. C. The client computer connected to an access port cannot see any VLAN tagging information. It is removed before the frame egresses the interface. An access port cannot carry VLAN tagging information because it is stripped. The client computer cannot request the VLAN that it wants to operate in. The administrator must manually configure the VLAN. A client computer cannot see the VLAN tagging information because it is stripped out as it egresses an access port.

20. C. The command used to configure an access port for VLAN 8 is `switchport access vlan 8`, and the command to configure the VOIP phone is `switchport voice vlan 6`. The command combination of `switchport vlan 8` and `switchport vlan 6 voip` is incorrect. The command combination of `switchport mode access vlan 8` and `switchport voice vlan 6` is also incorrect. The command `switchport access vlan 8 voice 6` is incorrect.

21. D. The port is set up as a trunk. The phone is not misconfigured since the phone is normally configured for 801.Q tagging of CoS values, and it will work for this example. The computer is also not misconfigured; computers normally do not tag traffic for data. In this example, the communications will be directed to the native VLAN on the configured trunk. Configuring the command `switchport nonegotiate` will only prevent the port from participating in Dynamic Trunking Protocol (DTP), but either way, the port will remain a trunk because it is manually configured as one.

22. A. When you are configuring port security on an interface, the switchport should have a mode of access configured. This will also protect the switch from transitioning into a trunk if another switch is connected. There is no such mode as dynamic mode. If the interface is configured in trunk mode, port security will not be effective since many different MAC addresses can traverse the link. Voice mode is not a mode; it is a function of an access port that tags traffic when a CoS value is detected.

23. D. All switches are configured by default with all interfaces in VLAN 1. This simplifies configuration if the switch is to be used as a direct replacement for a hub since nothing needs to be configured. All of the other options are incorrect.

24. C. VLANs 1 and 1002 through 1005 are protected by the IOS and cannot be changed, renamed, or deleted. VLAN 1 cannot be deleted, regardless of whether it is still configured on a port. The VLAN that serves as the switch's main management IP can be changed to any other VLAN; it only defaults to VLAN 1 from the factory. VLAN 1 cannot be deleted regardless of whether it is configured as a native VLAN on a trunk.

25. D. For security concerns, it should not be used in production. It is the default VLAN configured on all switches. Potentially, a computer can be plugged into an interface defaulted to VLAN 1 and expose resources such as the switch management network. VLAN 1 can be used as a production VLAN, and by default, all switches are configured to use VLAN 1 right out of the box. VLAN 1 can also be routed the same as any other VLAN via an SVI. VLAN 1 can also participate in VTP transfers, although its name cannot be modified.

26. B. VLAN 1 is the default VLAN and it is not permitted by the IOS to change the VLAN in any way. This includes name changes. VLAN 1 cannot be renamed regardless of whether it is used on another interface currently. All VLANs are configured numerically in Cisco IOS; a friendly name can be attached after it is configured. VLAN 1 cannot be renamed regardless of which configuration prompt you are in.

27. C. The port needs to be changed from trunk mode to access mode via the command `switchport mode access`. Although `switchport native vlan 12` would remedy the problem, it would be an improper configuration since you are expecting tagged traffic and directing untagged traffic to VLAN 12. Removing `switchport nonegotiate` mode would only allow the computer to negotiate a trunking protocol via DTP. Configuring the command `no spanning-tree portfast` would prevent the port from forwarding traffic right away.

28. B. The command to verify that a VLAN is created and the port(s) it is associated with is `show vlan`. The command `show vlans` is incorrect as it should be singular. The commands `show access vlan` and `show vlan database` are incorrect because they are not valid commands.

29. B. When the command is invoked inside of the interface, it will create the VLAN automatically. The command will not error, but if you are consoled into the device or you are monitoring the terminal, you can see the VLAN get automatically created. When the VLAN is auto-created, traffic will forward without the need of any other configuration. The original command of `switch access vlan 12` will be accepted, and the VLAN will be auto-created.

30. A. Creating the new VLAN will logically segment this workgroup. Creating a switched virtual interface (SVI) will allow routing on the layer 3 switch. The ACLs should only be applied to VLAN interfaces. Although the other solutions achieve a similar goal, they do not provide flexibility. Extended ACLs cannot be applied to the R&D switchports since they are layer 2 ports and extended ACLs are layer 3 entries. Creating a new VLAN for R&D and placing the R&D server in the VLAN will not accomplish the goal of restricting the server. Creating a new VLAN and using a trunk to connect the production and R&D network will not accomplish the task.

31. A. The Cisco Discovery Protocol (CDP) is required for Cisco VoIP phones. It allows the switch to learn capabilities and power requirements. The command `spanning-tree portfast` allows the interface on the switch to forward frames as it recalculates the switching topology. The command `switchport nonegotiate` stops the switch from participating in Dynamic Trunking Protocol (DTP) negotiation. The interface does not need to be configured as a trunk port for a VoIP phone to work; an access port is recommended.

32. D. The command `show interfaces switchport` will display the detail of all ports in respect to VLAN operational status. The command will show the operational mode of the interface, such as trunk or access mode. The command `show vlan` will show all VLANs configured on the switch. Although the command `show running-config` will display the running configuration of the port, it will not display the status of the interface. The command `show interfaces` will not display the VLAN configured on the port.

33. D. The proper way to enable a VLAN to forward traffic is to first enter the VLAN database for ID 3 and then issue the `no shutdown` command. On some IOS versions, this can also be done via the command `no shutdown vlan 3` from global config mode. The command `enable vlan 3` configured in privilege exec mode is not a valid command. The command `enable vlan 3` configured in global configuration is not a valid command. Although the command `no shutdown vlan 3` is valid on some IOS versions, it must be configured from global configuration mode.

34. C. The command `show interfaces FastEthernet 0/3 switchport` will show the switchport details for only Fa0/3, to include its operational mode. This command is similar to `show interfaces switchport`, which will show all ports. The command `show interfaces` will not show the operation mode of only Fa0/3. The command `show interfaces status | i 0/3` will filter the results and only display the line with the matching text of 0/3. These lines will not give you the operational mode of the interface.

35. B. The VLAN is disabled from forwarding traffic as shown in the VLAN database. The `no shutdown vlan 5` must be performed in global config. The VLAN interface being shut down would have no effect on traffic being forwarded on the VLAN, only routed. If the guest ports are associated with the proper VLAN in the figure, routing will function as normal. There could be a problem elsewhere, but the figure shows the VLAN as shut down.

36. A. You should first create the VLAN in the VLAN database and add its name. These actions should be performed on the VTP server when multiple switches are installed in the network. Then you need to enter the interface and configure the port for the VLAN. All other options are incorrect.

37. B. VLAN 4 is an active VLAN. However, it has not been given a name, so the default name is VLAN0004. The VLAN is not shut down as it has a status of active. The VLAN could have been created on a non-Cisco switch. However, the figure is from a Cisco switch, and the friendly name is not configured. VLANs cannot be suspended, only shut down, which is clearly not the problem in the figure.

38. B. You must manually configure the VLAN on the Cisco switch(s). VTP is a protocol that allows for VLAN autoconfiguration in the VLAN database. However, only Cisco switches support it. Setting the correct trunking protocol between the switches will help guarantee VLANs can traverse between switches. Configuring VTP is only possible on Cisco switches because it is a proprietary protocol. Assigning the VLAN to an interface on the other switch will not fix the problem.

39. B. When a VLAN is created, so is a broadcast domain. The broadcast domain/VLAN requires its own unique IP network addressing and a router to route between the networks. Therefore, you need a router for inter-VLAN communications. The VLANs will automatically be in a no shutdown mode when they are configured initially. The VLANs do not require VTP to be configured, although it is helpful. The interfaces associated with VLANs are automatically in a no shutdown mode.

40. C. The command show ip interface brief will display only the necessary information of interface, IP, and status to aid in the diagnostic process. The commands show ip interface, show interface, and show interface brief are incorrect.

41. B. Switch A and Switch B are participating in VLAN tagging. Therefore, Switch A interface Gi0/1 and Switch B interface Gi0/1 are both configured as trunk switchports. This will allow VLAN tagging across the trunk link. Switch A interface Gi0/1 cannot be configured as an access switchport because tagging of VLANs between switches would not occur. Switch B interface Fa0/1 shows no sign of being configured with a duplicate VLAN ID. Switch A interface Fa0/3 shows no sign of being configured with a duplicate VLAN ID.

42. B. Since the Dell switch cannot support the proprietary protocol of InterSwitch Link (ISL), both switches need to be set up to use 802.1Q. Although both switches need to have duplicate VLAN configurations, that will not prevent them from creating a trunk between themselves. VTP cannot be configured on both of the switches because VTP is a Cisco proprietary protocol.

43. B. The command show interfaces trunk will display all of the configured trunks on the switch. The commands show interfaces brief, show switchport trunk, and show switchport brief are incorrect.

44. A. All switches are configured by default as a VTP server. A switch configured as a client will receive and process VTP packets from a VTP server. A switch configured as transparent will not participate in VTP but will allow VTP to be forwarded to other switches. There is no such mode as master with VTP.

45. B. The command to display the mode settings for VTP is show vtp status. The commands show vtp, show vtp counters, and show running-config are incorrect.

46. B. When setting up VTP on a new switch connected to your existing VTP infrastructure, you need to change the mode of the switch. Then you must configure the VTP domain that is serving the VTP information. The transparent mode for VTP will not allow the switch to participate in VTP processing. Setting the VTP domain alone will not allow the switch to participate in VTP because it must be switched to the mode of client as well. The command vtp corpname is not a valid command.

47. C. The command switchport trunk allowed vlan remove 2-4 will remove VLANs 2 through 4 from the trunk. The commands switchport trunk remove vlan 2-4, switchport remove vlan 2-4, and switchport trunk allowed remove vlan 2-4 are incorrect.

48. D. The command `switchport trunk allowed vlan all` will restore the allowed VLAN list back to default. The commands `no switchport trunk allowed`, `no switchport trunk allowed all`, and `no switchport trunk allowed 1-4096` are incorrect.

49. A. The command `switchport trunk allowed vlan add 4` will add VLAN 4 to the existing list of VLANs already allowed on the interface. The commands `add allowed vlan 4`, `switchport trunk add vlan 4`, and `switchport trunk allowed add vlan 4` are incorrect.

50. C. The command will not complete because the interface is set to dynamic auto, which implies the trunk protocol will be negotiated. You cannot configure it with `switchport mode trunk` until you statically set the encapsulation via the command `switchport trunk encapsulation dot1q`. The commands `switchport mode trunk manual`, `no switchport mode dynamic auto`, and `no switchport trunk encapsulation auto` are incorrect.

51. B. VLAN Trunking Protocol (VTP) propagates the VLAN database from an initial master copy on the "server" to all of the "clients." VTP does not help facilitate the dynamic trunking between links. VTP does not detect trunk encapsulation and negotiate trunks. VTP allows for the propagation of the VLAN database, not the trunking database.

52. B. A switch in VTP transparent mode will not participate in VTP. However, if the VTP is v2, the switch will forward and receive VTP advertisements. The VTP server mode allows the switch to act as a master for the VTP domain. VTP proxy mode is not a real mode; therefore, it is incorrect. The VTP client mode allows the switch to act as a slave to the master server.

53. D. Both switches have a native VLAN mismatch. Since Switch B has an inactive VLAN, it would be recommended to change the native VLAN back to 1 on Switch B. When VLAN pruning is enabled, it will not affect traffic between switches. Both switches show that a link has been enabled with 802.1Q; therefore, there are no incompatibility issues.

54. B. VTP VLAN pruning removes forwarding traffic for VLANs that are not configured on remote switches. This saves bandwidth on trunks because if the remote switch does not have the VLAN configured on it, the frame destined for the VLAN will not traverse the trunk. VTP VLAN pruning does not remove VLANs from the database of other switches. VTP VLAN pruning also does not automatically change the allowed VLANs on interfaces.

55. B. The command `vtp pruning` in global configuration mode will enable VTP VLAN pruning. The commands `vtp mode pruning` and `vtp vlan pruning` are incorrect. The command `enable pruning` is an incorrect command when it is configured in a VLAN configuration prompt.

56. A. VTP pruning needs to be configured only on the VTP server. The clients will receive the update and turn on VTP pruning automatically. If VTP pruning is turned on at the VTP client, the setting will be ignored since the client is a slave to the master server. If the VTP pruning is configured on a VTP transparent, the configuration will be ignored since VTP transparent switches do not participate in VTP with other switches. VTP pruning only needs to be configured on the VTP server; all clients will receive the necessary configuration from the VTP server.

57. B. The VLAN is not allowed over the trunk because of the `switchport trunk allowed vlan 4,6,12,15` command. The native VLAN is used when frames are not tagged, and the problem states that traffic in the same VLAN is not being forwarded. The trunk encapsulation is set to 802.1Q, which is the default for many switches. Also, if encapsulation was not set properly, no traffic would be forwarded. VTP is not required for switching operation, although it is helpful.

58. D. The Dynamic Trunking Protocol can be turned off with the command `switchport nonegotiate`, which when configured states not to negotiate trunks via DTP. The commands `no dtp`, `no switchport dtp enable`, and `switchport dtp disable` are incorrect.

59. A. Switch B will need to have its interface set to either `switchport mode trunk` or `switchport mode dynamic desirable` for Switch A to turn its interface into a trunk. The commands `switchport mode dynamic trunk` and `switchport mode dynamic auto` are incorrect. The command `switchport nonegotiate` is incorrect as it will never negotiate a trunking protocol.

60. D. On Switch A, DTP is turned on and the encapsulation is set to 802.1Q. However, on Switch B, DTP is turned off and ISL encapsulation is manually set. Switch B will need to have 802.1Q configured in order to have trunking complete. Both Switch A and Switch B have their interfaces set to trunk mode already. DTP is running on Switch A, since the mode is set to auto in the figure. All VLANs do not need to be allowed first for trunking to happen.

61. A. Inter-Switch Link (ISL) is a proprietary protocol used for trunking of switches. If you need to connect non-Cisco switches to a Cisco switch, you must use 802.1Q, the IEEE standard. VTP is not a trunking protocol; it assists in populating VLANs across Cisco switches for conformity and ease of configuration. Cisco Discovery Protocol (CDP) is not a trunking protocol either; it negotiates power by communicating its capabilities with neighboring devices. It also allows for neighbor discovery, but CDP is proprietary to Cisco, so only Cisco devices can communicate.

62. C. 802.1Q inserts a field containing the 16-bit Tag Protocol ID of 0x8100, a 3-bit CoS field, a 1-bit drop-eligible indicator (used with CoS), and the 12=bit VLAN ID, which equals 32 bits, or 4 bytes. All of the other options are incorrect.

63. A. You must first set the encapsulation to 802.1Q, then you can statically set the mode to trunk. An alternative would be to set the port to `dynamic desirable` via the command `switchport mode dynamic desirable`. However, it is recommended to statically configure the link to trunk on one or both sides if possible. Configuring both sides with `switchport mode dynamic auto` will result in the negotiation of an access link. Turning DTP off by using the command `switchport nonegotiate` will result in an access link. The correct command to set encapsulation is `switchport trunk encapsulation dot1q`, not `switchport encapsulation dot1q`.

64. C. Native VLANs are only used for traffic that is not tagged, in which untagged frames are placed on a trunk link. A common use for native VLANs is management traffic between switches before both sides are configured as a trunk. Traffic that is tagged will traverse the trunk link and not use the native VLAN. Native VLANs are not used for disallowed VLANs on a trunk link. Any traffic that is tagged with ISL on an 802.1Q trunk will not be distinguishable on either side since the frame will be mismatched.

65. D. The switch is set up with a VTP mode of transparent. When a switch is set up with a mode of transparent, the VLAN information is stored in the `running-config` in lieu of the `vlan.dat` file. This is not the default mode of a switch; out of the box it is configured as a VTP server. The switch is not set up as a VTP client or server since the VLAN configuration is visible in the `running-config`.

66. B. If you issue the command `switchport nonegotiate`, the switch will not send Dynamic Trunking Protocol (DTP) frames for trunk negotiation. The default configuration for a port is the mode of access, so the port will remain an access port. This means the switchport will not transition to a trunk port, and it will remain an access port. The interface will not shut down, but it will be mismatched and not carry any tagged VLANs. The switchport will not enter an `err-disable` state.

67. A. Switch A must change its interface to an access port with the `switchport mode access` command, which will force Switch A's interface to remain an access port. Then you configure the access VLAN of 5 on Switch A with the `switchport access vlan 5` command. Configuring the port with the mode of a trunk on either switch will prevent the port from performing as an access port for VLAN 5. If you tried to configure this with a native VLAN, it would result in a native VLAN mismatch and improper configuration.

68. D. The command `switchport mode dynamic desirable` is similar to `switchport mode dynamic auto` with the exception that it is desirable to become a trunk. So if the neighboring port is set to auto, desirable, or trunk, it becomes a trunk.

69. A. The command `switchport mode dynamic auto` will cause the port to remain an access port if the neighboring port is configured the same. If both sides are configured with `switchport mode dynamic auto`, then the port will become an access link. If you configure the neighboring port as a trunk, it will become a trunk. If the native VLAN is changed, it will have no effect over the selection of switchport mode.

70. C. The command `show interfaces switchport` will show greater detail about the trunk than the command `show interfaces trunk`. Alternatively, you can specify a single port using the command `show interfaces Fa 0/5 switchport`, for example. The commands `show interfaces trunk detail`, `show switchport`, and `show running-config` are not similar.

71. B. When you configure the switchport to a mode of access, you are statically configuring the interface to remain an access switchport. When you configure the switchport to `nonegotiate`, you are turning off Dynamic Trunking Protocol (DTP). The switch will never negotiate its switchport. If the interface mode is specifically set with the command `switchport mode access`, it will never become a trunk. Regardless of what is plugged into the interface, the command `switchport mode access` will configure it as an access port.

72. B. The command to specify 802.1Q encapsulation on a trunk interface is `switchport trunk encapsulation 802.1q`. The commands `switchport mode trunk 802.1q`, `switchport 802.1q`, and `switchport encapsulation trunk 802.1q` are incorrect.

73. D. This error is very common when configuring Cisco switches since many switches only support 802.1Q and configuration is not necessary. The ISL trunking protocol is not supported on certain platforms, such as the older 2900 series switches. It is safe to assume that Cisco switches at minimum will support 802.1Q encapsulation, but ISL trunking protocol is usually a feature that must be added or purchased.

74. C. When a frame traverses a trunk and does not have VLAN tagging information in the 802.1Q encapsulation format (untagged), it is sent to the native VLAN configured on the trunk. This behavior is to prevent the untagged frame from being dropped. The terminology of default VLAN does not pertain to trunks. The default VLAN is the *default* VLAN configured on an access port. An untagged frame is only sent to the native VLAN and not the first VLAN ID configured on the trunk.

75. C. The 802.1Q protocol is supported by all switches' vendors for trunking. It is an open standard that was developed by the IEEE. Cisco Inter-Switch Link (ISL) is a proprietary protocol for trunking. VLAN Trunk Protocol (VTP) helps reduce configuration and maintenance of VLANs on Cisco switches. 802.1X is a security protocol used per port to allow and deny traffic based on credentials.

76. C. When implementing router on a stick (ROAS), you must first create a trunk to the router. Once the trunk is created, you must create subinterfaces for each VLAN to be routed and specify the IP address and 802.1Q encapsulation. A virtual interface is an interface that is configured inside of the IOS software and does not have a physical presence, such as a loopback interface. A switched virtual interface is a type of virtual interface inside of the IOS that allows for configuration of the traffic in the respective VLAN. The VLAN database is only kept on the switches and the router does not receive a copy.

77. B. An 802.1Q frame is a modified Ethernet frame. The type field is relocated after the 4 bytes used for 802.1Q tagging. Two of the bytes are used for tagging the frame, and 2 of the bytes are used for controls such as Class of Service (CoS). All of the other options are incorrect.

78. A. The default VLAN for all switches is VLAN 1. It is the default configuration for all access ports from the factory. A native VLAN is the VLAN that untagged frames are switched onto if the frames are received on a trunk. A default VLAN is not configured on all trunks for tagged frames. A native VLAN is not configured on all trunks for tagged frames.

79. C. The command `show interface fastethernet 0/15 switchport` will show the operational mode, and if configured as a trunk, it will show the native VLAN. The command `show running-config` is incorrect, as it will show all the interfaces. The command `show interface fastethernet 0/15` is incorrect as it will not show the native VLAN information. The command `show switchport fastethernet 0/15` is incorrect.

80. A. The command to change the native VLAN of a trunk to VLAN 999 is `switchport trunk native vlan 999`. The commands `native vlan 999` and `switchport` native vlan 999 are incorrect. Negating the command with no switchport native vlan 1 and then configuring switchport native vlan 999 is incorrect.

81. B. This error is normal if it is the first interface to be changed over to the new native VLAN since the other interface has not been changed yet. However, if the other interface was changed already and you received this error, then CDP is letting you know that the other side is mismatched. CDP must be running on both sides of the trunk; therefore, you would not see this error if it was disabled on either side. If the interfaces were running mismatched trunking protocols, a different error would be seen. The version of CDP on the other switch will not prompt the error of native VLAN mismatch.

82. D. The problems will not be apparent since the trunk will still function for tagged traffic. However, any traffic that is not tagged will be directed to the opposite side's native VLAN. So traffic expected for VLAN 1 will be directed to VLAN 10, and VLAN 10 traffic will be directed to VLAN 1 when the traffic is not tagged. Both CDP and VTP will continue to function over the trunk link. The misconfiguration will not allow any more broadcasts than normal over the trunk to Switch B.

83. B. Cisco Discovery Protocol (CDP) will alert you to a native VLAN mismatch. You will receive the error %CDP-4-NATIVE_VLAN_MISMATCH: Native VLAN mismatch discovered.... When a trunk is configured, the native VLAN is always used for CDP exchanges. VLAN Trunk Protocol (VTP) helps reduce configuration and maintenance of VLANs on Cisco switches. Cisco Inter-Switch Link (ISL) is a proprietary protocol for trunking. The 802.1Q protocol is a trunking protocol developed by the IEEE.

84. C. VLAN 1002 is reserved for use with an FDDI VLAN and not allowed for Ethernet traffic. All Ethernet traffic must be a VLAN between 1 to 1001. You cannot use 1002 to 1005 because they are used for legacy applications. The native VLAN does not need to be VLAN 1. The native VLAN can be an extended VLAN; however, this is not the problem.

85. B. Link Layer Discovery Protocol (LLDP) is an IEEE standard of 802.1ab. Most Cisco devices can perform LLDP, but it must be configured. The Cisco Discovery Protocol (CDP) is a proprietary protocol used to communicate neighbor devices' identities and capabilities. The IEEE 802.1a and 802.1b protocols are defunct protocols used for LAN management.

86. D. The command to turn off CDP globally on a switch is no cdp run. The commands cdp disable, no cdp enable, and no cdp are incorrect.

87. B. CDP frames are sent out all active interfaces every 60 seconds. All of the other options are incorrect.

88. C. Cisco Discovery Protocol (CDP) is a Cisco proprietary protocol used for gathering information from neighboring switches and routers. Link Layer Discovery Protocol (LLDP) is also called 802.1ab, which is an IEEE standard and performs identical functionality to CDP. 802.1a is a defunct IEEE protocol used for LAN management.

89. D. The default holddown timer for CDP entries is three times the advertisement timer of 60 seconds. So entries have a holddown timer value of 180 seconds. All of the other options are incorrect.

90. B. To turn off or suppress CDP advertisements on a single interface, you would enter the interface and enter the command no cdp enable. The commands cdp disable, no cdp, and no cdp run are incorrect.

91. D. The sh cdp entry * command will give output that's identical to that of the show cdp neighbors detail command. The commands sh cdp neighbors all, sh cdp neighbors *, and sh cdp entries all are incorrect.

92. B. The command lldp run entered in global config mode will enable LLDP on all interfaces. When enabled, LLDP-MED, or LLDP for Media, will read capabilities on the phone such as name and power level. The command in option A, lldp run, is incorrect as it needs to be configured in global configuration mode. The command lldp enable is incorrect, regardless of where it is configured.

93. C. The command show lldp neighbor detail will show output similar to the output of show cdp neighbor detail, but it will only include LLDP neighbors. The commands show lldp, show lldp devices, and show cdp neighbor detail are incorrect.

94. A. The default LLDP advertisement interval is 30 seconds. When turned on, it will advertise out all active interfaces every 30 seconds. All of the other options are incorrect.

95. B. When you use the command no lldp transmit, it will suppress LLDP messages from exiting the interface it is configured on. The commands no lldp, no lldp receive, and no lldp enable are incorrect.

96. D. The default value of the LLDP holddown timer for entries is 120 seconds. This holddown timer is set every time the switch hears an advertisement for a device. The holddown is four times the advertisement interval. All of the other options are incorrect.

97. C. Switch B is connected to Switch A via Gi0/2. Switch A Gi0/1 is the adjacent interface connecting the two switches. The holddown timer for this entry is at 162 seconds; it was not last seen 162 seconds ago. The IP address of Switch A is 192.168.1.1.

98. D. The command no cdp enable will turn off CDP advertisements on the interface that you configure it on. The commands cdp disable, no cdp, and no cdp disable are incorrect.

99. B. The command show cdp interface will display all of the interfaces CDP is enabled on along with their advertisement intervals. The command show cdp is incorrect as it will only show the timers for CDP. The commands show interface and show interface cdp are incorrect.

100. B. EtherChannel can aggregate 2 interfaces to 8 interfaces together on a single switch when using Port Aggregation Protocol (PAgP). All of the other options are incorrect.

101. D. When EtherChannel bonds interfaces together, they act as a single Ethernet link. Therefore, layer 2 and layer 3 see it as a single link. EtherChannel works independently of 802.1Q and does not block redundant links. EtherChannel can aggregate multiple links, but the links must have the same speed. EtherChannel cannot aggregate interfaces across multiple stand-alone switches.

102. A. The highest configurable bandwidth is going to be 2 Gb/s. This is because you cannot mix speeds and duplex settings. Therefore, 2.6 Gb/s is not possible, but 400 Mb/s is possible using four 100 Mb/s Fast Ethernet ports.

103. A. The Link Aggregation Control Protocol (LACP) is the IEEE standard 802.3ad. 802.1Q is an IEEE standard for VLAN trunking. The Port Aggregation Protocol (PAgP) is a Cisco-proprietary protocol used for port aggregation. 802.1X is a security protocol used with Ethernet ports.

104. B. LACP is an IEEE standard that is supported by non-Cisco devices to create aggregation links and negotiate the configuration. EtherChannel is a proprietary aggregation protocol that is also called PAgP. *Channel Group* is a configuration term used with Cisco for port aggregation.

105. C. EtherChannel can aggregate 2 interfaces to 16 interfaces together on a single switch when using LACP. Only eight ports can be used at any one time; the others are placed in standby mode. All of the other options are incorrect.

106. C. If you configure the EtherChannel to on mode, it forces the aggregation of links without the use of a control protocol. All of the other options are incorrect configurations.

107. A. The term *EtherChannel* is a Cisco-centric term. Most vendors will not recognize the term. PAgP is a Cisco-proprietary protocol used for port aggregation. LACP is an open standard for port aggregation. PAgP and LACP cannot bundle links with varying speeds and duplexes together.

108. C. The Port Aggregation Protocol (PAgP) is a Cisco-proprietary control negotiation protocol. LACP is an open standard for port aggregation. 802.1Q is an IEEE standard for VLAN trunking. 802.1ab is an IEEE standard that defines LLDP.

109. A. PAgP sends control notifications every 30 seconds to the adjacent switch. All of the other options are incorrect.

110. A. Using active mode on both sides ensures that the switches will start negotiation with only Link Aggregation Control Protocol (LACP). A configuration of passive mode on both sides will not form an LACP aggregation. Auto and desirable mode only pertain to PAgP.

111. C. When you use passive on one side and active on the other side of a port channel, the result is that Link Aggregation Control Protocol (LACP) will be used. *Passive* and *active* are synonymous with LACP configuration; therefore, PAgP is not configured with this terminology. EtherChannel is a Cisco term related to PAgP.

112. A. The command show etherchannel will display all EtherChannels on the switch along with their negotiated protocols. The command show port-channel is incorrect, as it is missing the summary argument. The command show interface is incorrect; it will show interface statistics. The command show run is incorrect; it will show the running configuration.

113. B. Since both interfaces are set to passive mode, neither side will initiate the LACP control notifications. Although the port channel is configured on the switch, it is not communicated between the switches. *Passive* and *active* are synonymous with LACP configuration; therefore, PAgP is not configured with this terminology. A port channel will not be unconditionally formed because both sides are set to passive and will not communicate with LACP.

114. D. When both sides of the port channel are configured with the on mode, an unconditional port channel is created. This means there is no control protocol assisting the port channel. The on mode is configured when you do not want to use a control protocol; therefore, PAgP and LACP will not be used.

115. C. The original version of STP was created by Digital Equipment Corporation (DEC). The IEEE ratified the specification of STP as 802.1D in 1990. 802.1X is the IEEE standard for port security that requires end devices authenticate before traffic will be allowed to pass. 802.1w is the IEEE standard for Rapid Spanning Tree Protocol (RSTP). 802.1s is the IEEE standard for Multiple Spanning Tree Protocol (MST).

116. B. Spanning Tree Protocol runs as a distributed process on each switch. Each switch creates and maintains its own topology database referencing and electing the root bridge. STP does not use routing protocols because it is a layer 2 protocol. STP uses bridge frames to check for switching loops.

117. A. STP monitors all interfaces for BPDUs, which carry switches' identities. When it sees the same switch ID in BPDUs on multiple interfaces, a redundant link is detected. STP will not listen to normal traffic frames or CDP on multiple interfaces. The STP protocol is only concerned with BPDUs since they are only generated by switches that can cause loops. STP can run independently on several different VLANs.

118. B. The original STP specification was revamped in 2004 with RSTP 802.1w. This revamping of STP was to fix problems with the original specification. 802.1X is the IEEE standard for port security that requires end devices to authenticate before traffic will be allowed to pass. 802.1s is the IEEE standard for Multiple Spanning Tree Protocol (MST). The original version of STP is the 802.1D IEEE specification.

119. D. The link cost is a numeric value that represents the cost in speed of a link. The higher the numbers, the lower the speed of the link, thus a higher cost. The link cost is not related to the latency of the frame traversing the link. The link cost is not a calculation of all the ports in the path to the root bridge; this is considered the path cost, not the link cost. There is also no monetary cost associated with a link because it pertains to STP link cost.

120. B. The RSTP path cost is the calculation of all of the link costs that lead back to the root bridge. The link cost is a numeric value that signifies the speed. The lower the cost, the higher the speed of the link. The path cost is not related to the latency of the frame traversing the link. There is also no monetary cost associated with a link because it pertains to STP link cost. The path cost is not a numeric value associated with the speed of a link; this would be the link cost, not the path cost.

121. B. Per-VLAN Spanning Tree+ (PVST+) elects a root bridge for each VLAN and creates a topology table for each VLAN. It is a Cisco-proprietary protocol due to the bridge ID calculation it must perform for each VLAN. The IEEE 802.1w specification details Rapid Spanning Tree Protocol (RSTP). The Common Spanning Tree (CST) protocol assumes one Spanning Tree instance for all VLANs. RSTP is the Spanning Tree Protocol that has superseded the original Spanning Tree Protocol.

122. A. Rapid Per-VLAN Spanning Tree+ elects a root bridge for each VLAN. It allows for fast convergence times and logical placement of the root bridge. However, it requires the most CPU and RAM of all implementations. Per VLAN Spanning Tree (PVST) operates similar to PVST+; however, it transmits 802.1D BPDUs. The Common Spanning Tree protocol assumes one Spanning Tree instance for all VLANs. There is no protocol called the RSTP+ protocol; therefore, it is an invalid answer.

123. B. Common Spanning Tree (CST) elects a single root bridge for the entire network and all of the VLANs. This creates a problem when the center of your network may vary upon VLAN placement. CST is a variant of STP; therefore, it has slower convergence times. CST should not be used in really large networks because the root switch for the various VLANs may be in different locations on the network. CST elects only one root bridge for all VLANs, which could cause a problem.

124. B. RSTP has three transition modes and converges faster than STP, which is 50 seconds. It is, however, backward compatible with STP 802.1D. RSTP by itself does not allow for multiple root bridges; however, the extension of Rapid PVST will allow for multiple root bridges. RSTP has an extremely fast convergence time, and STP has a convergence time of 50 seconds. STP has five port states to which an interface could possibly transition; RTSP has only three port states.

125. B. Each switch is responsible for sensing changes to the topology; it is not the sole responsibility of the root bridge. Whenever the topology changes, a topology change notification (TCN) is sent out all root ports and an acknowledgment is sent back. This happens until the root bridge sends back a notification. The root bridge does not poll each switch participating in STP for changes, and the switches participating in STP do not poll the root bridge for changes.

126. B. 802.1s, which is called Multiple Spanning Tree (MST), is a standard based on PVST+. It is an open standard created by the IEEE that will allow Per-VLAN Spanning in multivendor switched networks. 802.1X is the IEEE standard for port security that requires end devices to authenticate before traffic will be allowed to pass. The original IEEE specification of STP (802.1D) was revamped in 2004 with RSTP 802.1w. This revamping of STP was to fix problems with the original specification.

127. B. The switch with the MAC address of 0011.03ae.d8aa will become the root bridge. Its MAC address is the lowest of the four switches. All of the other options are incorrect.

128. D. All Cisco switches are defaulted to the Cisco-proprietary STP protocol extension of Rapid PVST+. 802.1D is the original IEEE specification for STP. 802.1w is the IEEE specification for RSTP. PVST+ is the Cisco-proprietary protocol extension for STP.

129. D. An alternate port is a port that is in a discarding state. If the root port fails on the switch with the alternate port, then the alternate port becomes the root port for that switch.

An alternate port is used only if the root bridge fails; it will not allow for an alternate path on a non-root bridge. An alternate port cannot replace a designated port if it fails. An alternate port is never placed in a forwarding state.

130. C. The root bridge is elected by all of the switches and has the lowest MAC address and priority of all the switches in the network. The root bridge is not elected based on a high or low IP address. Spanning Tree can function without an IP address, since it is a layer 2 loop avoidance.

131. A. The root bridge is a point of perspective for the rest of the STP network. It is important to have a point of perspective to calculate which ports are blocked and which remain in a forwarding mode. The root bridge has no influence on the forwarding decisions of frames. Each switch is responsible for its own calculation of STP; only the root bridge election is the consensus of all switches in the network.

132. C. The bridge ID is made up of a 2-byte bridge priority and a 6-byte MAC address for a total of 8 bytes. All of the other options are incorrect.

133. A. A designated port is a port that has the lowest cost compared to the higher cost of the redundant ports. It is placed into a forwarding state for a network segment. A designated port is determined to have the lowest cost, and not the highest cost, when it is placed into a forwarding state. A port that has the lowest cost to the root bridge is a root port and not a designated port. A port that has the highest cost to the root bridge is placed into a blocking state.

134. A. Every switch in the network segment must have at least one root port. This is the port that leads back to the root bridge. The root bridge will have a designated port on the adjacent link. Every switch will have an active link back to the root bridge; however, those ports leading back the root bridge are called root ports. A network may not have any alternate ports, depending on the topology and layout of the network. A network may not have any backup ports for the same reasons.

135. C. The root port is the port that leads back to the root bridge on the adjacent switch. It has the lowest cost of the redundant ports. A root port is determined to have the lowest cost to the root bridge, not a network segment. Root ports are always determined to have the lowest cost, not the highest cost.

136. A. The designated port is the port with the lowest cost of the redundant links to the network segment. The adjacent port is normally the root port leading back to the root bridge. A port that is determined to have the lowest cost or path cost to the root bridge is called the root port and not a designated port. The designated port will always have the lowest cost to a network segment, not the highest cost.

137. C. The PVST+ bridge ID comprises a 4-bit bridge priority calculated in blocks of 4096, a 12-bit sys-ext-id that is the VLAN ID for the segment, and a 6-byte MAC address for the switch. All of the other options are incorrect.

138. C. The default bridge priority for STP is 32,768. All of the other options are incorrect.

139. D. The root bridge always has all of its ports in a designated mode or forwarding mode. If there are redundant links, the adjacent switch to the designated port on the root bridge must be a nondesignated or blocking state. A designated port is always in a forwarding state. Every switch will not have at least one designated port; it is safe to say that every switch will have at least one port in a forwarding mode. Every switch will not have at least one nondesignated port since a switch might only have one link back to the root bridge.

140. A. A backup port is a port in a discarding state. It receives BPDUs from another port on the same switch. If the forwarding port fails, then the backup port will become designated so that connectivity to the segment can be restored. A backup port is another port on the same switch that receives BPDUs from itself. A backup port is placed into a blocking state and not a forwarding state.

141. D. 802.1D STP convergence takes 50 seconds to complete before the port is put into a state of forwarding or blocking. This is dependent on the STA, or spanning-tree algorithm. All of the other options are incorrect.

142. C. When a computer is connected to an STP-enabled interface, the port will transition between blocking, listening, learning, and forwarding. The time between the states of blocking and forwarding is called the convergence and is 50 seconds. Spanning Tree PortFast operates in a forwarding, listening, learning, and then possibly blocking state. All of the other options are incorrect.

143. C. An STP blocked port will block all frames from being forwarded. The blocking excludes BPDUs, which it will continue to listen for and calculate future topology decisions. When a port is in a blocking state, it will block all frames whether or not they are redundant, excluding BPDUs.

144. D. RSTP has three transitions when a computer is plugged in (no loops). The transitions are discarding, learning, and forwarding, which allow for rapid convergence times. All of the other options are incorrect.

145. A. RSTP has three port states: discarding, learning, and forwarding. Blocking and listening are both mapped to discarding in RSTP. When a port is in a state of discarding, it means the interface is discarding all frames except for BPDUs. A port in a learning state will learn incoming BPDUs to calculate redundant links. A port in a forwarding state will forward all packets as expected. A backup port is a port on the same network segment as another port on the same switch; this allows communication from the network segment if the designated port fails.

146. D. The new port state that RSTP has is discarding, which replaces the blocking state of STP. Learning in RSTP is the same as the learning state in STP. The forwarding state in RSTP is the same as the forwarding state in STP. The blocking state is not found in RSTP; it is found in STP.

147. D. The command `spanning-tree portfast` entered into the interface will turn on PortFast mode. This will allow the interface to forward first. The commands no `switchport spanning-tree`, `switchport spanning-tree portfast`, and `spanning-tree portfast default` are incorrect.

148. B. PortFast should only be configured on access links where end devices are plugged in because these devices will not typically create loops in the switch topology. If PortFast is configured on a trunk port, you have a very high risk of creating a loop if there is a mis-configuration on the switch being introduced. Voice ports have a lower probability of a network loop, but voice ports are usually connected to VoIP phones with built-in switches that can be looped. Designated ports are ports that are adjacent to a root port on the opposite switch that leads back to the root port.

149. B. This command turns on PortFast globally for only access ports on the switch. This command should be used on access switches because end devices are connected at this level in the hierarchy. The command `spanning-tree portfast default` is used to configure PortFast globally. This command does not turn off Spanning Tree for any ports.

150. A. You will create a temporary switching loop until the BPDUs are heard from each interface over the hub. However, during this period you will have a switching loop and degrade traffic over the entire switching topology until convergence happens. This is risky because the CPU could spike to 100% and not be able to detect the BPDUs and the loops will continue. With PortFast configured, the ports will not enter an `err-disable` state; they will forward traffic until the network connection is fully saturated with bandwidth. The port will not disable itself via Spanning Tree since the port transitions between forwarding, listening, learning, and then possibly changing into a blocking mode.

151. A. BPDU Guard will turn the interface to `err-disable` as soon as a BPDU is heard on the interface. This feature should be enabled on access switches when configuring PortFast. There is no feature called BPDU Detection. Loop Guard is used in conjunction with BPDU Guard for additional protection by monitoring and tracking BPDUs. UplinkFast is a Cisco-proprietary feature that improves convergence times for Spanning Tree.

152. A. PortFast mode allows an interface to bypass the blocking state and begin forwarding immediately. It then listens and learns of BPDUs on the interface and can make a decision to continue to forward frames or enter into a blocking state. All of the other options are incorrect.

153. C. The correct command to configure BPDU Guard on a single interface is `spanning-tree bpduguard enabled` entered into the interface you want to turn it on for. The commands `switchport mode bpduguard`, `switchport bpduguard enable`, and `spanning-tree bpduguard` are incorrect.

154. C. BPDU Guard was turned on the trunk link. When the BPDU of the adjacent switch was seen, the switch turned the port into `err-disable` mode. A Spanning Tree loop will not `err-disable` an interface; it will simply block the offending port. A switch uplink cable that is bad will not place the interface into an `err-disable` state. Flow control will not have any effect in placing an interface into an `err-disable` state.

155. B. Configuring BPDU Guard along with PortFast ensures that the end device will always be forwarding. BPDU Guard ensures that in the event a BPDU is heard on the interface, the interface will enter into an `err-disable` mode. You should only configure PortFast mode on access links. BPDU Guard should never be configured on a trunk line since it will place the interface into an `err-disable` state when a BPDU is seen. BPDU Guard and Uplink-Fast perform similar functions, such as preventing network loops.

156. D. Using the command `show spanning-tree interface fa 0/1` will show the Spanning Tree configuration for an interface. If PortFast has been configured, the last line will display `The port is in the PortFast mode`. The commands `show portfast`, `show interface fa 0/1`, and `show spanning-tree` are incorrect.

157. D. One way to disable BDPU Guard is to enter the command `spanning-tree bpdu guard disable`. Another way is to negate the command with `no spanning-tree bpduguard`. The commands `switchport bdpugaurd disable`, `spanning-tree bpduguard enable`, and `no switchport bpduguard` are incorrect.

158. C. The switch's interface will become err-disabled immediately. Once it is in `err-disable` mode, an administrator is required to reset the interface. When an interface is administratively disabled, an administrator has done it manually. The interface will not become disabled if a BPDU is advertised with BPDU Guard enabled; it will be err-disabled. Fortunately, a small switching loop will be averted as the interface will be placed into an `err-disable` mode.

159. B. The `show spanning-tree summary` command will show you which features are turned on globally or by default. The commands `show interface gi 0/1`, `show spanning-tree vlan 2`, and `show spanning-tree` are incorrect.

160. D. BPDU Guard will protect the edge switch from someone accidentally plugging in another switch to a port dedicated for end-user devices. Spanning Tree PortFast will allow the interface to enter into a forwarding mode as it listens and learns BPDUs converging. UplinkFast helps faster convergence when an uplink fails between switches. BackboneFast is a Cisco-proprietary protocol that improves convergence in the event an uplink fails.

161. B. To achieve density and/or bandwidth in a relatively small area, you will need to deploy lightweight WAPs with a wireless LAN controller (WLC). Although autonomous WAPs without a WLC would work, it would be problematic due to frequency coordination and roaming. Lightweight WAPs do not function without a WLC.

162. D. Cisco wireless access points can be placed into one of two modes: data serving mode or monitoring mode. In data serving mode, the AP will serve data and act as a normal wireless access point. When the AP is switched into monitor mode, the AP can scan the wireless spectrum and report on interference. It is important to note that when in monitoring mode, the AP will not serve data. The AP can be configured for both modes at the same time, with an impact on performance. All of the other options are incorrect.

163. C. An independent basic service set (IBSS), also known as an ad hoc network, does not require any wireless infrastructure. Clients connect directly to each other over the 802.11 wireless spectrum. A basic service set (BSS) is a small area with wireless coverage and is served by a single WAP. An extended service set (ESS) is a scaled-out BSS, where many WAPs support client roaming between the WAPs and channel selection. The distribution system (DS) is the connection between the wireless network and the wired network.

164. B. Non-root devices such as clients and repeaters connect to root devices such as access points (WAPs). Non-root devices cannot connect to other non-root devices in normal situations such as a network with infrastructure. Root devices do not connect to other root devices; they do connect to wired infrastructure. Repeaters are considered non-root devices.

165. D. An autonomous WAP has a full operating system and controls its own functions independently. A lightweight WAP requires a wireless LAN controller (WLC) to function. A mesh wireless access point communicates with other wireless access points to extend distance and signal.

166. C. A point-to-multipoint wireless bridge will allow you to connect all three buildings together, tying them back to a central location. A mesh network is usually designed for endpoints (clients) and not the interconnection of buildings. Point-to-point bridges would allow all the buildings to connect to each other, but it would not network them together to a central point. Autonomous wireless access points are used for endpoint connectivity and not building-to-building connectivity.

167. B. A service set identifier (SSID) can be a maximum of 32 characters in length. The wireless access point will associate a MAC address to the SSID so clients can associate to the SSID. All of the other options are incorrect.

168. D. The cheapest and most effective solution you could recommend is to install a wireless repeater. A wireless repeater will do just that: It will repeat the current wireless signal and allow for extra distance. A wireless bridging system is used for connecting buildings or locations where running wire is just not possible. A mesh wireless system is probably the most expensive option, since it requires infrastructure such as a controller and lightweight WAPs. Adding just a wireless LAN controller will not add any benefit.

169. A. A lightweight WAP requires a wireless LAN controller (WLC) to function because all data forwarding is controlled by the WLC. A basic service set (BSS) is not a type of wireless access point; it is a deployment of wireless. Wireless bridges allow for buildings or locations where running cable is not possible to bridge the locations. An autonomous WAP is a WAP that can act independently without a WLC.

170. A. A mesh wireless network will allow for coverage of the large area. A mesh network will provide the highest bandwidth possible. An autonomous wireless network is composed of several wireless access point, but they require direct connection to the wired network. A point-to-multipoint wireless bridge is used for connecting buildings together to a central point. Wireless repeaters could possibly achieve the coverage, but they would do so at the cost of bandwidth.

171. B. Wireless LAN controllers allow trunks to be used so that multiple VLANs can be used. Once the VLANs are accessible to the WLC, you need to create one SSID tied to the VLAN configured for production and another SSID tied to the VLAN configured for guests. Access control lists won't work because they are implemented at layer 3 and wireless signaling operates at layer 2. Dynamic VLANs are VLANs that are associated with a host dynamically based on authentication. Although this option would satisfy the segmentation of traffic, it is not the simplest solution to the problem.

172. C. You can build an EtherChannel between routers and wireless controllers to obtain more bandwidth when using router on a stick (ROAS). It is supported on certain models of routers, such as 4000 series routers. The Routing Information Protocol (RIP) will not balance bandwidth between the wireless controller and the router. Wireless controllers will not perform inter-VLAN routing; this job requires a router or firewall with routing capabilities.

173. B. You should configure a trunk port on the switch so that several different VLANs can be tagged and carried over the link. This will allow the forwarding of both voice and data, with expansion for other applications in the future. An access port will only allow one VLAN of traffic and you would need a separate access port for each type of traffic, eventually running out of physical ports. Although this setup sounds like a voice port would fit the application, a WLC does not have the ability to use a voice port. A routed switchport is nothing more than an interface on the switch with an IP address for routing purposes.

174. C. Link Aggregation (LAG) must be used between the WLC and the switch, regardless of the brand. Wireless LAN controllers do not support the use of LACP or PAgP; they only support vanilla EtherChannel configurations, also known as LAG. *PortChannel* is a term synonymous with Cisco devices only.

175. B. When a LAG is created between a switch and a WLC, the method of load balancing used is hash-based, using layer 4 source and destination ports. Round-robin load balancing cannot be configured on the WLC or switch side of a LAG. First in, first out (FIFO) is a buffer mechanism used to send data out as it comes in, and it is not used in load balancing scenarios. Spill and fill is a method of saturating one link before the other link is used; it is not used in load balancing scenarios.

176. B. The maximum number of ports that can be bundled in a LAG is 8 ports. All of the other options are incorrect.

177. A. When a wireless system spans a town, city, or large metropolitan area, it is considered a wireless metro area network (WMAN). These can be found in many cities today but are not limited to public use. Many wireless systems are used by municipalities to facilitate connectivity to cameras and traffic monitoring systems. A wireless personal area network (WPAN) is a wireless network designed for personal use, usually for personal connectivity to the Internet through a hot spot. Wireless LAN (WLAN) is a term used to describe a wireless network that extends a wired network to wireless. The term is used to describe a campus-sized wireless network and not a wireless network that spans a public area. Wireless wide area network (WWAN) is a term used to describe cellular networks and not typical 802.11 wireless.

178. C. The simplest and cheapest way to accommodate this new requirement is to convert one of the current access ports to a trunk. This will allow several VLANs to be carried across the one port to the switching equipment. Upgrading is always an option that could get you more ports, but at some point, you will hit the end of the line and run out of money in the process. Converting the current access ports to LAGs will only load-balance the traffic across one network, and it will not accommodate the new requirements. Adding a second WLC to accommodate the new departments can become an expensive endeavor in money and time, since you will have two systems to administer.

179. A. A wireless personal area network (WPAN) is a small wireless network that usually has a maximum distance of 30 feet. It is used for personal wireless connectivity to the Internet via wireless. Wireless LANs (WLANs) are traditional wireless networks that we use to connect to our home and work networks. Bluetooth is a common WPAN; it allows for hands-free calling, monitoring of your pulse with wearable devices, and many other services we have come to rely on. Wireless metro area networks (WMANs) are wireless networks that span a fairly large geographic area like a city or suburban area. A wireless wide area network (WWAN) is used for Internet connectivity and usually delivered over cellular networks.

180. C. When installing a wireless access point onto a WLC, the port should be configured as a trunk port. Configuring the port as a trunk port will allow management traffic and data traffic to be tagged. This type of configuration will also future-proof the design for additional networks in the future. Wireless access points are configured with access ports when a controller is not being used and the AP is running in an autonomous mode. There is no such thing as a wireless port configuration. Configuring the port as a LAG port is not possible since APs normally only have one interface and LAGs require two or more for aggregation.

181. B. Telnet is used for terminal emulation over a network to a device expecting terminal emulation, such as a router, switch, or access point. Simple Network Management Protocol (SNMP) is a management protocol for sending and receiving network events and statistics. Hypertext Transfer Protocol (HTTP) allows for web-based configuration of devices. Trivial File Transfer Protocol (TFTP) is a network utility that allows for file transfer, usually for the maintenance of devices such as uploading a new IOS.

182. A. The IP address or hostname entered in privileged exec mode will create a direct Telnet request. Alternatively, you can specify the command `telnet 198.56.33.3`. The commands `connect 198.56.33.3`, `remote 198.56.33.3`, and `vty 198.56.33.3` are incorrect.

183. D. TACACS+ uses TCP and port 49 for communications between the switch or router and the AAA server. All of the other options are incorrect.

184. C. Secure Shell (SSH) is a secure console emulation method for the administration of network devices. It allows for both the sender and receiver to create an encrypted session, so data cannot be intercepted. Remote Authentication Dial-In User Service (RADIUS) is a protocol that authenticates users, and it does not provide encryption. Hypertext Transfer Protocol (HTTP) is a method for relaying Hypertext Markup Language (HTML) from a server to a requesting host; it does not provide encryption. SSH File Transfer Protocol (SFTP) is a protocol that provides encryption for file transfers, but it does not provide management access.

185. D. The use of a cloud controller such as the Cisco Application Policy Infrastructure Controller (APIC) allows for easier deployment of Cisco devices and a consolidated view for management. Configuration via the command-line interface (CLI) will be slower than a cloud-based deployment and the CLI will not provide a consolidated view. The Simple Network Management Protocol (SNMP) is used to monitor network devices and it is not used for provisioning devices. The Secure Shell (SSH) protocol is another method of connecting to a network device's command-line interface.

186. A. Using the Meraki dashboard, you can manage multiple Catalyst 9000-M series switches. The Meraki dashboard is a cloud-based management system that provides automatic firmware upgrades and configuration management. Using the Trivial File Transfer Protocol (TFTP) is a tactic for manual firmware upgrade. The Secure Shell (SSH) protocol is used for command-line interface (CLI) connectivity. The Remote Authentication Dial-In User Service (RADIUS) is an authentication and authorization protocol.

187. D. The Secure Shell (SSH) protocol uses asymmetrical encryption with the use of public and private key pairs. This not only provides encryption, but it also provides authentication of clients. Symmetrical encryption means that the same key that encrypts the information also decrypts it, and this method is not commonly used with any remote technologies. Code block ciphers (CBCs) are used with wireless technology to encrypt the data several times. *At-rest encryption* is a term used to describe the protection of data stored and not data in transit.

188. A. When a wireless access point is being debugged, the information is displayed by default to the console. This information can be extended to the remote SSH or Telnet session by using the command `terminal monitor`. Logging servers must be configured and are not created by default. Although on some higher-end switches local storage provides a method of storage for logging, it is not the default for wireless access points.

189. A. Remote Authentication Dial-In User Service (RADIUS) was originally proposed by the IETF and became an open standard for authentication, often used with 802.1X. TACACS+ is a standard that was originally developed by Cisco. Kerberos is an authentication protocol used for Active Directory authentication and was originally created by MIT. Lightweight Directory Access Protocol (LDAP) is not an authentication protocol; it is a helper protocol used by authentication protocols to look up objects.

190. A. Secure Shell (SSH) can use a multitude of encryption protocols; one of the encryption protocols is Advanced Encryption Standard (AES). TACACS+ is used to authenticate users only and provides no encryption. Hypertext Transfer Protocol Secure (HTTPS) uses Secure Sockets Layer (SSL) to transmit data, but it does not provide AES encryption. Remote Authentication Dial-In User Service is similar to TACACS+; both provide authentication and do not provide encryption.

191. C. When setting up an autonomous wireless access point for the first time, you need to connect via the console port. The network services for management are not set up by default on a wireless access point right out of the box. HTTPS can be configured, but by default, it is not configured since the wireless does not have an IP address right out of the box. SSH and Telnet are also inaccessible for a wireless access point right out of the box.

192. C. The universal console speed for all Cisco devices is 9600 baud. The connection for Cisco equipment should be set up as 9600 baud, 8 bits of data, no flow control, and 1 stop bit. This connection is also known as 96008N1 and should be committed to memory. All of the other options are incorrect.

193. C. A trust boundary is the point in the network where the QoS markings are trusted from the devices connected to it. A network administrator will create a trust boundary where a VoIP phone will be placed. Since the VoIP phone will be trusted, the markings will be accepted and used for priority throughout the network. The trust boundary should always be placed closest to the IT-controlled equipment.

194. A. WLAN Quality of Service (QoS) is de-fined by IEEE 802.11e. The definitions align with the 802.1p, which is the wired equivalent called Architecture for Voice, Video and Integrated Data (AVVID). The IEEE 802.11r specification is used for BSS fast transition (FT) and does not pertain to QoS. The IEEE 802.11k specification is used for roaming clients to locate the closet WAP and does not pertain to QoS.

195. C. MAC-based filtering is the best way you can achieve the goal of only allowing corporate hosts to connect to the network. You would need to preload into the WLC all of the MAC addresses that you want to allow access. Disabling the SSID from broadcasting is security through obscurity and only a deterrent; a savvy user can manually create a connection to the hidden SSID. Setting a unique preshared key (PSK) is only as secure as the people who know it; unfortunately at some point, it will leak out to others. Adding an LDAP server is the first step in setting up the web portal for user authentication and will not prevent users from joining their personal devices.

196. C. 802.11k should be enabled; it will allow client devices to download a list of neighboring wireless access points and their associated wireless bands. 802.11r is used for BSS fast transition (FT) by allowing authentication to be bypassed. 802.11e defines Quality of Service (QoS) for wireless communications. 802.11ac is a wireless standard for communication speed and equipment and does not pertain to neighboring WAP lists.

197. D. The QoS profile of Platinum should be associated with the wireless VoIP phones. The Platinum QoS profile is normally associated with network control traffic and highly sensitive protocols such as VoIP. The Bronze QoS profile should be used for bulk data transfer, such as file transfers. The Silver QoS profile should be associated with transactional traffic, such as basic user forms. The Gold QoS profile should be reserved for lower priority time-sensitive protocols such as interactive video.

198. A. The administrative status of the WLAN is disabled. This means that the WLAN will not allow associations. To fix the problem, it must be reenabled and applied. Changing the Radio Policy value will not affect the solution because the WLAN is effectively administratively disabled. Enabling the Multicast VLAN feature will not correct the issue since many WLANs never need multicast support. Enabling the Broadcast SSID option would not accomplish anything because it could have been disabled already.

199. C. This WLAN is configured for WPA2 personal; you can see that because the Pre-Shared Key (PSK) option is enabled and is filled out. The original WPA is not enabled. WPA2 enterprise mode requires the use of certificates that cannot exist with PSK mode. 802.1X is not enabled, as you can see in the figure.

200. B. Local mode creates a Control And Provisioning of Wireless Access Points (CAPWAP) tunnel to the wireless LAN controller to allow switching of VLANs local to the WLC. All traffic in Local mode must traverse back to the WLC to get switched into the respective VLANs. Flex Connect mode does not create a CAPWAP tunnel to mode data, only control information. Local mode allows for the switching of VLANs at the WLC only. Flex Connect mode is the opposite, where VLANs can be switched at the WAP.

201. A. The Bronze QoS profile should be used for bulk data transfer, such as file transfers of this nature. The Gold QoS profile should be reserved for lower priority time-sensitive protocols such as interactive video. The QoS profile of Platinum should be associated with the wireless VoIP phones and time-sensitive protocols. The Silver QoS profile should be associated with transactional traffic, such as basic user forms.

202. B. 802.1X is a control protocol that can be configured on Cisco and non-Cisco wireless LAN controllers to allow only hosts that present a valid certificate on the network. The server that arbitrates the authentication is normally a Remote Authentication Dial-In User Service (RADIUS). MAC filtering is normally a manual process in which the MAC address of the client is entered into a database that the WLC checks before allowing access to the wireless network. WPA2 PSK only uses a simple key that is punched into both the WLC and the client. Fast Transitioning (FT) allows a client to roam between access points without further authentication.

Chapter 3: IP Connectivity (Domain 3)

1.   D. The scalability of routes between routers should always be considered when choosing a static routing design vs. a dynamic routing design. A few subnets over many routers creates a lot of work when a new subnet is created and static routing is being used. However, when one router is being used, the administrative overhead is low.

2.   A. Routers are grouped into the same autonomous system (AS). When they are within the same AS, they can exchange information such as routes to destination networks and converge their routing tables. Routing protocols are not normally redistributed between ASs because the network is usually managed as one AS. All routers do not necessarily use the same routing protocols; many different portions of the network can use different protocols. All network IDs are not advertised with the same autonomous system number. Routers are normally grouped into one AS logically, such as an organization. Inside that organization (AS), many different autonomous system numbers can be used.

3.   A. The maximum hop count for RIP is 15. A hop count over 15 hops is considered unroutable or unreachable, so the other options are incorrect.

4.   C. By default, RIPv2 multicasts the full routing table on all active interfaces every 30 seconds. RIPv2 does not allow for neighborship through hello packets, as link-state and hybrid dynamic routing protocols do. RIPv2 uses multicasts, not broadcasts. RIPv2 multicasts the full routing table every 30 seconds, not every 60 seconds.

5.   B. RIPv2 uses the multicast address 224.0.0.9 to advertise routes. The multicast address 224.0.0.5 is used by OSPF for hello messages. The multicast address 224.0.0.6 is also used by OSPF for hello messages for designated routers (DRs) and backup designated routers (BDRs). The multicast address 224.0.0.2 is a special multicast group for all routers and it is not used by any particular routing protocol.

6.   B. To route packets over the higher-speed link, you would need to configure a static route for both Router A and Router B. If these links went down, then the lower-speed link would become active. This is due to administrative distance. Configuring passive interfaces on Router A and Router B will only restrict the two routers from trading their route tables between each other. Setting the cost on the interface will not affect the routing with RIPv2. You cannot set the metric of 2 for each of the routers; it is an invalid command.

7.   B. Routing Information Protocol (RIP) does not contain a topology table. RIP compiles its table from multiple broadcasts or multicasts in the network from which it learns routes. However, it never has a full topological diagram of the network like OSPF, EIGRP, and BGP.

8.   D. The split horizon method prevents routing updates from exiting an interface in which they have been learned. This stops false information from propagating in the network, which can cause a routing loop. Routing to infinity is a way of advertising a downed route as unreachable because of the number of hops. Route poisoning is similar to routing to infinity as it advertises a downed route as over the routable hop count. Holddowns can help stabilize a network by holding off changes until a specific amount of time has passed.

9. B. Although this is a static route, it is a very special static route called a default route or gateway of last resort. The S signifies that it is static and the ⋆ signifies that it is the default route. Most all default routes are static, but default routes can also be populated with dynamic routing protocols. The S signifies that the route is a static route; therefore, it cannot be populated with a dynamic routing protocol such as OSPF.

10. C. The 4 represents the metric for this route statement. Since this is a RIP entry, the metric is the number of hops for this particular route. The administrative distance is 120 in the figure. The protocol in the figure is RIP. The position in the routing table cannot be derived from a single statement in the routing table.

11. A. The command show ip route 160.45.23.0 255.255.255.0 longer-prefixes will detail all of the specific routes contained in the route for 160.45.23.0/24. The command show ip route 160.45.23.0 255.255.255.0 will show the specific route of 160.45.23.0/24. The command show ip route bgp is not a valid command. The command show ip route will show the entire route table.

12. B. The network of 192.168.1.0/24 is directly connected via Serial 0/0. The packet will be delivered out the exit interface of Serial 0/0. The administrative distance (AD) is the lowest on directly connected routes. The gateway address of 172.16.1.200 would only be valid if the example in the figure was only using OSPF. The gateway of 172.16.1.100 would only be valid if the example in the figure was only using RIP. The exit interface of Ethernet0 is valid for OSPF and RIP routing.

13. B. The IP address of 203.80.53.22/19 belongs to the network of 203.80.32.0/19. No other answers are correct because they do not belong to the 203.80.32.0/19 network.

14. B. The top line in the figure is the summarization of all three routes below. This is also called a supernet, since it is the opposite of a subnet and groups networks together rather than dividing them. It groups the networks that are independently routable into one statement, summarizing them. The 10.0.0.0/8 is not a route in the routing table; the routes are grouped under this summarization. The 10.0.0.0/8 is a network address and therefore cannot be the router's network address. The 10.0.0.0/8 is not populated from another router directly; it is summarized from the routes learned from other routers.

15. C. The number represents the time the route had been in the routing table and signifies when the route had last been updated. This route is populated via a dynamic routing protocol; when the protocol updates the route, it will be reset to zero. The time represented in this figure is not the current time. The delay is not represented in the form of time; it is normally a component of the metric. The route statement will not display the amount of time an interface or route has been up.

16. C. When routers select the next hop, the rule of most specific first is always used. Since there are three routes to 192.168.4.0/24 (including the gateway of last resort), the most specific of 192.168.4.0/24 via Serial 0/0/1 is selected. The interface Serial 0/2/0 would only be right if the destination address was not in the other route statements. The IP address of 192.168.4.2 would only be right if the destination address was in the 192.168.5.0/24 network. The IP address of 198.22.34.3 would only be right if the destination address was in the 192.168.0.0/16 network and no other specific routes existed.

17. D. Nothing needs to be done since the IP address of 198.44.4.5/24 is configured on Fa0/1. This shows that the network of 198.44.4.0/24 is connected to Fa0/1. Configuring the command `ip route 198.44.4.0 255.255.255.0 198.44.4.5` would not achieve anything because the network is configured on the interface already. Configuring the command `ip route 198.44.4.0 255.255.255.0 fast 0/1` would not achieve anything because the interface already belongs to the network of 192.168.4.0/24. The command of `ip route 198.44.4.0/24 fast 0/1` is normally not a valid command because the network mask is expressed in dotted-decimal form.

18. B. The network of 205.34.54.85/29 is written out as 205.34.54.85 255.255.255.248. The next hop is 205.34.55.2, so the command would be `ip route 205.34.54.85 255.255.255.248 205.34.55.2`. The command `ip route 205.34.54.85/24 205.34.55.2` is invalid because it is not normally entered with a CIDR notation. The command `ip route 205.34.54.85 255.255.255.240 205.34.55.2` is invalid because the network mask is wrong when written out in dotted-decimal format. The command `ip route 205.34.55.2 255.255.255.248 205.34.54.85` is invalid because the next hop and the network are in the wrong place on the command.

19. A. Static routes are highly trusted routes, since an administrator created them. Therefore, they have the lowest administrative distance (AD) with a number of 1. The administrative distance of 0 is used for connected interfaces. The administrative distance of 2 is a wrong answer and does not map to a route source. The administrative distance of 255 is reserved for unknown sources and is entered into the route process.

20. D. The administrative distance of the Routing Information Protocol (RIP) is 120. The administrative distance of 90 is used for internal Enhanced Interior Gateway Routing Protocol (EIGRP). The administrative distance of 100 is used for Interior Gateway Routing Protocol (IGR). The administrative distance of 110 is used for Open Shortest.

21. B. Administrative distance (AD) is an order of reliability between dynamic routing protocols and static routes. Administrative distances do not define protocol standards; they only reference them. Administrative distances do not allow for the shortest distance between routers; they allow the router to choose the best path to the destination network. Although administrative distances are programmed into route statements by administrators, they do not calculate path selection.

22. A. A directly connected network has an administrative distance (AD) of 0 and is the most highly reliable. The administrative distance of 1 is used for static entries. The administrative distance of 5 is used for Enhanced Interior Gateway Routing Protocol summary routes. Directly connected networks have an AD of 0 that is trusted over all other router sources.

23. A. Internal EIGRP has an administrative distance (AD) of 90. The AD of 100 is used for Interior Gateway Routing Protocol (IGRP). The administrative distance of 110 is used for Open Shortest Path First (OSPF). The administrative distance of the Routing Information Protocol (RIP) is 120.

24. C. The administrative distance (AD) determines how the routing table is built and which route is more preferable than others. This preference is important when multiple routes exist to the same destination. Directly connected routes have ADs with the highest level of trust. Route statements populated by the same dynamic routing protocol will be calculated for the best route upon their metric and not their administrative distance. The administrative distance is not assigned by the administrator for route selection. The administrative distance value is not associated with the cost to the destination, only the trust of a route statement.

25. A. Enhanced Interior Gateway Routing Protocol (EIGRP) uses bandwidth and delay by default for calculating routes. The bandwidth should be set to the actual bandwidth of the link so that routing protocols such as EIGRP can calculate the best route based on throughput. Delay is typically not set because it is a variable of the interface based upon the delay of a packet traversing the interface. Reliability is typically not set because it is a variable of the interface based upon the reliability of the link. Load is typically not set because it is also a variable of the interface, based upon the load of the interface.

26. C. The administrative distance (AD) of EIGRP is 90. The most common ADs are 90 for EIGRP, 100 for IGRP, 110 for OSPF, and 120 for RIP. The mnemonic of 90 Exotic Indian Oval Rubies will help you remember the order; then starting with EIGRP with a value of 90, increment the following values by 10.

27. C. The routing protocol with the lowest administrative distance (AD) is always chosen. Within that protocol, if there are multiple routes to the same network, then the lowest metric is chosen. The route is chosen with the lowest administrative distance, not the highest administrative distance. The route with the lowest metric will be selected as the best route, but only when within the same routing protocol. The route with the highest metric will not be selected as the best route.

28. C. EIGRP metrics are bandwidth, delay, load, reliability, and MTU, while RIP is a distance-vector protocol and only takes hop count into consideration for the metric. BGP is not suited for optimal performance since a large amount of resources need to be dedicated for the protocol.

29. A. Cisco uses a metric for OSPF that is calculated as 10^8 / bandwidth. This cost value is of 100 Mb/s (reference bandwidth) divided by the interface bandwidth. Delay, bandwidth, reliability, and load are used as a composite metric with EIGRP. K metrics are used to weight the calculation of the composite metric used with EIGRP. Bandwidth is used by OSPF, but only when used with the formula of 10^8 / bandwidth.

30. A. It identifies the administrative distance (AD) of 110 for OSPF. The cost calculation is the reference bandwidth of 100 Mb/s di-vided by the link bandwidth. This calculation would result in a cost of 1. The calculation of the OSPF metric is 10^8 / bandwidth, or 100,000,000/ bandwidth. Therefore, a metric of 1 would equal 100,000,000/100,000,000, and all of the other options are wrong.

31. C. The destination address of 0.0.0.0/0 is a special route called the default route or gateway of last resort. The 0.0.0.0/0 addresses are all hosts, and if a specific route is not matched in the routing table, then this route is the last resort. IOS and IOS-XR have local host routes; the routes provide a local routing path to an interface or internally configured IP address. Dynamic routes are routes that have been discovered by a dynamic routing protocol. There is no such thing as a loopback route.

32. B. ICMP notifies the sending host if there is no viable route to the destination. The ICMP message sent to the sending host is a destination unreachable message. ICMP is not used to populate routing tables. ICMP does not maintain the routing table; dynamic routing protocols populate and maintain the routing table. ICMP is used to diagnose problems with an internetwork, but ICMP does not continuously diagnosis network paths.

33. B. When a route table contains overlapping destination prefixes such as 192.168.0.0/16 and 192.168.1.0/24, the route with the longest matching prefix is selected. The cost is not a consideration unless there are two routes with the same prefix length; then metrics are taken into consideration. The administrative distance (AD) is not a factor in deciding the destination path to be taken unless the routes have equal length prefixes with different route sources.

34. A. Since both routes are default routes, the route with the lowest administrative distance (AD) will be selected. The route with the highest administrative distance will never be selected first. The route with the lowest metric will only be used if two routes exist to the same destination network and have equal administrative distances. The RIP routing protocol has an administrative distance of 120; therefore, it has a higher administrative distance over a statically defined default route and will not be selected.

35. C. A host route is used when you need to route packets to a different next hop for a specific host. A host route is configured as a long prefix of /32 so that it is selected when network prefixes are overlapped. The route table will not create host routes; host routes must be manually configured by the administrator. Hot Standby Router Protocol (HSRP) is not used with host routes, and therefore, it is an incorrect option.

36. B. The routing protocol code is in the form of a single letter at the beginning of each route statement. A legend that depicts each route source precedes the route table. The prefix and network mask are learned from the route source. The metric will not identify where a route was learned, such as its route source. The next hop will not identify where a route was learned, such as its route source.

37. B. All routing decisions are based on the destination IP address. The router examines the IP address and routes the packet to the next closest hop for the network it belongs to. The source IP address is not used during the route process and will not change throughout the process. The time to live (TTL) is used to limit how many times a packet is routed throughout a network or the Internet. The TTL is decremented by 1 as it passes through a router; when it reaches 0, the packet will be dropped and will no longer be routable. The destination MAC address is not used for routing decisions.

38. C. Static routing requires a network administrator to intervene and create a route in the routing table. Dynamic routing is the opposite of static routing because routes are learned dynamically. Link-state and distance-vector routing are forms of dynamic routing protocols and do not require administrator intervention.

39. A. The subnet mask is used by the host to determine the immediate network and the destination network. It then decides to either route the packet or try to deliver the packet itself without the router's help. The subnet mask of the destination network is not used to determine routing decisions because the sending host does not know the destination subnet mask.

The router does not use the network mask for routing decisions because it is not transmitted in the IP packet. The destination computer will check only the destination IP address in the packet because the network mask is not transmitted with the IP packet.

40. C. The Address Resolution Protocol (ARP) is employed by the host or router when a destination IP address is determined to be local on one of its interfaces. The Internet Group Management Protocol (IGMP) is used to build multicast sessions for switches and routers. Reverse Address Resolution Protocol (RARP) is used to obtain an IP address assigned for a specific MAC address. RARP has been replaced with DHCP and is no longer used outside of networking theory. The Internet Control Message Protocol (ICMP) is used with connectivity tools such as ping and tracert. ICMP is also used to notify a sender when the destination network is unreachable.

41. C. The destination MAC address is changed to the router's MAC address and the destination IP address is untouched. The destination IP address is not changed throughout the routing process. The destination MAC address is only changed to the destination host's MAC address if the traffic is deemed to be local. The source IP address is not changed throughout the routing process unless NAT is being used.

42. B. The TTL, or time to live, is decremented usually by one. When the TTL reaches zero, a packet is considered unroutable. This prevents packets from eternally routing. The destination IP address is not changed throughout the normal routing process. The source MAC address is not changed, since the originator of the frame has no need to forge the frame.

43. B. When a packet is determined to be local to the sending host, ARP is used to resolve the MAC address for the IP address of the destination host, and the frame is sent directly to the host. The destination IP address is not changed throughout the network delivery process. The destination MAC address is only changed to the MAC address of the router if the packet is deemed to be remote from the immediate network. The source IP address is not changed throughout the routing process unless NAT is being used, and NAT is not used for local communications.

44. B. The sending host ANDs its subnet mask against the destination IP address, then against its IP address, and this gives a frame of reference for where it needs to go and where it is. The host compares the remote IP to its internal routing table after the calculation of local vs. remote is performed and the host is ready to route the packet. The host does not perform the ANDing process against the destination IP address and destination subnet mask because the destination subnet mask is often unknown and irrelevant to the calculation. ICMP is not used in the calculation of local vs. remote networks.

45. D. The current method of packet forwarding used by Cisco routers is Cisco Express Forwarding (CEF). CEF creates several cache tables used for determining the best route for the destination network. Process switching is the original method used with routing packets and is no longer used. Fast switching is also an older method used with routing packets on Cisco devices, and it too is no longer used. Intelligent packet forwarding is not a packet forwarding method, and therefore, it is an invalid option.

46. B. The layer 2 process is called frame rewrite. When a packet hops from router to router, the destination frame is rewritten for the next destination MAC address. IP routing is the process

the router actually performs for the selection of a route or path to the destination. Packet hopping is not a valid process in the routing of packets, and therefore, it is an invalid option. Packet switching is the concept of moving packets of data over a digital network, and therefore, it is an incorrect option.

47. C. When a MAC address is unknown for the destination IP address or the default gateway, the ARP request is sent in the form of a broadcast. If the destination MAC address was the router's MAC address, the router would be the only device to receive the ARP request frame. The host's MAC address is what we need to process the framing of data; therefore, it is the reason for the ARP request to all listening nodes. In IPv4, ARP uses broadcasts to forward the ARP request to all listening network devices. Multicast is used in IPv6 for node discovery, but it does not use ARP.

48. A. Every host contains an ARP cache. This cache allows for lookups of MAC addresses for destination IP addresses when the host frequently sends packets to the destination. Therefore, there are fewer ARP packets. IP multicasting is used with network discovery (ND) packets in IPv6 and not ARP. There is no such thing as frame casting; therefore, it is an invalid option. There is also no such thing as an IP cache; therefore, it is also an invalid option.

49. B. After the frame is verified to be addressed to the router and the FCS has been checked, the router decapsulates the packet and strips off the frame. The router will only accept frames that are unicast directly to the router's MAC address, multicasted to the router multicast group, or broadcast to all devices. Routers must decapsulate packets to inspect the destination IP address. Routing decisions are never made by examining the source MAC address, since the source of the traffic is irrelevant to the destination.

50. D. The command to display the router's ARP cache is show ip arp. The commands show arp, show arp table, and show arp cache are incorrect.

51. B. By default, all entries have a time to live, or TTL, of 240 seconds. They will be removed after that period if not used during the 240 seconds. All other options are incorrect.

52. D. Dynamic routing allows for the population of routing tables from advertisements of other routers. There are several dynamic routing protocols, such as, for example, EIGRP, RIP, and OSPF. Default routing forces all traffic that is unknown to a specific next hop. Stub routing is similar to default routing. Stub routing is often used to describe a default route on a stub network, where any remote network address is through a specific next hop. Static routing is the method of manually configuring route statements in router versus dynamic routing protocol processes.

53. B. When a route is found in the routing table, the router will find the gateway for the next hop and change the packet's destination MAC address for the next router. The packet's TTL will always be decremented by one as it passes through a router and is not increased. When packets travel through a router, the layer 4 transport information is not inspected; only the layer 3 destination IP address is inspected. The packet is never changed throughout the routing process, such as adding the destination IP address of the next hop.

54. D. The Internet Control Message Protocol (ICMP) is a layer 3 protocol that allows for end-to-end testing with a command such as traceroute. The Internet Group Management Protocol

(IGMP) is used to allow hosts to join a multicast group on a switch. The RARP is used to resolve an IP address from a MAC address; its operation closely resembles DHCP. Address Resolution Protocol (ARP) is used to resolve a MAC address from an IP address for the purpose of framing data.

55. B. The Routing Information Protocol (RIP) is a distance-vector protocol. Open Shortest Path First (OSPF) is a link-state protocol. Enhanced Interior Gateway Routing Protocol is a hybrid protocol that more closely resembles a link-state protocol. Border Gateway Protocol (BGP) is a path-vector protocol used for Internet routing.

56. D. The last router will send an ICMP packet back to the originating host, which has the result code of destination unreachable. The router will discard the packet, but a notification is still sent back to the originating host. The router will not change the TTL of the packet; it will just drop the packet and notify the originating host. The router will not bother with sending the original packet back to the originating host.

57. A. When packets are routed out one interface and come back in on a different interface, this is considered asynchronous routing and not typical of a routing loop. Packets transmitted within a series of routers never reaching the destination is the typical description of packet loss. Packets reaching the expiry TTL could mean that there are too many hops to the destination network, but not that a routing loop is occurring. Packets being routed via an inefficient path is not a symptom of a routing loop.

58. A. Open Shortest Path First (OSPF) is a link-state protocol. A link-state protocol tracks the state of a link between two routers and chooses the most efficient routes based upon the shortest path. Routing Information Protocol (RIP) is a distance-vector protocol. Enhanced Interior Gateway Routing Protocol (EIGRP) is considered a hybrid protocol. Interior Gateway Routing Protocol (IGRP) is a distance-vector protocol.

59. A. Dynamic routes are stored in RAM. When the power is taken away from a router, all routes must be repopulated by neighboring routers. Flash is where the IOS of the router is stored. The startup configuration is stored in nonvolatile random-access memory (NVRAM). The running configuration is stored in RAM along with tables such as dynamic routes.

60. A. Latency is lower with SVI inter-VLAN routing because of the use of ASICs. This is usually why IVR switches are more expensive. Latency is not higher because the SVI inter-VLAN routing uses ASICs. SVI inter-VLAN routing is not always a cheaper alternative to router on a stick (ROAS) because of licensing and the requirement of a layer 3 switch. Bandwidth is not limited like ROAS and is usually substantially higher, which is one of the main motivations to use SVI inter-VLAN routing.

61. C. The lack of scalability of ROAS is a major disadvantage. It does not scale well when a large number of VLANs are configured. ROAS can be used with Inter-Switch Link (ISL) protocol for VLAN support. With 802.1Q or ISL trunking, you can tie several VLANs to a physical port. All dynamic routing protocols are supported with ROAS.

62. A. The use of VLANs requires a unique IP network for each VLAN. This is how broadcast domains are increased, since all VLANs are behind a router interface (default gateway). IVR does not reduce the number of broadcast domains; it increases the number of broadcast domains. You'll have several different VLANs in which you can broadcast as the scale of your network grows. IVR supports access control lists (ACLs) because you are creating network interfaces as you add VLANs. IVRs promote the use of subnetting because you need a unique IP network for each VLAN.

63. B. When a router's interface is used to allow routing, the method is called router on a stick, or ROAS. Interface routing is used when an IP address is assigned to an interface and routing is enabled between the interfaces. Switched Virtual Interface (SVI) routing allows for the layer 3 router inside a switch to provide necessary routing between VLANs. There is no such thing as bridge routing; bridges are limited interface switches, and routing is a layer 3 function.

64. B. Bandwidth is often a consideration because everything you send to the router must come back on the same port for routing to work. Routing between two VLANs on a 1 Gb/s interface will allow for the bandwidth of 1 Gb/s up and 1 Gb/s down. When a third VLAN is introduced, they must all share the 1 Gb/s. Routers can handle large amounts of traffic, but the same interface used to receive is also used to send the traffic, thereby reducing the bandwidth by half. Security can be implemented with ROAS with the use of ACLs. Broadcast traffic is not increased by using a single router interface to route several VLANs.

65. C. When you perform inter-VLAN routing on a layer 3 switch, it is called SVI VLAN routing. Interface routing is used when an IP address is assigned to an interface and routing is enabled between the interfaces. ROAS is used when a router only has one interface and you need to route multiple VLANs. There is no such thing as bridge routing; bridges are limited interface switches, and routing is a layer 3 function.

66. A. Dynamic routing does not require any administrator intervention when routes go down. This is because dynamic routes send route notifications and recalculate the routing tables of all participating routers. Directly connected routes will require administrator intervention if the admin is relying upon the connected route as the route source and an interface goes down. Default routing requires administrator intervention if the default route goes down; the admin will need to pick a new default route and configure it. Static routing always requires an amount of administrator intervention for setup and maintenance of the routes since they are all done manually.

67. C. Static routing requires increased time for configuration as networks grow in complexity. You will need to update routers that you add with all of the existing routes in the network. You will also need to update all of the existing routers with the new routes you add with the new router. RIP is a dynamic routing protocol and therefore requires less time as a network grows. OSPF is a dynamic routing protocol and therefore requires less time as a network grows. Default routing is used on stub networks and requires no additional time if the network remains a stub network.

68. D. Default routing requires the least amount of RAM consumption because one routing statement is required for all of the upstream networks. This type of routing technique is best used on stub network routers. RIP routing requires an amount of RAM to hold its learned routes. OSPF requires a substantial amount of RAM because it holds learned routes and calculates the shortest path to remote networks. Static routing requires RAM for each route configured manually compared to default routing, which only requires one static entry.

69. C. Routing Information Protocol (RIP) has the lowest overhead of all of the routing protocols. However, it is not very scalable; the maximum number of hops is 15. BGP has tremendous overhead because of the storage and calculations on best path. OSPF has a large overhead as well because of storage and calculations to the shortest path. EIGRP is similar to OSPF in regard to storage and calculations for the next hop.

70. A. The benefit of a dynamic routing protocol is that it creates resiliency when routes become unavailable. It does this by recalculating the best route in the network around the outage. When using dynamic routing protocols there is a higher RAM usage because of the route tables collected. CPU usage is also higher with dynamic routing protocols because of calculations. Bandwidth usage is also higher with dynamic routing protocols because of the traffic involved learning the various routes.

71. A. The Routing Information Protocol version 1 (RIPv1) broadcasts updates for routing tables. OSPF exclusively uses multicast to send updates. EIGRP uses multicast to send updates as well and has a backup of direct unicast. BGP uses unicast to retrieve updates on network paths.

72. B. Optimized route selection is a direct advantage of using dynamic routing protocols. A protocol such as OSPF uses the shortest path first algorithm for route selection. Routing tables will not be centralized since all routers participating in dynamic routing will contain their own routing tables. Dynamic routing is not easy to configure due to the upfront planning and configuration. A portion of the available bandwidth will also be consumed for the dynamic routing protocol.

73. C. EIGRP has a default hop count of 100 and can be configured for up to 255 hops. The Routing Information Protocol (RIP) is a distance-vector routing protocol that has a maximum of 15 hops. OSPF is an extremely scalable routing protocol, and therefore, OSPF isn't limited to a hop count. BGP is the routing protocol that routes the Internet; it does, however, have a maximum hop count of 255.

74. C. The Enhanced Interior Gateway Routing Protocol (EIGRP) is a hybrid protocol. It has features of a vector-based protocol and a link-state protocol; hence it is considered a hybrid protocol. RIP is a distance-vector routing protocol that is used for small networks. OSPF is an extremely scalable link-state protocol. BGP is the routing protocol that is used to route packets on the Internet, and it is considered a path-vector protocol.

75. B. Protocols such as RIP re-advertise routes learned. This can be problematic since it is the equivalent of gossiping about what they have heard. Routes learned through this method are never tracked for status or double-checked for validity. Distance-vector protocols do not keep a topology database; they just feed routes to the route table. Distance-vector protocols never check the routes they learn because of the method of routing through rumor.

76. B. RIP, which is a distance-vector protocol, is best suited for networks containing fewer than 15 routers. This is because RIP is limited to a 15 hop count. Any route that is more than 15 hops away is considered unreachable. All other answers are incorrect and describe networks that are best suited for a hybrid, link-state, or path-vector protocol.

77. A. Routing loops are the most common problem when you're using a distance-vector routing protocol. Although they can occur with any dynamic routing protocol, distance-vector protocols are most susceptible due to how they converge routes. RIP is extremely compatible with all router implementations, and it is a light protocol; therefore, it is found on many different routers. RIP is a very simple protocol to configure compared to other dynamic routing protocols. RIP also supports the advertisement of a default route.

78. B. The diffusing update algorithm (DUAL) is used by EIGRP to calculate the best route for the destination network. RIP uses the Bellman–Ford algorithm for calculations of routes. OSPF uses the Dijkstra algorithm to calculate the shortest path between two networks. BGP uses the best path algorithm that determines the best path between two networks.

79. B. Slow convergence of routing tables is a major disadvantage for distance-vector protocols like RIP. It could take several announcement cycles before the entire network registers a routing change. RIP is an extremely compatible and light protocol; therefore, it is found on many different routers. Because RIP is extremely lightweight as a routing protocol, it uses very little CPU and RAM. RIP is not best suited for complex networks, and therefore, it is very easy to configure.

80. A. The RIP uses the Bellman–Ford routing algorithm to calculate the shortest path based on distance. The distance is computed from the shortest number of hops. EIGRP uses the DUAL algorithm to calculate the best route for the destination network. OSPF uses the Dijkstra algorithm to calculate the shortest path between two networks. BGP uses the best path algorithm that determines the best path between two networks.

81. B. The use of holddown timers allows the convergence of the network routing tables. This is used to hold down changes to the routing table before convergence can happen and a routing decision is hastily made by RIP. Although the topology database helps stop routing loops, it is not a functional component of distance-vector protocols. There is no such thing as anti-flapping ACLs; therefore, it is an incorrect answer. Counting-to-infinity is another name for a routing loop, and therefore, it is not a design concept used to stop routing loops.

82. D. The Border Gateway Protocol (BGP) is an exterior gateway routing protocol, which is used on the exterior of your network. RIPv1 is an internal gateway routing protocol. OSPF is an internal gateway routing protocol. EIGRP is a Cisco-proprietary internal gateway routing protocol.

83. C. Enhanced Interior Gateway Routing Protocol (EIGRP) is a Cisco-proprietary interior gateway protocol. RIPv1 is an open source interior gateway protocol. OSPF is also an open source interior gateway protocol. BGP is an open source interior or exterior gateway protocol.

84. C. Interior routing protocols are used internally inside of a network. The functional difference is that IGPs exchange information within an autonomous system, and EGPs exchange information between autonomous systems. Interior routing protocols are used to exchange information between routers within the same autonomous system. Exterior routing protocols can be used to exchange routing information between autonomous systems. Exterior routing protocols are used on the edge of a network, usually facing the Internet.

85. B. Interior gateway protocols function with-in an administrative domain. This administrative domain is defined with a common autonomous system number or area ID. IGPs, like OSPF, can require a large amount of resources, such as CPU and RAM. An EGP is by definition an exterior gateway routing protocol and not an interior gateway routing protocol. EGPs use autonomous system numbers (ASN) that have been assigned by ARIN.

86. D. The only time you need to use an exterior gateway protocol such as Border Gateway Protocol (BGP) is when you have a dual-homed connection between two ISPs. An example of this would be routing between the Internet and Internet 2. You would need to know the fastest path to the destination network via the Internet connection. You don't need to use an exterior gateway protocol to connect to the Internet; default routing is normally used. When you are delegated a large number of IP addresses, conventional static routing can be used. Fast routing to the Internet does not require the use of an exterior gateway protocol; static routing can be used.

87. D. When you're configuring RIP on a router, the RIP process will default to RIPv1, which is classful. The command `version 2` must be configured in the router instance of RIP to allow for RIPv2. The command `ip classless` is incorrect, when configured in the global configuration prompt or the config-router prompt. The command `router rip v2` is also incorrect.

88. A. The command `network 192.168.1.0` will configure the RIPv2 route process to advertise the network 192.168.1.0. The commands `network 192.168.1.0 0.0.0.255`, `network 192.168.1.0/24`, and `network 192.168.1.0 255.255.255.0` are incorrect.

89. B. When an IP address is configured on an interface, the entry in the routing table is called the local route. The local routes always have a prefix of /32. *IP address route* is not a valid term and therefore is an invalid option. A dynamic route is dynamically learned and not manually configured. A static route is manually configured, but it is a route to a remote network and not an IP address on the local router.

90. C. RIPv2 uses hop count to calculate routes. When a router sends its routing table, the next router adds a +1 to the metric for the entries in the table. Delay, bandwidth, and combinations are not used by RIPv2 to calculate routes. Minimum bandwidth, delay, load, reliability, and maximum transmission unit (MTU) are used to calculate routes with EIGRP.

91. B. The command `show ip rip database` will display all of the discovered routes and their calculated metrics. The commands `show ip protocols rip`, `show ip interface`, and `show ip rip topology` are incorrect.

92. B. The command `show ip cef` will display all of the network prefixes and the next hop that Cisco Express Forwarding (CEF) has in the forwarding information base (FIB). The command will also display the exit interface for the next hop. The commands `show cef`, `show cef nop` and `show cef route` are incorrect.

93. A. The destination MAC address changes on the layer 2 frame, leaving the layer 3 packet intact; this process is known as packet switching. The destination IP address will not change throughout the entire routing process. The source IP address will not change throughout the entire routing process, as the destination will need the source IP address to respond back to answer the request. The internal routes of the router(s) will not change based on the routed packet.

94. C. The router will drop the packet if no matching route is present. The router will not flood all active interfaces; only switches perform flooding in an attempt to discover the destination MAC address. Routers will not multicast the packet if no route is known. The router will not send the original packet back to the originating host; it will, however, send an ICMP destination network unreachable packet to the originating host.

95. D. By default, directly connected routes are used automatically on routers to create routes in the route table. Default routing is a type of static routing, and it is not configured by default or automatically. Dynamic routing must be configured on routers, and therefore, it is not used automatically. Static routes must be configured on routers, and therefore, they are not used by default.

96. D. When you configure routers, always use the rule of major/minor. The major protocol is IPv6 and the minor command is route. So the correct command is `ipv6 route ::0/0 s0/0`, specifying the ::0/0 s0/0 to mean everything out of the existing interface of s0/0. The commands `ip route 0.0.0.0/0 s0/0`, `ipv6 route 0.0.0.0/0 s0/0`, and `ipv6 unicast-route ::0/0 s0/0` are incorrect.

97. D. RIPng, OSPFv3, and EIGRPv6 are all dynamic routing protocols that work with IPv6.

98. C. The command `show ipv6 route` will display only the IPv6 routes in the routing table. The commands `show route`, `show ip route`, and `show route ipv6` are incorrect.

99. C. When traffic is remote to the immediate network, the host sends an ARP packet for the IP address of the default gateway. This determines the destination MAC address for the frame. The destination IP address is never replaced throughout the entire routing process. The host will not broadcast packets that are deemed remote; it will use the ARP process as described above. The host will not create a dedicated connection with the default gateway.

100. A. The command to view the routing table is `show ip route`. The commands `show route`, `show route table`, and `show routes` are incorrect.

101. C. The Address Resolution Protocol (ARP) is used by TCP/IP to resolve a MAC address from a known IP address. This in turn allows TCP/IP to packet switch from router to router by sending the packet to the next destination MAC address. The Internet Group Management Protocol (IGMP) is used in conjunction with multicast to join clients to a multicast group. The Reverse Address Resolution Protocol (RARP) is a legacy protocol that maps an IP address from a MAC address, similar to DHCP. The Internet Control Message Protocol (ICMP) is a layer 3 protocol that allows for end-to-end testing with a command such as `traceroute`.

102. C. The `ping` command uses ICMP to check the status of a router. It also gives the round-trip time of the packet. Simple Network Management Protocol (SNMP) traps are alerts sent from an SNMP agent to an SNMP collector when a specific event is triggered. SNMP trap notifications are messages that are sent to a network management station (NMS) and are defined with severity levels. The Address Resolution Protocol (ARP) helps map a MAC address to an IP address for the framing of data.

103. C. When you're using the `ping` command, the exclamation marks signify that the ping was successful and the router is responding. If the distant router is not responding, you will see periods. A high or low response time cannot be identified with the `ping` command.

104. B. The correct command sequence is `ip route` followed by the network ID, the subnet mask, and then the gateway. In this case, the gateway is a serial line. The commands `ip route 192.168.4.0/24 serial 0/1`, `ip route 192.168.4.0/24 interface serial 0/1`, and `ip route Router(config-rtr)#192.168.4.0/24 serial 0/1` are incorrect.

105. B. The command `ip default-gateway` allows the management plane of the router to egress the network the router is configured upon through a different gateway. The command `ip default-gateway` is not used for dynamic routing; it is strictly used for the management traffic of the router. Although the specified gateway could be wrong, correcting it will not allow for the routing of data, only management traffic.

106. C. Router A needs to be pointed to the adjacent router's far IP address. Imagine a hall with two doors; one door leads to Network A and the other leads to Network B. To get to Network B, you need to get to the router's IP interface (door). The commands `ip route 192.168.3.0 255.255.255.0 serial 0/1`, `ip route 192.168.3.0 255.255.255.0 192.168.2.1`, and `ip route 192.168.3.0 255.255.255.0 192.168.3.1` are incorrect.

107. D. When an IP address of 192.168.1.1/24 is configured, for example, the router will create a summary route for 192.168.1.0/24 as well as a route for 192.168.1.1/32. Both of these changes to the routing table will trigger an update depending on which dynamic routing protocol is being used.

108. B. The command `show ip interfaces brief` will display all of the interfaces and their configured IP addresses. The commands `show ip`, `show interfaces`, and `show ip brief` are incorrect.

109. A. A route for the interface will not be populated in the routing table until the interface is in an up/up status. If the link was disconnected, this would create the same symptoms. Although the speed could be incorrect, the route would still be populated in the route table. Setting the bandwidth on an interface will only help routing protocols such as EIGRP make better route decisions. Saving the configuration will have no effect on route entries in the route table.

110. C. Static routing is suited for small networks, where the central admin has a good understanding of the network layout. It does reduce router-to-router communications because the overhead of routing dynamic protocols will not use up bandwidth. Adding networks in a static routing environment can be a time-consuming task for a network administrator because of all the routers that will need to be updated. Static routing is best suited for small networks and not large networks. There is not an advantage of easy configuration or easier accessibility by any network admin with static routing.

111. C. When you configure a static route, it is temporarily stored in the `running-config`. After it is saved by using `copy running-config startup-config`, it is stored in the startup configuration and can survive reboots. The startup configuration is located on the NVRAM. When a router loads, the IOS is loaded into RAM from the flash. The router will then load the startup configuration into RAM. The routing database is also held in RAM.

112. C. The easiest way to accomplish this is to super-net the addresses together. The network of 192.168.0.0/30 or 255.255.240.0 would capture traffic for the range of 192.168.0.1 to 192.168.3.254. The commands `ip route 192.168.0.0 255.255.0.0 198.43.23.2`, `ip route 192.168.0.0 255.255.255.0 198.43.23.2`, and `ip route 192.168.0.0 255.255.0.240 198.43.23.2` are incorrect.

113. B. Secondary routes with higher administrative distance (AD) are used for failover. If the physical interface fails, the route statement will be taken out of the routing table. Then the second route will become active. Route tables unfortunately do not adjust based on the success or failure of a packet being routed. A router will not know to use a secondary route if the primary route fails to route a packet. If a dynamic protocol is used, such as OSPF or EIGRP, the routing protocol can sense high amounts of traffic and adjust route paths. However, statically configured routes are not managed by these dynamic routing protocols; therefore, the secondary route will not be used. A router will not be aware of routing loops; it will not respond with a change in the routing of packets.

114. A. The IP address of 208.43.34.17/29 belongs to the network of 208.43.34.16/29. In addition to the statement for the network that owns the IP address, the individual IP address will be configured as a local route with a /32. All other options are incorrect.

115. D. The 192.168.4.0/24 network is routable via the Serial 0/0/1 interface. There is no route statement in the route table for the 172.30.0.0/16, 192.168.128.0/24, or 192.168.0.0/16 networks.

116. D. The route you will need should address the 198.44.4.0/24 network with the network mask of 255.255.255.0. The exit interface is Serial 0/1, which is directly connected to the other router. The commands `ip route 198.44.4.0/24 198.55.4.9`, `ip route 198.44.4.0 255.255.255.0 198.55.4.10`, and `ip route 198.44.4.0 255.255.255.0 Serial 0/0` are incorrect.

117. A. The IP address of 194.22.34.54/28 belongs to the network of 194.22.34.48/28. All other options are incorrect.

118. C. When entering IPv6 routes. you must use the command `ipv6 route`. It is then followed by the IPv6 prefix and mask and then the gateway. The default route would be `ipv6 route ::/0 serial 0/0`. The command `ip route 0.0.0.0 0.0.0.0 serial 0/0` is incorrect because it's specific to IPv4. The command `ipv6 route 0.0.0.0 0.0.0.0 serial 0/0` is incorrect because it's a mix of IPv6 and IPv4. The command `ip route ::/0 serial 0/0` is incorrect because it's a mixture of IPv4 and IPv6.

119. B. When configuring an IPv6 route, you use the `ipv6 route` command. You then must specify the network and mask using CIDR notation. Last, you specify the exit interface or next hop of `serial 0/0/0`. The complete command will be `ipv6 route fc00:0:0:1/64 serial 0/0/0`. The command `ip route fc00:0:0:1 serial 0/0/0` is incorrect because it's a mixture of IPv4 and IPv6. The command `ip route` fc00:0:0:1/64 serial 0/0 is incorrect because it's a mixture of IPv4 and IPv6. The command ipv6 route fc00:0:0:1 serial 0/0/0 is incorrect because it is missing the subnet mask.

120. A. The packet will be routed to the IP address of 192.168.4.2. This will occur because the administrative distance is lower than the route for the gateway of 192.168.4.5. Interface Serial 0/0/1 and Interface Serial 0/2/0 will not be used because no matching route exists in the route table.

121. D. The command no switchport does the opposite of configuring a port as a switchport. It turns the port into a routed interface in which an IP address can be configured. A Switched Virtual Interface (SVI) is created when a VLAN interface is created and it is not related to a switchport. An access port is configured with the switchport mode access command. A trunk port is configured with the switchport mode trunk command.

122. B. Router on a stick (ROAS) is created by configuring a trunk between the switch and the router. ROAS will receive tagged frames and route them, then send them back down the interface to the respective connected VLAN. Although you could purchase a router with additional interfaces, this would not be the most efficient method of completing the task. Configuring a dynamic routing protocol will not accomplish this task.

123. C. The ip routing command must be entered in global config. When this command is entered, a routing table will be created and populated. The commands routing, ip router, and ip route are incorrect.

124. B. 802.1Q is the trunking protocol that should be used for tagging VLANs when you are routing between VLANs on a router. 802.1x is a protocol that authenticates layer 2 communications. Inter-Switch Link (ISL) is a Cisco-proprietary protocol and it's not always supported. The VLAN Trunking Protocol (VTP) is a Cisco-proprietary protocol that helps propagate VLAN configuration to other switches.

125. D. The command encapsulation dot1q 2 will associate the subinterface with VLAN 2. If you specify the native tag after the command, it will make this subinterface the native VLAN for the trunk. The commands switchport native vlan 2, interface gi 0/1.2 native, and native vlan 2 are incorrect.

126. A. When configuring an IP address on an SVI, you must enter the interface of the VLAN. Once in the pseudo-interface, you enter the **ip address** command and then enter **no shutdown**. Entering the command interface vlan 10 and then configuring ip address 192.168.10.1/24 will not work because the commands are not followed by a no shutdown command. The IP address is also entered in CIDR format and not the proper dot-decimal notation. When entering vlan 10, you will be placed inside the VLAN configuration prompt and not the SVI.

127. A. When you are configuring a router on a stick (ROAS), the switchport of the switch must be in trunk mode. This is so that traffic can be tagged as it gets sent to the router, which will see the tag and route it accordingly by the destination IP address. In an access mode, the VLAN information is stripped from the frame before it enters or leaves the interface.

In routed mode, the interface performs as a routed interface. In switched mode, the interface can perform as an access mode or trunk mode switchport.

128. B. A best practice is to always name the subinterface the same as the VLAN number you are going to route. An example is if you are connected to Fa0/1 on the router and you want to create an IP address on the subinterface for VLAN 2. Then you would name the subinterface **Fa0/1.2**. The subinterface will not allow you to name it with a friendly name, unlike Cisco switches that allow for a friendly name to be associated with VLANs. Although you can configure a subinterface from 1 through 65535 and higher with various IOS versions, the default gateway cannot be sensibly represented. Naming the subinterface the same as the switch's interface number is not very useful in identifying the VLAN.

129. C. The command `encapsulation dot1q 5`, when configured inside of the subinterface, will program the subinterface to accept frames for VLAN 5. The commands `interface gi 0/1.5`, `vlan 5`, and `switchport access vlan 5` are incorrect.

130. B. On 2960-XR switches, you must enable the Switching Database Manager (SDM) for LAN Base routing to enable routing. The switch then requires a reload before you can configure routable SVIs. The commands `ip lanbase`, `sdm lanbase-routing`, and `sdm routing` are incorrect.

131. A. The same command used to verify physical interfaces on a router is used to verify SVI interfaces on a switch. The command `show ip interface brief` will pull up the configured IP address on each VLAN interface. The commands `show interfaces status`, `show svi`, and `show switchports ip` are incorrect.

132. C. The command `ip address 192.168.2.0 255.255.255.0` only defines the 192.168.2.0 network. Although the subnet is correct, the statement does not specify a valid host IP address for the SVI. Nothing prevents you from using the 192.168.2.0 subnet on the SVI, but a valid IP address contained in the network must be configured. The VLAN does not need to be configured first, but it is a good idea to configure it first. The VLAN will automatically be created when the VLAN interface is configured.

133. B. The LAN Base feature supports IP routing between SVIs. However, it must be enabled first via the Switching Database Manager (SDM) by using the `sdm prefer lanbase-routing` command. There is no prerequisite of IP addresses preconfigured before configuring the `ip routing` command. If there is not enough memory for the routing table, you will not receive an "Invalid input detected" error. The IP Base feature is not required; the base license will cover IP routing.

134. C. The `no switchport` command will configure a physical port of a switch to act as a routed interface. Once the physical port is configured as a non-switchport, you will be able to configure an IP address directly on the interface. The commands `switchport routed`, `no ip-routing`, and `ip address 192.168.2.1 255.255.255.0` are incorrect.

135. A. The command `show interface gi 0/2 switchport` will show the state of a port. It will display if the port is switched or routed among several other attributes. The commands `show interface gi 0/2 state`, `show switchport interface gi 0/2`, and `show status interface gi 0/2` are incorrect.

136. D. The command `encapsulation isl 5` configured in the subinterface will achieve this. It specifies the encapsulation as ISL and a VLAN of 5 that it will be tagged with. The command `encapsulation 5` configured in the interface is incorrect. The command `encapsulation isl 5` configured in the interface is also incorrect. Although the command `switchport encapsulation isl 5` is configured in the correct subinterface, the command itself is incorrect.

137. B. After configuring a VLAN and the respective SVI interface, a route will not show until at least one port is configured with the new VLAN and it is in an up status. The VLAN will be taken out of a shutdown state when the command `no shutdown` is configured. The `show ip route` command will not display the SVI as a directly connected route until an interface is configured with the VLAN. Dynamic routing protocols are not a prerequisite for configuring SVIs.

138. B. Using router on a stick (ROAS) is a cheaper alternative to IVR if the current switch does not support layer 3 routing. Using ROAS is highly inefficient because all traffic that is routed to the router must be routed back, diminishing the bandwidth of the link by 50%. ROAS can be used with ISL or 802.1Q. ROAS is not limited to a maximum of 16 routes.

139. B. When configuring ROAS on a router's interface, you should always issue the `no ip address` command. No IPs can be configured on the main interface. All IPs are configured on the subinterfaces. The commands `ip routing`, `ip encapsulation dot1q`, and `sdm routing` are incorrect.

140. C. Verifying the proper operation of the switch would start with verifying that the port is correctly set as a trunk to the router. If it is not set as a trunk, it would not be able to tag frames for the router to direct to the proper interfaces. The commands `show ip route`, `show interface status`, and `show switchport` are incorrect.

141. C. When you're configuring a router interface to accept VLAN tagging, the subinterface numbering does not matter. It is recommended that the subinterface match the VLAN for readability. However, `encapsulation dot1q 10` is the command that allows the subinterface to accept the frames for VLAN 10. The commands `encapsulation vlan 10 dot1q`, `interface Fa 0/0.10`, and `ip address 192.168.10.1 255.255.255.0` are incorrect.

142. A. When ROAS is implemented, only the physical interface has a unique MAC address. All ARP requests for the IP addresses configured on the subinterfaces respond with the same MAC address. They are not unique MAC addresses, but on each VLAN they are unique in the sense that no other machines on the VLAN share the same MAC address.

143. A. Each IP address on a subinterface is the routed gateway for the VLAN on that subinterface. The main interface should be configured with the `no ip address` command when ROAS is configured. The default native VLAN of 1 is configured on the switch side only unless you explicitly configure a native VLAN on the router.

144. C. Default routing is a form of static routing. It is used on the edge of a network to direct all traffic to the inner core of the network. OSPF, EIGRP, and RIP are dynamic routing protocols.

145. B. Static routing is extremely secure because it does not need to broadcast or multicast routing updates. These updates can be intercepted or injected into a network to create problems. Static routing requires a higher degree of administrative overhead because all possible routes must be configured and maintained manually. All routing protocols have the potential to create resiliency on a network. Static routing is not scalable because it is all manually entered.

146. D. Static routing has the lowest bandwidth overhead because there is no bandwidth required to maintain static routes. RIP routing has the highest bandwidth overhead because it uses either broadcasts or multicasts to transmit the entire routing table. OSPF and EIGRP routing both have higher bandwidth overhead than static routing.

147. A. Most dynamic routing protocols will summarize routes. They do this for efficiency, so the least number of route statements will need to exist in the routing table. Directly connected routes do not perform auto-summarization. Default routing is a technique of sending all traffic that does not specifically match to a default router interface. Static routing requires manual intervention, and because of this, it does not auto-summarize.

148. D. Static routing requires administrator intervention when a route goes down. Dynamic routing will automatically update routes when a route goes down. Directly connected routes will be pulled out of the routing table if the link goes down. Default routing is generally used for stub networks where the only route out of the network is the default route.

149. C. The `show ip routes static` command will display all of the routes that are configured as static routes. The commands `show static routes`, `show ip static routes`, and `show ip routes` are incorrect.

150. C. The network ID of 2000:0db8:4400:2300::/64 will be calculated and assigned to the directly connected route of Serial 0/0. The network ID will not be shortened to 2000:0db8:: because there is a network of /64 defined. The IPv6 address of 2000: 0db8:4400:2300:1234:0000:0000:0000/128 will not be assigned to Serial 0/0 because it is a network ID. The network ID should be 2000:0db8:4400:2300::/64; therefore, 2000:db8:4400:2300:0000/64 is a wrong option.

151. B. The second address on an interface with the prefix of ff80::/64 is the link-local address for Duplicate Address Detection (DAD) and Stateless Address Autoconfiguration. Link-local addresses are nonroutable, so they will not get added to the routing table. Multicast addresses will not get added to the routing tables, but this would not explain why the statement does not appear in the routing table. Multiple route statements can be active for a particular interface. Broadcast addresses will not get added to the routing tables, but this would not explain why the statement does not appear in the routing table.

152. B. The backup route to network 192.168.3.0/24 is though the gateway of 192.168.2.6. However, the administrative distance of a normal static route is 1. So the AD must be higher than RIP, which is 120. An AD of 220 is higher than 90, so the RIP route will be the main route and the static route will become the backup floating route. The command `ip route 192.168.2.8 255.255.255.252 192.168.2.6` is incorrect because the AD is not higher than 90. The command `ip route 192.168.3.0 255.255.255.0 192.168.2.6 90` is incorrect because the AD is 90. The command `ip route 192.168.3.0 255.255.255.0 192.168.2.10` is incorrect because it will assume an AD of 1.

153. C. The command `ipv6 address auto-config default` configures the interface of Serial 0/3/0 with an IP address via SLAAC. When the default subcommand is used, it allows the router to inherit the default route discovered via NDP RS/RA messages. The commands `ipv6 address default`, `ip route ::/0 serial 0/3/0`, and `ipv6 address slaac` are incorrect.

154. D. The command `default-information originate` will advertise the default route to all other RIPv2 routers. The commands `network 0.0.0.0`, `default-route advertise`, and `network 0.0.0.0 default` are incorrect.

155. C. The correct command to implement a default route for routing is `ip route 0.0.0.0 0.0.0.0 192.168.2.6`. The commands `ip default-network 192.168.2.6`, `ip route default-gateway 192.168.2.6`, and `ip route 0.0.0.0 255.255.255.255 192.168.2.6` are incorrect.

156. D. You can conclude the ping packet was routed through 3 routers, because the default TTL is 255. If the packet started with a TTL of 255 and a TTL of 252 was reported, 3 routers routed the ping packet (255 – 252 = 3). Time has nothing to do with TTL; therefore, the time and delay are not reported in the resultant TTL. The TTL decrements by one as the packet is routed by each router to its destination. Therefore, the answer of 252 routers is invalid.

157. D. The command `show ip route rip` will display only the route entries for the RIP protocol that exist in the route table. Always remember that the Cisco commands should be from left to right, least specific to most specific; therefore, `show ip` pertains to the IPv4 stack, `route` pertains to the route table, and `rip` specifies only those entries in the table. The commands `show ip rip`, `show ip route`, and `show ip rip route` are incorrect.

158. B. Open Shortest Path First (OSPF) is a true link-state protocol. Link-state protocols keep track of the state of the links as well as the bandwidth the links report. Routing Information Protocol (RIP) is a distance-vector routing protocol. Enhanced Interior Gateway Routing Protocol (EIGRP) is a hybrid routing protocol. Border Gateway Protocol is a path-vector routing protocol.

159. C. The Dijkstra algorithm is used by OSPF to calculate the shortest path based on a cost calculation of the bandwidth of the link vs. distance vector, which is based on hop count. RIP uses the Bellman–Ford algorithm to calculate distance. EIGRP uses the diffusing update algorithm to calculate a best route. BGP uses the best path algorithm to determine the best path for a packet.

160. A. Link-state protocols such as OSPF require all routers to maintain their own topology database of the network. This topology database is why routing loops are less likely to occur. Distance-vector protocols don't really have a topology of the network and thus suffer from routing loops. Each router is responsible for maintaining its own topology database and therefore does not share its topology. A router will only create a neighbor database for the neighboring routers, and OSPF will not track the state of all other routers as well. Link-state protocols can use multiple routes to the same destination, but by default, only one successive route will be entered in the route table.

161. D. OSPF employs link-state advertisement (LSA) flooding and triggered updates. When these occur, every participating router will recalculate its routing tables. Link-state routing protocols do not use hop count as a metric. Link-state routing protocols support CIDR and VLSM, but all other routing protocols also support CIDR and VLSM; therefore, it is not an advantage. OSPF requires a rather large amount of CPU and RAM to calculate and retain databases.

162. C. Link-state protocols such as OSPF are best suited for large hierarchical networks such as global networks, since they can separate out the participating routers with areas and border area routers. Extremely small networks do not warrant the planning and maintenance of OSPF and are best suited for static routing. Networks with routers that have a limited amount of RAM and CPU are best suited for static routing. OSPF requires a network admin with the knowledge of OSPF so it is properly configured.

163. B. Open Shortest Path First (OSPF) is an interior gateway protocol and a nonproprietary standard. Exterior gateway protocol (EGP) is a class of protocols used externally on an organization's network. Enhanced Interior Gateway Routing Protocol (EIGRP) is a Cisco-proprietary protocol. Border Gateway Protocol (BGP) is an EGP.

164. B. Although you have different administrative units, all of the administrative units are in the same company. In this situation, it is recommended to use an interior gateway protocol that can segment each administrative unit. OSPF will perform this requirement with the use of area IDs. Border Gateway Protocol (BGP) is an EGP used to work with different autonomous routing organizations. RIPv2 does not have the ability to segment administrative units. Exterior Gateway Protocol (EGP) is a class of protocols used externally on the organization's network.

165. A. Area 0 must be present in an OSPF network. It is the backbone area and all other areas must connect to it. All other options are incorrect.

166. C. Router A is on the boundary of the autonomous system, which OSPF manages; therefore, it is an autonomous system boundary router (ASBR). Area border routers (ABRs) are routers that sit between one or more OSPF areas. Autonomous system routers (ASRs) are routers that sit between one or more autonomous systems. Area backup routers is not a type of router for OSPF.

167. B. OSPF uses 224.0.0.5 for neighbor discovery via link-state advertisements (LSAs). Routing Information Protocol version 2 (RIPv2) uses 224.0.0.9 for routing updates. OSPF uses 224.0.0.6 for DRs and backup designated routers (BDR). EIGRP uses 224.0.0.7 for neighboring routers.

168. A. Routers C, D, and E are called area border routers (ABRs). They border both the backbone area and areas 1, 2, and 3, respectively. Autonomous system routers (ASRs) are routers that sit between one or more autonomous systems. Router A is on the boundary of the autonomous system, which OSPF manages; therefore, it is an autonomous system boundary router (ASBR). Area border routers (ABRs) are routers that will take over for a router covering a routing area.

169. D. OSPF updates are event triggered. These events could be a neighbor router not responding or a route going down. OSPF is a link-state protocol and not a distance-vector protocol.

OSPF does not perform auto-summarization of routes. OSPF multicasts changes to links, and each router calculates changes to its own routing table.

170. B. The highest IP address configured on all of the loopback interfaces is chosen first. If a loopback is not configured, then the highest IP address on an active interface is chosen. However, if a RID is statically set via the OSPF process, it will override all of the above. The RID is always the highest IP address configured, not the lowest. The MAC address is not relevant to OSPF for the calculation of the RID.

171. C. A link is a routed interface that is assigned to a network and participates in the OSPF process. This link will be tracked by the OSPF process for up/down information as well as the network with which it is associated. Just because two routers are participating in OSPF does not mean they form a link. Routers sharing the same area ID does not dictate that they will form a link. Autonomous system (AS) numbers are not used with OSPF; therefore, this is an incorrect option.

172. B. Adjacencies are formed between the designated router (DR) and its neighbors in the same area. This is done to ensure that all neighboring routers have the same Link State Database (LSDB). Adjacencies are not formed between routers on the same link, same autonomous system (AS), and same OSPF area unless one is the DR and they are connected on the same LAN.

173. D. The designated router (DR) is elected by the highest priority in the same area. If the priorities are all the same, then the highest RID becomes the tiebreaker. OSPF will elect a DR for each broadcast network, such as a LAN. This is to minimize the number of adjacencies formed. A DR is never elected by the lowest priority or lowest RID.

174. B. The neighborship database is where all of the routers can be found that have responded to hello packets. The neighborship database contains all of the routers by RID, and each router participating in OSPF manages its own neighborship database. The route table database is what the router's route decisions are based on. The topological database is the link-state database in OSPF. The link-state database contains all the active links that have been learned.

175. C. OSPF uses areas to create a hierarchal structure for routing. This structure begins with the backbone area of 0. All other areas connect to it to form a complete autonomous system (AS). This enables scalability with OSPF, since each area works independently. OSPF operates within an autonomous system such as an organization. OSPF uses process IDs so that OSPF can be reset by clearing the process. OSPF uses router IDs (RIDs) so that a designated router can be elected.

176. D. A LAN is an example of a broadcast multi-access network. All nodes in a network segment can hear a broadcast and have common access to the local area network (LAN). In OSPF, a broadcast (multi-access) network requires a DR and BDR. An X.25 network is a legacy network connectivity method that can provide packet switching. Frame Relay by default is a non-broadcast multi-access (NBMA) connectivity method. Asynchronous Transfer Mode (ATM) is a legacy network connectivity method that acts as an NBMA network.

177. C. The multicast address of 224.0.0.6 is used to communicate between the designated router and the adjacencies formed. This multicast address is used for LSA flooding on broadcast networks. RIP version 2 uses 224.0.0.9 for routing updates. OSPF uses 224.0.0.5 for neighbor discovery via link-state advertisements (LSAs). EIGRP uses 224.0.0.7 for neighboring routers.

178. A. The command `router ospf 20` configures a process ID of 20. This process identifies the databases for an OSPF process as well as its configuration. The process ID is only locally significant to the router on which it is configured. It can be an arbitrary number from 1 to 65535. The area for OSPF is set with the network command, such as `network 192.168.1.1 0.0.0.255 area 0`. Autonomous systems (ASs) are not used with OSPF. Cost is not set with the `router ospf 20` command; it is set with the `ip ospf cost` command.

179. B. The command `show interface` will display the reported bandwidth or configured bandwidth of an interface. The command `show ospf interface` will only display the calculated cost. The commands `show ospf` and `show running-config` are also incorrect.

180. D. When you're configuring Cisco routers to participate in OSPF with non-Cisco routers, each interface on the Cisco router needs to be configured. The `ip ospf cost` command can be tuned between 1 to 65535 and will need to be matched with the other vendor. The command `ip cost 20000` is incorrect. The command `ip ospf cost 20000` is also incorrect when configured in a global configuration prompt.

181. D. The first command sets up the process ID of 1 via `router ospf 1`. The next command advertises the network of 192.168.1.0 with a wildcard mask of 0.0.0.255 and specifies area 0 via `network 192.168.1.0 0.0.0.255 area 0`. The command `network 192.168.1.0 0.0.0.255` is incorrect, as it should follow with an area number as the last argument. The `ospf 0` argument must follow after the `router` argument, such as `router ospf 0`, which is why option B is incorrect. The command `network 192.168.1.0 255.255.255.0` is incorrect, as it should follow with an area number.

182. A. By default, Cisco routes will load-balance 4 equal-cost routes with OSPF. All other options are incorrect.

183. C. The wildcard mask is 0.0.0.31 for a network advertisement of 131.40.32.0/27. A wildcard mask is a bitwise calculation that matches the bits that change. The /27 has subnets with multiples of 32. The easiest way to calculate wildcard masks for configuration is to subtract 1 from the subnet you are trying to match; for example, matching a subnet of 32 in the third octet minus 1 equals 31, and you want to match all bits in the fourth octet with 255.

184. D. The command `maximum-paths 10` will configure a maximum of 10 routes of equal cost for load balancing. This command must be entered under the OSPF router process. The command `ospf equal-cost 10` is incorrect when configured in both the global configuration prompt and the config-router prompt. The command `ospf maximum-paths 10` is incorrect when configured in a global configuration prompt.

185. D. The maximum number of equal-cost routes that can be configured for load balancing with OSPF on a Cisco router is 32. By default, Cisco routers will use 4 equal-cost routes.

186. A. The command `show ip ospf` will allow you to verify the currently configured router ID (RID) or the IP address acting as the router's RID. The commands `show ip interface`, `show ip ospf rid`, and `show ip ospf neighbor` are incorrect.

187. C. The wildcard mask is 0.0.0.15 for a network advertisement of 192.168.1.16/28. A wildcard mask is a bitwise calculation that matches the bits that change. The /28 has subnets with multiples of 16. The easiest way to calculate wildcard masks for configuration is to subtract 1 from the subnet you are trying to match; for example, matching a subnet of 16 in the fourth octet minus 1 equals 15.

188. A. The command `show ip ospf neighbor` will show all of the adjacencies formed as well as the routers discovered. The commands `show router adjacency`, `show ip ospf`, and `show ip ospf router` are incorrect.

189. B. The default hello interval is 10 seconds for a broadcast (multi-access) network such as a LAN. All other options are incorrect.

190. B. The command `passive-interface gigabitethernet 0/1` must be configured under the router process. This command will suppress hello packets from exiting the Gi0/1 interface. The command `passive-interface` is incorrect when it is configured inside an interface. The command `passive-interface gigabitethernet 0/1` is incorrect when it is configured in global configuration mode. The command `passive-interface default` is also incorrect.

191. C. The command `show ip ospf interface` will show all interfaces in which OSPF is configured and sending hello packets. The command `show interfaces` is incorrect as it will only show the interface on the router. The command `show ip routes` is incorrect as it will show the route table. The command `show ip ospf brief` is also an incorrect command.

192. D. Although all of these are valid methods of possibly setting the router ID (RID) of the router for OSPF, the configuration of `router-id 192.168.1.5` will override all others. Entering interface fa 0/1 and then `ip address 192.168.1.5 255.255.255.0` will configure an IP address on an interface. Entering `interface loopback 0` and then `ip address 192.168.1.5 255.255.255.0` will configure an IP address on the loopback interface 0. The command `rid 192.168.1.5` is incorrect.

193. C. The command `passive-interface default` configured under the OSPF process will cease hello packets by default on all interfaces. The command `no passive-interface gigabitethernet 0/2` will allow hello packets to exit the interface and allow Gi0/2 to become a neighbor. The command `active-interface gigabitethernet 0/2` is an incorrect command. Therefore, any combination of `active-interface` is incorrect. If `passive-interface gigabitethernet 0/2` is configured, then `gigabitethernet 0/2` will not send hello packets.

194. A. After the OSPF configuration is changed, OSPF needs to be restarted. This is achieved at the privileged exec prompt by typing `clear ip ospf`. The router configuration prompt will not allow `shutdown` and `no shutdown` commands. The commands `clear ip ospf` and `clear ospf` are incorrect.

195. D. Type 3 link-state advertisements (LSAs) contain summary information about the networks on the other side of the area boarder router (ABR). These LSA announcements are called summary link advertisements (SLAs). ABRs sit between areas within OSPF. ABRs listen to Type 1 link-state advertisements but do not exchange. ABRs listen to Type 2 link-state but do not exchange link state advertisement messages.

196. B. The network IDs of 128.24.0.0/24, 128.24.1.0/24, 128.24.2.0/24, and 128.24.3.0/24 can be summarized as 128.24.1.0/22. The wildcard-mask for /22 is 0.0.252.255. The commands `network 128.24.0.0/22 area 0` and `network 128.24.0.0/22 area 1` are incorrect because they require a bitmask, not a CIDR notation. The commands `128.24.0.0 0.0.254.255 area 0` and `network 128.24.0.0 255.254.255 area 1` are incorrect because the bitmask is incorrect. The command `network 128.24.0.0 0.0.255.255` is incorrect because it does not specify the area.

197. A. The command `show ip ospf database` will show you a summary count of all the LSAs in the database. The commands `show ip ospf states`, `show ip ospf neighbors`, and `show ip ospf topology` are incorrect.

198. D. Interface GigabitEthernet 0/0 is not participating because it is in a different network than what the wildcard mask is advertising. The wildcard mask of 0.0.0.63 is a /26 network mask with the range of 197.234.3.0 to 197.234.3.63. The interface Gi0/0 is in the 197.234.3.64/26 network and therefore will not participate.

199. D. Interface GigabitEthernet 0/0 is not participating because it is in a different network than what the wildcard mask is advertising. The wildcard mask of 0.0.0.63 is a /26 network mask with the range of 197.234.3.0 to 197.234.3.63. The interface Gi0/0 is in the 197.234.3.64/26 network and therefore will not participate.

200. A. Fast convergence of the Link State Database (LSDB) that feeds the routing tables is a direct result of a hierarchical OSPF design. The use of areas allows for routers within an area to converge and send summary link advertisements (LSAs) to other areas. OSPF design is much more complex than static routing or other dynamic routing protocols such as RIP. Bandwidth will not be increased with the implementation of OSPF. Security does not improve with OSPF.

201. B. Designated routers (DRs) are only elected on broadcast (multi-access) networks such as a LAN. The router with the highest IP address will become the designated router. Since Router B has IP addresses of 192.168.10.2/30, 192.168.10.5/30, and 192.168.2.1/24, it will become the DR. Router C is on a non-broadcast multi-access (NBMA), and therefore, it will not be elected to be a designated router. Router D and Router E have IP addresses of 192.168.2.2/24 and 192.168.2.3/24, respectively, which are lower than Router B's interfaces.

202. B. Router B is called the area border router (ABR) since it sits between area 0 and area 1. An autonomous system border router (ASBR) is a router that sits between two or more autonomous systems (ASs), such as the Internet and an organization. A designated router (DR) is a router that is elected in a LAN to form neighborships with other routers. A backup designated router (BDR) is a router that is next in line if the DR fails.

203. C. The subnet mask is incorrect because it should be at least 8 bits starting with 255.0.0.0 or a higher number of bits. The process ID would not affect the operation of OSPF. The area number will only affect a router if it is not participating with another bordering router or router within its area. The network ID is correct in this example, but the bitmask is incorrect.

204. A. In order to form an adjacency, the area IDs must match as well as the hello and dead timers. If the hello timer is changed on one router, it must be changed on the other router to form an adjacency. Although the link is a point-to-point connection, the two routers will form an adjacency because it supports multicast/broadcasts. The process IDs do not need to match to form an adjacency. Areas are not configured with an IP address; therefore this is an incorrect option.

205. A. The FULL state is only achieved after the router has created an adjacency with a neighbor router and downloaded the LSAs to form its topological database. The EXSTART state means that the DR and BDR routers have been elected and are awaiting the exchange of link state information. The INIT state is the first step in the creation of an adjacency. The EXCHANGE state means that the exchange of the LSA information is in progress.

206. D. Both routers have formed an adjacency. However, the LSDB on each router has not yet been fully synchronized. Once the LSDBs have been synchronized, the state will become FULL and OSPF will calculate costs. The figure does not detail any information to conclude that the neighbors are having problems forming an adjacency. The neighbor or router OSPF recalculation of cost would not show in the show ip ospf neighbor output.

207. C. The command ip ospf cost 25 should be configured on the interface that will act as the backup route. This adjustment of cost will allow the router to prefer the other route first. The commands ip ospf priority 25, ip ospf route primary, and passive interface gi 0/0 are incorrect.

208. D. The router ID of 192.168.2.2 is neither a designated router (DR) nor a backup designated router (BDR). Since it is neither, it will only form an adjacency with the DR or BDR and will participate in future elections. The figure does not show any evidence that the router is in the process of forming an adjacency since all of the states show FULL. The DROTHER state means that the router is not a designated router or backup designated router. It is participating in OSPF because it shows up in the neighbor table for OSPF.

209. B. The command ip ospf priority 10 will change the interface's default priority of 1 to 10. This router will always become the designated router (DR) on the LAN. The commands ospf priority, ip address 192.168.5.2 255.255.255.0, and ip ospf cost 15 are incorrect.

210. D. The command `show ip ospf interface` will display the interface details of each interface for OSPF. In this information, the DR and BDR router ID (RIDs) will be displayed. The commands `show ip ospf neighbor`, `show ip ospf database`, and `show ip ospf dr` are incorrect.

211. D. In order to form an adjacency, the area IDs must match. In this figure, Router A has an area of 0 and Router B has an area of 1 configured. The hello and dead timers on both routers match at 10 seconds for the hello and 40 seconds for the dead timer. The existence of a designated router (DR) will not restrict the two routers from forming an adjacency. The process IDs do not need to match for the two routers to form an adjacency.

212. C. The command `default-information originate` will propagate a default route originating from router 172.16.1.1. All OSPF routers will calculate their default routes back to this router. The commands `ip route 0.0.0.0 0.0.0.0 serial 0/0`, `default-route originate`, and `network 0.0.0.0 0.0.0.0 area 0` are incorrect.

213. A. Bandwidth is always specified in kilobits per second (Kb/s), so 2.048 Mb/s would be 2,048,000 bits per second, or 2,048 Kb/s. The command `bandwidth 2048000000` is incorrect because it is configured in Kb/s, not b/s, although this would be 2,048 gigabits. The command `bandwidth 2.048` is incorrect because it cannot be notated with a period. The command `bandwidth 2048000` is incorrect because it is configured in Kb/s, not b/s.

214. D. All routers by default have an OSPF priority of 1. If you set the priority to 0, the router will never become a designated router (DR). This command must be set in the interface. The command `no ospf designated` is incorrect regardless of which configuration prompt it is configured in. The command `passive interface gi 0/0` is also incorrect.

215. B. The command `interface loopback 0` will configure and create a pseudo-interface called loopback 0. The loopback number must be specified, and the loopback should not overlap a loopback already configured. The command `ip address 192.168.1.2 255.255.255.0` will configure the IP address on the loopback interface. The command `ip address 192.168.1.2/24` is an incorrect command because you cannot configure CIDR notation in this prompt. When configuring loopback interfaces, you must supply a number between 0 and 1023.

216. D. Both the customer edge (CE) routers and the provider edge (PE) routers can host area 0. However, the service provider must support area 0, called the super backbone, on its PE routers since all areas must be connected to area 0. The customer chooses whether the CE participates in area 0. Although the PE and the CE can host area 0, they are not exclusively configured for area 0. The CE does not need Generic Routing Encapsulation (GRE) to support OSPF.

217. A. The Open Shortest Path First (OSPF) priority for a router is a value of 1. This priority is used when electing a designated router (DR) and backup designated router (BDR). The higher the value, the higher the chances of the router becoming a DR or BDR. All other options are incorrect.

218. D. When configuring OSPF for the designated router (DR), if you configure another router with a higher priority, the original DR will remain the current DR. OSPF does not allow for preemption, and therefore you must force the election by clearing the OSPF process on the DR. This will force the DR to relinquish its status. Using the shutdown command on the interface with the highest IP address will not restart the OSPF process. The command ospf election force is invalid; there is no such command. Executing the command clear ip ospf process on any router other than the DR will only restart the OSPF process on the router on which it is executed.

219. A. In order to form an adjacency, the two neighbors must have the same hello timer of 30 seconds. The routers can be configured with multiple area IDs, and this will not affect their ability to form an adjacency. The default hello interval on a LAN is 10 seconds; for non-broadcast networks such as Frame Relay, the hello timer is 30 seconds. In order to form an adjacency, the hello and dead intervals must match.

220. B. The administrative distance for OSPF is 110. Internal Enhanced Interior Gateway Routing Protocol (EIGRP) has an administrative distance (AD) of 90. RIP has an administrative distance of 120. Internal Border Gateway Protocol (BGP) has an administrative distance of 200.

221. B. Virtual Router Redundancy Protocol (VRRP) is an IEEE open standard that is supported freely on many router products. Proxy ARP is not considered an FHRP but is used in conjunction with FHRPs as a helper protocol. Gateway Load Balancing Protocol (GLBP) is a Cisco-proprietary FHRP for load-balancing multiple gateways. Hot Standby Router Protocol (HSRP) is also a Cisco-proprietary FHRP for highly available gateways.

222. D. The well-known HSRP ID is 07.ac. Whenever you see 07.ac in the second part of the MAC address along with the Cisco OUI, you can identify that HSRP is being employed. The first 24 bits of the MAC address, in this example 0000.0c, compose the default organizationally unique identifier (OUI) for Cisco. The oc07 in the MAC address is part of the OUI and part of the well-known HSRP ID. The 0a in the MAC address is the HSRP group number.

223. C. Gateway Load Balancing Protocol (GLBP) is a Cisco-proprietary protocol that supports redundancy and per-subnet load balancing. Proxy ARP is not considered an FHRP but is used in conjunction with FHRPs as a helper protocol. Virtual Router Redundancy Protocol (VRRP) is an IEEE open standard that is supported freely on many router products. Hot Standby Router Protocol (HSRP) is also a Cisco-proprietary FHRP for highly available gateways, but it does not support load balancing.

224. C. The HSRP group number in the MAC address 0000.0c07.ac01 is 01. After the Cisco organizationally unique identifier (OUI) and well-known HSRP ID, the last two digits are the HSRP group identifier. The first 24 bits of the MAC address, in this example 0000.0c, compose the default OUI for Cisco. The 0c07 in the MAC address is part of the OUI and part of the well-known HSRP ID. The well-known HSRP ID is 07.ac. Whenever you see

07.ac in the second part of the MAC address along with the Cisco OUI, you know that HSRP is being employed.

225. A. The default priority of HSRP is 100. All other options are incorrect.

226. D. You can create up to 256 HSRP groups on a router. This would include group 0 to 255 for a total of 256 groups. All other options are incorrect.

227. B. HSRP routers communicate with each other on port 1985 using UDP. All other options are incorrect.

228. B. Only one router can be active at a time in an HSRP group. All other routers are standby routers, until the active router fails. The virtual router does not send hello packets to the HSRP group; each HSRP member sends its own hello packets. HSRP does not allow for per-packet load balancing; GLBP can load balance on a per-packet basis.

229. C. HSRP uses multicasting to communicate among HSRP group members. For HSRPv1, the address is 224.0.0.2, and for HSRPv2, the address is 224.0.0.102. Unicast is an incorrect option, although most of the communication flowing through HSRP is unicast traffic. Broadcasts are dropped by routers, and HSRP is not different in this respect. Layer 2 flooding is a technique used by switches to discover hosts, and it is not used by HSRP.

230. A. The virtual router is responsible for host communications such as an ARP request for the host's default gateway. Technically, this is served by the active router since it is hosting the virtual router. However, it is the virtual router's IP address and MAC address that are used for outgoing packets. The standby router will not respond unless the active router is down; then the standby will become the active router. A monitor router is a router that is not participating in HSRP.

231. C. The hold timer must expire for the standby router to become an active router. The hold timer is three times the hello timer, so three hello packets must be missed before the standby becomes active. The hello timer sets the time between hello packets outgoing to all other HSRP members. The standby timer is a timer on the standby router that expires in sync with the hello timer. There is no such timer as the virtual timer; therefore, this is a wrong option.

232. D. Gateway Load Balancing Protocol (GLBP) use the port number 3222 and the protocol UDP for router communications. All other options are incorrect.

233. D. Hot Standby Router Protocol version 2 (HSRPv2) allows for timers to be configured in milliseconds in lieu of seconds. This allows for quicker failover between active and standby routers. Both HSRPv1 and HSRPv2 use hello packets to maintain a healthy state among other HSRP members. HSRPv1 and HSRPv2 both use multicasts for management and hello packets. HSRPv1 does not support IPv6; only HSRPv2 supports IPv6.

234. C. The active virtual gateway (AVG) is responsible for responding to ARP requests from hosts. The AVG will reply with the MAC address of any one of the active virtual forwarders (AVFs). The active router is a concept used with Virtual Router Redundancy Protocol (VRRP) or Hot Standby Router Protocol (HSRP), and it does not apply to Gateway Load Balancing Protocol (GLBP). The active virtual gateway will respond with the MAC address of the next active virtual forwarder or router that is available. The virtual router is not responsible for tracking requests; the AVG is responsible.

235. D. The router with the highest priority will become the AVG. However, if all routers have the same priority, then the router with the highest IP address configured becomes the tie-breaker. The router with the highest priority and highest IP address will become the AVG, not the one with the lowest priority and lowest IP address.

236. B. Gateway Load Balancing Protocol (GLBP) supports up to 4 active virtual forwarders per GLBP group. All other options are incorrect.

237. A. The command `standby 1 priority 150` will set the HSRP group of 1 on this router to a priority of 150. As long as all other routers are set to the default of 100, this router will become the default router on the next election. The commands `standby 1 priority 70`, `hsrp 1 priority 150`, and `hsrp 1 priority 90` are incorrect.

238. D. You can create up to 4,096 HSRP groups on a router with HSRPv2. This would include group 0 to 4095 for a total of 4,096 groups. HSRPv1 is limited to 256 HSRP groups. All other options are incorrect.

239. C. Hot Standby Router Protocol version 2 (HSRPv2) is being employed. It uses an OUI of 0000.0c and a well-known identifier of 9f.f, and the last three digits identify the HSRP group, which has been expanded from two digits in version 1. HSRPv1 has a well-known identifier of 07.ac. Gateway Load Balancing Protocol (GLBP) and Virtual Router Redundancy Protocol (VRRP) do not have well-known identifiers.

240. D. Preemption allows for the election process to happen for a newly added HSRP router. If preemption is not enabled, then the newly added HSRP router will become a standby router. HSRP does not load-balance per packet; Gateway Load Balancing Protocol (GLBP) will load-balance per packet. Object tracking effectively watches an upstream interface and recalculates HSRP if the interface fails. HSRP uses both the priority and highest IP address to elect an active router.

241. B. Hot Standby Router Protocol (HSRP) allows for only one active router per HSRP group. However, you can configure multiple VLANs with HSRP groups. You can then alternate a higher-than-default priority to force an active router per VLAN. This will give you a rudimentary way of balancing traffic. Configuring version 2 for all HSRP groups will not achieve load-balancing. Configuring PPPoE on the router interfaces is an incorrect option as it will pin a host to a specific interface. You cannot configure all the routers in an HSRP group as active routers.

242. C. The command `show standby` will allow you to verify the state of the current router for HSRP. The commands `show hsrp`, `show ip standby`, and `show ip hsrp` are incorrect.

243. C. The HSRP group is not set for preemption, which is the default behavior for HSRP. You need to enable preemption, which will allow a reelection when the priority is changed or if a new standby router comes online. If preemption is disabled, the active router will have affinity. The default priority for HSRP is 100. The hold timers will have nothing to do with the election of the active router unless there is a failure. Router A's IP address will not matter if the priority is higher than that of the other routers (default of 100).

244. D. The command standby 1 preempt will configure HSRP group 1 for preemption. This command must be configured under the interface on which HSRP has been enabled. The command show standby will allow you to verify this. The command standby 1 preemption is incorrectly configured in the global configuration prompt or an interface configuration prompt. The command hsrp 1 preempt is incorrect.

245. B. The command vrrp 1 ip 10.1.2.3 will configure the interface with VRRP with a virtual IP address of 10.1.2.3. The commands vrrp 1 10.1.2.3 gi 0/0, vrrp 1 10.1.2.3, standby 1 10.1.2.3, and standby 1 vrrp are incorrect.

246. C. Interface tracking is configured on the interface in which the HSRP group has been configured. The command standby 1 track serial 0/0/1 tells the HSRP group of 1 to track the status of interface serial 0/0/1. The commands standby 1 interface tracking serial 0/0/1, standby 1 tracking serial 0/0/1, interface serial 0/0/1, and standby 1 interface tracking are incorrect.

247. C. The command debug standby will allow you to see real-time information from HSRP on the router on which you have entered the command. The commands show ip hsrp, debug ip hsrp, and debug ip standby are incorrect.

248. A. GLBP allows for per-host load balancing. It does this by allowing the active virtual router to respond for the virtual IP address. The AVG then hands out the MAC address in the ARP request for one of the active virtual forwarders. It does this in a round-robin fashion. The active virtual gateway will respond with the active virtual forwarder; an active router is a concept used with HSRP. GLBP will not load balance per-subnet; HSRP can be set up with a different HSRP group for each VLAN. The virtual router is not responsible for responding to the tracking requests; the active virtual router is responsible for this task.

249. A. The command standby 1 timers msec 200 msec 700 will set the HSRP group of 1 with a hello timer of 200 milliseconds and a hold timer of 700 milliseconds. This is configured inside of the interface in which the HSRP group was created. The commands standby 1 timers 200 msec 700 msec, standby 1 timers 700 msec 200 msec, and standby 1 timers msec 700 msec 200 are incorrect.

250. C. Router C will become the active router since it has the highest priority. The default priority of HSRP is 100, and therefore, the router with the highest priority will become the active router. It is important to note that nothing will change if preemption is not configured on the routers. Router A, Router B, and Router D all have lower HSRP priorities compared to Router C with a priority of 140.

Chapter 4: IP Services (Domain 4)

1. C. Network Address Translation (NAT) was created to slow the depletion of Internet addresses. It does this by translating RFC 1918 privatized addresses to one or several public IP addresses. It allows the packets to masquerade as the public IP address on the Internet until it is translated back to the private IP address. Classless Inter-Domain Routing (CIDR) is a notation used to express the network for a host. Classful addressing is the original addressing scheme for the Internet. Virtual private networks (VPNs) are used for remote access.

2. A. The inside local address is the address local to the enterprise (private), and the address is inside the enterprise. The inside local address will almost always be an RCF 1918 address unless NAT is being used for purposes other than enterprise Internet access. If NAT is used for Internet access, then the inside local address is any host address destined for the Internet through NAT. 192.168.1.1 is the router's interface address used to communicate with inside local hosts during the NAT process. 179.43.44.1 is the inside global address for the NAT process. 198.23.53.3 is the outside global address for the NAT process.

3. C. The inside global address is the address public to the enterprise. The address is inside of or controlled by the enterprise. The inside global address in this case is the public side of the NAT, which is Router A's S0/0 IP address. 192.168.1.2 is the inside local address of the host computer. 192.168.1.1 is the router's interface address used to communicate with inside local hosts during the NAT process. 198.23.53.3 is the outside global address for the NAT process.

4. D. The outside global address is the address public to the enterprise. The address is outside of the enterprise or outside of its control. When using NAT for Internet access, the outside global address is the destination host on the Internet. The outside global address in this figure is the web server. 192.168.1.2 is the inside local address of the host computer. 192.168.1.1 is the router's interface address used to communicate with inside local hosts during the NAT process. 179.43.44.1 is the inside global address for the NAT process.

5. A. The command `show ip nat translations` will allow you to view the active NAT translations on the router. The command `show nat translations` is incorrect. The command `debug ip nat translations` will turn on debugging for NAT. The command `show translations nat` is also incorrect.

6. D. The command `show ip nat statistics` will display an overview of the number of active NAT translations on the router, as well as other statistical information for the NAT process. In addition, it will provide you with the current inside and outside interfaces. The command `show ip nat translations` will allow you to view the active NAT translations on the router. The commands `show ip nat summary` and `show ip nat status` are incorrect.

7. A. After you define the inside and outside for each respective interface, the command `ip nat inside source static 192.168.1.3 179.43.44.1` will statically create a NAT (Network Address Translation) entry for the inside and outside interfaces the inside local address of 192.168.1.3 to the inside global address of 179.43.44.1. The commands `nat source static 192.168.1.3 179.43.44.1`, `ip nat static 192.168.1.3 179.43.44.1`, and `ip nat source static 192.168.1.3 179.43.44.1` are incorrect.

8. D. The command `ip nat pool EntPool 179.43.44.2 179.43.44.15 netmask 255.255.255.0` will configure the pool called EntPool with the range of IP addresses from 179.43.44.2 to 179.43.44.15 and the network mask of /24. The /24 is used in lieu of the /28 because the serial interface is a /24, and therefore, all IP addresses in that network are /24. The commands `ip nat pool EntPool 179.43.44.0/28` and `ip pool EntPool 179.43.44.2 179.43.44.15 netmask 255.255.255.0` are incorrect. The command `ip nat pool EntPool 179.43.44.1 179.43.44.15 netmask 255.255.255.240` is incorrect because the serial interface is a /24 IP address.

9. B. The access list is used to identify IP addresses that are allowed to pass through the NAT process; these are considered the inside local addresses. The access list does not restrict incoming access from the outside global. The access list does not restrict outgoing access from the outside local. The access list does not restrict outgoing access from the inside global.

10. C. The command `clear ip nat translation *` will clear all IP NAT translations out of the NAT table. The asterisk is used as a wildcard for all addresses. You can alternatively specify a specific inside or outside NAT address. The commands `no ip nat translation`, `clear ip nat translation`, and `clear ip nat` are incorrect.

11. B. The command `debug ip nat` will allow you to see real-time NAT translations. When you issue this command, you should know that each NAT translation will log to the screen or logging server and will spike CPU usage. The commands `show ip translations`, `debug ip translations`, and `show ip nat` are incorrect.

12. C. The first command required is `access-list 1 permit 192.168.1.0 0.0.0.255`, which defines the allowed networks. The next command creates the NAT pool with `ip nat pool EntPool 179.43.44.1 179.43.44.1 netmask 255.255.255.0`. The last command, `ip nat inside source list 1 pool EntPool overload`, ties the access list together with the pool and defines PAT with the overload command. All other command configurations are incorrect.

13. A. The command `ntp server 129.6.15.28` will configure your router to connect to the server 129.6.15.28 as an NTP source. This command must be entered in global configuration mode. The command `ntp server 129.6.15.28` entered from the `Router#` prompt (Privileged Exec mode) is incorrect. The command `ntp client 129.6.15.28` is incorrect. The command `ntp client 129.6.15.28` entered from the `Router#` prompt is incorrect.

14. B. The command `ntp master` configures the router or switch to trust its internal time clock. The commands `ntp server`, `ntp clock source`, and `ntp trusted` are incorrect.

15. A. The command `show clock detail` will display either `no time source` or `time source is NTP` if the router or switch is configured to slave off a server for time. The commands `show ntp`, `show time`, and `show time source` are incorrect.

16. C. The command `show ntp associations detail` will allow you to view the NTP clock details from the master NTP server. The commands `show clock detail`, `show ntp detail`, and `show ntp skew` are incorrect.

17. D. The Network Time Protocol (NTP) uses UDP port 123 for time synchronization. Network Management Protocol (SNMP) uses TCP/161 to listen for incoming SNMP messages. TCP/123 can be configured for NTP, but it is normally not used by default. UDP/69 is used by Trivial File Transfer (TFTP) for file transfers.

18. C. The command debug ntp packets will allow you to verify packets received from an NTP server. The commands show ntp, show ip ntp, and debug ntp messages are incorrect.

19. A. A best practice is to configure the main router in your network to a known good trusted time source by its DNS address. All devices in your network should then be configured to point to this trusted router. All time sources should pyramid out from the central source of time in your network. Configuring all devices to a public NTP server is not a best practice because multiple firewall entries will need to be configured. Configuring all devices to different NTP servers for redundancy is not a best practice because all devices should synchronize to the same master. Configuring all devices as master servers is not a best practice; only one master should exist.

20. C. The command show ntp status will allow you to see the current time source, the precision of the time source, and the drift from your internal time clock. The commands show ntp, show ip ntp, and debug ntp drift are incorrect.

21. B. The command clock timezone pst -8 0 will set the time zone to Pacific Standard Time with an offset of –8 from Coordinated Universal Time (UTC) with a minute offset of 0. The commands clock timezone pacific, timezone pacific, and timezone pst -8 are incorrect.

22. C. You should configure a loopback interface on the switch with the IP address of the NTP server the NTP clients will use. A tunnel interface and an NTP interface are incorrect options. Although a Switched Virtual Interface (SVI) would work, it is not active until at least one port is configured with the VLAN. Therefore, the SVI is still tied to a physical interface state.

23. A. The command ntp source loopback 0 will configure the NTP service to respond to clients from the source address of the loopback 0 interface. The commands ntp loopback 0, ntp master loopback 0, and ntp clock loop-back 0 are incorrect.

24. B. The command clock set 2:24:00 1 august 2024 will set the clock to 2:24 a.m. (24-hour format) and August 1, 2024. The command clock set 2:24:00 1 august 2024 is incorrect when configured from a global configuration prompt. The commands clock set 2:24:00 august 1 2024 and clock 2:24:00 1 august 2024 are incorrect.

25. B. A reverse lookup is when the fully qualified domain name (FQDN) is resolved from an IP address. This is useful when you want to identify an IP address. From the IP address, you can derive the FQDN. A reverse lookup is not when the request needs to be reversed to another DNS server. A reverse lookup is not when the DNS queried can answer the request without asking another DNS server. A reverse lookup is not the resolution of an FQDN to an IP address; it is the resolution of an IP address to an FQDN.

26. C. The PTR, or pointer record, is used to look up IP addresses and return FQDNs that are mapped to them. This is helpful to identify an IP address, and in the case of SSH, it is used to positively identify the host which you are connecting. The A record is used to look up an IP address for a given hostname. The CName record is used to look up the alias for a given hostname. The AAAA record is used to look up an IPv6 address for a given hostname.

27. A. The configured DNS domain name is appended to the hostname query. As an example, if you query a hostname of routera and the configured domain name is network.local, the DNS server will see a query for routera.network.local. The DNS zone is the database of records contained in DNS. *Host header* is a term used with web servers and therefore not relevant to DNS resolution. The hostname PTR record is the reverse DNS record for a given IP address.

28. C. Static hostname entries are the most secure name resolution method for routers and switches because they are configured locally on the device. This is because the switch or router does not need to forward-query a server. However, static hostname entries are not scalable. DNS is not considered as secure as static hostname entries because it is publicly accessible. PTR records are reverse DNS records and therefore not relevant to security. Link Local Multicast Name Resolution (LLMNR) is the protocol that the Windows operating system uses for local name queries.

29. A. The A record is the DNS record that is queried when you want to resolve a hostname to an IP address. The CName record is used to look up the alias for a given hostname. The PTR, or pointer record, is used to look up IP addresses and return FQDNs that are mapped to them. The AAAA record is used to look up an IPv6 address for a given hostname.

30. B. The time to live (TTL) limits the amount of time a DNS entry will be available in the DNS cache. The TTL can be defined by the DNS administrator on the entry, or it can be defined in the SOA record as the default TTL. An A record is used to look up an IP address for a given hostname with DNS name resolution. The Start of Authority (SOA) is the first record in a DNS zone that explains where to find other servers and parameters for zone operation. The TTL does not default to 5 minutes; the default TTL is defined in the SOA record.

31. A. The DHCP acknowledgment message is sent from the DHCP client to the DHCP server to acknowledge that the IP address offered will be used by the client. The Discover message is the first message that is sent by the client to discover a DHCP server on the local network. The Offer message is sent by the DHCP server to offer an IP address lease to the client. The Request message is sent from the client to the DHCP server to formally request the offered IP address lease.

32. A. DHCP uses layer 3 broadcasts by sending packets to 255.255.255.255 for initial DHCP discovery. Layer 3 multicast is not used for DHCP clients. Layer 3 802.1Q is an incorrect answer because 802.1Q is used for switch trunks. Layer 3 unicasts are the form of communication clients use after obtaining an IP address.

33. B. DHCP clients request a renewal of the lease halfway through the lease time of the IP address. One-quarter of the lease is an incorrect answer. Seven-eighths of the lease is called the rebind time, where the client will accept a new IP address from any DHCP server. The end of the lease is when the client must relinquish the IP address.

34. C. After the initial Discover, Offer, Request, and Acknowledge, it is the client's responsibility to maintain the lease of the IP address. This includes release and renewal. The DHCP server

is not responsible for maintaining the life cycle of an IP address. DHCP does not use multi-casting between the client and server. The DHCP lease is mandated by the configuration on the DHCP server.

35. A. DHCP uses UDP as a connectionless protocol for the Discover, Offer, Request, and Acknowledge packets. ICMP is used by ping and traceroute to verify the response and path of a packet. TCP is not used by DHCP. RARP is not used by DHCP; it is considered an alternate method of assigning an IP address to a client.

36. B. When DHCP detects a duplicate IP address in the pool, it will remove the duplicate IP address from the DHCP pool and place it into the conflict table. It will require manual inter-vention to reserve the IP address. The IP address is placed into a conflict table, and there-fore, it is not served to any client. The DHCP server will continue to serve other available IP addresses in the DHCP pool. The duplicate IP address can only be served in the future if it is cleared from the conflict table.

37. D. SNMP version 3 introduced message integrity, authentication, and encryption to the SNMP suite. SNMP version 1 was the first release of SNMP and is considered deprecated. SNMP version 2e is not a valid version of SNMP. SNMP version 2c is an amendment of SNMP version 2 that added the SET command and other improvements.

38. B. The management information base (MIB) is a database of variables in which SNMP allows retrieval of information. The attributes in the MIB are the description, variable type, and read-write status. Object identifiers (OIDs) are the addressable counters that are arranged in a hierarchical fashion. The SNMP agent is the software on the client that allows SNMP to collect or pass information. The SNMP community string is used to restrict com-munications to only the clients or servers that have a matching SNMP community string.

39. B. The network management station (NMS) is a server to which SNMP is polled back or in which SNMP information is trapped. The NMS can escalate problems via email, text mes-sage, or even visual indicators. Examples of NMS systems are SolarWinds Orion and Open-NMS. The syslog is a logging file where system messages are sent. The object identifier (OID) is used to describe the SNMP counter being requested. The management information base (MIB) is a sort of database of counters that SNMP can use for a specific device.

40. D. Trap messages are sent from the network device to the SNMP network management station when an event has triggered over a set threshold on the device. An example of an event to be trapped is an interface going down or a restriction by port security. The get-request message is used by an NMS to request information from an SNMP agent. The get-response message is the message sent back from the client to the NMS after a get-request message is received. The set-request message is sent by the NMS to the SNMP client request-ing a specific writable counter be set to the specified value.

41. A. OIDs are the variables that make up the management information base. Each object has a unique ID in a hierarchical format in the form of a tree. As an example, 1.3.6.1.4.9.2.1.58.0 is the object that holds the router CPU utilization variable. The SNMP community string is used to restrict communications to only the clients or servers that have a matching SNMP community string. The SNMP agent is the software on the client that allows SNMP to collect or pass information. SNMP messages are the data relayed with the various SNMP verb com-mands, such as GET, SET, and INFORM, to name a few.

42. D. Inform messages differ from trap messages with respect to acknowledgment. Trap messages employ a best effort delivery utilizing UDP. Inform messages employ acknowledgments; while they use the User Datagram Protocol (UDP), they rely on the Application layer for acknowledgments. Trap messages are not always encrypted and can be sent with plaintext. Inform messages use acknowledgments at the Application layer. Trap messages do not use acknowledgments.

43. C. SNMP version 2c is identical to SNMP version 1 with respect to security. Both transmit information in clear text and use the security of community strings to authenticate users for access to information. SNMP version 2c does not employ encryption. SNMP version 2c does not employ user authentication. SNMP version 2c does not employ message integrity.

44. B. Standard access control lists (ACLs) can be used in conjunction with the SNMP agent configuration. First a standard ACL is created containing the NMS IP. Then, when the `snmp-server` command is used, it becomes the last argument. For example, a standard ACL of 2 would be added as follows: `snmp-server community snmpreadonly read-only 2`. There is no such thing as encrypted communities. There is no such thing as SNMP callback security; callback security is related to PPP. SNMP does not employ SHA-256 as its encryption protocol.

45. C. The first portion of the command, `snmp-server host 192.168.1.5`, will configure the SNMP agent to send traps to the host 192.168.1.5. The second portion of the command, `version 2c C0mmun1ty`, sets the SNMP version to 2c and the community to "C0mmun1ty." All of the other command configurations are incorrect.

46. C. SNMP uses UDP port 162 for communication from an SNMP agent to the network management station for trap and inform messages. SNMP agents listen on UDP/161. SNMP does not use TCP for messaging. UDP/514 is used for syslog messaging.

47. C. The command `show snmp host` will display the host that is configured to receive notifications of trap or inform messages from the router or switch. The commands `show snmp`, `show snmp community`, and `show snmp notifications` are incorrect.

48. B. When you begin to configure SNMPv3 for a restricted OID, the first step is configuring a view. The view allows or restricts what the user will have access to. All of the other options come after configuring a view.

49. D. The router or switch sends syslog messages to the syslog server on port 514 with UDP. SNMP agents listen on UDP/161. SNMP does not use TCP for messaging. SNMP sends traps on UDP/162.

50. C. The command `logging trap debugging` will configure syslog events to be sent to the syslog server for the severity levels of debugging (7) through emergency (0). The commands `syslog debugging`, `logging debugging`, and `log-level debugging` are incorrect.

51. B. The command `logging trap 4` will trap all messages with warnings to the syslog server. The command `logging server 4` is incorrect. The command `logging trap 5` is incorrect, as it will send all notice messages. The command `logging server 5` is also incorrect.

52. D. The command `service timestamps log datetime` will configure syslog messages to be logged with the date and time rather than the arbitrary sequence number. The commands `logging timestamps log datetime`, `logging timestamps datetime`, and `service datetime timestamps` are incorrect.

53. A. The command `logging console 0` will configure the logging to the console for the severity level of facility 0, which is alerts. The `logging` command is not configured in the config-line prompt; therefore, both options B and D are incorrect. The command `logging console 7` is incorrect because it sets the logging level to debug.

54. A. The command `logging buffered 1` will configure the logs stored in RAM, which is buffered to a severity of 1. This command will include severity levels 1 and 0. The command `logging 1` is incorrect. The command `logging buffered 2` will set the logging level to critical events. The command `logging 2` is also incorrect.

55. C. The command `show history` will show the last commands typed, which are kept in the buffer. The history normally includes the last 10 commands. The command `show commands` is incorrect. The command `show log` is incorrect as it will display the logs. The command `show buffer` is also incorrect.

56. B. Line protocol up/down messages are logged to the notifications (5) severity level. This can be determined by looking up the 5 that appears after the affected component of line protocol in the syslog severity chart. For example, `%LINEPROTO-5-UPDOWN` specifies the severity level of 5 for the line protocol. All of the other options are incorrect.

57. C. The command `show processes` will display the utilization of the CPU. The first line of the output is broken down by 5 second utilization, 1 minute utilization, and 5 minute utilization. The commands `show cpu`, `show cpu-stats`, and `show environment cpu` are incorrect.

58. A. The command `logging buffered` will direct buffering of log messages to RAM. This command can be undone by using the no directive in front of `logging buffered`. The command must be entered in global configuration mode. The commands `logging internal`, `logging ram`, and `logging console` are incorrect.

59. B. By default, all syslog messages are sent to the console of the router or switch. It is recommended to configure a syslog server, because once the router or switch is powered off, the information is lost. Syslog messages are never broadcast, but they can be directed to a syslog server. Syslog messages can only be sent to the connected TTY if the command `terminal monitor` is entered. Syslog messages cannot be sent to NVRAM.

60. D. The default syslog facility level is debugging (7). All debugging messages are logged to the internal buffer by default. Notification (5), Informational (6), and Warning (4) are not the default level for syslog logging.

61. A. The command `show dhcp lease` will help you verify the IP address configured on the router, the DHCP server that served the lease, and the lease time in seconds. The commands `show ip dhcp lease`, `show ip lease`, and `show ip interface` are incorrect.

62. C. The DHCP Offer packet is a broadcast packet from the DHCP server to the DHCP client, which will contain the MAC address of the server. The layer 3 packet and layer 2 frame are both broadcasts. The layer 3 destination to the DHCP client is not a unicast. The layer 2 destination of the Offer packet is a broadcast and therefore not the destination MAC address of the client. Link-local addressing is not used for DHCP.

63. D. The command `ip helper-address 10.10.1.101` will configure the interface to become a DHCP relay agent. This command must be configured on the interface in which you want the DHCP relay agent to listen and respond. The command `ip dhcp server 10.10.1.101` configured in the global configuration prompt is incorrect. The command `ip dhcp server 10.10.1.101` configured in the interface configuration prompt is incorrect. The command `ip relay-agent 10.10.1.101` is also incorrect.

64. B. The Gateway Address (GIADDR) field is filled out by the DHCP relay agent before the DHCP packet is sent to the DHCP server. This field helps the DHCP server decide which scope to send an Offer message back for. The CIADDR field is used for the client IP address and not used to determine scope selection. The SIADDR field is used for the server IP address and not used to determine scope selection. The CHADDR is the client hardware address and not used to determine scope selection.

65. D. A DHCP relay agent installed on Router A interface Gi0/0 will allow clients on Host A's network to obtain IP addressing from DHCP. A second DHCP server on the network where Host A is located will not satisfy the requirement of using the existing DHCP server. A DHCP relay agent on the interface Gi0/0 located on Router B will not help serve IP addresses on the Host A network. A DHCP relay agent cannot be configured on a layer 2 switch.

66. C. The command `debug ip dhcp server packet` will show the details of a DHCP relay agent conversation. It will detail conversation between the client and router and the router and the DHCP server. The commands `debug dhcp`, `show ip dhcp detail`, and `debug ip dhcp` are incorrect.

67. C. Stateless Address Autoconfiguration (SLAAC) allows for the client to learn the network ID and calculate a host ID that is unique. However, SLAAC lacks the ability to configure options such as DNS time servers. DHCPv6 allows for the configuration of these options when used in conjunction with SLAAC. DHCPv6 configured for SLAAC is not used for stateful configuration of client IPv6 addressing. DHCPv6 configured for SLAAC will not provide network IDs. IPv6 by default provides stateless configuration of clients with IPv6 addressing; DHCPv6 complements this stateless configuration.

68. D. They will lose their IP addresses after their entire lease has expired. Until the lease expires, they will have functioning IP addresses. Clients will not lose their IP addresses immediately because the server is only needed for renewals after the initial IP address lease is obtained. The host requests a renewal for the lease at one-half of the lease time, but if a response is not heard, the host will retain its original lease. After seven-eighths of the lease time, the host will attempt to find a new server to rebind the original lease of the IP address. If a rebind does not occur, the IP address will remain active until the end of the lease.

69. A. Stateful DHCPv6 supplies the network ID and host ID. The default router is discovered through the Neighbor Discovery Protocol (NDP). Stateful DHCPv6 only supplies the network ID and host ID to the client; the default router is also discovered through the Neighbor Discovery Protocol. IPv6 uses multicasts, not broadcasts, to communicate. Stateful DHCPv6 is a replacement for the process of Stateless Address Autoconfiguration (SLAAC).

70. C. The command `ipv6 address dhcp` will configure the interface to obtain its IP address via stateful DHCPv6. The commands `ipv6 address dhcp gi 0/0`, `ipv6 address dhcpv6`, and `ipv6 address stateless` are incorrect.

71. C. When the lease for a node is deleted on the DHCP server, the DHCP server is free to hand out the lease to another node. This happens independently from the client, as there is no communication from server to client about the lease. The client will retain the IP address until the renewal period, which will cause a duplication of IP addressing. The client is responsible for the management of the lease cycle; therefore, the server has no obligation to contact the client when the lease is deleted. The client will not know to contact the server for a renewal of the lease until the halfway point of the lease cycle. If or when the server issues the lease to another client, the existing client will still maintain the original lease.

72. A. At seven-eighths of the lease cycle, the DHCP client will perform a rebinding. The rebinding process means that the original DHCP server was down at the one-half mark of the lease, so now the client will try to rebind with any responding DHCP server. The DHCP client will retain the lease until the end of the lease cycle. During the rebind, the DHCP client will attempt to renew a new lease with any DHCP server. The DHCP client will not relinquish the IP address until the very end of the lease.

73. A. QoS classifies traffic with access control lists (ACLs) and applies markings to the packets. Layer 2 ASICs help process the QoS but do not classify the QoS for traffic. Route tables are used for routing and therefore have no effect on QoS. Frame filters are used to forward/filter frames to their destination port; they are part of the switching process.

74. C. Jitter is the measurement of variation between consecutive packet times from source to destination (one-way delay). For example, if the first packet takes 10 ms and the second, third, and fourth take 10 ms, the jitter, or variance, is 0 ms. The simple calculation is an average of packet times. However, data size has an influence on jitter, so the more accurate calculation is $J = J + (D (I - 1, I) - J) / 16$. Bandwidth is the total width of data that can be passed for a specific interval. Delay is the measurement of how long a packet takes to travel from source to destination. Loss is the total number of packets that are not delivered from source to destination.

75. B. The Class of Service (CoS) field (802.1p) is only found in layer 2 transmissions, specifically only across trunks due to the dependency of 802.1Q. The CoS field is a 3-bit field in the 802.1Q frame type. The CoS field does not need to be present from end to end of a transmission because the transmission can traverse a router. The CoS field is a 3-bit field, not a 6-bit field.

76. D. Loss is the measurement of discarded packets. The measurement is a percentage of transmitted packets. For example, if 100 packets are transmitted and 3 packets are dropped, then the loss is 3%. Loss can be attributed to congestion, faulty wiring, EMI, or device queue congestion. Bandwidth is the total width of data that can be passed for a specific interval. Delay is the measurement of how long a packet takes to travel from source to destination. Jitter is the measurement of variation between consecutive packet times from source to destination (one-way delay).

77. B. The standardized marking of DSCP EF, or Expedite Forwarding, is a decimal equivalent of 46. This marking has the highest priority and should be used for VoIP traffic and video. DSCP AF 43 is an incorrect answer. DSCP AF 11 is an incorrect answer. DSCP AF 00 is an incorrect answer.

78. C. The maximum delay that VoIP traffic should not exceed is 150 ms. At 150 ms, you will have call disruption. 10 ms can normally only be achieved on the same LAN; therefore, it is not a recommended maximum. 90 ms is the far end of the scale and sometimes seen in WAN communications. 300 ms is roughly one-third of a second and traffic will experience echoes and drops.

79. B. Low Latency Queuing (LLQ) overrides Class Based Weighted Fair Queuing (CBWFQ). CBWFQ uses a weighted round-robin scheduling of packets. LLQ has priority override when packets come in matching the classification for LLQ. FIFO queues work on a first in, first out system but do not have a concept of priority. Committed information rate (CIR) is a term used with Frame Relay.

80. B. QoS queue starvation occurs when the Low Latency Queuing (LLQ) is given priority over the Class-Based Weighted Fair Queuing (CBWFQ). Therefore, policing of the LLQ will help limit queue starvation and allow those queues an equal share of the total output bandwidth. Class-Based Weighted Fair Queuing is not a method to combat queue starvation. First in, first out (FIFO) is not a method to combat queue starvation.

81. A. Shaping monitors the bit rate of packets. If the bit rate is exceeded for a configured queue, then shaping holds packets over the configured bit rate, causing a delay. Shaping of packets does not drop packets when the bandwidth is over the configured bit rate. Shaping will not use jitter as a control method when the bandwidth is over the configured bit rate. Shaping has no mechanism to control speed, only the rate at which packets are released.

82. C. Class-Based Weighted Fair Queuing (CBWFQ) is driven by a round-robin scheduler. The queues are weighted for priority in the scheduler and the packets are put into the queues upon classification. Low Latency Queueing (LLQ) does not use a round-robin scheduler. First in, first out (FIFO) does not use a round-robin scheduler. Priority Queueing (PQ) does not use a round-robin scheduler.

83. B. Policing monitors the bit rate of packets. If the bit rate is exceeded for a configured queue, then policing drops packets over the configured bit rate, causing loss. In some cases, it can be configured to remark the packets. Policing does not hold packets in the queue over the configured bit rate to cause delay. Policing does not hold packets in the queue over the configured bit rate to cause jitter. Policing will not slow packets in the queue over the configured bit rate to adhere to the bit rate.

84. B. QoS policing should be implemented to adhere network traffic to a contracted committed information rate (CIR). As an example, if your enterprise contracted a Metro Ethernet connection with an access link of 1 Gb/s and a CIR of 400 Mb/s, you would need to make sure that traffic does not exceed the CIR except for occasional bursts. QoS policing is not used to police LAN applications. QoS policing is not used to police WAN applications. QoS will not help with maintaining a contracted burst rate.

85. D. When the queue depth is above the minimum threshold, a percentage of TCP packets are dropped. This allows the TCP window to shrink and allows a normal slowdown of TCP transmissions. This is done in hopes that the queue will fall under the minimum threshold and return to normal. Congestion avoidance tools drop all packets when the queue depth is full, but this is a cause of total congestion and not prevention of tail drop. When the queue depth is empty, nothing is dropped. When the queue depth is below the minimum threshold, nothing is dropped since this is optimal.

86. B. AF41 marked traffic has a better position in the queue than traffic marked AF31. During high congestion times, traffic with lower positions in the queues (AF3x, AF2x, AF1x) would have more chances of being dropped than AF41. AF31 marked traffic is placed in a lower queue than traffic marked with AF41. AF31 and AF41 markings of traffic are not the same. During high congestion, traffic in the AF31 queue will be dropped before the AF 41 queue.

87. B. The hostname and domain name are required before you attempt to generate the encryption keys for SSH. Although setting the time and date is good practice, it is not required for the generation of SSH encryption keys. Setting the key strength is not required for the generation of SSH encryption keys. Setting the key repository is not required for the generation of SSH encryption keys.

88. A. The command `ip ssh version 2` will set your SSH version to 2. This command is to be entered at a global configuration prompt. The command `version 2` configured in the config-line prompt is incorrect. The command `version 2` configured in the config-ssh prompt is incorrect as there is no config-ssh prompt. The command `ssh version 2` is also incorrect.

89. C. The command `transport ssh telnet` will configure the VTY line to accept SSH as a login protocol and fall back to Telnet. The command `login ssh telnet` is incorrect. The command `login ssh telnet` configured in the config-line prompt is incorrect. The command `transport ssh telnet` configured in the global configuration prompt is incorrect.

90. D. SSH is encrypted and Telnet is in clear text. To keep passwords and configuration safe, SSH should always be used. Telnet has no encryption; therefore it cannot have weak encryption. Although files can be transferred via SSH, replacing Telnet with SSH does not enable this feature. SSH does not make it easier to create ACLs for access.

91. B. When you're configuring a switch or router for SSH version 2, the key strength must be at least 768 bits for the modulus. The default is 512 bits, and it is standard practice to double the number to 1024 bits. The time and date do not need to be corrected to enable SSH version 2. The DNS server does not need to be configured for SSH version 2. Host records for the switch or router do not have to be configured for SSH version 2.

92. A. The command `username user1 password Password20!` will create a user account called user1 with a password of Password20!. All of the other commands are incorrect.

93. B. The command `crypto key generate rsa` will generate the encryption keys for SSH. You will be asked for the key strength, called the modulus, which should be over 768 bits to support SSH version 2, or you can supply the modulus with the full command of `crypto key generate rsa modulus 2048`. The command `generate crypto key` rsa is incorrect. The command `crypto generate key rsa` entered in the global configuration prompt is incorrect. The command `crypto key generate rsa` entered in privilege exec mode is incorrect.

94. D. After configuring the username and password combinations that will be used on the switch or router, you will need to configure the line(s) that will use local authentication. The command used inside of the line is `login local`. This will apply to all the transport methods configured on the line. The command `new aaa model` is incorrect. The command `local authentication` entered in global configuration mode is incorrect. The command `local authentication` entered in the config-line prompt is incorrect.

95. B. The login banner will be displayed during initial connection to a Cisco device via SSH. The MOTD banner will be displayed when a user logs in locally. After a user logs in, the exec banner or incoming banner will be displayed.

96. C. The command `copy tftp: running-config` will ask for the TFTP server address, source filename, and destination filename. It will then proceed to copy the file over the network from the TFTP server. The commands `archive tftp: running-config`, `restore tftp://192.168.1.2 running-config`, and `copy server: running-config` are incorrect.

97. A. The command `copy tftp flash` will begin an interactive upgrade prompts. The prompts will ask for the IP address of the TFTP server, the source filename on the TFTP server, and the destination filename. It will then begin transferring the image. The commands `copy tftp ios`, `copy tftp nvram`, and `upgrade tftp flash` are incorrect.

98. D. The command `boot system c2900-universalk9-mz.SPA.151-4.M4.bin tftp://192.168.1.2` will configure the router for booting of the image named `c2900-universalk9-mz.SPA.151-4.M4.bin` from the 192.168.1.2 TFTP server. Under normal circumstances, this should not be used in production environments since the router boot process is dependent on the availability of the TFTP server. The commands `boot tftp://192.168.1.2`, `boot tftp://192.168.1.2 c2900-universalk9-mz.SPA.151-4.M4.bin`, and `boot system tftp://192.168.1.2 c2900-universalk9-mz.SPA.151-4.M4.bin` are incorrect.

99. B. The IOS is stored on the flash card. Since the flash card is brand-new, nothing is on it. When the router boots, it will not find the IOS and will boot into ROMMON mode. From ROMMON mode, you will configure an IP address, subnet mask, gateway, TFTP server, and image and initiate a TFTP download to flash. Once the IOS is downloaded to flash memory, you can boot the router and verify operations. New flash memory will not contain a mini-IOS installed from the factory. You cannot format the flash card with the FAT filesystem, as the IOS requires its own filesystem to be formatted.

100. C. The command `ip ftp username USER` will configure the username USER for FTP connections. The command `ip ftp password USERPASS` will configure the password USERPASS for FTP connections. The commands `ip ftp username USER password USERPASS`, `ftp USER password USERPASS`, and `username USER password USERPASS` are incorrect.

Chapter 5: Security Fundamentals (Domain 5)

1. B. The perimeter area, or perimeter network, is outside of the corporate firewall. The perimeter area generally holds equipment necessary for routing to the ISP. The DMZ is in between the perimeter network and the internal network. The internal area is the area or network inside of your organization. A trusted area is an area or network that has a high level of trust; generally your internal area is a trusted area.

2. A. The DMZ is an area that is protected by the corporate firewall. The DMZ area is in between the perimeter network and the internal network. However, it allows servers such as web servers, email servers, and application servers to be accessible via the Internet. The perimeter area, or perimeter network, is outside of the corporate firewall. The perimeter area generally holds equipment necessary for routing to the ISP. The internal area is the area or network inside of your organization. A trusted area is an area or network that has a high level of trust; generally your internal area is a trusted area.

3. C. An intrusion prevention system (IPS) can detect and prevent attacks based on their signature. They are commonly found in firewall systems such as Firepower Threat Defense (FTD) devices. Honeypots are server or network appliances that have been security weakened to attract bad actors so their actions and tactics can be examined. An IDS is a system that can detect an attack based on a signature. They too are found in firewall systems such as FTD devices. Although similar to an IPS, the IDS will only notify someone in the event of a detection. A host intrusion detection system (HIDS) is an application that runs on a host to detect intrusions. An HIDS is similar to an IDS, but it is all software based and resides on the host it is to protect.

4. A. The internal network is defined by the firewall. Anything protected by the firewall on the internal network is considered to be the trusted network. The Internet is an untrusted network, because it is outside of your control and outside of your organization. The DMZ area is in between the perimeter network and the internal network. A network with SSL encryption is not considered trusted; it is considered encrypted. A network with SSL can travel over an untrusted network such as the Internet.

5. B. Distributed denial of service (DDoS) is a common attack technique used to deny others of service. It is performed by overwhelming the service with bogus traffic. When it is performed from multiple hosts on the Internet, it is very difficult to prevent and stop. A denial of service (DoS) attack is typically carried out by one source and is relatively easy to mitigate. IP address spoofing is a tactic in which the source IP address is spoofed in a packet in an attempt to bypass security. Session hijacking is an attack in which a conversation between two hosts is hijacked by an attacker.

6. B. An intrusion detection system (IDS) can detect an attack based on its signature. They are commonly found in firewall systems such as Firepower Threat Defense (FTD). Although similar to an IPS, the IDS will only notify someone in the event of a detection. Honeypots are server or network appliances that have been security weakened to attract bad actors so their actions and tactics can be examined. An intrusion prevention system (IPS) can detect and prevent attacks based on their signature. They too are commonly found in firewall systems such as FTD. A host intrusion detection system (HIDS) is an application that runs on a host to detect intrusions. An HIDS is similar to an IDS, but it is all software based and resides on the host it is to protect.

7. D. Ping sweep scans are used by attackers to discover hosts on a network. The scan sends a flood of ICMP echo requests to the perimeter network and awaits echo replies. When ICMP is blocked at the perimeter, an attacker would not be able to scan the network via ICMP. Although deploying a host intrusion detection system (HIDS) and intrusion detection system (IDS) is a good idea, these systems will only notify you of a ping sweep scan and will not prevent it. Blocking RFC 1918 addresses at the perimeter is also a positive security measure. However, RFC 1918 addresses are not Internet routable, and this measure does not prevent an internal ping sweep scan.

8. C. An intrusion prevention system (IPS) will help mitigate denial-of-service (DoS) attacks. Common features of IPS can be found in the Cisco Adaptive Security Appliance. Honeypots are server or network appliances that have been security weakened to attract bad actors so their actions and tactics can be examined. An intrusion detection system (IDS) can detect an attack based on its signature. They are also commonly found in firewall systems such as Firepower Threat Defense (FTD) devices. Although similar to an IPS, the IDS will only notify someone in the event of a detection. A host intrusion detection system (HIDS) is an application that runs on a host to detect intrusions. An HIDS is similar to an IDS, but it is all software based and resides on the host it is to protect.

9. C. IP address spoofing is a common attack method used to attempt to gain access to a system by spoofing the originating IP address. A denial-of-service (DoS) attack is typically carried out by one source and is relatively easy to mitigate. Distributed denial of service (DDoS) is a common attack technique used to deny others of service. It is performed by overwhelming the service with bogus traffic. When it is performed from multiple hosts on the Internet, it is very difficult to prevent and stop. Malware is malicious software that can perform malicious activities on a system or network.

10. C. Secure Sockets Layer (SSL) communications offer both encryption and authentication of the data via certificate signing. This would prevent tampering of the data end to end. Access control lists (ACLs) are used to control traffic by either allowing, denying, or logging traffic depending on specific conditions. Spoofing mitigation is the action of inspecting the source IP addresses of a packet to block packets from outside the network spoofing internal addresses. Encryption of the data alone will not prevent tampering; SSL provides encryption and authentication.

11. D. This attack is called an on-path attack. The attacker sits in the middle of communications and relays it back while capturing it and possibly modifying it. A Smurf attack is an attack where a number of computers are told to respond to a victim IP address via a spoofed packet. A compromised key attack involves a key pair that has been tampered with or copied, such as SSL or SSH key pairs. A sniffer attack is a passive attack where an attacker will collect packets with a network sniffer for later playback or analysis.

12. A. Access control lists (ACLs) are an effective way to mitigate spoofing of internal IPs from outside the trusted network. ACLs are used to control traffic by either allowing, denying, or logging traffic depending on specific conditions. An intrusion detection system (IDS) can be used to notify you if it detects an attack, but it will not prevent an attack. Secure Sockets Layer (SSL) communications offer both encryption and authentication of the data via certificate signing. This would prevent tampering of the data end to end, but it will not prevent spoofing. A host intrusion detection system (HIDS) is an application that runs on a host to detect intrusions. An HIDS is similar to an IDS, but it is all software based and resides on the host it is to protect.

13. A. A requirement of DHCP snooping is that the device is on the VLAN that DHCP snooping is monitoring. There is nothing that requires the DHCP server to run on a layer 2 switch. The device that is being protected must be on a layer 2 switched port on the same VLAN and not a layer 3 routed port. DHCP snooping does not require a dedicated IP address to be configured for its operations.

14. D. Any service that allows the user to create a connection or access to information can be used as an attack vector. In the case of DHCP, the attacker will set the gateway to their IP address. In the case of DNS, the attacker could spoof a request to redirect the traffic. In the case of wireless, the attacker can spoof the Service Set Identifier (SSID).

15. A. Double tagging is an attack that can be used against the native VLAN. The attacker will tag the native VLAN on a frame and then tag another inside that frame for the VLAN that the attacker intends to compromise. When the switch receives the first frame, it removes the default VLAN tag and forwards it to other switches via a trunk port. When the other switch receives the frame with the second VLAN tag, it forwards it to the VLAN the attacker is targeting. VLAN traversal is not an attack; it is a term to describe a VLAN traversing a trunk link between two switches. Trunk popping is not a valid attack; it is not a term used in networking, and therefore, it is an invalid answer. A denial-of-service (DoS) attack is an attack in which an attempt to exhaust services resources is launched to knock a service offline.

16. A. The command `ip dhcp snooping trust` will configure the interface as a trusted port. The commands `dhcp snooping trust`, `ip dhcp snooping trust interface gi 2/3`, and `ip dhcp trust` are incorrect.

17. C. The native VLAN is the default configuration on all switches. It is very possible that a user could be configured by accident for the native VLAN of 1. This would allow management access to switching and routing. The native VLAN will not contain frames from all VLANs. The native VLAN will only contain frames that are placed onto a trunk that have not been tagged. The native VLAN is not configured on all switches for logging; logging can be transmitted over any VLAN. All VLANs provide no encryption, regardless of whether they are the native VLAN.

18. A. End-user training and vigilance is the best way to protect users from phishing attacks. A phishing attack is an email or site that looks legitimate and baits the user to enter their credentials. If a user can identify a phishing attempt that looks like a legitimate request, they can protect themselves by ignoring the phishing attempt or deleting it. Antimalware and antivirus software will not protect you from phishing attacks since they are engineered to protect you from malware or viruses. Certificates can be used internally to sign emails, but external vendors do not normally use certificates to sign emails.

19. A. A hardware or software token creates a numeric password that is only valid for a specific amount of time before a new one is displayed. Certificate authentication is not time-limited for a session. Smartcard authentication is not time-limited for a session. *License* is a term used with the licensing of software and therefore an incorrect answer.

20. C. This is most likely a phishing attack aimed at the user. Spam would not have links to a bank website for login. Password cracking is the act of trying several different passwords in an attempt to gain access. A worm is malware that replicates itself and infects other systems.

21. B. Privacy filters are either film or glass add-ons that are placed over a monitor. They prevent the data on the screen from being readable when viewed from the sides. Security is the overall goal and not the correct answer. Degaussing is associated with magnetic media erasure. Tempered describes a type of glass that does not prevent side viewing.

22. A. Shoulder surfing involves looking over someone's shoulder as they enter information. Phishing is the act of attempting to steal credentials by sending an email that takes you to a fraudulent login. Tailgating is the act of following a person through an access control point and using their credentials. Whaling is a form of phishing that targets high-profile individuals.

23. D. By implementing least privilege and removing the administrative privileges from the office workers, you can easily secure the network. Biometric authentication will secure the network, but it is not easily implemented. Hardware tokens will secure the network, but they are not easily implemented. Active Directory will not add security to the network anymore because it is only a centralized authentication system.

24. C. Antimalware software covers a wide array of security threats to users, including Trojans, viruses, and phishing emails. Multifactor authentication combines two or more single-factor authentication methods to create very secure authentication for users. Software firewalls will not prevent threats such as Trojans, viruses, and phishing emails. Antivirus software protects you only from viruses and Trojans, not phishing emails.

25. B. Using access control vestibules (small rooms that limit access to one or a few individuals) is a great way to stop tailgating. User authentication will not prevent or stop tailgating. Strong passwords will not prevent tailgating because tailgating is a physical security problem. Changing SSIDs will not stop tailgating because tailgating does not pertain to wireless.

26. C. The command `enable secret Password20!` will set the enable password and encrypt the Password20! password. The commands `password enable Password20!`, `enable Password20!`, and `secret enable Password20!` are incorrect.

27. D. The command `line vty 0 5` will enter you into the line for the virtual teletype, which is where you configure your Telnet password. The command `interface vlan 1` is incorrect; it will set the focus to the switched virtual interface (SVI) of VLAN 1. The command `line console 1` is incorrect; it will set the focus to the console line 1. The command `line aux 1` is incorrect; it will set the focus to the auxiliary line 1.

28. B. If the enable password is set and the enable secret is set, the enable password will be ignored. Therefore, the enable secret is being used to authenticate the user, and you are typing the wrong password. The command `enable password` exists for backward compatibility with pre-10.3 IOSs and should no longer be used. Although the originally entered password could be wrong, the enable password is ignored. The password Password20! contains a special character, but this is encouraged to promote better security. The password Password20! is not too long. The maximum length is 64 characters, which can differ from version to version of IOS.

29. C. The command `password Password20!` will set the login password to Password20!. The subcommand `login` will require login for the line. The commands `set password Password20!` and `request login` are incorrect. The commands of `password Password20!` and `login password` are incorrect. The command `login password Password20!` is incorrect.

30. C. The VTY line login password is not set when you receive the error `Password required, but none set`. If the enable secret or enable password was not set, you would just not be able to get to a privileged exec prompt, but you would still be able to get to a user exec prompt. A VTY line cannot be administratively shut down.

31. B. The hostname and domain name are required before you attempt to generate the encryption keys for SSH. Setting the time and date is recommended but not required for generating the encryption keys for SSH on a router or switch. Setting the key strength is also recommended but not required. The key strength should be set over 768 bits so that SSH version 2 can be used. The key repository does not need to be set; it normally defaults to NVRAM on routers and switches and differs from platform to platform.

32. A. The command `ip ssh version 2` will set your SSH version to 2. This command is to be entered at a global configuration prompt. The command `version 2` is incorrect, regardless of where it is configured. The command `ssh version 2` must be preceded with the `ip` command.

33. C. The command `transport ssh telnet` will configure the VTY line to accept SSH as a login protocol and fallback to Telnet. The command `login ssh telnet` is incorrect regardless of where it is configured. The command `transport ssh telnet` is incorrect when it is configured from a global configuration prompt.

34. D. SSH is encrypted and Telnet is in clear text. To keep passwords and configuration safe, SSH should always be used. Telnet contains no encryption whatsoever, and all usernames, passwords, and commands are sent in clear text. SSH allows for file copy if it is turned on in the IOS, but it is not a main reason to replace Telnet. Telnet and SSH make it equally easy to create ACLs for access.

35. C. You must first create an access list to permit the host that will manage the router or switch with the command `access-list 1 permit host 192.168.1.5`. Then enter the VTY line in which it will be applied with the command `line vty 0 5`. Then apply it with the command `ip access-class 1 in`, which differs from the command `ip access-group`, which is used on interfaces. All of the other options are incorrect.

36. B. When you're configuring a switch or router for SSH version 2, the key strength must be at least 768 bits for the modulus. The default is normally 512 bits, and it is standard practice to double the number to 1024 bits. The time and date do not necessarily need to be correct to enable SSH version 2. The DNS server does not need to be configured to enable SSH version 2. DNS and host records are used strictly for connectivity and will not affect enabling SSH version 2.

37. A. The command `username user1 password Password20!` will create a user account called user1 with a password of Password20!. The commands `account user1` and `password Password20!` are incorrect. The commands `user user1 Password20!` and `user-account user1 password Password20!` are incorrect.

38. B. The command `service password-encryption` should be entered in global config. It should not be kept in the configuration as it will use CPU cycles. So after it is configured, you should perform a `show running-config` to double-check if the encryption worked and then perform a `no service password-encryption` to turn it off. The commands `password encryption`, `service encryption`, and `password-encryption service` are incorrect.

39. B. The command `crypto key generate rsa` will generate the encryption keys for SSH. You will be asked for the key strength, called the modulus, which should be over 768 bits to support SSH version 2. The commands `generate crypto key rsa` and `crypto generate key rsa` are incorrect. The command `crypto key generate rsa` is also incorrect when configured from the privileged exec prompt.

40. A. The command `exec-timeout 0 0` will disable auto-disconnect for idle privileged exec sessions. The commands `exec-timeout 0` and `timeout 0 0` are incorrect. The command `no exec-timeout` is incorrect as it will remove any configured `exec-timeout` from the configuration.

41. B. The line on which you are connected is always preceded by an asterisk. In this example, you are connected to the router via line VTY 0. All other lines are remotely connected for other administrative sessions on the switch.

42. D. After configuring the username and password combinations that will be used on the switch or router, you will need to configure the line(s) that will use local authentication. The command used inside of the line is `login local`. This will apply to all the transport methods configured on the line. The command `new aaa model` is incorrect. The command `local authentication` is incorrect regardless of where it is configured.

43. D. The command `enable algorithm-type scrypt secret Password20!` will change the enable password to Password20! and use the scrypt algorithm type. The commands `enable secret 9`, `service password-encryption scrypt`, and `enable secret algorithm-type scrypt` are incorrect.

44. D. The default encryption method for passwords configured for lines is clear text. If you want to encrypt the password, you should use the `service password-encryption` command. When the command `service password-encryption` is used, the password will be encrypted with an MD5 hash, otherwise known as a Cisco level 7 encryption. All of the other options are incorrect.

45. B. The command `exec-timeout 30 0` will change the idle time to 30 minutes and zero seconds. If a privileged exec session is idle for 30 minutes, the network admin will be disconnected. The command `exec-timeout 30 0` is incorrect when configured from a global configuration prompt. The command `exec-timeout 0 30` is incorrect because it will time out a user after 0 minutes and 30 seconds. The command `timeout 30 0` is incorrect.

46. D. The command `clear line vty 2` will disconnect a remote admin connected to the switch. Nothing stops the admin from reconnecting to the switch again. The command `no enable secret` is incorrect because it will only prevent future enable sessions. The command `no line vty 2` is incorrect; you cannot negate a physical line. The command `disconnect line vty 2` is incorrect.

47. C. The exec banner will display a message to authenticated users who have successfully logged in, regardless of whether they are connected via Telnet or SSH. The message of the day (MOTD) banner is displayed when a user attempts to login. The login banner is displayed after the MOTD but before initial login. An incoming banner is used for reverse Telnet connections and does not normally apply.

48. C. 802.1X allows selective access to a network at layer 2. It allows this on the switch because the switch acts as an authenticator to an AAA server, only allowing access after the user or device has been authenticated. 802.1Q is a trunking protocol used for transporting multiple VLANs over a layer 2 connection, and it does not provide authentication. An access control list (ACL) is a condition and action statement used to allow, deny, or log traffic. Firewalls contain ACLs and policies to allow, deny, and log traffic, but normally firewalls will not authenticate traffic.

49. B. The end device that sends credentials is called the supplicant. The supplicant is a piece of software in the operating system that supplies the credentials for AAA authentication. The authenticator is the wireless access point (WAP) or switch configured for 802.1X. The AAA server is normally a RADIUS server or TACACS+ server that is configured for 802.1X.

50. A. The switch is responsible for communicating with the supplicant and sending information to the authenticating server. This device is called the authenticator. The end device that sends credentials is called the supplicant. The supplicant is a piece of software in the operating system that supplies the credentials for AAA authentication. The AAA server is normally a RADIUS server or TACACS+ server that is configured for 802.1X.

51. A. The protocol used to communicate between the supplicants (OS) and the authenticator (switch) is 802.1X, the Extensible Authentication Protocol (EAP). 802.1X EAP is a layer 2 protocol used specifically for authenticating devices to switch ports and wireless. UDP ports 1812 and 1813 are commonly used between the authenticator and the AAA RADIUS server. TCP is not commonly used with 802.1X. IP is used for logical addressing when an authenticator needs to talk with the AAA RADIUS server.

52. C. The Extensible Authentication Protocol (EAP) is used for authentication between the supplicant and the authenticator. It is also used inside of the requests to the RADIUS server from the authenticator. The process begins by the EAP frame first being transmitted over the layer 2 connection via EAP over LAN (EAPoL). The switch (authenticator) then sends the EAP message to the RADIUS server encapsulated in a UDP packet for authentication. 802.1X authentication headers are used between the supplicant and the authenticator, such as the switch or wireless access point (WAP). IPsec is not commonly used with 802.1X. The RADIUS server is commonly the AAA authentication server.

53. A. The device requesting access is the supplicant. The supplicant is built into the operating system in which it is authenticating. The server that is providing authentication is the authentication server, which is commonly the AAA RADIUS server. The device that is controlling the access via the 802.1X protocol is the authenticator. The device connecting the layer 3 network is normally a router or layer 3 switch.

54. C. A smartcard is an example of multifactor authentication because you must have the smartcard and know the passphrase that secures the credentials stored on the card. Single-factor authentication would only require having something or knowing something, but not both in this instance. RADIUS authentication requires an authentication server for validating usernames and passwords. Active Directory authentication requires a username and password.

55. A. Turning on password complexity would reduce the risk of a password attack. Password expiration would be secondary to password complexity to reduce the risk, since without complexity the user could create a simple password. Phishing protection would not prevent a password attack. Time restrictions would not prevent a password attack.

56. D. Generic Routing Encapsulation (GRE) tunnels provide packet-in-packet encapsulation. It takes the original IP packet and encapsulates it, adding another IP packet for the GRE tunnel. GRE tunnels alone do not provide any encryption. GRE does not use IPsec security by default. It must be configured to use this security protocol inside of the GRE packet; this is commonly called an IPsec security transform. GRE uses a layer 3 IP protocol of 47, not 57. GRE does not provide per-packet authentication; IPsec can provide this service.

57. A. Generic Routing Encapsulation (GRE) is a Cisco-proprietary standard for encapsulating layer 3 protocols over an IP network, such as the Internet. Point-to-Point Protocol (PPP) is an IEEE standardized protocol for point-to-point links. IP Security (IPsec) is an IEEE standardized protocol for encryption of IP packets. Secure Sockets Layer (SSL) is an IEEE standardized protocol for mutual authentication and encryption between two hosts using certificates.

58. C. GRE uses the layer 3 protocol 47, which is the protocol that is stated in the layer 3 header. These protocol numbers are IP layer protocol numbers and should not be confused with TCP/UDP layer 4 port numbers. All of the other options are incorrect.

59. C. The network is unrouteable, since interface G0/1 on Router A is configured with a 192.168.1.0/24 network and interface G0/1 on Router B is configured with a 192.168.1.0/24. The `route` statement that needs to be configured will not pass any traffic since 192.168.1.0/24 is directly configured on both routers. The destination on Router A of the tunnel is correct, but the interface G0/1 on Router B is incorrectly addressed. The serial interfaces are on different addresses but most likely correspond to the IP network in the WAN cloud.

60. D. The correct route statement is `ip route 192.168.3.0 255.255.255.0 192.168.2.2`, because the network of 192.168.2.0/24 is built between these two routers. The tunnel acts as a routed interface between the routers. The route statements `ip route 192.168.3.0 255.255.255.0 tunnel 0`, `ip route 192.168.2.0 255.255.255.0 tunnel 0`, and `ip route 192.168.3.0 255.255.255.0 serial 0/0/1` are incorrect.

61. A. The maximum transmission unit of a GRE tunnel is 1476 because there are 24 bytes of overhead for the GRE header; 20 bytes are used by the public IP header and 4 bytes are used for GRE. Ethernet is commonly set to an MTU of 1492 or an MTU of 1500. An 802.1Q packet is commonly set to an MTU of 1528 because of the additional VLAN tagging information.

62. B. The command `show interface tunnel 0` will show in the output the source and destination of the tunnel. The commands `show ip tunnel 0`, `show ip gre`, and `show ip route` are incorrect.

63. A. If a traceroute is performed to 192.168.3.50 on Router A, it will show one hop. This is because the 192.168.3.0 network is on the other side of the tunnel interface, which is one hop away. All of the other options are incorrect.

64. C. The routes are wrong. They should be set to the destination of the opposite tunnel IP address and not the serial WAN address. The tunnel numbers do not need to match since they are locally significant to the configuration. The destination on Router A of the tunnel is correct because it points to the serial WAN address on Router B. The serial interfaces do not need to match because they are locally significant to the configuration on each router.

65. B. The Next Hop Router Protocol (NHRP) is responsible for resolving and directing traffic for Dynamic Multipoint VPN (DMVPN) traffic. Hot Standby Router Protocol (HSRP) is a first hop redundancy protocol (FHRP) used to failover to another standby router in the event the active router is offline. Address Resolution Protocol (ARP) is an IP helper protocol to determine the destination MAC address according to a destination IP address. Generic Router Encapsulation (GRE) is a Cisco-proprietary standard for encapsulating layer 3 protocols over an IP network, such as the Internet.

66. C. The problem is a layer 2 problem because both routers are in an UP/DOWN state for the connecting serial interfaces. Router A has a protocol of HDLC configured and Router B has a protocol of PPP configured. The output of the `show interface` command for both serial 0/0 and serial 0/1 on both routers does not show that the interfaces have been administratively disabled. The output of the `show interface` command on both routers does not support the theory that a wiring problem exists. If there was an IP address mismatch, the line protocol would still be in an UP state.

67. B. Dynamic Multipoint VPN (DMVPN) is an example of a hub-and-spoke or point-to-multipoint topology. All of the satellite connections terminate back to the central location. A single VPN site-to-site connection would be an example of a point-to-point topology. A full-mesh topology is commonly found on the core layer of an enterprise network. A dual-homed topology is commonly found on the WAN of enterprises that have two or more redundant connections to the Internet.

68. B. Data integrity is one of the benefits of using a secure VPN protocol. To ensure its integrity, a packet is sealed with a hash that must be calculated to the same hash on the other side when it is received and decrypted. Authentication is a benefit to using a VPN in that both parties are authenticated before network transmission begins. Anti-replay is a byproduct of authentication and data integrity; packets cannot be replayed without authentication between both parties and a rehashing of the packets. Confidentiality is created with any VPN because of the end-to-end encryption.

69. C. Cisco Firepower Threat Defense (FTD) devices are used to create VPN tunnels between sites. FTD devices run the Cisco FTD software, which allows for firewall, intrusion prevention, and VPNs, among other security-related functions. Catalyst switches and Cisco routers are not commonly used to create VPN tunnels between sites. Policy-based routing is a way to selectively route packets depending on specific criteria.

70. C. Since you have several remote workers who telecommute, the best connectivity option would be client SSL/VPN connectivity. A product called Cisco Any Connect Secure Mobility Client allows for SSL encryption for VPN tunnels back to the main site. A GRE tunnel is often use for site-to-site connectivity where an IPsec tunnel is also implemented. Wireless WAN can be used to connect clients to the Internet, but the client-to-site connection would be a VPN or SSL connection over the Internet. Site-to-site VPN connections are intended for connecting sites to each other via an encrypted tunnel over the Internet.

71. B. IPsec uses the Encapsulating Security Payload (ESP) protocol to encrypt data. The Authentication Headers (AH) protocol is used with IPsec for the integrity of data. Internet Key Exchange (IKE) is used between two IPsec members so they can build a security association (SA). Internet Security Association and Key Management Protocol (ISAKMP) uses IKE to build an SA so that encryption keys can be exchanged in the second phase of encryption.

72. C. Site-to-site IPsec VPNs offer scalability as a benefit. This is because each remote office only needs an Internet connection to create a VPN tunnel back to the main office. There is a certain overhead when using VPN; therefore, higher bandwidth requirements may exist after deploying site-to-site IPsec VPNs. Latency is affected and will be higher due to the level of encryption each packet must undergo as it passes through the site-to-site VPN. Support for multicast is not a common benefit of site-to-site IPsec VPNs.

73. A. Standard access control lists (ACLs) are within the range of 1 to 99. Extended access control lists are within the range of 100 to 199. All of the other options are incorrect.

74. C. Standard access control lists (ACLs) can be based on only the source address of the packet. Extended access control list conditions can be based on the destination address. When using standard access control list conditions, the source address can solely be used to create a condition, but a source port cannot be defined. Extended access control list conditions allow for combinations of source or destination address and source or destination port.

75. C. Extended access lists are within the range of 100 to 199. Standard access lists are within the range of 1 to 99. All of the other options are incorrect.

76. B. At the end of every access list there is a deny any any rule. If a permit is not configured in the access list, the ACL does not serve a purpose. All ACLs must contain at least one permit statement to be considered an actionable ACL. All of the other options are incorrect.

77. B. When packets are compared to an access control list, they are compared in a sequential order. When the first rule is found to match, the action is acted upon. There is no further rule processing after the first match. There is an explicit deny any any rule at the end of each ACL. Therefore, if none of the conditions matches the packet, it is discarded due to the conditions matching the deny any any rule at the end of the list.

78. B. An advantage of a standard access control list (ACL) is that they require less processing overhead from the ASIC or CPU (depending on the platform). Since they only inspect layer 3 headers, no further decapsulation is required for layer 4. The level of security is not increased or decreased when using standard access control lists. If a higher level of specificity for the condition is required, then extended access lists should be used. Blocking of specific applications can only be achieved with extended access lists because the source and destination ports can be specified.

79. C. The expanded range of a standard access list is 1300 to 1999. The range for an expanded extended access list is 2000 to 2699. All of the other options are incorrect.

80. C. A wildcard mask is the opposite of a network mask. The easy way to calculate a wildcard mask is to figure out what the subnet is and deduct 1 for the octet. For example, if the network address is 172.16.0.0/12 Classless Inter-Domain Routing (CIDR) or 255.240.0.0 (dotted decimal notation), and each network number is a multiple of 16, the wildcard mask should be 0.15.255.255. 255.240.0.0 is the network mask for the 172.16.0.0/12 network. All of the other options are incorrect.

81. A. The command `ip access-list 20 192.168.1.0 0.0.0.255` will configure an access list of 20, which is a standard access list. The source address of 192.168.1.0 is wildcard masked with 0.0.0.255. The commands `ip access-list 100 192.168.1.0 0.0.0.255`, `ip access-list 1 192.168.1.0/24`, and `ip access-list 2 192.168.1.0 255.255.255.0` are incorrect.

82. D. A rule with an address of 0.0.0.0 and wildcard mask of 255.255.255.255 defines all addresses. Effectively, it is another way to specify the "any" source or destination. All of the other options are incorrect.

83. D. Access lists can be applied per a port, per a protocol, or per a direction. For example, you could apply only one ACL per the interface of Fa 0/1, per the protocol of IP in the inbound direction.

84. B. An extended access list allows you to filter traffic by port, which defines an application being used, since web traffic is communicated on 80 or 443. A standard access list can only filter by the source IP address. A dynamic ACL is an ACL that is controlled by some dynamic factor such as traffic patterns or time of day. An expanded ACL is not really a type of ACL; it specifies the expanded numbering for standard and extend-ed ACLs.

85. D. The expanded range of a standard access list is 2000 to 2699. The expanded range of a standard access list is 1300 to 1999. The other options are incorrect.

86. C. A wildcard mask is the opposite of a network mask. The easy way to calculate a wildcard mask is to figure out what the subnet is and deduct 1 for the octet. For example, if the network address is 192.168.1.0/25 Classless Inter-Domain Routing (CIDR), or 255.255.255.128 (dotted decimal notation), and each network number is a multiple of 128, the wildcard mask should be 0.0.0.127. The network mask 255.255.255.128 is the network mask used with the 192.168.1.0/25 network. The other options are incorrect.

87. D. A named access control list (ACL) allows for removing and adding entries by their line number. Standard and extended access lists require the entire ACL to be removed and reconfigured if one entry needs to be removed. Dynamic access lists are special access lists that are used with the condition of time or traffic and by default do not allow for per-entry editing.

88. B. Once a successful login is performed at the router, the dynamic access control list (ACL) is activated. This is also called lock and key security. Standard access lists can execute actions based on the condition of a source IP address only. Extended access lists can execute actions based on the condition of a source and destination IP address as well as source and destination port numbers. Named access lists are nothing more than standard or extended access lists and use a name in lieu of a specific number.

89. A. The statement `access-list 20 deny 172.16.0.0 0.255.255.255` configures a standard access list for two reasons: The first is that the access list number is 20, which falls within the standard access list range of 1 to 99. The second reason is that you are depicting traffic by source address. The commands `access-list 180 permit udp any 172.16.0.0 0.255.255.255 eq 161`, `access-list 130 permit permit ip any any`, and `access-list 150 deny any 172.16.0.0 0.255.255.255` are incorrect.

90. C. The command `access-list 5 permit host 192.168.1.5` specifies the traffic coming from the host 192.168.1.5. The statement `access-list 5 permit 192.168.1.5 0.0.0.0` achieves the same thing. The commands `access-list 5 permit 192.168.1.5`, `access-list 5 permit 192.168.1.5/24`, and `access-list 5 permit 192.168.1.0 0.0.0.255` are incorrect.

91. B. The command `access-list 101 deny tcp host 192.168.2.6 host 192.168.1.3 eq 80` denies access from the host 192.168.2.3 to the host 192.168.1.6 for port 80. The next command, `access-list 101 permit ip any any`, allows all IP traffic from any to any. With extended access lists, the protocol needs to be described. The commands `access-list 101 deny tcp host 192.168.2.6 host 192.168.1.3 eq 80` and `access-list 101 permit any any` are incorrect. The commands `access-list 101 deny host 192.168.2.6 host 192.168.1.3 eq 80` and `access-list 101 permit any any` are incorrect. The commands `access-list 101 deny tcp host 192.168.2.6 host 192.168.1.3 eq 80` and `access-list 101 permit ip any any eq 80` are incorrect.

92. D. Standard access lists only allow you to describe traffic by source address. This helps the processing of the access list because the router or switch does not need to decapsulate packets further than layer 3. Extended access lists can execute actions based on the condition of a source and destination IP address as well as source and destination port numbers. Named access lists are nothing more than standard or extended access lists that use a name in lieu of a specific number. Dynamic access lists are ACLs that are triggered by a specific traffic pattern or a time of day.

93. D. The command `access-list 199 deny tcp any host 192.168.1.5 eq 22` will create an extended access list of 199 and deny TCP communication from any computer to the host of 192.168.1.5 for port 22. The commands `access-list 90 deny ip host 192.168.1.5 eq 22`, `access-list 90 deny tcp any host 192.168.1.5 eq 22`, and `access-list 199 deny tcp host 192.168.1.5 any eq 23` are incorrect.

94. C. An extended access list is required because you want to block by the destination address of the HR web application server. If you blocked only by source using a standard access list, then all host network traffic would be blocked to all servers. A dynamic access list does not work in this situation because a specific traffic pattern or time of day is not required. Expanded access lists allow for higher numbers to be used with access lists but do not work in this example.

95. C. The command `access-list 143 permit tcp host 192.168.8.3 eq 80` any is a valid statement. All extended access lists that describe a port must also describe the protocol. The commands `access-list 99 deny tcp host 192.168.2.7 eq 443`, `access-list 189 deny any host 192.168.1.5 eq 22`, and `access-list 153 permit any host 192.168.4.5 eq 22` are incorrect.

96. D. The command `ip access-group 198 in` will apply access list 198 to the interface in which it is configured in the inbound direction. The commands `ip access-list 198 in fast 0/1`, `ip access-list 198 in`, and `ip access-class 198 in` are incorrect.

97. D. The access list must be placed on the Gi0/2 interface outbound. Whenever you are evaluating access list placement, remember that packets are evaluated as they leave the interface, which is outbound. When packets enter the interface, they are evaluated inbound. It is always in the perspective of the router. The commands `interface gi 0/0` and `ip access-group 2 in` are incorrect because they are applied to the wrong interface. The commands `interface gi 0/0` and `ip access-group 2 out` are incorrect because they are applied to the wrong interface. The commands `interface gi 0/2` and `ip access-group 2 in` are incorrect because they are applied to the wrong direction on the interface.

98. D. The command `show ip access-list` will show all access lists with the line numbers. If the command is specific, such as `show ip access-list named_list`, you will see the ACL lines but no line numbers. The commands `show access-list named_list`, `show ip access-list`, and `show running-configuration` are incorrect.

99. A. Extended ACLs should always be placed closest to the source of traffic since they are extremely granular. Standard ACLs should always be placed closest to the destination of traffic since they only specify the source IP address. Dynamic ACLs can be placed in either location because they can be standard or extended access lists, with the addition of traffic-based rules or time of day–based rules. An expanded ACL is not really a type of ACL; it specifies the expanded numbering for standard and extended ACLs.

100. C. The command `ip access-list extended named_list` will create an extended named access list. The commands `access-list 101 allow host 192.168.1.5 any`, `ip access-list named_list`, and `ip access-list 101 named_list` are incorrect.

101. B. Standard ACLs should always be placed closest to the destination of traffic since they are broad in the traffic they control. Extended ACLs should always be placed closest to the source of traffic since they are extremely granular. Dynamic ACLs can be placed in either location because they can be standard or extended access lists, with the addition of traffic-based rules or time of day–based rules. An expanded ACL is not really a type of ACL; it specifies the expanded numbering for standard and extended ACLs.

102. A. When you're trying to diagnose port security, the first command should be `show port-security`. This will detail all of the ports with port security and their expected behavior when port security is violated. The commands `show mac address-table`, `show interface`, and `show security` are incorrect.

103. B. Since the remote office has no onsite IT personnel, there is a risk of workers plugging in unauthorized equipment such as a WAP. If port security is implemented, the interface can be secured to allow only the MAC address of the computer to pass; all other traffic can be dropped. Dynamic VLANs will not prevent unauthorized equipment from being plugged into the network, such as a WAP. ACLs can mitigate what is accessible on servers but will not prevent unauthorized equipment from being plugged in. VLAN pruning is a good overall practice to minimize traffic across trunk links, but it does nothing for end device security.

104. B. Port security can restrict a port to a single device by MAC address. This will effectively make plugging in a wireless access point (WAP) a non-event for a corporate network. Access control lists (ACLs) cannot restrict a wireless access point from being plugged into the corporate network. Wired Equivalent Privacy (WEP) is a very insecure wireless encryption protocol and will not prevent a wireless access point from being plugged into the corporate network. Static MAC addresses will not stop a wireless access point from being plugged into the corporate network.

105. A. Port security blocks unauthorized access by examining the source address of a net-work device. The destination MAC address is used for forward filter decisions. The source and destination IP addresses are used by access control lists (ACLs) to filter traffic.

106. C. Port security is enabled by configuring the command `switchport port-security`. This command must be configured on the interface in which you want to enable port security. The command `switchport port-security` is incorrect when it is configured in a global configuration prompt. The command `port-security enable` is incorrect regardless of where it is configured.

107. A. By default, only a single MAC address is allowed on an interface when port security is enabled. All of the other options are incorrect.

108. C. Port security operates at layer 2 by inspecting the source MAC addresses in frames. It allows the configured number of source MAC addresses to be switched into the port and onto the switch processor. All of the other options are incorrect.

109. C. Configuring port security helps a network administrator prevent unauthorized access by MAC address. VLANs can be allowed or disallowed only on a trunk link and not on an access link. ACLs can be used to allow or disallow IP addresses. Port security cannot be used to prevent unauthorized access by users.

110. C. Port security works best in static environments where there is minimal change to the environment. It does not require any more memory since the results are pulled from the MAC address table. Port security can work in mobile environments, but depending on the configuration, it may become an administrative burden. Port security does not require a higher amount of memory. Port security can be configured so that admin intervention to reset an err-disabled port is not required.

111. B. Both the computer and the VoIP phone have MAC addresses, and therefore you will need to allow the port to have two MAC addresses, one for the phone to communicate and the other for the computer to communicate on the port. All of the other options are incorrect.

112. B. By default, when port security is configured on a port, the violation method is err-disabled shutdown. Administratively shutdown ports can only be configured by an administrator. You can configure port security to restrict access to a MAC address with and without logging.

113. C. When port security is configured, the port cannot be in dynamic mode for Dynamic Trunking Protocol (DTP) mode. You must configure the port as an access port first, then turn off DTP with the command `switchport nonnegotiate`. You can then configure switchport security. The commands `no switchport dynamic` and `switchport port-security` are incorrect. The commands `switchport mode access` and `switchport port-security` are incorrect. The commands `switchport mode access`, `no dynamic`, and `switchport port-security` are incorrect.

114. B. The command `switchport port-security maximum 2` will configure the port with a maximum of two MAC addresses that shall pass through the port. The commands `switchport maximum 2`, `port-security maximum 2`, and `switchport port-security limit 2` are incorrect.

115. D. The command `switchport port-security violation restrict` will set the violation mode to restrict. This will drop frames over the maximum number of learned MAC addresses and will log security violations to the counters. The command `switchport port-security violation shutdown` is incorrect; this is the default mode in which it will enter an err-disabled state upon a violation. The command `switchport port-security restrict` is incorrect as it is missing the violation argument. The command `switchport port-security violation protect` is incorrect because it will not increment the `security-violation` count while it is dropping frames.

116. B. The command `show port-security interface gi 2/13` will allow you to see a detailed view of an individual port configured for port security. The command `show running-configuration` is incorrect; it will not show the status of a port, only the configuration. The commands `show port-security details interface gi 2/13` and `show port-security gi 2/13` are incorrect.

117. A. The command `switchport port-security violation shutdown` puts the interface into the err-disable state immediately and sends an SNMP trap notification to a syslog server. The commands `switchport port-security restrict`, `switchport port-security violation protect`, and `switchport port-security violation restrict` are incorrect.

118. C. The command `switchport port-security violation protect` will set the violation mode to protect. This will drop frames over the maximum number of learned MAC addresses but will not log security violations to the counters. The commands `switchport port-security violation shutdown`, `switchport`

port-security restrict, and switchport port-security violation restrict are incorrect.

119. C. The command show port-security will show all ports that have logged port security violations. The commands show violations, show port-security violations, and show psec violations are incorrect.

120. C. When you configure sticky port security, the first MAC address seen by the switch will become bound to the port. Any other MAC addresses will trip the access violation set. Static port security will require you to enter the MAC address of each computer paired with each port. Dynamic port security and time limit port security are not types of port security that can be implemented.

121. B. The default configuration for port security results in an access violation of shutdown. When a port security violation occurs, the port will be shut down in an err-disable status. Because the port is in an err-disabled state, the figure does not support the theory that a port has been administratively shut down. The figure also does not support the theory that the port has bad wiring. You cannot tell from the output in the figure that the port is configured as a trunk or access link, but neither will place the port into an err-disabled state.

122. A. The command switchport port-security mac-address sticky will configure the port to learn the first MAC address and allow only the first MAC address to pass traffic. The commands switchport port-security mac-address dynamic, is switchport port-security mac-address static, and switchport port-security mac-address learn are incorrect.

123. D. One way to clear an err-disable status is to issue the shutdown command and then the no shutdown command on the port. This will reset the port so that traffic can flow again. However, if the access violation still exists, then the port will enter an err-disable status again. The command no port-security is incorrect and will not clear the err-disable state. The command no shutdown is incorrect and will not clear the err-disable state. The command no switchport port-security is incorrect and will not clear the err-disable state.

124. B. The command switchport port-security mac-address 0334.56f3.e4e4 will configure the interface with a static MAC address of 0334.56f3.e4e4. The command switchport port-security mac-address sticky is incorrect as it will configure itself with the first MAC address learned. The command switchport port-security mac-address static 0334.56f3.e4e4 is incorrect. The command switchport port-security static 0334.56f3.e4e4 is incorrect.

125. D. The command show port-security will show all of the ports that are actively participating in port security. In addition, you can see the maximum number of addresses configured, current addresses, security violations, and action. The commands show port-security details, show mac address-table secure, and show port-security address are incorrect.

126. D. The global config command `errdisable recovery cause psecure_ violation` will reset all ports with an err-disable status. The commands `clear err-disable`, `clear switchport port-security`, and `clear port-security violation` are incorrect.

127. A. The command `show running-config` will show you the learned MAC addresses from port security. The commands `show port-security`, `show port-security details`, and `show port-security status` are incorrect.

128. B. The AAA server will centralize authentication for Cisco routers and switches. AAA stands for authentication, authorization, and accounting. It is pronounced "triple A." An Active Directory server can be used in conjunction with authentication, but the AAA server will facilitate the authentication. 802.1X is a protocol and not a type of server; therefore, this is incorrect. Terminal servers are servers that extend applications or the server desktop to remote users and have nothing to do with authentication of Cisco routers and switches.

129. B. RADIUS authentication uses the UDP protocol and port 1645 for communications between the switch or router and the AAA server. All of the other options are incorrect.

130. B. TACACS+ is a protocol used for communications between a switch or router and the AAA server for authenticating users. 802.1X is used to secure ports on a switch or access to wireless access points (WAPs). Active Di-rectory (AD) is a Microsoft directory of computers and users that is used for authentication purposes. Extensible Authentication Protocol (EAP) is a protocol that allows for passwords, certificates, biometrics, and any other extensible method for authentication.

131. A. The command `aaa authentication log-in default group tacacs+ local` will configure AAA authentication for login using the default list and a group of TACACS+ servers for TACACS+ login first and a backup of local for authentication. The other options are incorrect.

132. C. The router will lock you out since you have not provided a local account to log in with. The password recovery procedure would need to be performed if the configuration was saved. The enable secret will be overridden by the configuration, since you configured default local and it will not work. The console will also not be available because the default local was configured. Once the default local is configured, the authentication will be based upon the local AAA configuration; if no user exists, then you will be locked out of the router or switch.

133. A. Routinely looking at a log file and discovering that a security incident has occurred is an example of passive detection. Active detection would be if you were actively notified when the incident occurred. Proactive detection is where you find the security incident before it occurs. Auditing is the act of reading through a log file, not detecting an incident.

134. D. Remote Authentication Dial-In User Service (RADIUS) servers are authentication servers. DNS servers perform name resolution for clients. Email servers deliver and receive email on the Internet. Proxy servers fetch requests on behalf of clients.

135. B. Enabling MAC filtering on the access point will allow the devices that she specifies. Disabling WPA2 encryption will not prevent unauthorized access to the SOHO network and creates other security concerns. Port Security is enabled on wired network switches to prevent unauthorized access. Disabling the SSID from broadcasting will not prevent unauthorized access.

136. B. A certificate infrastructure is required for WPA2-Enterprise mode. WPA2-Enterprise mode is not compatible with a preshared key (PSK) method of security. 192-bit key strength was introduced with WPA3-Enterprise mode. WPA2-Enterprise can be used with any of the 802.11 wireless coverage technologies since it operates independently.

137. B. Message Integrity Check (MIC), also known as Michael, is responsible for the protection of messages by including an integrity check that the other side can verify. Temporal Key Integrity Protocol (TKIP) was used as an encryption protocol for WPA as a quick replacement of Wired Equivalent Privacy (WEP). Advanced Encryption Standard (AES) is an encryption protocol first introduced with WPA2. A cyclic redundancy check (CRC) is a simple calculation to assure that data is not damaged in transit.

138. C. WPA3-Enterprise offers a 192-bit security mode that uses 192-bit minimum strength security protocols. Although WPA3-Enterprise can use the authentication encryption of 256-bit Galois/Counter Mode Protocol (GCMP-256), it employs 192-bit AES for the encryption and transmission of data, which is where it gets its name. All of the other options are incorrect.

139. C. After the weaknesses in WEP encryption were discovered, the Wi-Fi Alliance rushed the release of the WPA security protocol. The WPA security protocol incorporated the 802.11i standard of TKIP, which allowed for better integrity of 802.11 transmissions. The WPA security protocol was released after the WEP security protocol. The WPA security protocol did not address any problems related to coverage. It was not a rebranding of the WEP security protocol; it was intended to be a replacement.

140. B. The 802.11i standard added the feature of per-frame encryption. The use of certificates and preshared keys (PSKs) are features of WPA and not the 802.11i standard. CRC checking is part of the 802.11 standard, and therefore, it was not added with 802.11i or the WPA security protocol.

141. C. The 802.11i (WPA2) specification introduced a specific mode of Advanced Encryption Standard (AES) encryption called Counter Mode with Cipher Block Chaining Message Authentication Code Protocol (CCMP). The Rivest Cipher 4 (RC4) algorithm is used by Wired Equivalent Privacy (WEP) and Wi-Fi Protected Access (WPA) as an encryption protocol. Message-Digest algorithm 5 (MD5) and Secure Hash Algorithm 1 (SHA1) are popular hashing algorithms but not related to wireless communications.

142. C. The WPA3 protocol introduced the feature of Simultaneous Authentication of Equals (SAE) authentication, also known as the Dragonfly handshake. Certificate support, per-frame encryption, and Temporal Key Integrity Protocol (TKIP) were all features introduced with the original WPA standard.

143. B. When configuring WAP2-Enterprise mode on a wireless LAN controller, you must configure a RADIUS server for authentication of the users or computers joining wireless. Setting a Network Time Protocol server is optional when configuring WPA2-Enterprise.

WPA-Personal uses a preshared key (PSK), whereas WPA-Enterprise uses a certificate pair for authentication. Captive portals are not required for WPA2-Enterprise because the user or computer should be authenticated by the certificate pair.

144. C. You should disable the Temporal Key Integrity Protocol (TKIP) when configuring WPA2. This will ensure that the WAP and client do not fall back to the older WPA protocol. 802.1X will operate independently from the WPA2 and WPA fallback mechanism. Advanced Encryption Standard (AES) is an encryption protocol that is used in conjunction with WPA2; therefore, it should not be disabled. MAC filtering is not related to WPA or WPA2 and works independently as a security mechanism.

145. A. A preshared key (PSK) is the mechanism used for configuring authentication with WPA2 using a symmetrical key. Advanced Encryption Standard (AES) is an encryption protocol that is used in conjunction with WPA2. AES is not used for authentication of hosts. Certificates are used with WPA2-Enterprise; they are asymmetrical keys used for authentication. The Temporal Key Integrity Protocol (TKIP) is used along-side the RC4 protocol to provide encryption for WPA; it is not used for authentication.

146. D. When the status of a configured WLAN is set to disable or unchecked in the GUI, the SSID will be broadcast and active for clients. SSID beaconing is enabled by default; if it were disabled, the clients would not see the SSID. Multicast support is used for multimedia applications and would not prevent the SSID from being seen by clients. The Radio Policy could possibly restrict clients from seeing the SSID depending on what it is set to. However, when it is set to all, there are no restrictions.

147. A. A single preshared key (PSK) is configured for a WPA2 WLAN. The PSK can be either one hex or one ASCII key, but it cannot be both. If you need multiple keys, then WPA2-Enterprise should be used. Keep in mind that a PSK is symmetrical encryption, whereas WPA2-Enterprise uses certificates and asymmetrical encryption. All of the other options are incorrect.

148. D. The Wi-Fi Protected Access 2 (WPA2) protocol can be configured with Advanced Encryption Standard (AES) encryption to provide the highest level of security. Wi-Fi Protected Access (WPA) cannot be configured with AES encryption; therefore, this is a wrong answer. WPA2 cannot be configured with Temporal Key Integrity Protocol (TKIP); only WPA uses the RC4 encryption algorithm and TKIP.

149. B. In order to satisfy the requirements of the client, WPA2-Personal should be configured for the wireless network. WPA2-Personal will allow for 128-bit AES-CCMP encryption and work with a preshared key (PSK) to minimize infrastructure. WPA-Enterprise and WPA3-Enterprise require certificate services and an AAA server. WPA-Personal is weaker encryption than WPA2-Personal.

150. B. When a WLAN is configured with WPA-TKIP, it will not be able to achieve over 54 Mbps. The Counter Mode with Cipher Block Chaining Message Authentication Code Protocol (CCMP) is based on of the Advanced Encryption Standard (AES) encryption protocol and will not hinder throughput. Configuring a preshared key (PSK) will also not hinder throughput.

Chapter 6: Automation and Programmability (Domain 6)

1. B. A reason to automate a process for the configuration of several routers is to create a positive outcome that can be reproduced. Automating processes for configuration decreases the possibility for misconfiguration. Automation of configuration does not decrease problems from the new configuration; if anything, it automates the increase of possible problems. Although it might seem like automating a process for configuration allows you to do less work, it is not always the case.

2. C. Creating a Python script to configure each router is the best way to complete this task. You can automate the process and save time since the entry of the route is a repetitious process. Copying and pasting scripts from Notepad++ or Excel into each router will require you to log into each router. Doing this increases the chances of missing a router. You could also work with a partner and start at different ends of the list, but again, this approach introduces the possibility of errors and ties up two technicians.

3. C. The number one motivating factor to use network automation is to reduce the human error factor when creating bulk changes. Network automation will not reduce the number of changes to be made. As an example, an updated ACL on all the routers will still need to be updated on all the routers. Network automation also does not reduce the complications that arise from changes; it actually increases them. Network automation also increases the planning time for changes. A network automation script can change everything rapidly; if it's wrong, it can even lead to an outage of services.

4. B. The term *DevOps* is used to describe the framework responsible for assisting in network automation. It is usually written in conjunction with network operations, but it is considered a development function using the DevOps framework. The term *NetOps* refers to the network operation team's responsibility. The term *SysOps* is used to describe the control of network systems such as DNS, Active Directory (AD), and DHCP, just to name a few. The term *SecOps* refers to the security operation as it pertains to the network.

5. A. The management methodology that is commonly used by developers for network automation is Lean and Agile. Agile focuses on an adaptive approach for simultaneous workflows, such as the configuration of a default route on several routers. The Waterfall management methodology is used for projects in a linear process that does not allow for going back to a prior phase. The Kanban management methodology is used to improve existing processes. Scrum is primarily focused on getting more work done more quickly.

6. D. After a network automation script is released to production, the very next process should be to monitor its effects on the network. This step should already be considered with prebuilt metrics so that you can positively conclude its intended function. The testing step should have been done prior to the deployment phase. The building phase is done when you are ready to test a completed configuration change. The planning phase is the first phase before anything is put into motion; it is where you have determined the metrics for the project, which determines if the changes are successful.

7. B. The YAML Ain't Markup Language (YAML) markup language uses mapping to define keys and values as pairs. *Definition* is not a term used with YAML; therefore, option A is an invalid answer. Lists are keys with multiple values in the form of a list. Keys are categories that contain a value in the key-value pair.

8. A. A YAML file will always begin with three dashes. This is how you know you are working with a YAML file structure. Files that start with a hashbang preprocessor are normally scripts, and the hashbang describes to the operating system which command interpreter to use. A file that has its content contained between curly braces or square braces is normally a JSON file.

9. D. Extensible Markup Language (XML) was adopted from Hypertext Markup Language (HTML) as a storage method for systems to interchange data. YAML Ain't Markup Language (YAML) is a white space–structured file that is also used to store data for the interchange of information. JavaScript Object Notation (JSON) is another structured storage method for data and was originally created for use with JavaScript and gained popularity with other languages. Comma-separated values (CSV) is a flat data storage method that is popular when lists of information must be passed from system to system.

10. A. YAML Ain't Markup Language (YAML) is a white space–structured file that is also used to store data for the interchange of information. JavaScript Object Notation (JSON) is structured with curly and square brackets. Extensible Markup Language (XML) was adopted from Hypertext Markup Language (HTML), which uses opening and closing tags. Comma-separated values (CSV) is a flat data storage method that uses commas to delimit the fields of information held on each line.

11. B. The application programming interface (API) on the device that is to be controlled through automation should be researched. The API is a method for controlling devices with programmability control; this includes the import and export of information. The user interface layout is more accustomed to users and manual configuration, since programs do not use the user interface. The source code and data storage methods for the device are not normally attainable and do not really get you what you need to control the device.

12. B. The Simple Network Management Protocol (SNMP) was originally created to allow retrieval of information from network devices and can be programmatically controlled, similar to an application programming interface (API). The command-line interface (CLI) is what the user will interface with; therefore, it is considered a type of user interface (UI). Syslog is a method of sending logging information to remote syslog servers. Secure Shell (SSH) is a method for connectivity and not used as an API.

13. A. The NETCONF protocol was created as a replacement for the dated Simple Network Management Protocol (SNMP). Syslog is a system of formatted messages for log file storage, either local or remote, via the syslog protocol. Representational state transfer (REST) is a set of constraints used for sending data to and from services. Secure Shell (SSH) is a method of connecting to network devices through a console-based terminal emulator.

14. A. The NETCONF protocol was created to interface with network devices over the SSH protocol. Data transferred to and from network devices with the NETCONF protocol must adhere to the Yet Another Next Generation (YANG) data model. Representational state transfer (REST) is a set of constraints used for sending data to and from services. Simple Network Management Protocol (SNMP) is a network management protocol used to retrieve and send information to remote network devices. YAML is a markup language used to store and transfer data between applications.

15. B. The RESTCONF protocol is used with a Hypertext Transfer Protocol Secure (HTTPS) transport protocol. RESTCONF is the successor of NETCONF, which uses SSH for device access. RESTCONF now uses a common transport of HTTPS to send and retrieve information from network devices. Simple Network Management Protocol (SNMP) defines its own standard of information set and retrieval and does not use HTTPS. Syslog is a system of formatted messages for log file storage either local or remote via the syslog protocol.

16. A. A benefit of controller-based networking is increased security. When ACLs and filters are applied, they are applied informally to all nodes that are controlled by the controller. There is not a reduction of problems that can be encountered in a network with the introduction of controller-based networking. Throughput will not increase magically because of the introduction of controller-based networking. Complexity should be reduced with the introduction of controller-based networking because all of the configuration is centralized.

17. B. Controller-based networking has a logically centralized control plane to centrally control the data plane. The data plane is not centralized because switching and routing of data must be done very fast, usually with the use of application-specific integrated circuits (ASICs). Controller-based networking comes in many different forms, ranging from applications to hardware appliances. Both controller-based network switching and autonomous network switching use ASICs, but controller-based network switches do not centrally switch frames.

18. B. *Software-defined wide area network (SD-WAN)* is the term commonly used to describe the combination of multiple sites to act as one single network. Use cases of SD-WAN are disaster recovery and remote office and branch office planning. Software-defined networking (SDN) is the term used to describe local area network (LAN) controller-based networking. *SD-LAN* is not a term commonly used, and therefore, option C is an invalid answer. A virtual private network (VPN) will allow multiple sites to act as one single network, but it is not centrally controlled with controller-based networking.

19. C. Controller-based networking, also known as software-defined networking (SDN), is roughly 15 years old. Many see this maturity as a disadvantage when comparing it to traditional networking equipment that is much older in theory. Scalability, security, and centralized provisioning are advantages to using controller-based networking and far outweigh the disadvantage of the youth of SDN.

20. C. Quality of service (QoS) can be directly controlled with an SDN controller. The SDN controller will push programming to the SDN-enabled switch so that the switch can control the flow of traffic. CPU and memory utilization can be reported on, and arguably programming can be pushed out to alleviate central processing unit (CPU) and memory utilization, but CPU and memory utilization is not directly controlled with an SDN controller. The forwarding of traffic is a responsibility of the data plane, which can be changed by the control plane. However, the SDN controller does not forward packets explicitly; that is the function of the switch.

21. B. All software-defined network (SDN) switches are stateless with respect to their configuration. The configuration is applied from the central controller, and therefore, any configuration contained on the switch does not matter if it is lost during a reboot. Data is not centrally switched at the SDN controller; this would make data transfer too slow and overburden the SDN controller. The data flowing through the switch is not consequential to the SDN controller; some data flows can be stateless, such as UDP, and some can be stateful, such as TCP.

22. A. The Simple Network Management Protocol (SNMP) allows for the central monitoring of switches and routers by using traps and polling of network metrics. Syslog is a method of collecting logs for passive analysis after an event has been brought to your attention. Software-defined networking (SDN) allows for the centralized control of switches and routers. The Cisco Discovery Protocol (CDP) is used to discover Cisco devices on the immediate network.

23. D. The Simple Network Management Protocol (SNMP) utilizes a component called the network management station (NMS) to collect all messages and poll metrics from all managed devices. An SNMP trap is a message generated from an SNMP agent installed on a host. An SNMP agent is a piece of software that monitors the operating system and hardware and either reports to the NMS or is polled by the NMS. A syslog server is a centralized server that collects logs for passive analysis of problems.

24. A. The Simple Network Management Protocol (SNMP) along with Telnet and Secure Shell (SSH) are used to configure network devices with Cisco Prime. Control And Provisioning of Wireless Access Points (CAPWAP) and Lightweight Access Point Protocol (LWAPP) are used with wireless LAN controllers for the configuration of wireless access points (WAPs). RESTCONF is used with Cisco Digital Network Architecture (DNA) for network device configuration.

25. B. The Spine/Leaf architecture model has been adopted in controller-based networks. The Leaf switch acts as the access and distribution, and the Spine acts as the core or backbone for the network. The three-tier network model and the collapsed core network model are used with controller-based networking. However, the concepts of the Cisco three-tier model are still applicable, such as the access, distribution, and core concepts as described. A storage area network (SAN) fabric is not used in a network or controller-based network, as it is applicable only to storage area networks.

26. D. Leaf switches never connect to other Leaf switches; they only connect to Spine switches. There can be many Spine switches per network; they are considered the backbone of the network. Although nothing stops you from connecting a host to a Spine switch, Spine switches should only provide core/backbone services.

27. A. Traffic flow in a Spine/Leaf network flows from the host connected to the Leaf to the Spine, eventually to the destination Leaf and the awaiting host. Leaf switches are connected only to the Spine; therefore, traffic cannot flow from the host to a Leaf to another Leaf directly. Hosts should not be connected to Spine switches, so traffic will not flow from the host to the Spine to a Leaf and then a Spine switch.

28. D. The Cisco Application Centric Infra-structure (ACI) software-defined networking (SDN) solution is data center–focused to deliver applications to end users. The Cisco Application Policy Infrastructure Controller - Enterprise Module (APIC-EM) is a legacy SDN solution that is not part of Cisco Digital Network Architecture (DNA). OpenDaylight (ODL) is an open platform used for SDN solutions; it is not provided or maintained by Cisco. The Cisco Software-Defined Wide Area Network (SD-WAN) is a scalable SDN solution for networks that operate over several data centers.

29. B. Cisco Software Defined - Wide Area Network (SD-WAN) is a solution that will allow remote office/branch office (ROBO) personnel to access cloud-based applications directly. The Cisco Application Policy Infrastructure Controller - Enterprise Module (APIC-EM) is a legacy SDN solution that is not part of Cisco Digital Network Architecture (DNA). Cisco Prime Infrastructure is a legacy management tool for deployment of switches, routers, and wireless. OpenDaylight (ODL) is an open platform used for SDN solutions; it is not provided or maintained by Cisco.

30. B. The campus networking model is a traditional networking model that is deployed as either a three-tier model with a core, distribution, and access layer or a collapsed core model. In the collapsed core model, the core and distribution layers are the same functional equipment. The Spine/Leaf, also known as the CLOS model, is commonly found in software-defined networking (SDN).

31. C. The software-defined network (SDN) controller replaces the control plane on SDN devices. The SDN devices in the network do not contain a control plane locally and instead are controlled by the SDN controller. The SDN controller does not configure the management plane of the network devices; it replaces the management plane of the network devices. The SDN controller does not monitor the data plane of traffic; it only controls the traffic. The SDN controller does not complement the control plane of the SDN device; it replaces the control plane of the SDN device.

32. A. Application Policy Infrastructure Controller - Enterprise Module (APIC-EM) is a Cisco SDN controller. This package is freely downloadable from the Cisco DevNet website as of this writing. It comes with several built-in apps, such as a plug-and-play module and a path trace module. Many other apps can be built on top of the APIC to extend functionality of the controller. However, the product has been largely replaced with Cisco DNA and is now licensed. OpenSDN is an open source SDN controller platform that utilized the open source OpenDaylight (ODL) protocol. OpenStack is another open source SDN controller aimed at data centers.

33. B. The control plane refers to any mechanism that controls the data plane. STP is used to control the data plane by removing redundant links. The data plane is responsible for switching and routing data. Any data that is destined for endpoints is switched or routed on the data plane. The management plane is any mechanism that helps in the management of a router or switch. *Switch plane* is not a term normally used to describe data types; therefore, option D is an invalid answer.

34. C. The management plane is any mechanism that helps in the management of a router or switch. Some of the common mechanisms are SSH and Telnet. However, any mechanism that the router uses for management is considered part of the management plane. The control plane refers to any mechanism that controls the data plane. The data plane is responsible for switching and routing data. Any data that is destined for endpoints is switched or routed on the data plane. *Switch plane* is not a term normally used to describe data types; therefore, option D is an invalid answer.

35. A. The data plane is responsible for switching and routing data. Any data that is destined for endpoints is switched or routed on the data plane. For example, when one computer pings another, the ping is switched and routed on the data plane. The control plane refers to any mechanism that controls the data plane. The management plane is any mechanism that helps in the management of a router or switch. *Switch plane* is not a term normally used to describe data types; therefore, option is an invalid answer.

36. B. Routing protocols such as OSPF and EIGRP would perform their function on the control plane since they are controlling the routing of the data plane. The data plane is responsible for switching and routing data. Any data that is destined for endpoints is switched or routed on the data plane. For example, when one computer pings another, the ping is switched and routed on the data plane. The management plane is any mechanism that helps in the management of a router or switch. *Routing plane* is not a term normally used to describe data types; therefore, option D is an invalid answer.

37. D. The Cisco Discovery Protocol (CDP) functions on the management plane of the SDN model. It helps with management of the routers and switches and does not directly impact the data plane. The data plane is responsible for switching and routing data. Any data that is destined for endpoints is switched or routed on the data plane. *Network plane* is not a term normally used to describe data types; therefore, option C is an invalid answer. The management plane is any mechanism that helps in the management of a router or switch.

38. B. The southbound interface (SBI) directly communicates with the SDN devices. This control is done via several different types of SBI protocols, such as OpenFlow, OpFlex, and CLI (Telnet/SSH). The northbound interface (NBI) is responsible for allowing communication between applications and the core of the controller. The core of the controller is the mechanism that connects the NBI to the SBI. Applications hosted on the controller interface with the NBI.

39. C. An application program interface (API) is a method the programmer has created to allow other programs to communicate with their program. The interprogrammability is required when another program wants to share data with the API. Although an API allows data transfer, it is not a program specifically written for the transfer of data. An API is used for network programmability, but it is not a language for network programmability. An API does not allow for a program to be virtualized.

40. C. The northbound interface (NBI) is responsible for allowing communication between applications and the core of the controller. Applications therefore directly communicate with the core through the northbound interface. The southbound interface (SBI) directly communicates with the SDN devices. The core of the controller is the mechanism that connects the

NBI to the SBI. The Simple Network Management Protocol (SNMP) is used for the monitoring and collection of device metrics.

41. B. The data plane is responsible for the routing of packets to specific destinations. The control plane would be responsible for the management of the routes for the functional routing of packets. The management plane would be responsible for the management of all functions of the router. There is no plane called the routing plane; therefore, option D is an invalid answer.

42. B. The maximum hop count on fabric switching is a total of 3 hops. When a host transmits, it will enter a Leaf switch; the Leaf switch will then forward traffic to the Spine switch. The Spine switch will in turn forward traffic to the corresponding Leaf switch and to the destination host. Of course, traffic could be 1 hop away, if both hosts are on the same Leaf switch. However, the maximum hop count is 3 hops.

43. D. The underlay is where you will set the maximum transmission unit (MTU). The overlay is where the tunnel or virtual circuit is built using the underlay as the transport. A Leaf switch is a part of the software-defined network (SDN), along with the Spine switch; both need to have the same MTU set.

44. D. When you configure access control lists (ACLs) through any interface, you are affecting the control plane. This is because you are controlling the flow of data with the ACL. You are accessing the router through the management plane when you are connected to either the web interface or the command-line interface (CLI). The data plane is what you are controlling with the control plane. The data plane is the actual flow of information.

45. A. Dynamic Multipoint Virtual Private Network (DMVPN) is a wide area network (WAN) technology that allows for virtual private networks (VPNs) to be created using the overlay of software-defined networking (SDN). Virtual Extensible LAN (VXLAN) is used to transport virtual local area network (VLAN) traffic over routed connections. Equal-cost multipath routing (ECMP) is used by Leaf and Spine switches to provide a next-hop packet forwarding decision.

46. C. The Virtual Extensible LAN (VXLAN) protocol is used to create layer 2 tunnels over a layer 3 network. The VXLAN protocol functions by encapsulating layer 2 traffic inside of a layer 3 packet. The Equal Cost Load Balancing Protocol (ECMP) is used by Leaf and Spine switches to provide next-hop packet forwarding decisions. Dynamic Multipoint Virtual Private Network (DMVPN) is a point-to-multipoint VPN technology used for layer 3 connectivity over a wide area network (WAN) connection. The Enhanced Interior Gateway Routing Protocol (EIGRP) is a Cisco-proprietary layer 3 routing protocol.

47. A. The Simple Network Management Protocol (SNMP) is a protocol used on the management plane. SNMP is used for the management of routers and switches because it can be writeable and allow for configuration. The Cisco Discovery Protocol (CDP) is a control protocol because it communicates port properties via layer 2 frames, such as power requirements. The Internet Control Message Protocol (ICMP) is a control protocol, because it is used to send control messages back to the originating device. The VLAN Trunking Protocol (VTP) is used to communicate the control information of VLANs to other participating switches.

48. A. The equal-cost multipath routing (ECMP) packet forwarding protocol is used to calculate next-hop forwarding with SDN switching networks. The Open Shortest Path First (OSPF) protocol is a layer 3 routing protocol and not used with SDN switching networks. The Multi-protocol Label Switching Protocol (MPLS) is a protocol used with MPLS wide area network (WAN) providers and not used with SDN switching networks. The CLOS network is also known as a Leaf/Spine network, but it is the topology and not a next-hop packet forwarding protocol.

49. C. The Cisco DNA Center is Cisco's next-generation software-defined network (SDN) controller; it replaces Cisco's Application Policy Infrastructure Controller - Enterprise Module (APIC-EM) platform. OpenFlow is a protocol used to configure software-defined networks. Cisco Prime Infrastructure (CPI) is a network management software suite, but it does not provide SDN functionality. Cisco Software Defined - Wide Area Network (SD-WAN) is an SDN controller for building WAN connections.

50. D. After the Cisco Digital Network Architecture (Cisco DNA) discovery process has found a device, it will use SSH, Telnet, SNMPv2, SNMPv3, HTTP, HTTPS, and NETCONF. The discovery process will not use OpenFlow, since this is a configuration protocol that is mainly used by open platforms.

51. B. Artificial intelligence is a broad term that explains the simulation of human intelligence to include learning, reasoning, and self-correction. Machine learning is a term that explains the act of teaching a data model to a computer so that it can recognize patterns. Data analytics is the analysis of data, which is the first step in training data for machine learning or artificial intelligence.

52. A. Machine learning is a term that explains the act of teaching a data model to a computer so that it can recognize patterns. Artificial intelligence is a broad term that explains the simulation of human intelligence to include, learning, reasoning, and self-correction. Data analytics is the analysis of data, which is the first step in training data for machine learning or artificial intelligence.

53. A. Predictive artificial intelligence uses historical data to forecast and predict future outcomes, such as potential failure or congestion of a network. Generative artificial intelligence uses data models and reasoning to develop new models to develop insight into a problem or event. Anomaly detection is typically an outcome of machine learning. Root cause analysis is typically an outcome of artificial intelligence analyzing data across many different network elements.

54. D. ChatGPT and many other GPT models are generative pretrained transformer artificial intelligence models Machine learning does not transform outcomes. Predictive artificial intelligence uses historical data to predict an outcome. Although GPT models are generative artificial intelligence in nature, generative artificial intelligence will not transform by itself.

55. C. Reinforcement learning uses trial and error to fine-tune the outcome of the artificial intelligence decisions. Supervised learning uses labeled dataset to train the artificial intelligence model. Unsupervised learning uses unlabeled datasets to train the artificial intelligence model. Controlled learning is similar to supervised learning in which the dataset is strictly controlled.

56. A. Cisco Meraki uses machine learning to automate provisioning, management, trouble-shooting, connectivity optimization, and uptime of network devices. Cisco Thousand Eyes uses artificial intelligence and machine learning to deliver applications and services over the Internet. Cisco Secure Network Analytics uses machine learning to monitor network traffic in real time and respond to anomalies. Cisco AppDynamics uses both machine learning and artificial intelligence to enhance visibility in applications and infrastructure.

57. B. Generative artificial intelligence uses data models and reasoning to develop new models to develop insight into a problem or event. Predictive artificial intelligence uses historical data to forecast and predict future outcomes, such as potential failure or congestion of a network. Anomaly detection is typically an outcome of machine learning. Root cause analysis is typically an outcome of artificial intelligence analyzing data across many different network elements.

58. B. Unsupervised learning uses unlabeled datasets to train the artificial intelligence model. Supervised learning uses labeled dataset to train the artificial intelligence model. Reinforcement learning uses trial and error to fine-tune the outcome of the artificial intelligence decisions. Controlled learning is similar to supervised learning in which the dataset is strictly controlled.

59. A. System-generated insights will appear in the Cisco Catalyst Center and suggest improvements to the network. Proactive exploration allows you to investigate parts of the network with tools like heat maps. Artificial intelligence (AI) and machine language (ML) power the Cisco Catalyst Center to provide insight. Analytics is a wrong answer.

60. B. Representational state transfer (REST) APIs normally utilize Hypertext Transfer Protocol (HTTP) for moving data. It performs this via a `get` URI and it receives a response in XML, JSON, or another data transfer language. Although you can encrypt the HTTP traffic with SSL (HTTPS), its core language is still HTTP. Simple Network Management Protocol (SNMP) and Simple Network Time Protocol (SNTP) are not used with REST APIs. Simple Object Access Protocol (SOAP) is considered an alternate technology to REST for API access.

61. B. You will authenticate with Cisco DNA Center by sending a `POST` request to the API for an authentication token. You can then use the authentication token for all subsequent requests to Cisco DNA Center. You will not pass the username and password; the username and password must be encoded in Base64 to obtain the authentication token. The `dna/system/api/v1/auth/token` API requires a `POST` request to obtain the authentication token, not a `GET` request. The Cisco DNA Center does not use public-private key pairs for API authentication.

62. D. The CREATE, READ, UPDATE, DELETE (CRUD) framework describes the various actions that can be performed on data via the REST-based API. Although CRUD sounds like it might clean up memory, it has nothing to do with memory cleanup. It works in conjunction with REST-based APIs as a framework for the manipulation of data. The Base64 algorithm is used for data encoding when it is needed.

63. A. Basic authentication is used for token requests with the Cisco DNA Center. Active Directory (AD) integrated authentication and passthrough authentication are Microsoft-only types of authentication, and the Cisco DNA Center does not support them. Secure Sockets Layer (SSL) is a method of encryption for authentication requests, but it is not an authentication method.

64. B. After the initial POST to obtain the authentication token, it should be placed in the header of subsequent requests as an X-Auth-Token element. You will most likely use a variable to store the token, but a variable by itself is not enough to authenticate subsequent requests. The token is not passed in the URI of subsequent requests. Although performing a POST within 10 seconds of the subsequent request is a good idea, if the token is not placed in the header, it will not authenticate you.

65. C. When you process the POST to obtain the X-Auth-Token from a device such as Cisco Catalyst Center, you will pass the username and password encoded in Base 64 encoding. Although you will request the X-Auth-Token over Secure Sockets Layer (SSL), it is an encryption protocol and not an encoding method. Authentication, authorization, and accounting (AAA) services are a means for authentication and often used with 802.1X; AAA is not an encoding method. When you request an X-Auth-Token, you will request it via basic authentication; this is a Hyper-Text Transfer Protocol (HTTP) method of submitting the username and password and not an encoding method.

66. B. You will perform this task using the RESTCONF protocol. RESTCONF will encapsulate the YANG data model containing the configuration in a RESTCONF transport protocol. OpenFlow is used with the OpenDayLight Protocol and not commonly used with Cisco switches. The Simple Network Management Protocol (SNMP) does not support the YANG data model. A REST-based API is another API style that switches do not support directly, but Cisco DNA Center does.

67. A. When a request is made with RESTCONF, the data is sent via the Hypertext Transfer Protocol (HTTP) using the Multipurpose Internet Mail Extensions (MIME) content type of application/yang-data+json. This MIME type is used because the request is interfacing with an application and the data is encapsulated inside of the Yet Another Next Generation (YANG) data model in the form of JavaScript Object Notation (JSON).

68. D. The most likely course of action is to restart the REST-based service, since a 500 status code means that there is an internal server error. If a 400 status code was returned, it would most likely be the formatting of your request. If a 403 status code was returned, it would suggest that you have not authenticated to the software-defined network (SDN) controller or you are not authorized to access the API. A 200 status code means that everything was successful and the request is OK.

69. D. RESTCONF requests are used outbound to network devices on the southbound interface (SBI). REST-based APIs are accessible via the northbound interface (NBI) so that programmability can be achieved. The eastbound interface is used for events and notification on controller. The westbound interface is used for integration with third-party management products.

70. A. The status code is passed back to the client via the Hypertext Transfer Protocol (HTTP) header. Web-based browsers do not show HTTP headers, and this is why using a tool such as Postman is recommended. The HTTP body is where the returned data of the request can be found. Script variables are used internally by the script so that data can be loaded into the variable and passed to other procedures within the script. Script data objects are also used internally by the script to load and pass complex data structures called objects.

71. A. A status code of 201 means that the item has been created; normally only a POST command can create a data item. A GET Hypertext Transfer Protocol (HTTP) verb will read an item and return a 200 status code. A PATCH HTTP verb will update an existing item and return a 200 status code. A DELETE HTTP verb will delete an item and return a 200 status code.

72. C. The question mark signifies the starting point for a series of request query parameters in a Uniform Resource Identifier (URI) string. For example, the URI string might look something like this: `https://server/path/api?para1=test1&para2=test2`. The backslash is not used in a URI. The forward slash helps delimit the various components of a URI. The ampersand delimits the various request query parameters if there is more than one.

73. C. The Hypertext Transfer Protocol (HTTP) action verb POST will insert or create a data item when referencing an application programming interface (API). The HTTP action verb GET will read data from an API. The HTTP action verb UPDATE is not a valid verb; therefore, this is an invalid answer. The HTTP action verb PUT will only replace or update a data item; it will not insert a data item.

74. B. A status code of 504 means that the command that was sent to the server did not return in a timely fashion and timed out. A status code of 400 would depict that the command is missing parameters. If a command is restricted for the authentication supplied, a status code of 403 would be returned. If a service is down or improperly responding, a status code of 500 would be returned.

75. B. Ansible a configuration management tool operates by applying specific configurations to server or network devices. A network management station (NMS) is typically used with the Simple Network Management Protocol (SNMP) to centralize polling of SNMP counters and allow for devices to send alerts. Software-defined networking (SDN) is a method of centralizing the control and management planes of a network so that the network device can focus on the data plane. Centralized logging is used with syslog so that all logs can be sent to a centralized area for analysis.

76. A. Ansible uses the YAML format to store configuration. The Cisco DNA Center stores configuration internally inside of its database, but many things are exportable via JavaScript Object Notation (JSON). Chef and Puppet both use Embedded Ruby (ERB) templates to store configuration.

77. C. The Inventory component defines the various hosts and their connection information in an Ansible setup. The Playbook component defines the script to execute to perform the configuration management. The `ansible.cfg` file controls the settings for the Ansible server. The Modules component allows Ansible to connect to and understand various systems.

78. A. Ansible does not require an agent to apply changes to a Linux-based server or other network device. It uses Secure Shell (SSH) TCP port 22 to apply the configuration. Puppet and Chef both require agents to be installed on the managed hosts. Although Cisco DNA Center is installed on top of a Linux distribution, Cisco DNA Center does not support Linux servers; it is primarily used for the management of Cisco devices. You could certainly create an extensible package to send commands to a Linux box through an SNMP agent, but currently it would need to be developed. Ansible supports Linux-based servers without an agent and without any development for communications.

79. A. The overarching to build cloud infrastructure Terraform is called infrastructure as code (IaC). Desired State Configuration (DSC) is a Microsoft technology that allows configuration of Windows servers. The application program interface (API) is a method of interfacing with applications with code. Representational State Transfer (REST) is a method for programmatically interfacing with APIs.

80. C. Terraform uses (HCL). The HCL language is a declarative language and recommended over JSON.

81. C. The `provider` Terraform block adds functionality for vendors, such as Azure, AWS, and Cisco Catalyst Center, just to name a few. The `resource` Terraform block is how you address resources inside of a provider, such as the credentials for a provider. The Terraform command `terraform plan` creates an execution plan from the configuration files. `vendor` is not a valid block or command.

82. B. The variable `ANSIBLE_CONFIG` is used to determine the location of the Ansible setting file named `ansible.cfg`. The variable `ANSIBLE_SETTINGS` is not used with Ansible and therefore option A is an invalid answer. The `ansible_connection` variable is used inside of the Inventory file to explain to Ansible how to connect to a remote system. The file `/etc/ansible/hosts` is not a variable; it specifies the various target nodes, also called the Inventory.

83. D. The command `ansible-doc` will give you detailed information on Ansible modules. The command is followed by the module name to give specific information on a particular module. For example, `ansible-doc ios_vlan` will display all of the configuration for VLANs on Cisco IOS. The man command will give Linux/Unix manual information of the command of `ansible-doc`, but not the individual modules. The `cat` command is short for concatenate; it allows you to display or create the contents of a file. Ad hoc is not a command; it is a configuration mode in which you can test commands before they are run network wide.

84. C. The Ad hoc interface allows you to try commands against a host without making a Playbook. The Knife interface is a command-line interface (CLI) for the Chef configuration management utility. The `ansible_playbook` command is used to execute an Ansible playbook. Ansible Tower is a paid version of Ansible supported by Red Hat that adds central management.

85. C. The command `terraform init` will initialize a workspace and prepare it for configuration. The command `terraform plan` will create the execution plan. The command `terraform validate` will validate your configuration and is typically run before you create the plan. The command `terraform apply` will create or update infrastructure based on the configuration.

86. C. The `resource` Terraform block is how you address resources inside of a provider, such as the URL for the provider. The Terraform command `terraform plan` creates an execution plan from the configuration files. The `provider` Terraform block adds functionality for vendors, such as Azure, AWS, and Cisco Catalyst Center, just to name a few. `vendor` is not a valid block or command.

87. A. Ansible Tower is a paid version of Ansible supported by Red Hat that adds central management. Ansible Tower also allows for role-based access control (RBAC) for the execution of Playbooks. The addition of RBAC adds greater security to Ansible while allowing users a specific role to administer their responsibilities inside of Ansible. All of the other options are incorrect.

88. A. The Ansible configuration management utility allows for easy configuration of Cisco network devices because it has many modules dedicated to Cisco IOS. Ansible also does not require the installation of an agent, which Puppet and Chef require. Python can be used for configuration management, but it will not allow for periodic checks to make sure that the configuration does not drift.

89. D. The Cisco Intersight product is often used with Terraform to create infrastructure for both public and private cloud resources. Cisco Meraki is a cloud-based networking platform for small to large enterprise. Cisco Catalyst CenterCisco Application Centric Infrastructure (ACI) is used to automate software-defined network (SDN) solutions.

90. C. Configuration management uses infrastructure as code (IaC) to prevent drift with the applied theory of Idempotence. Idempotence states that only required changes will be applied to servers that fall outside of the desired system state. Infrastructure as a service (IaaS) is a cloud model that defines components that can be purchased for a period, such as virtual router, switches, and virtual machines (VMs), just to name a few. Configuration management can install the Network Time Protocol (NTP) so time does not drift, but NTP will not prevent configuration drift. Configuration management software does not always require per-host licensing. Most configuration management utilities offer a community edition that is free; if you want enterprise features, you can then purchase licensing from the parent company.

91. C. Ansible is the easiest configuration management utility to set up as well as use. Chef and Puppet are a bit more involved to set up because they require clients to be installed on the hosts being managed. Cisco DNA Center is not a configuration management utility outside of Cisco devices; therefore, option D is an invalid answer.

92. C. Ansible is installed with a number of modules compiled already. However, if you want to make custom modules, they must be created in JSON format. All of the other options are incorrect.

93. D. A JavaScript Object Notation (JSON) element always starts with a curly bracket, sometimes called a brace. If a file contains an array of JSON elements, it will start with a square bracket or square brace. If the file starts with three dashes, the file is most likely YAML.

94. B. When a square bracket is in place of a value inside a JavaScript Object Notation (JSON) file, it means there is a series of key-value pairs for the initial value. These key-value pairs are often called collections. All of the other options are incorrect.

95. C. There is a missing curly bracket that ends the address value. The capitalization of Fa0/1 is fine because it is within double quotes, so therefore it is read literally. The address does not need to have square brackets unless there will be more than one address.

96. D. JavaScript Object Notation (JSON) allows for a hierarchical structure that allows for programmability; this is somewhat similar to Extensible Markup Language (XML). Both JSON and comma-separated values (CSV) can contain spaces, because the values are enclosed within double quotes. Both JSON and CSV can have multiple values for a particular key. Only CSV can be read line by line; JSON files must be read in their entirety.

97. A. SDN controllers, such as the Cisco DNA Center will return REST-based requests in JavaScript Object Notation (JSON) format. All of the other options are incorrect.

98. B. The collection of routes contains two individual route statements that are named route (singular). All collections must be contained within square brackets, also called braces. All of the other options are incorrect. The corrected JSON is shown in the following:

```
{
  "ipaddress": "192.168.1.2",
  "subnet_mask": "255.255.255.0",
  "defaultgw": "192.168.1.1",
  "routes": [
    {
      "route": "10.0.0.0/8 via 192.168.1.10"
    },
    {
      "route": "0.0.0.0/0 via 192.168.1.1"
    }
  ]
}
```

99. D. Nothing is wrong with the JSON data. The IP address is defined as a collection of IP addresses using the JSON tag of ipaddress. Although for completeness a second subnet mask should be stated in the JSON data, it may be in the proper format that is expected. The last comma is not needed in JSON files, as it defines the end of the hierarchy. The underscore in a JSON key or value data is not considered an illegal character.

100. B. The JavaScript Object Notation (JSON) data is incorrect because it is missing a closing square bracket after the IP addresses. The last comma is not needed in JSON files, as it defines the end of the hierarchy. The underscore in a JSON key or value data is not considered an illegal character.

Chapter 7: Practice Exam 1

1. **B.** A hub is a multiport repeater. When a hub receives a frame, it will repeat the frame on all other ports, whether or not the port is the destination host. A firewall is a network device that can protect a network from malicious traffic and/or restrict access. A router is a network device that routes layer 3 packets. A switch is a layer 2 device that creates microsegmentation.

2. **B.** Switches break up collision domains by allowing microsegmentation. Switches are set to auto-negotiate duplex and speed by default, and they do not force full-duplex. Routers break up broadcast domains; switches will not break up broadcast domains. Switches also don't always allow for a fast uplink port; it always depends on the type of switch and the application in which it is marketed.

3. **A.** When a firewall matches a Uniform Resource Identifier (URI), such as a URL, it is operating at layer 7. This is known as a web application firewall (WAF). Layer 5 communications are session based; one such application that is session based is Structured Query Language (SQL). Layer 4 communications are port based; many basic firewall rules are built to block and allow specific ports. Layer 3 communications are IP address based; many basic firewall rules are also built to block and allow specific IP addresses.

4. **A.** An autonomous WAP acts similarly to an access layer switch. However, WAPs normally do not have redundant links back to the distribution switches. So it acts more like a star topology, connecting the Ethernet and wireless clients together. A full-mesh topology is often found between the core and distribution layers of the Cisco three-tier design model. A partial-mesh topology is often found between the distribution and access layers in the Cisco three-tier design model. A hybrid topology is found in many networks today because one topology does not fit all needs throughout the network.

5. **B.** High-Level Data Link Control (HDLC) is the default encapsulation on a serial connection for Cisco. Multiprotocol Label Switching (MPLS) is becoming a popular WAN connectivity method, but it is not an encapsulation method. Point-to-Point Protocol (PPP) is an open standard layer 2 protocol used for point-to-point connections, such as WAN serial connections. Point-to-Point Protocol over Ethernet (PPPoE) is the PPP protocol encapsulated into an Ethernet frame. Its most notable use is in Digital Subscriber Line (DSL) communications, where it is mainly used for its authentication methods.

6. **B.** The Point-to-Point Protocol (PPP) is an open standard. Cisco routers default to the HDLC protocol. However, HDLC is a proprietary standard for Cisco. So, PPP should be used for compatibility. Point-to-Point Protocol over Ethernet (PPPoE) is the PPP protocol encapsulated into an Ethernet frame. The X.25 protocol is one of the first WAN protocols for packet switching; it has largely been deprecated for newer protocols, such as PPP, that offer more features.

7. **C.** The central office, sometimes referred to as the CO, is the local switching office. The CO is where your data lines meet the public network for data and voice. The demarcation point, or demarc as it is also referred to, is the point at which the provider responsibility for wiring

and maintenance ends. *Network edge* is not a term typically used for WAN networking; therefore, it is an invalid answer. The main data frame (MDF) describes the location where network equipment is concentrated and connects to external networks.

8. B. *Point of presence (PoP)* is the term that defines the access point of the provider's services. These services might be Internet, private WAN, or cloud resources. The demarcation point, or demarc as it is also referred to, is the point at which the provider responsibility for wiring and maintenance ends. *Customer edge* is a term often used with Multiprotocol Label Switching (MPLS) WAN terminology to describe the end of the customer's network before a packet enters the MPLS network. *Network edge* is not a term typically used for WAN networking; therefore, it is an invalid answer.

9. C. Lowering bandwidth between the premises and your virtual machines (VMs) on the public cloud is a direct benefit of locating a Network Time Protocol (NTP) virtual network function (VNF) on the public cloud for VM time synchronization. Using an NTP server regardless of where it is located will yield you precision time. Implementing the NTP VNF in the cloud will not allow for better response time from VMs. An NTP VNF will not overcome different time zones; this is a function of the time offset on the VM.

10. A. Bandwidth is the primary decision factor for moving the Domain Name System (DNS) closer to the application in the public cloud. However, if the majority of DNS users are on premises, then it should remain on premises for bandwidth reasons. Response time should not increase, since DNS is a lightweight service for looking up resource records. DNS resolution should not be affected when migrating DNS to a public cloud. Although the cloud provider has certain requirements, DNS functionality is relatively the same.

11. C. Flow control is synonymous with the Transport layer of the Open Systems Interconnection (OSI) model. User Datagram Protocol (UDP) operates at the Transport layer, but UDP does not provide flow control for communications. UDP provides a program with a connectionless method of transmitting segments. The Internet Protocol (IP) is logical addressing for the routing of information. Transmission Control Protocol (TCP) is a connection-based protocol and maintains a state throughout the transfer of data. The Internet Control Message Protocol (ICMP) is used as an error-reporting tool for IP packets as well as a diagnostic protocol for determining path problems.

12. C. The network seems to be configured properly. You have received a valid address in the Class A space of the RFC 1918 private address range. The network jack is obviously working because you have been assigned an IP address. The network is configured properly, and no evidence exists to determine it is not configured properly. The DHCP server is obviously working because it assigned you an IP address where there was no prior IP address.

13. C. The network 192.168.4.32/27 has a valid IP address range of 192.168.4.33 to 192.168.4.62. The /27 CIDR notation, or 255.255.255.224 dotted-decimal notation (DDN), defines networks in multiples of 32. Therefore, the address 192.168.4.28/27 is part of the 192.168.4.32/27 network. All of the other options are incorrect.

14. D. Stateless DHCPv6 servers are used to configure DHCP options only. The one option that all clients need is the DNS server. The default gateway and the IPv6 address are configured via the Router Solicitation (RS) and Router Advertisement (RA) packets when a client starts up in the network. The IPv6 prefix length is fixed to a 64-bit prefix.

15. B. Duplicate Address Detection (DAD) uses Neighbor Solicitation and Neighbor Advertisement messages to avoid duplicate addresses when SLAAC is being used. Neighbor Discovery Protocol (NDP) is a protocol that is used to discover neighboring devices in an IPv6 network for layer 2 addressing. Stateless Address Autoconfiguration (SLAAC) is an IPv6 method used to assign the 64-bit network ID to a host. ARPv6 is not a valid protocol; the Address Resolution Protocol (ARP) in IPv4 has been replaced with NDP in IPv6.

16. B. The IPv6 address 2202:0ff8:0002:2344:3533:8eff:fe22:ae4c is an EUI-64 generated address. The host portion of the address is 3533:8eff:fe22:ae4c; the fffe in the middle of it indicates that the address was generated from the MAC address. The MAC address of this host would be 37-33-8e-02-ae-4c. When EUI-64 is used, an ffee is placed in the middle of the MAC address, and then the 7th bit from the left is flipped. This changes the first two hex digits of the MAC address from 35 to 37. Multicast addresses will always start with ff00. Anycast addresses are not visibly different because they are normal addresses with special regional routing statements that direct communications to the closest server. Link-local addresses will always start with fe80.

17. B. The store and forward method of switching allows the switch to receive the entire frame and calculate the CRC against the data contained in the frame. If the CRC does not match, the frame is dropped, and the sending node must retransmit after an expiry timer or upper-protocol timer times out. Switches cannot perform error correction from the CRC calculation; they can only detect that there are errors and discard the frame. Switches will never send a frame back; they will discard the frame and wait for retransmission from upper-layer protocols. Switches do not store frames for longer than it would take for a forward filter decision to be made.

18. A. In the figure, a broadcast storm is occurring due to improper configuration of Spanning Tree Protocol (STP) for loop avoidance. MAC table thrashing could occur due to the loop in the figure; however, the figure does not show evidence to prove MAC table thrashing is occurring. Although STP is not configured, duplication of unicast frames is not evident in the figure. STP is a loop avoidance mechanism; it will not propagate loops.

19. B. The command to show the current MAC address entry count in the MAC address table is `show mac address-table count`. This command will also show the maximum number of entries the table can hold. The command `show mac address-table` is incorrect, as it will show the contents of the MAC address table in the switch. The commands `show mac count` and `show cam count` are incorrect.

20. A. Forward filter decisions are made upon the destination MAC address in the frame. The source MAC address is used for MAC address learning to build the forward/filter table. The source and destination IP address in the frame is no concern of the switch. Only a router would decapsulate the frame further to make routing decisions upon the destination IP address.

21. C. The computer is on another switch connected via a trunk link since there are multiple VLANs on the interface of Gi0/1. This is also evidence that the computer is not the only device on port Gi0/1. It cannot be concluded that the computer is on a hub connected to port Gi0/1. The computer's MAC address has not aged out of the table yet because it can still be seen in the figure.

22. B. Access ports strip all VLAN information before the frame egresses the destination interface. The endpoint on an access switch port will never see any of the VLAN information that was associated with the frame. A trunk port will carry the frame along with the VLAN information until it gets to the other side of the trunk link. Voice ports also carry the frame along with VLAN tagging information. A Dynamic Trunking Protocol (DTP) port will form a trunk port to another switch; therefore, it is a trunking protocol, not a switchport type.

23. B. The switch has negotiated with the adjacent switch to become a trunk and set its trunking protocol to 802.1Q. The letter n in front of 802.1Q specifies it was negotiated. When a switch is set to auto for the Dynamic Trunking Protocol (DTP), it will respond to trunking requests but will not initiate DTP messages. The adjacent switch must be set to desirable since the desirable mode will send DTP messages. The native VLAN does not show it has been changed, since VLAN 1 is the default native VLAN as it is configured in the figure. The figure does not show evidence that the switch is sending DTP frames. Evidence also does not exist in the figure to support the theory that the adjacent switch is also set for auto DTP.

24. C. The command `show running-config interface gi 3/45` will show the running-configuration for only interface Gi3/45. The command `show interface gi 3/45` is incorrect, as it will display the interface details for Gi3/45 and not the configuration. The command `show running-config | include 3/45` is incorrect as it will only display lines matching 3/45. The command `show running gi 3/45` is incorrect.

25. A. The command `show version` will display the serial number of the switch or router. This is usually required when calling into support to open a support ticket. The commands `show serial`, `show board`, and `show controller` are incorrect.

26. D. The command `show running-config | begin 4/45` will show the running-config and begin when the text 4/45 is found. It is important to note that after the | begin, everything is case sensitive. The commands `show running-config begin 4/45` and `show filter running-config 4/45` are incorrect. The command `show running-config interface gi 4/45` is incorrect, as it will only display the running-config for interface Gi4/45.

27. B. By default, Cisco devices do not participate in Link Layer Discovery Protocol (LLDP). The first command that needs to be configured is `lldp run`, which starts the switch participating in LLDP. You then need to enter the command `show lldp neighbors detail` in the privileged exec mode prompt, by exiting global configuration mode. This command will show all of the neighboring LLDP devices. The command `enable lldp` is incorrect and will not enable LLDP. Because LLDP is not enabled by default, the command `show lldp neighbors detail` by itself will not display anything.

28. A. The interface Gig 0/1 is used for the interface of es-switch2, which connects cs-main. ntw via its interface of Gig 0/40. The Gig 0/1 interfaces on cs-main.ntw, es-layer2.ntw, and es-switch3.ntw are not depicted in the figure because we are examining the Cisco Discovery Protocol (CDP) on es-switch2.

29. C. The EtherChannel has been configured with no control protocol, which is a result of configuring each side of the EtherChannel with the command `channel-group 1 mode on`. The figure shows no evidence that the EtherChannel is configured with either Port Aggregation Protocol (PAgP) or Link Aggregation Control Protocol (LACP). The figure also shows no evidence that the EtherChannel is configured as an access port.

30. B. Since the auto mode was used on the first switch (Switch A), desirable should be used on the second switch to assure forming of an EtherChannel by using the command `channel-group 1 mode desirable`. If both sides are set to auto with the command `channel-group 1 mode auto`, then the EtherChannel will not be built. The commands `channel-group 1 mode active` and `channel-group 1 mode passive` are used for Link Aggregation Control Protocol (LACP) configuration.

31. D. If the other switch is set to passive mode, an EtherChannel will not form. The recommended mode for the other side is active mode. The figure also shows no evidence that the EtherChannel is configured as an access port. The Cisco Discovery Protocol (CDP) has no effect on an EtherChannel. The EtherChannel has been configured for Link Aggregation Control Protocol (LACP), noted by the `channel-group 1 mode passive` command.

32. C. Switch B has the lowest MAC address of all of the switches. Therefore, Switch B will become the RSTP root bridge. All ports leading back to Switch B will become the root ports. Switch A interface Gi1/8, Switch D interface Fa2/16, and Switch C interface Gi1/3 will become root ports. All of the other options are incorrect.

33. C. The 802.1w Rapid Spanning Tree Protocol (RSTP) defines that designated switchports always forward traffic. The designated port is a port that is forwarding traffic and is opposite of the root port or blocking port if it is a redundant link. A disabled switchport does not participate in RSTP or the forwarding of traffic. A backup port is a redundant port on the same switch and segment that is placed in a blocking mode in the event the forwarding port is unable to forward traffic. An alternate port is a redundant port on the same segment, but different switches. The alternate port is placed in a blocking mode, and in the event the forwarding port is unable to forward traffic, the alternate port will forward traffic.

34. A. The command `spanning-tree portfast default` will configure all access ports on the switch as PortFast enabled. The commands `switchport spanning-tree portfast`, `spanning-tree portfast enable`, and `spanning-tree portfast` are incorrect.

35. A. Monitor mode can be used for analysis of the radio spectrum. Analysis mode is not a real mode; therefore, it is an incorrect option. FlexConnect mode is a switching mode on the wireless access point (WAP) in which traffic is switched directly to the intended destination. Local mode is a switching mode on the wireless access point in which all traffic is directed to the wireless controller before being switched to the intended destination.

36. D. WorkGroup Bridge mode allows you to connect an AP to another AP via an SSID. The Ethernet connection is then bridged over to allow other wired connections to share the wireless bridge. A wireless mesh is used for wireless coverage where wired APs cannot be installed. LightWeight mode is a wireless AP mode in which the wireless LAN controller controls the AP. Local mode is a switching mode on the wireless access point (WAP) in which all traffic is directed to the wireless controller before being switched to the intended destination.

37. B. When an EtherChannel is configured to an "on mode," it means that no negotiation protocol will be used to build the EtherChannel. If the mode of auto or desirable is configured on the EtherChannel interfaces, then the EtherChannel will participate in Port Aggregation Protocol (PAgP). If the mode of passive is configured on the EtherChannel interfaces, then the EtherChannel will participate in Link Aggregation Control Protocol (LACP).

38. C. TACACS+ is a Cisco-defined protocol. One of the useful features it has is that it can authenticate a user and only allow that user to access certain commands on the router or switch. The TACACS+ protocol is not an open standard. The TACACS+ protocol encrypts the passwords for the user but does not support authenticating a user for a specific length of time.

39. B. The local second method should always be configured. This will ensure that if the router's connection to the AAA server is down, you can still gain access to diagnose or repair. If properly secured, a second method of local authentication does not create a backdoor because it creates a backup of authentication. The local second method is not required, but it is a good idea so that you can log in during outages of the AAA server.

40. A. A captive portal will allow you to require all guests to register for wireless Internet access before granting them access. When they connect to the Service Set Identifier (SSID), they will be presented with the captive portal web page. An AAA server is required if you have a list of already established users and want to authenticate them via the AAA server. An extended service set (ESS) is two or more access points covering a common SSID or serving multiple SSIDs. Radio resource management (RRM) is a service on the wireless LAN controller (WLC) that adjusts the radio output and channels used by an ESS.

41. D. When an IP address is configured on a router's interface, the network is automatically put into the route table. The IP address is also added to the route table. When the route table changes, this normally tells the routing protocol it should perform an update.

42. A. In the route table there is a static route for 192.168.4.0/24 via Serial 0/0/1. Interface Serial 0/0/0 has a route of 172.16.0.0/16 configured. The IP gateway of 192.168.4.1 does not appear in the figure. Interface Serial 0/2/0 has a route of 10.0.0.0/8 configured.

43. C. The route will exit the Serial 0/2/0 interface, since the gateway of last resort is set to Serial 0/2/0. This statement is identified by the S* 0.0.0.0/0 entry. Interface Serial 0/1/1 has a route of 198.23.24.0/24 configured. Interface Serial 0/0/1 has a route of 192.168.1.0/24 configured. Because there is a gateway of last resort configured, any route not specifically in the route table will follow the gateway of last resort.

44. C. The administrative distance (AD) of Open Shortest Path First (OSPF) is 110. The administrative distance of Internal Enhanced Interior Gateway Routing Protocol (EIGRP) is 90. The administrative distance of the legacy routing protocol of Interior Gateway Routing Protocol (IGRP) is 100. The administrative distance of Routing Information Protocol (RIP) is 120.

45. A. The command show ip protocols will display the next interval when RIPv2 advertisements are sent out. The commands show ip rip database, show ip rip, and show ip interface are incorrect.

46. D. The command debug ip rip will allow you to see advertisements in real time. The commands show ip protocols, debug rip, and show ip rip are incorrect.

47. B. The three Class C networks need to be advertised separately. RIPv2 uses the default class network mask when configuring networks. The command network 192.168.0.0 is incorrect as it will not advertise the individual networks of 192.168.1.0, 192.168.2.0, and 192.168.3.0. The commands network 192.168.0.0/16 and network 192.168.0.0 0.0.255.255 are incorrect.

48. C. The command `passive-interface serial 0/0` configured in the router instance will suppress updates from exiting interface Serial 0/0. The commands `ip rip passive-interface`, `rip passive-interface`, and `ip rip suppress-advertisement` are incorrect.

49. B. RIPv2 has extremely slow convergence time. This is because the advertisement of routes is every 30 seconds. So a router 4 hops away could take 120 seconds before discovering the route. Configuration for RIPv2 is rather simple compared to other protocols, such as Open Shortest Path First (OSPF). RIPv2 uses multicasts to send the complete route table to other participating routers; RIPv1 uses broadcasts. The RIPv2 protocol supports classless networks; RIPv1 does not support classless networks.

50. A. Split horizons are used to stop routing loops with RIPv2. Split horizons prevent a router from advertising a route to a router in which the original route was discovered. Advertisement intervals can be adjusted to allow RIPv2 to converge faster. Zoning is not a design concept for RIP; therefore, it is an invalid answer. The invalid timers can be adjusted for faster convergence as well.

51. C. RIPv2 uses the Bellman–Ford algorithm to calculate its metrics. The Open Shortest Path First (OSPF) protocol uses the Shortest Path First (SPF) algorithm, which is also called the Dijkstra algorithm. The diffusing update algorithm (DUAL) is used by Enhanced Interior Gateway Routing Protocol (EIGRP).

52. D. The command `no auto-summary` will stop the router process of RIPv2 from auto-summarizing network addresses. In a discontiguous network, this is problematic and should be turned off. The command `network discontiguous` is incorrect, regardless of which prompt it is configured in. The command `no auto-summary` is incorrect when configured from the global configuration prompt.

53. B. Configuring RIPv2 begins with configuration of the router instance of RIP via the command `router rip`. RIPv2 is configured inside of the router instance with the command `version 2`. Then the network of 192.168.20.0/24 is advertised with the command `network 192.168.20.0`. All of the other options are incorrect.

54. C. Static routing is best suited for small networks in which there is not a lot of change. It should be chosen when administrators want absolute control over the routing process. Open Shortest Path First (OSPF) is suited for large-scale networks because of its scalability. The Enhanced Interior Gateway Routing Protocol (EIGRP) is also a relatively scalable dynamic routing protocol. The Routing Information Protocol (RIP) is well suited for medium-sized to smaller networks, where administrators do not want to control routing.

55. C. The command `show ipv6 interfaces brief` will show all of the IPv6 addresses configured for each of the interfaces on the router. The commands `show ipv6`, `show ip interfaces brief`, and `show ipv6 brief` are incorrect.

56. A. The command `show ipv6 route` will display only the entries in the route table for IPv6. The command `show ip route` will only display the entries in the route table for IPv4. The commands `show ipv6 route summary` and `show ipv6 route brief` are incorrect.

57. C. You will need two route statements, one on each router. Each route should point to the far side network through the serial interface. Since the IP address is an IPv6 address, the easier way to configure the routes is to direct the packets to the exit interface of Serial 0/3/0. All of the other options are incorrect because the commands specify either the wrong protocol or the wrong routes.

58. B. The command show ipv6 route connected will display only the directly connected routes on the router. The commands show ipv6 interface summary, show ipv6 interface brief, and show ipv6 summary are incorrect.

59. C. The route statement ipv6 route ::/0 serial 0/3/0 will route any network that is unknown by Router B to Router A via the exit interface of Serial 0/3/0. The command ipv6 route 0.0.0.0 0.0.0.0 serial 0/3/0 is incorrect because it mixes IPv4-style IP addresses and the ipv6 route command. The commands ipv6 route 2002:ea34:4520:3412::/64 serial 0/3/0 and ipv6 route ::/0 2001:db8:1500::/64 eui are incorrect.

60. D. You will need two route statements, one on each router. Each route points to the far side network through the gateway in the ff80::/64 network. Router A has a gateway of ff80::ff:f200:2/64 to the 2001:db8:4::/64 network, and Router B has a gateway of ff80::ff:f200:1/64 to the 2001:db8:400/64 network. All other options are incorrect because the commands specify either the wrong protocol or the wrong routes.

61. B. The ping command will allow basic connectivity testing at layer 3. The command show ip route is incorrect. The command pathping 192.168.4.1 is incorrect; the pathping command is only available on Windows operating systems. The command ip ping 192.168.4.1 is incorrect; the ip command does not need to be specified.

62. D. The command traceroute will allow you to verify the path on which a packet gets routed. The command show ip route is incorrect. The command tracert 192.168.7.56 is incorrect; the tracert command is only available on Windows operating systems. The command pathping 192.168.7.56 is incorrect; the path-ping command is only available on Windows operating systems.

63. C. Both routers have passive interfaces for OSPF. In order to fix this, the command no passive-interface serial 0/0 would need to be entered. This command would need to be configured in the OSPF router process. The routers are within the same network with a common serial line connecting the routers. The process IDs do not matter and are locally significant to the routers. The hello/dead intervals for both routers match each other.

64. A. The command show ip protocols will list the router ID of the current router as well as the networks that are being advertised via OSPF on the current router. The commands show ip ospf, show ip ospf database, and show ip ospf neighbors are incorrect.

65. C. When Hot Standby Router Protocol (HSRP) is used, the default gateway the client is issued is an IP address for the virtual router. The virtual router is not a physical router, but it is mapped to a physical router via HSRP. The active router processes requests for the virtual router IP address by responding to the virtual MAC address associated with the virtual router IP address. The standby router only becomes active if the active router is no longer responding with hello packets for 10 seconds. Support routers are any routers used outside of HSRP to support routing of the network.

66. C. The flexibility of Internet connections is usually a driving factor for PAT (NAT Overloading). Memory is significantly higher with PAT, since the source and destination port numbers must be recorded in the NAT table. There is no effect on packet loss, and jitter is marginally affected. Memory usage is actually higher than with other types of NAT because it must account for ports in the NAT table.

67. D. The command to configure the private side of the network interface for NAT is `ip nat inside`. This command is configured on the interface in which you want to define it as the "inside" of your network. The configuration of the command `ip nat outside` is incorrect. The commands `ip nat inside gi0/0` and `ip nat private` are incorrect.

68. C. Time synchronization is important for logging accuracy. Serial communication frame alignment is timed via clocking and packet queues are timed by how fast they can respond. The serialized communication for frame alignment comes from the DCE side of the link, which provides clocking signals. Time synchronization has no effect on quality of service queuing or the delivery of packets via timed queues.

69. D. Fully qualified domain names (FQDNs) are significant from right to left, starting with a period to signify the root. The period is normally not visible on the FQDN, but it is processed as the root lookup. A DNS server will not always process the entire FQDN if there is a cached entry for the resource record requested. FQDNs are not always registered with a registrar because organizations used them for authentication and internal purposes. FQDNs are resolved from right to left starting with the root, not left to right.

70. A. Simple Network Management Protocol (SNMP) uses UDP port 161 for communication from an SNMP network management station to a network device for information requests. SNMP uses UDP and TCP port 162 for traps and not polling. Syslog uses UDP and TCP port 514 for sending log entries.

71. A. The command `show logging` will display the configured syslog server and the current severity level for logs to be sent to the syslog server. The commands `show syslog`, `show log-server`, and `show ip logging` are incorrect.

72. B. The command `show ip interface` will display the IP addresses configured on the router's interfaces. It will detail which are static and which have been allocated through DHCP. The command `show ip dhcp bindings` is incorrect because it will show the internal table for the local DHCP server. The commands `show ip lease` and `show ip dhcp lease` are incorrect.

73. A. QoS marking should always be performed closest to the source of the traffic. All switches and routers in the network should be configured to properly prioritize markings of traffic in queues. If it is performed closest to the Internet router, you may not get any effectiveness from the configuration because Internet routers may not process QoS. Not every device in the network needs QoS marking, such as infrastructure services like DHCP and DNS. QoS marking should also not be performed on the core router in the network; a good rule of thumb is don't implement anything on the core router that could slow it down. The act of QoS marking could slow the core router down; already marked packets are fine.

74. A. A malicious user can mark all of their traffic as high priority. Therefore, the network administrator must establish a trust boundary. A common trust boundary device is the IP phone, but it is any device that the network administrator controls. If the switch is set as a trust boundary, a malicious user could plug in and start marking their packets with a higher than normal QoS. Routers are not the only devices that create trust boundaries, and IP phones are not the only devices that can become trust boundaries.

75. B. The command `ip scp server enable` needs to be configured to enable the Secure Copy Protocol (SCP). This command is entered in the global configuration. The commands `ip ssh server enable`, `service scp enable`, and `service scp-server` are incorrect.

76. B. VLAN hopping is an attack in which DTP is exploited. The attacker negotiates a trunk with the switch via DTP and can hop from VLAN to VLAN. Native VLAN will carry any frame that is not tagged; the native VLAN should be configured to something other than VLAN 1. VLAN *traversal* and *trunk popping* are not terms used with VLANs, and therefore, they are invalid answers.

77. B. Point-to-Point Protocol (PPP) is a layer 2 wide area network (WAN) protocol. PPP supports Challenge Handshake Authentication Protocol (CHAP), which secures connections. High-Level Data Link Control (HDLC) is a serial control protocol used on WAN links and it provides no security. The IPsec protocol is a layer 3 security protocol used to encrypt traffic and not a layer 2 protocol. Although Metro Ethernet is built site to site by the service provider, there is no guarantee of security in the form of authentication.

78. B. Antivirus software is an application that is installed on a system and is used to protect it and to scan workstations for viruses as well as worms and Trojan horses. Malware is malicious software that once installed on a system causes malicious activity. Software firewalls will not detect Trojan horses and worms. Spyware is software that monitors user activity and offers unsolicited pop-up advertisements.

79. C. The command `banner login ^CCNA Routing and Switching^` will configure the login banner to read "CCNA Routing and Switching." The marks at the beginning and end of the text are delimiters to mark the beginning and end of the banner. The commands `login banner CCNA Routing and Switching` and `banner login CCNA Routing and Switching` are incorrect. The command `banner login ^CCNA Routing and Switching^` is incorrect when it is configured in the line configuration prompt.

80. A. When a user is connecting to a router via SSH, the MOTD banner is not displayed until after the user has authenticated to the router or switch. A login banner is always displayed pre-login. When connecting with the Telnet protocol, you must specify a login password first. When connecting via the console, the MOTD will not be displayed. The MOTD banner will show before the enable password is entered.

81. B. Extensible Authentication Protocol/Transport Layer Security (EAP-TLS) uses certificates to authenticate end devices. It also provides a layer of encryption via the certificate infrastructure. Although EAP can be configured to use MD5 symmetrical authentication, it is not used with TLS. Secure Shell (SSH), and passwords are not used with EAP-TLS.

82. A. Multiprotocol Label Switching (MPLS) allows for varied access links such as serial leased lines, Frame Relay, Metro Ethernet, and so on. You can leverage the existing connectivity methods to form a private WAN. PPPoE and GRE tunnels are connectivity methods used on top of a WAN technology, so they are invalid answers.

83. A. IPsec uses the Authentication Header (AH) protocol to check data integrity. This is done by creating a numerical hash of the data via SHA1, SHA2, or MD5 algorithms. The Encapsulating Security Payload (ESP) protocol is part of the IPsec suite of protocols, and it is responsible for encryption of packets. The Internet Security Association and Key Management Protocol (ISAKMP) is part of the Internet Key Exchange (IKE) protocol suite and is responsible for creating a security association between two participating computers in IPsec.

84. C. You can have only one access control list (ACL) per direction, per protocol, and per interface. Therefore, each of the two interfaces can have both an inbound and outbound ACL, per the protocol of IPv4. This allows for a total of four ACLs, which can be used to control access through the router. If you added IPv6 to both interfaces, you could apply a total of eight ACLs. All of the other options are incorrect.

85. B. The command `access-list 2 permit 192.168.2.3 0.0.0.0` will perform the same function as `access-list 2 permit host 192.168.2.3`. The command configures the host 192.168.2.3 with a bit mask, which will only match the single IP address. Although it can be configured as a bit mask, it should be configured via the host parameter for readability. The commands `access-list 2 permit 192.168.2.3 255.255.255.255`, `ip access-list 2 permit host 192.168.2.3`, and `access-list 2 permit 192.168.2.3` are incorrect.

86. C. Ports that are connecting to trusted infrastructure devices such as routers and switches should be trusted. This is because legitimate DHCP traffic could originate from these ports. You would not want ports connecting to clients to be trusted, since this is the purpose of enabling DHCP snooping. Web servers and DNS servers should also not be trusted, since they are not facilitating DHCP.

87. C. The untrusted ports drop Offer and Acknowledgment DHCP messages. The only device that should offer and acknowledge IP addresses is the DHCP server on a trusted port. The untrusted ports do not allow Offer or Acknowledgment messages but will allow Discover messages. All of the options except C are incorrect.

88. B. The command `radius-server host 192.168.1.5 key aaaauth` will configure the radius server 192.168.1.5 with a secret key of aaaauth. The commands `radius host 192.168.1.5 key aaaauth`, `radius-server 192.168.1.5 key aaaauth`, and `radius-server host 192.168.1.5 secret aaaauth` are incorrect.

89. A. Wi-Fi Protected Access (WPA) was rushed out and released to fix weak security in the Wired Equivalent Privacy (WEP) wireless security protocol. WPA2 was formally released to address weaknesses in the RC4-TKIP security protocol. WPA3 is the newest wireless security protocol to be released and offers the highest level of security for wireless.

90. C. MAC filtering will allow you to set up a WLAN with Wi-Fi Protected Access (WPA) with a preshared key (PSK) and restrict certain devices. A captive portal will not allow you to restrict devices but will only capture guests with a web page so they must log in. Although you can restrict a user; you cannot restrict a particular device. A Remote Authentication Dial-In User Service (RADIUS) server works in conjunction with AAA authentication and is not implemented alongside WPA PSK. Disabling broadcasting of the SSID is security through obscurity and not a sufficient mechanism to restrict devices.

91. A. You can speed up the changing of all 50 router passwords with a Python script. JavaScript Object Notation (JSON) is used for input and output of data; although it can be used in conjunction with a script, it by itself is not a script language. You cannot apply YAML or JSON templates to routers unless there is another mechanism, such as a script, that is being used.

92. B. A negative outcome from automation of configuration across an enterprise is that you increase the odds of configuration conflicts. You decrease the odds of typographical errors when using automation because redundant commands do not need to be entered. The time spent building configurations should be no more or no less than normal once an automated system is established.

93. A. The Cisco Discovery Protocol (CDP) can be used to map out all of the Cisco devices connected to the network. If you issue the command show cdp neighbors detail or show cdp entry *, the output will display all of the Cisco devices connected to the switch or router the command is issue from. The running configuration will not display the current devices connected. The Open Shortest Path First (OSPF) or Enhanced Interior Gateway Routing Protocol (EIGRP) protocol will not display the directly connected devices.

94. B. The OpenFlow protocol is an open standard used to configure network devices via the southbound interface (SBI) of the software-defined networking (SDN) controller. Python is a common programming language that is used for the programming of an SDN controller via the northbound interface (NBI) of the SDN controller. Representational State Transfer (REST) is an architecture for moving data using the Hypertext Transfer Protocol (HTTP). JavaScript Object Notation (JSON) is a data-interchange format used with many different SDN controllers.

95. B. The fabric of a software-defined network switches packets on layer 3. All of the other options are incorrect.

96. A. You can configure the upgrade of IOS for network devices from the Provision section of the Cisco DNA Center. The Design section allows you to create a hierarchical design of the network, with a graphical map. The Policy section allows you to create policies based on applications, traffic, and IP-based access control lists (ACLs), just to name a few. The Assurance section of the Cisco DNA Center allows you to see the overall health of network devices managed by DNA Center.

97. C. When a status code of 401 is returned, it means that the method was unauthorized. A status code of 200 or 202 means the method was okay or accepted; these are the two most common.

98. D. Ansible uses a configuration file and can be programmed with Python. Desired State Configuration (DSC) is a Microsoft-centric product that is programmed in PowerShell. Chef uses Domain Specific Language (DSL) with Ruby. Puppet uses DSL with the PuppetDSL language.

99. B. A requirement for using Ansible for configuration management is root Secure Shell (SSH) access to the remote system. Internet access is only required if you are managing a system across the Internet. An unrestricted firewall is not required because you only need port 22 TCP (SSH) for Ansible to access the remote machine. Ansible is scripted with Python and not Ruby.

100. A. The command show interface status | json-pretty native is used to convert the output of a command to JSON in a Cisco router or switch. You will enter the command first, such as show interface status, and then pipe the output to the | json-pretty command and specify native formatting. The commands json interface status, show interface status | json, and show interface status json are incorrect.

Chapter 8: Practice Exam 2

1. **C.** A router will stop broadcasts by default. If you add a router to a flat network, which is a single broadcast domain, you effectively raise bandwidth by reducing the number of broadcasts. A firewall is a network device that can protect a network from malicious traffic and/or restrict access. A hub is nothing more than a multiport repeater and does not create broadcast domains. A switch is a layer 2 device that creates microsegmentation.

2. **D.** Switches create collision domains by isolating the possibility of a collision to the segment it is transmitting to or receiving frames from. This in turn raises effective bandwidth for the rest of the segments. A firewall is a network device that can protect a network from malicious traffic and/or restrict access. A hub is nothing more than a multiport repeater and does not create broadcast domains. A router is a network device that routes layer 3 packets.

3. **D.** Since the email server needs access to the Internet to send and receive mail, it should be placed in the demilitarized zone (DMZ). This will also allow access to internal clients in the inside zone. The inside zone is the private, or internal, network. The outside zone contains access for the public Internet, also called the perimeter or external network. A DNS zone is a database that serves resource records for an FQDN and has nothing to do with firewalls.

4. **C.** Generally, office buildings do not have direct runs to each switch closet from the other closets. Although a full mesh is desirable, sometimes only a partial mesh is achievable. Traditional Ethernet-based networks function in a star topology, starting with a switch and connecting each client as a point on the star. A full-mesh topology is often found between the core and distribution layers of the Cisco three-tier design model. A hybrid topology is found in many networks today because one topology does not fit all needs throughout the network.

5. **B.** The Network Control Protocol (NCP) works at layer 3, tagging the network protocols from end to end when PPP is used. This gives PPP the ability to offer multiprotocol transport. Multiprotocol Label Switching (MPLS) is a routing technique in which the labels on the packets are tagged and packet switched throughout the provider's network. The Link Control Protocol (LCP) is responsible for connection setup, authentication, and header compression, among other things. PCP is not a protocol commonly used, and therefore, it is an invalid answer.

6. **A.** The command `encapsulation ppp` configures the serial interface with the Point to Point Protocol (PPP). PPP is an encapsulation protocol. The commands `protocol ppp`, `ppp enable`, and `ppp protocol` are incorrect.

7. **A.** DSL access multipliers, or DSLAMs, share the local loop with analog phone traffic to intercept communications from the DSL modem. DSLAMs provide the switching of data to the Internet. A DSL concentrator is normally installed at a housing complex or hotel and allows for individual DSL lines to be created. The 5ESS switching system is used for switching plain old telephone system (POTS) calls. A digital cross-connect system is used to connect circuits between the local loop and the provider.

8. **C.** The committed information rate (CIR) is the sustainable speed which the customer can communicate on the Ethernet virtual circuit. This CIR is directly tied to the price of the Monthly Recurring Charge (MRC), since the service provider must dedicate this bandwidth for the customer agreement. The IP addresses and routing protocols used are agreed upon by the connecting parties and are not part of the Metro Ethernet connection. The use of quality of service (QoS) is agreed upon by the connecting parties as well.

9. **C.** Platform as a service (PaaS) is commonly used by software developers. It provides a development platform that the software developer can use to create applications. An example of this is a web server with PHP and MySQL, which is hosted in the cloud. Software as a service (SAAS) is a software product similar to email or social networking software in which you use the software provided as a service. Infrastructure as a service (IaaS) allows you to rent infrastructure such as virtual machines (VMs), virtual networks, or even DNS, just to name a few. Disaster recovery as a service (DRaaS) is another popular service; you can rent storage and compute power to facilitate a disaster recovery site.

10. **D.** Rapid elasticity is the ability to add and remove compute capability in the cloud. As demand increases, compute power can be increased by adding more CPUs or servers. As demand for compute power decreases, CPUs or servers can be removed. Resource pooling is the concept that all of the physical hosts the provider has are pooled together to provide a customer with resources. Measured services is the concept that the provider can determine the amount of computing, network, or storage a customer has used so that they can be billed or a report can be created. Broad network access is the concept that the resources can be accessed from anywhere on the Internet.

11. **B.** During the three-way handshake, Computer A sends a SYN flag along with its receiving window size and initial sequence number. Then Computer B sends a SYN flag and ACK flag along with its receiving window and acknowledgment of the sequence number. Finally, Computer A sends an ACK flag, which acknowledges the synchronization of Computer B's receiving window. Communication begins and is considered to be in an established state. All of the other options are incorrect.

12. **D.** The summary route of 172.16.32.0/21 contains 172.16.38.0/24 as a valid network route. The /21 CIDR mask defines networks in multiples of 8 in the third octet of the network address. Therefore, the next summary network address is 172.16.40.0/21. All of the other options are incorrect.

13. **D.** The IP address 225.34.5.4 is a multicast IP address. Multicast IP addresses are defined as Class D addresses in the range 224.0.0.1 to 239.255.255.254. Class A defines any address with the first octet of 0 to 127. Class B defines any address with the first octet of 128 to 191. Class C defines any address with the first octet of 192 to 223.

14. **B.** Stateful DHCPv6 uses a process similar to DORA for IPv4. However, IPv6 uses multicast in lieu of broadcasts via the DHCPv6 Solicit multicast address. The Discover, Offer, Request, and Acknowledge (DORA) process only happens with IPv4 via broadcasts. Neighbor Solicitation (NS) and Neighbor Advertisement (NA) messages are used with the Neighbor Discovery Protocol (NDP). Router Solicitation (RS) and Router Advertisement (RA) messages are used with Stateless Autoconfiguration (SLAAC).

15. C. Before a host can communicate via an RS packet, it first needs a valid IP address. The first address is a link-local address so that it can send an RS packet and receive an RA packet. The client performs Duplicate Address Detection (DAD) on the link-local address. Then a Router Solicitation (RS) message is sent from the client. A Router Advertisement (RA) message is sent from the router to the client with the network ID. The host portion is then configured and DAD is checked again to make sure that the host does not have a duplicate IP address.

16. C. In IPv6, the solicited-node multicast message is used for resolution of the MAC address for an IPv6 address. The first 104 bits of the 128-bit IPv6 address is ff02::1:ff, and the last 24 bits comprise the last 24 bits of the IPv6 address that needs to be resolved. The solicited-node multicast message is also used for Duplicate Address Detection (DAD). All of the other options are incorrect.

17. B. The first field after the preamble and start frame delimiter (SFD) is the destination MAC address. The destination MAC address is always first because switches need to make forwarding decisions upon reading the destination MAC address. The source MAC address is in field B in the figure. The type field is in field C in the figure, and the frame checking sequence (FCS) is in field E in the figure.

18. B. Field C in the figure is the Type field. The Type field is used to define the upper-layer protocol the data belongs to. The destination MAC address in field A of the figure is used for forward filter decisions. The 7-byte preamble and start frame delimiter (SFD) of the frame in the figure are used to synchronize timing of the data. The frame checking sequence (FCS) is a cyclical redundancy checksum (CRC) value that can be seen in field E of the figure.

19. B. The command used to reset the MAC address table is `clear mac-address-table dynamic`. The commands `reset mac address-table`, `clear mac-address-table`, and `clear mac table` are incorrect.

20. A. The command to see all of the MAC addresses on a single interface is `show mac address-table interfaces fast 0/1`. This command can be entered in either privileged exec mode or user exec mode. The commands `show address-table interfaces fast 0/1`, `show mac interfaces fast 0/1`, and `show address-table fast 0/1` are incorrect.

21. D. The details of the output show that monitor session 1 is configured to capture interface Fa0/1 and VLAN 2 in both directions. The destination interface is Fa 0/2. All of the other options are incorrect.

22. C. Under normal circumstances, when VLANs are configured, they are stored in a file separate from the startup or running configuration. The VLAN database is stored in a file called `vlan.dat` on the flash. When decommissioning a switch, if you were to erase the configuration of a switch, you would also need to delete the `vlan.dat`. VLANs are configured in the running configuration when the switch is in VTP transparent mode. The VLAN configuration can then be stored for survivability of reboots in the startup configuration by writing the running configuration to the startup configuration. The `vlan.dat` file is not stored on the NVRAM; it is always stored on the flash.

23. B. The command `interface range gigabitethernet 1/1 - 12` will allow you to configure the interfaces Gigabit Ethernet 1/1 to 1/12. The commands `interface gigabitethernet range 1/1 - 12`, `interface range gigabitethernet 1/1 1/12`, and `interface range gigabitethernet range 1/1,12` are incorrect.

24. D. The command `switchport trunk allowed vlan 12` will remove all other VLANs and only VLAN 12 will be allowed on the trunk interface. The proper command to add an additional VLAN would be `switchport trunk allowed vlan add 12`. This command will add a VLAN to the already established list. All of the other options are incorrect.

25. D. The VLAN Trunking Protocol (VTP) assists in synchronizing a VLAN database across all Cisco switches participating in VTP. You must initially configure the VTP domain on the switch that will hold the master database. Then all other switches must be configured as clients and the VTP domain must be configured as well. The Network Time Protocol (NTP) synchronizes time on the switch or router with a known precision source. The Internet Group Management Protocol (IGMP) is used to facilitate multicast snooping on switches by allowing join and leave requests for the multicast group. The Inter-Switch Link (ISL) protocol is a Cisco proprietary protocol for VLAN trunking.

26. C. The two switches have a duplex mismatch. The duplex mismatch is a direct result of statically configuring only one side of the link to full-duplex. Switch A is not participating in port negotiation. Both sides must be configured statically the same or set to auto. There is no evidence of a wiring fault from the figure. There is also no evidence that interface Gi1/1 is operating nominally from the figure. The two switches could not have a VLAN mismatch because they are both configured as trunk links.

27. D. The device has the capability of both a switch and a router. It is most likely a switch that is performing SVI routing or has routing enabled. If the capability showed a B, the device would have source route bridge capabilities. If either S or R showed as a capability by itself, it would mean the device had switch capability or route capability, respectively.

28. C. The command `show cdp neighbors detail` will display all connected switches along with their IP addresses, hostnames, and IOS version. If this command is used from the central switch, you can quickly assess which switches need to be upgraded. The commands `show version`, `show running-config`, and `show lldp neighbors` are incorrect.

29. A. When one side is configured with on mode, it uses no control protocol. If a control protocol is sensed from the adjacent switch, the port will enter err-disabled mode to protect it from a loop. If one switch was configured with the auto mode and the other switch was configured with desirable mode, a Port Aggregation Protocol (PAgP) EtherChannel link would be formed. If both switches were configured with active mode, then a Link Aggregation Control Protocol (LACP) EtherChannel would be formed. When both switches are configured with passive mode, then LACP would not form an EtherChannel.

30. C. When you configure the `channel-group 1 mode active` command on the first interface, a pseudo interface is created called `port-channel 1`. All statistics and configuration should be referenced by this interface. All of the other options are incorrect.

31. A. The command `channel-group 1 mode passive` configures the port to be placed in a passive negotiating state. The other switch must be placed into an active negotiating state for LACP to become the control protocol for the channel group. If the other switch is configured with desirable mode, there will be a mismatch and the interface will enter an err-disabled state. If the other switch is configured with on mode, then it will not form an EtherChannel link. If the other switch is configured with auto mode, there will be a mismatch and the interface will enter an err-disabled state.

32. B. The long delay for the device to become active on the interface is the wait time for convergence of Spanning Tree Protocol (STP). If the interface will only connect a device to the port, then the port should be configured with Spanning Tree PortFast mode. This will skip the blocking mode during convergence of STP. Turning off auto-negotiation on the interface will not do anything other than statically set the speed and duplex. Configuring BPDU Guard mode for Spanning Tree is a good idea, but it will not speed up convergence of STP. Turning off port security will not speed up convergence of the STP protocol.

33. B. When all of the ports on a switch are in designated mode, it means that the switch is the root bridge for the Spanning Tree Protocol (STP). If the switch was connected to a root bridge, you would see the ports as being root ports. The switch is obviously participating in STP because it is displaying a status for the STP port state. The switch is already the root bridge, and it cannot be a backup root bridge as well.

34. B. When BPDU Guard is configured on a port, it guards the port from creating a loop. It also guards STP so that the STP calculation of redundant links is not affected by the device connected to the interface. If a BPDU is seen on the interface, the interface will immediately enter into an err-disabled state. The most likely cause was that another switch was plugged into the interface. If a neighboring switch recalculates its Spanning Tree Protocol (STP), it will not affect this switch. If a device is disconnected for a long period of time, the port will not enter into an err-disabled state. Although an interface that is flapping should enter into an err-disabled state, it is not common for this to happen from a flapping port.

35. B. Local mode is a centralized switching mode in which all traffic is first sent to the wireless LAN controller (WLC) to be centrally switched to its intended destination. Monitor mode can be used for analysis of the radio spectrum. FlexConnect mode is a switching mode on the wireless access point (WAP) in which traffic is switched directly to the intended destination. Central mode is not a valid mode, and therefore, it is an invalid answer.

36. B. Monitor mode will help support location-based services when used with a wireless LAN controller (WLC), but it will not serve client requests. FlexConnect mode is a switching mode on the wireless access point (WAP) in which traffic is switched directly to the intended destination. Local mode is a centralized switching mode in which all traffic is first sent to the wireless LAN controller to be centrally switched to its intended destination. Locate mode is not a valid mode, and therefore, it is an invalid answer.

37. B. When a link in a link aggregation (LAG) fails, the remaining traffic will be migrated over to the active link. No packet loss should be noticed, except for the initial failover. The links will not enter an err-disabled mode or be administratively disabled; this can only happen if there is a mismatch of protocols or the interfaces are shut down manually. All traffic is

migrated to the active link, so no degradation should be seen on the active interface unless it is at peak capacity.

38. D. The TACACS+ protocol will encrypt the entire packet from the switch or router to the AAA server. This is performed with the use of a pre-shared key (PSK) that is configured on both the TACACS+ device and the AAA server. 802.1X will not encrypt the entire packet from the switch or router to the AAA server. IPsec is an open standard for encryption of packets, but it is not commonly used to encrypt the transmission of a switch or router to an AAA server. A Remote Authentication Dial-In User Service (RADIUS) server is an AAA server and, therefore, is an invalid answer.

39. D. The Secure Copy Protocol (SCP) will encrypt the IOS over the network during an upgrade from the client computer. The Hypertext Transfer Protocol (HTTP) is an unencrypted protocol normally used to transfer web pages across the Internet. The Trivial File Transfer Protocol (TFTP) is an unencrypted protocol for transferring files without any security. TFTP is often used to copy configuration or upgrade firmware on network devices. The File Transfer Protocol (FTP) is a legacy protocol used to transfer files between hosts. FTP operates in clear text and provides no encryption for the file transfers.

40. B. When you configure a WLAN and use the default QoS settings, the effective QoS is silver. Gold is used for video application on a wireless network. Bronze is the lowest level of traffic for unimportant traffic. Platinum is the highest level of traffic, and it is usually reserved for voice traffic over wireless.

41. D. Your packets are most likely making it to the destination host. However, there is no route back to your host on the other network's router. You must enter a network route on Router B to get to Network A. You would not have been able to configure a route if the `ip routing` command was needed. The hosts on Network A and Network B are most likely not the problem.

42. A. Enhanced Interior Gateway Routing Protocol (EIGRP) has the lowest administrative distance (AD) of the three protocols. Therefore, regardless of the metric, the lowest AD will always be chosen. All of the other options are incorrect.

43. A. Serial interfaces are point-to-point connections. Any traffic directed down the interface will automatically appear on the adjacent router. Routers will not process traffic normally unless Proxy ARP is configured for the interface. All of the other options are incorrect.

44. B. The administrative distance (AD) can be added to the end of the route statement. Since RIP has an administrative distance of 120, 130 will be chosen if the RIP route is not present. The commands `ip route 192.168.2.0 255.255.255.0 192.168.4.1 110`, `ip route 110 192.168.2.0 255.255.255.0 192.168.4.1`, and `ip route 130 192.168.2.0 255.255.255.0 192.168.4.1` are incorrect.

45. B. The holddown timer's job is to allow the network to stabilize after a route had become unreachable via an update. This limits the potential problems related to a flapping port and allows RIPv2 to converge route updates in the entire network. The default holddown timer is set to 180 seconds. The flush timer defines the time between when the route becomes invalid and it is flushed or deleted from the route table. The default flush timer is set to 240 seconds.

The invalid timer defines when a route is declared invalid. The default invalid timer is set to 180 seconds. The update timer is the timer that defines how often multicasts are sent with the complete route table. When the update is multicast to all listening neighbors, the route table will be populated with the new entries. The default update timer is set to 30 seconds.

46. C. The ARP request took time for the ARP reply, and during this time, the ICMP timeout threshold was exceeded. This is common on a router, and the following pings should not time out unless the ARP entry is cleared after its TTL expires. The local router will not drop the first packet, mainly because routers don't normally drop traffic unless instructed to do so. Although the route table could be updating at that moment, it is not probable because this behavior can be replicated. The remote router, like the local router, will not normally drop packets unless instructed to do so.

47. A. The command `network 203.244.234.0` will advertise the 203.244.234.0 network. When you're configuring RIP, only the network address needs to be configured with the `network` command. The commands `network 203.244.234.0 255.255.255.0`, `network 203.244.234.0 0.0.0.255`, and `network 203.244.234.0/24` are incorrect.

48. C. In the figure, packets are being sent to the router via a trunk link. A setup where the packets for VLANs are sent to a router for routing between VLANs is called router on a stick (ROAS) routing. Default routing, also known as stub routing, is normally used on stub networks, where all networks are available through the gateway of last resort. Switched virtual interface (SVI) routing is performed on layer 3 switches. A virtual interface is created that will have an IP address and routing capabilities.

49. D. When you want to turn on the layer 3 functionality of a switch, you must configure the command `ip routing` in global configuration. This is required when you want to create Switched Virtual Interfaces (SVIs) for VLANs and want to route on the switch between the VLANs. This method of routing is much more efficient, since the traffic is routed in the ASICs on the switch. The commands `ip route svi`, `feature svi routing`, and `svi routing` are incorrect.

50. C. The entries with the dash in the Age column represent the physical interfaces of the router. If the entries were configured statically, their type would reflect a status of `static`. Entries that have just been added to the ARP table will have an initial timer set. All entries in the ARP table will be displayed with their remaining time in seconds. Therefore, any entry with less than a minute left before it expires will be under 60 seconds.

51. C. Time to live (TTL) is a field in the IP header that prevents packets from endlessly routing in networks. Each time a packet is routed, the router's responsibility is to decrement the TTL by 1. When the TTL reaches 0, the packet is considered unrouteable and dropped. The checksum field is used to check for a damaged packet in transit. The flags field in the IP packet is to signal if the packet has been fragmented. The header length field defines the length of the header of the IP packet.

52. A. Cisco Express Forwarding (CEF) allows the CPU to initially populate a sort of route cache called the forwarding information base (FIB). Any packets entering the router can be checked against the FIB and routed without the help of the CPU. Process switching and fast switching both use the processor directly to make routing decisions. Expedited forwarding is not a packet routing technique; it is a quality of service (QoS) method and therefore an invalid answer.

53. C. The multicast address of ff02::a is the multicast address for IPv6 EIGRP updates. Updates for routers participating in IPv6 EIGRP will be multicast to the IPv6 address of ff02::a. Routing Information Protocol Next Generation (RIPng) uses a multicast address of ff06::9. Open Shortest Path First version 3 (OSPFv3) uses multicast addresses of ff05::5 and ff05::6. Stateless Autoconfiguration (SLAAC) uses the link-local address that starts with fe80.

54. B. When you see an exclamation mark, it means that the packets were successfully acknowledged on the other side and an ICMP response was received. If you see five periods returned, it means that the packets have never made it back to the router. Congestion in the path will not be visible with the ping command. If the packets are received on the far router but ICMP times out, periods will be displayed.

55. C. The extended ping command allows you to specify a number of parameters such as repeat count, datagram size, and source address or exit interface. There are several other parameters that can be adjusted. You use the extended ping command through the privileged exec prompt and not the global configuration mode. Configuring a temporary route for the router exit interface will affect all traffic on the router.

56. C. The three times are the minimum response time, average response time, and maximum response time of the ICMP echo and reply. All other options are incorrect.

57. C. The Ctrl+Shift+6 key sequence will cause a break during a network command such as ping or traceroute. The key sequences Ctrl+C, Ctrl+4, and Ctrl+Shift+1 are incorrect.

58. B. When you are diagnosing a network connectivity issue, you always start testing the closest IP address. In this case, the default gateway of Router A is the closest IP address. The switches are irrelevant because they are not layer 3 devices that can be tested at layer 3. The fact that it has an IP address and can return a ping means that you can communicate with its management plane. The Internet Control Message Protocol (ICMP) packet will traverse the data plane, also called the forwarding plane. All of the other options are incorrect.

59. C. The command debug ip packet will turn on debugging for IP packets. The output will display the exit interface that the traffic is taking, to include the source and destination IP addresses. This command should be used with caution because it could create high CPU utilization on the router. It is recommended to be used with an ACL. The commands ping 192.168.3.5 Gi 0/1, ping Gi 0/1 192.168.3.5, and debug ip ping are incorrect.

60. B. The third hop (router) is not responding to ICMP echo requests. The traceroute completes since the fourth hop responded and the user did not need to perform a break on the command. Therefore, it can be concluded that the third hop is not down. The traceroute completes after 4 hops; only the third hop is not responding with ICMP replies. The figure does not show evidence that packets have been rerouted.

61. D. An extended ping allows for the source interface or IP address to be specified. You can access the extended ping by entering the command ping without an IP address and then

following the prompt until it asks if you want extended commands. Datagram size, repeat counts, and timeout can be set when using the normal ping command options.

62. A. The probe count attribute must be changed to allow multiple packets to be sent to each hop. The default is three packets. Numeric display defaults to both numbers and symbols for the output. The maximum time to live (TTL) is used to set the number of hops before a ping request is considered unrouteable. Packet type is not an option for an extended traceroute; therefore, this is an invalid answer.

63. C. An area defines a topology inside of the OSPF hierarchy. Since each router in an area calculates its own costs, they all contain the same topological database, or link state database (LSDB). It is not true that all the routers in the same area have the same neighbor table. All routers in the same area do not need to share the same hello/dead timers; only their adjacent routers must be configured with matching hello/dead timers. All routers do not need the same process ID, since this is a local value to define the process OSPF is running on the local router.

64. B. Link-state advertisement (LSA) packets communicate the topology of the local router with other routers in the OSPF area. The information contained in the LSA packet is a summary of links the local router's topology consists of. Hello packets are used to notify adjacent routers that the link is still valid. The Link State Acknowledgment (LSAck) packets verify that an LSA has been received. Dead packets are not a real type of packet because when a link goes down, there will be an absence of hello packets, tripping the dead time.

65. C. When interface tracking is turned on and a link that is being tracked fails, the priority of the active router is lowered and an election is forced. This will make the standby router become the active router. However, if the link is repaired, the priority will recover to its normal value, but the current active router will remain the active router. Preemption allows for the value to instantly reelect the original router as the active router. Interface tracking resets, failback options, and priority tracking are not valid options for interface tracking; therefore, these are invalid answers.

66. A. Network Address Translation (NAT) creates packet switching path delay. This is because each address traveling through the NAT process requires lookup time for the translation. NAT does not introduce security weaknesses; it can actually be used to strengthen security, since private IP addresses are masqueraded behind a public IP address. NAT is often used so that address renumbering is not required when two networks are merged together with identical IP addressing. NAT does not increase bandwidth utilization at all.

67. B. Static Network Address Translation (NAT) is a one-to-one mapping between a local (private) and global (public) IP address. This is used for servers, such as web servers and email servers so that they are Internet reachable. Dynamic NAT creates a dynamic association between local and global addresses for a specific period of time. NAT Overloading, also known as Port Address Translation (PAT), creates a dynamic mapping to a pool of IP addresses or an individual IP address using the source and destination ports of the packet. Symmetric NAT is NAT Overloading where the source port and destination port are mapped to the same matching global source port and destination port.

68. B. The Network Time Protocol (NTP) is used to synchronize time for routers and switches. Simple Network Management Protocol (SNMP) is used to transmit and collect counters on network devices. Syslog is used to transmit and collect messages from network devices. Internet Control Message Protocol (ICMP) is used by many diagnostic tools such as `ping` and `traceroute` to communicate round-trip time and reachability.

69. A. Domain Name Services (DNS) direct queries are performed over the UDP protocol to port 53. The queries do not require the TCP setup and teardown because the queries are simple request and reply messages, so UDP is used for direct queries. TCP port 53 is used for DNS zone transfers between DNS servers. UDP port 55 is not used for any popular protocols. UDP port 68 is used with the Dynamic Host Configuration Protocol (DHCP).

70. C. The introduction of SNMP version 2c added the Inform and Get-bulk messages for SNMP. SNMP version 1 was the first release of SNMP, and it did not support Inform and Get-bulk messages. SNMP version 2 was promptly replaced with SNMP version 2c; therefore, it is an invalid answer. SNMP version 3 introduced many new features such as security and encryption, to name a few.

71. C. The command `logging host 192.168.1.6` will configure all logs to be sent to the syslog server 192.168.1.6. The commands `logging server 192.168.1.6`, `logging 192.168.1.6`, and `syslog server 192.168.1.6` are incorrect.

72. C. The command `ip address dhcp` will configure the router to use DHCP for IP address assignment. This command needs to be issued on the interface in which you want the IP address to be configured, similar to static IP address assignment. The command `ip address dhcp` is incorrect when it is configured in the global configuration prompt. The command `ip address auto` is incorrect, regardless of which prompt it is configured in.

73. B. Delay is the time it takes for a packet to travel from source to destination, which is a description of one-way delay. Round-trip delay is the time it takes for the packet to travel from source to destination (one-way delay) plus the time it takes for the destination computer to send the packet back to the originating node to form a round trip. Bandwidth is the measured maximum of throughput for a connection. Jitter is the difference between the delay of packets. Loss is the measurement of packets lost in the transfer of data.

74. A. The Differentiated Services Code Point (DSCP) is a 6-bit value in the Type of Service (ToS) field of the IP header. The DSCP value defines the importance of packets at layer 3. 802.1Q is a layer 2 trunking protocol that accommodates CoS markings. Class of Service (CoS) is a 3-bit field in an 802.1Q Ethernet frame. QoE is not a valid term used with Ethernet and therefore is an invalid answer.

75. C. The command `username scpadmin privilege-level 15 password Sybex` must be configured. This command will configure a user named scpadmin with a privilege level of 15 (enable access) and a password of Sybex. The commands `ip scp user scpadmin password Sybex`, `username scpadmin password Sybex`, and `ip scp user scpadmin privilege-level 15 password Sybex` are incorrect.

76. D. An attacker will take advantage of the automatic trunking configuration of Dynamic Trunking Protocol (DTP). This will allow the attacker to create a trunk with the switch and tag packets so that they can hop onto different VLANs. An open Telnet connection can be eavesdropped on since it is in clear text. *Automatic encapsulation negotiation* is not a valid term used with switching; therefore, it is an invalid answer. Forwarding of broadcasts is not really an exploit; it is a function of switching. Routers will stop the forwarding of broadcasts.

77. C. Port security can prevent MAC address flooding attacks by restricting the number of MAC addresses associated to an interface. This will prevent the content-addressable memory (CAM) from being overrun by bogus entries. Access control lists (ACLs) will allow you to control layer 3 and layer 4 network traffic but are not used to prevent MAC address flooding attacks. Network Address Translation (NAT) is also not used to prevent MAC address flooding attacks. VLAN access control lists (VACLs) can be used to control layers 2, 3, and 4 traffic, but they are not used to prevent MAC address flooding attacks.

78. A. Locking doors is a recommended physical security method. Installing antivirus software is a form of digital protection. Firewalls are considered logical security. Directory-level permissions are considered a form of logical security.

79. C. The command `logging synchronous` will configure console logging messages to synchronize with what is being typed so they will not disrupt the user's input. The command must be configured for the line that it will be applied to. The command `no logging inline` is incorrect. The command `logging synchronous` is incorrect when configured from a global configuration prompt. The command `logging synchronous` is incorrect when configured from a privileged exec prompt.

80. D. Once the password has been forgotten, a password recovery must be performed on the router. Although you have the encrypted password, it cannot be reversed, since the configuration now contains a one-way hash of the password. A one-way hash is a form of symmetrical encryption of the password; only the same combination of letters and numbers will produce the same hash. The Cisco Technical Assistance Center (TAC) cannot reverse the password. The hash cannot be used as the password; only the password can be used, and it is then checked against the hash. There is also no `decrypt-password 06074352EFF6` command in the operating system to decrypt the password.

81. C. The AAA server listens for requests on UDP port 1812 for authentication of credentials. UDP port 49 is not correct and is not associated with a popular protocol. UDP port 1821 is not correct and is also not associated with a popular protocol. UDP port 1813 is used for AAA servers listening for accounting information.

82. B. ACLs are a major consideration since they are neither TCP nor UDP; they are a layer 3 protocol of their own. The ACL required for the tunnel creation is `permit gre {source} {destination}`, which would be for a named access list. The tunnel interface number is only locally significant to the router. The adjoining router will never know the tunnel interface number. Speed of the tunnel is not a consideration that can restrict tunnel creation. Generic Routing Encapsulation (GRE) is expressly used to reduce the number of hops between the source and destination. When employed, it allows the remote network to look like it is one hop away, so the number of hops between the source and destination is not a consideration that can restrict tunnel creation.

83. B. Internet Protocol Security (IPsec) does not support multicast packets. If you require both, you can set up a Generic Routing Encapsulation (GRE) tunnel for the multicast and broadcast traffic, then encrypt only the data over IPsec. However, by itself IPsec does not support multicast or broadcast traffic. The Point-to-Point Protocol (PPP) does not support multicast packets. Multiprotocol Label Switching (MPLS) does not natively support multicast packets.

84. A. The command `access-list 101 deny tcp 192.168.2.0 0.0.0.255 any eq 23` will deny TCP traffic from 192.168.2.0/24 to any address with a destination of 23 (Telnet). The command `access-list 101 permit ip any any` will permit all other traffic. The commands `access-list 101 deny 192.168.2.0 0.0.0.255 eq 23` and `access-list 101 permit ip any any` are incorrect; the deny statement is incorrectly formatted. The commands `access-list 101 block tcp 192.168.2.0 0.0.0.255 any eq 23` and `access-list 101 permit ip any any` are incorrect; the block argument is not a valid argument. The commands `access-list 101 deny 192.168.2.0 0.0.0.255 any eq 23` and `access-list 101 permit any any` are incorrect; the `permit any any` command does not specify a protocol and therefore is incorrect.

85. B. Conventional access lists don't give you the ability to edit a single entry. The entire ACL must be removed and re-added with the correct entry. An alternative to conventional access lists is named access lists. A named access list is referenced by line numbers, which allows for removal and addition of single entries. Unfortunately, the Cisco IOS does not provide an ACL editor for conventional access lists. You can remove the line number and add a new line number back when you use named access lists. However, this functionality is not available for conventional access lists. Conventional access lists can be completely negated with the `no` command, but you cannot negate a single entry.

86. D. The command `show ip dhcp snooping binding` will display the DHCP snooping database. This database will have entries for the MAC address, IP address, lease time, VLAN, and interface. The commands `show dhcp binding`, `show ip dhcp binding`, and `show ip dhcp snooping database` are incorrect.

87. C. The computer will not be allowed to communicate, and the port will enter an err-disabled state. The defaults for port security allow for only one MAC address, and the default violation is shutdown. The violation of shutdown will shut the port down and place it into an err-disabled state, which will require administrative intervention. Port security cannot be configured in a fashion where it only provides logging and does not restrict the violating MAC address (host).

88. A. TACACS+ will allow for authentication of users, and it also provides a method of restricting users to specific commands. This allows for much more granular control of lower-level administrators. Authentication, authorization, and accounting (AAA) servers, also known as Remote Authentication Dial-In User Service (RADIUS) servers, are generally configured to enable access for routers or switches. The 802.1X protocol is not used to authenticate users for management access in routers or switches. The 802.1X protocol is used to control access to layer 2 switched ports.

89. C. Wi-Fi Protected Access 2 - Lightweight Extensible Authentication Protocol (WPA2-LEAP) is a Cisco-proprietary protocol that allows for user accounts to be authenticated via a RADIUS server to Active Directory (AD). WPA2-LEAP will provide both encryption and user authentication. Wi-Fi Protected Access 2 - Preshared Key (WPA2-PSK) and WPA3-PSK will not provide user authentication, since they use a preshared key (PSK). Wi-Fi Protected Access 2 - Extensible Authentication Protocol (WPA2-EAP) uses certificates to authenticate the computer account connecting to the wireless network.

90. B. When configuring WPA2 PSK using the GUI of a wireless LAN controller (WLC), you should select the WPA2 Policy-AES for the WPA+WPA2 Parameter policy. This policy will ensure the highest level of security for the WLAN. 802.1X and PSK are authentication key management options and therefore not valid answers. The WPA Policy uses the RC4 encryption algorithm, and thus, it is weaker than the AES encryption protocol.

91. B. The most important aspect to understand when automating a change across an enterprise is the effect of the changes being automated. Although the way the change is to be automated is important, the effects outweigh the method of the change. The topology of the devices and the connection between them are not that important to the automated change unless the topology and connections are being changed through the automation.

92. B. The Python scripting language has been adopted as the most popular language to automate changes in a network. This is mainly due to its support by major providers and easy syntax. Administrators can easily focus on the task at hand and not the nuances of the language. C++ and C# are much more involved because they are considered programming languages and not scripting languages. JavaScript Object Notation (JSON) is not a programming or scripting language; it's a data storage/transfer method used with programming and scripting languages.

93. B. The Cisco License Manager (CLM) can be installed on Windows, Solaris, or Linux. It allows for discovery of Cisco devices and inventory of Cisco device licenses and connects to Cisco for access to current and new licenses purchased. The CLM allows for management of the software activation process through its user interface.

94. A. The Virtual Extensible LAN (VXLAN) protocol is commonly found on the overlay of a software-defined network (SDN). It allows for the transport of layer 2 frames over a layer 3 network. The Open Shortest Path First (OSPF) protocol is a layer 3 networking protocol commonly found on the underlay of SDN. OpenFlow is a protocol that is used for the programming of network devices from the Southbound interface (SBI) of the SDN controller. JavaScript Object Notation (JSON) is a data-interchange format used with many different SDN controllers.

95. C. The Python programming language is commonly used with the northbound interface (NBI) of a software-defined network (SDN) controller. The term *CLOS* describes Spine/Leaf network switching. The Open-Flow and NETCONF protocols are commonly used with the southbound interface (SBI) of an SDN controller for programming the SDN devices.

96. A. The Design section allows you to create a hierarchical design of the network with a graphical map. In addition, the Design section also allows you to specify the default servers that will be applied after discovery. The Discovery tool is not a major section of Cisco DNA Center, and it is not used to specify server defaults. The Provision section allows you to view and edit the discovered inventory of network devices. The Policy section allows you to create policies based upon applications, traffic, and IP-based access control lists (ACLs), just to name a few. The Platform section allows you to perform upgrades and search the API catalog.

97. D. The REST-based HTTP verb PUT is used to update or replace data via the API. The POST verb is used to create data. The GET verb is used to read data. The UPDATE verb does not exist within the CREATE, READ, UPDATE, DELETE (CRUD) framework; therefore, it is an invalid answer.

98. C. A 400 status code from the REST-based service means that it is a bad request. The data being sent to the REST-based service could be wrong or wrongly formatted. A 200 status code is used to signify that everything is okay and nothing is wrong. A forbidden request will return a 403 status code. On rare occasions, you may receive a 500 status code; this signifies that there is an internal server error.

99. A. The Chef configuration management utility uses Ruby as its reference language. Python is used by Ansible as its reference language. PowerShell is used by Microsoft's Desired State Configuration (DSC) as its reference language. YAML is not a reference language; it's a mechanism to transfer data and store data in a structured manner.

100. D. A JavaScript Object Notation (JSON) file starts with curly brackets and ends with curly brackets, also called braces. Inside of the curly brackets, the keys and values are encapsulated in double quotes. Single quotes are not used for formatting purposes with JSON. Square brackets can signify that more than one key-value pair exists for a specific item.

Index

100 Mb/s hub, switches, 21
802.1X, security, 168
802.11 wireless, 33
2.4 GHz, 34

A

AAA authentication, 186, 216, 245, 247, 360.
   See also authentication
ABR (area border router), 326
access
   registration, 216
   unauthorized, 8
access control vestibules, 347
access layer, switches, 11
access points
   service providers, 209
   wireless, restricting, 181
   wireless roaming, 9
ACI (Application Centric Infra-structure), 367
ACLs (access control lists), 174, 353–354
   configuring, 176, 178
   entry removal, 176
   extended, 180, 355–356
   interfaces and, 175
   modifications, 246
   placement, 356
   range, 173–175
   spoofing and, 346
   traffic source address, 177
   traffic source and, 180
AD (administrative distance), 91–92, 394
   EIGRP, 328
   OSPF, 129, 217, 328
   RIP, 91
   static routes, 91

administrative privileges, 163
ADSL (Asymmetrical Digital Subscriber
   Line), 259
   remote router, 14
AES (Advanced Encryption Standard), 80
AF31 traffic, 155
aggregation protocols, 66–67
AI (artificial intelligence), 197, 370–371
   ChatGPT, 197
   data models, 198
   learning models, 198
   training datasets, 198
Ansible, 201, 202–203, 373–374
antimalware, 347
anycast addresses, 31, 270
AP modes, 236
APIC (Application Policy Infrastructure), 298
APIC-EM (APIC Enterprise Module), 197, 367
APIs (application program interfaces), 195, 364
   REST APIs, 198
   YANG data model, 199
ARIN (American Registry for Internet
   Numbers), 30
ARP (Address Resolution Protocol),
   306–307, 313
   cache, 96, 112
   packets, 96
ASA (Adaptive Security Appliance), 8
ASBR (autonomous system border router), 326
attacks. *See also* security
   DDoS (distributed denial of service), 344
   DoS (denial-of-service), 161
   double tagging, 346
   DTP (Dynamic Trunking Protocol), 224
   IP address spoofing, 345
   MAC address flooding, 244
   on-path attacks, 162, 345

passwords, 169
phishing, 162, 163, 346–347
ping sweep scans, 160
sniffer, 345
social engineering, 163
spoofing, 161
traffic and, 160
VLANs, native, 162
WAP (wireless access point), 161
authentication
    802.1X, 168
    centralized, 185, 254
    encryption, 246
    IETF and, 80
    limited, 162
    local, 167
    PPP (point-to-point protocol), 12
        nonces, 13
    RADIUS, 245
    REST-based token requests, 199
    selective access and, 168
    smartcards, 168
    SNMP, 147
    SSL, 345
    symmetrical keys, 188
    tokens, 199
    types, 163
    wireless standards, 34
    WPA2, 188
automation
    billing, 259
    configuration, routers, 190, 363
    network, 190, 191, 363
auto-negotiation, 20, 21
AVG (active virtual gateway), 329–330
AWS (Amazon Web Services), 14, 259
    EC2 (Elastic Compute), 260

B

BaaS (backup-as-a-service), 259–260
bandwidth, 327, 378
    broadcast domains and, 230
    collision domains and, 230
    setting, 128

banners, 167
BDR (backup designated router), 326
Bell-Ford algorithm, 100
BGP (Border Gateway Protocol), 311–312
    AD (administrative distance), 328
binding, 22
Bluetooth, wireless frequency spectrum, 34
BPDU, 294–295
BPDU Guard, 74, 236, 295
bridges
    ID calculation, 71
    root bridge, 292–293
    switches, 70
broadcast addresses, 26
broadcast domains, 3, 230
broadcast networks, 119
broadcast storm, 379

C

cabling, 261–262
    Cat5e, 17
    crossover, 17
    fiber optic, 16
    straight-through, 17
    types, switches, 16, 17
    UTP (unshielded twisted pair), 261
CAPWAP (Control And Provisioning of
    Wireless Access Points), 300
Cat5e cabling, 17
CBWFQ (Class-Based Weighted Fair
    Queuing), 341
CDP (Cisco Discovery Protocol),
    287–288, 388
    frames, 63
    output details, 65
    turning off, 63
CE (customer edge) router, 327
CEF (Cisco Express Forwarding), 395
    hop information, 102
CHAP (Challenge Handshake Authentication
    Protocol), 258
ChatGPT, 197, 370
CIDR (Classless Inter-Domain Routing), 332
    subnet masks, 23

CIR (committed information rate), 390
Cisco
  connection speed, 81
  device licensing, 247
  interior gateway protocols, 101
  machine language, 198
  OSPF, 93
  packet forwarding and, 95
  router ID, 118
  trunks, 58
  tunnel protocols, 169
Cisco AP, Bluetooth devices and, 76
Cisco Catalyst Center, 198
Cisco Prime Infrastructure,
    configuration, 193
CLM (Cisco License Manager), 401
cloud computing
  compute capability increase, 231
  criterion, 15
  hosted environments, 15
  intercloud exchange, 260
  public clouds, connectivity, 16
  virtualization and, 15
cloud providers, colocation sites, 15
cloud services
  BaaS (backup-as-a-service), 259
  catalog, 15, 259
  IaaS (infrastructure-as-a-service), 259
  IaC (infrastructure as code), 374
  PaaS (platform-as-a-service), 259,
    390
  SaaS (software-as-a-service), 259
  SLBaaS (server load balancing as a
    service), 273
  software development, 231
collapsed core design model, 11, 256
collision domains, 4, 230, 250–251
compute resource distribution, 34
configuration, Cisco Prime
    Infrastructure, 193
configuration management, 201, 203
connectionless protocol, 209
connectivity
  layer 3, 221

  low cost, 17
  public clouds, 16
  security, 173
controller-based networking,
    192–193, 365–366
  architecture, 193
core layer, 10
  switches, 11, 256
core switch, 252
CoS (Class of Service), 340
CRC checksums, 36, 275
crossover cables, 17
CRUD framework, 199, 371
CST (Common Spanning Tree), 69, 291
customer responsibility, 18

D

DAD (Duplicate Address Detection), 269,
    319, 379
data format, white space, 191
data in transit, security, 161
databases, VLANs, 52
DCE (data communications equipment),
    260
DDoS (distributed denial of service)
    attack, 344
demarc (demarcation point), 262
designated ports, 71
devices
  access, unauthorized, 8
  information collection, 63
  switches, 236
DevOps, 363
DHCP (Dynamic Host Configuration
    Protocol), 335–336, 339–340
  down server, 152
  IP address duplicates, 146
  Offer packet, 338–339
  snooping, 161, 226, 346
    database, viewing, 246
  transport protocol, 146
DHCP server, 33

lease, deleting, 152
relay agents, 151
DHCPv6
  stateful, 152, 232, 339, 390
  stateless, 210
Dijkstra routing algorithm, 115, 320
disconnection from network, 167
discontinuous networks, 218
distance-vector protocols, 100
  routing loops and, 101
distance-vector routing protocol, 97
distribution layer, 194
  switches, 11, 256
distribution switches, 6
DMVPN (Dynamic Multipoint Virtual
    Private Network), 257, 352, 369
  topologies, 172
DMZ (demilitarized zone), 253, 344, 389
  server placement, 8
DNA (Digital Network Architecture),
    367, 370
DNA discovery, 197
DNS (Domain Name System), 32
  bandwidth, 378
  cloud, 209
  default servers, 247
  direct queries, 243
  entry time in cache, 146
  hostname queries, 145
  name resolution, 33, 145
  UDP and, 23
domains
  broadcast, 3
  collision domains, 4
DoS (denial-of-service) attacks, 161
double tagging, 346
DR (designated router), 325
  command, 126
  displaying, 127
  OSPF, 118–119
DS1 connection speed, 18
DSCP (Differentiated Services Code
    Point), 398
  marking priority, 153

DSL modem, 230
DSLAMs (DSL access multipliers), 389
DTP (Dynamic Trunking Protocol), 57,
    284, 285
  attacks, 224, 398
DUAL (diffusing update algorithm), 311
duplex issues, 18
dynamic routing protocol, 87, 93, 307
  advantages, 99
  Bellman-Ford algorithm, 100
  Dijkstra, 115
  IPv6, 103
  overhead, 99
  update algorithms, 100

E

EAP (Extensible Authentication
    Protocol), 350
EAP-TLS, 225, 386
EC2 (Elastic Compute), 260
EGPs (exterior gateway protocols), 101
EIGRP (Enhanced Interior Gateway Routing
    Protocol), 304, 310, 368, 394
  AD (administrative distance), 328
elasticity, 390
email
  phishing, 163
  zones, servers, 230
enable password, 164
encapsulation
  serial connections, 208
  serial links, 13
encryption
  AES (Advanced Encryption Standard),
    80
  authentication, 246
  IOS, 237
  keys, 164, 166
  packets, 173, 237
  passwords, 167, 348–349
  per-frame, 361
  SNMP, 147

SSH, 80
SSL, 345
wireless, 24-bit initialization, 34
enterprise, automated changes, 247
error counts, resetting, 19
ESP (Encapsulating Security Payload), 353
ESS (extended service set), 254
EtherChannel, 65–66, 213–214, 288, 289, 380–381
Ethernet frames, 232
Ethernet switches, wire speed, 6
EUI-64 method, 32, 270
exterior gateway routing protocols, 101

F

fabric switching hop count, 196
fames, MTUs, 47
Fast Ethernet, routers, 20
FHRP (first hop redundancy protocol), 130
fiber optics, 16
firewalls, 160, 253, 344
    DMZ (demilitarized zone), 344
    Internet-facing services, 7
    management, 8
    placement, 7
    stateful, 8
    trusted networks, 160
    URIs, 208, 377
    virtual firewalls, 273
flash memory, 157, 343
Flex Connect mode, 83
flooding frames, 7
flow control, 21
FQDNs (fully qualified domain names), 223, 334, 385
frames
    flooding, 7
    VLANs and, 46
FTD (Firepower Threat Defense), 344, 352
FTP servers, configuration backup, 157
full-mesh topology, 10, 255

G

gateway
    default, 222
    verifying, 32
GIADDR (Gateway Address), 339
GLBP (Gateway Load Balancing Protocol), 131–132, 135, 328
    per-host load balancing, 331
global unicast addresses, 30
GRE (Generic Routing Encapsulation), 169–170, 351
    tunnel configuration, 171
    tunnel creation restriction, 245

H

hardware, virtualization, 35
HDLC (High-Level Data Link Control), 258, 377
hello timer, 328
HIDS (host intrusion detection system), 344–345
hop count
    fabric switching, 196
    RIP maximum, 87
host readers, 335
hosted environments, cloud computing, 15
HSRP (Hot Standby Router Protocol), 130–131, 328–331, 352, 384
    preemption, 133
    real-time diagnostics, 134
    router state, 133
hub-and-spoke topology, 12
hubs, 5, 377
hybrid protocols, 100
hybrid topologies, three-tier design model, 10
hypervisor, 272

I

IaaS (infrastructure-as-a-service), 259–260
IaC (infrastructure as code), 374

IANA (Internet Assigned Numbers
  Authority), 267
IBSS (independent basic service set), 295
ICMP (Internet Control Message
  Protocol), 305
  packet routing and, 93
  packets, 242
  router status, 104
idle time before disconnection, 167
IDS (intrusion detection system), 160,
  254, 344
IEEE standards
  aggregation protocols, 66–67
  FHRP (first hop redundancy
    protocol), 130
  protocols, 63
  Rapid PVST+ and, 70
IETF (Internet Engineering Task Force),
  authentication and, 80
IGMP (Internet Group Messaging
  Protocol), 267
IGPs (interior gateway protocols), 101
IGRP (Interior Gateway Routing
  Protocol), 303
incident detection, 186
inside addresses, 332
intercloud exchange, 260
interfaces
  bandwidth, setting, 128
  error count reset, 19
  EtherChannel and, 65
  loopback, 128
  PAgP and, 65
interference tracking, 331
interior gateway routing protocols, 87
  nonproprietary, 116
internal clock, 143
IOS, encryption, 237
IOS restoration, flash memory and, 157
IP addresses, 25, 266–267
  classes, 23, 231, 265
  inside local IP address, 138–139
  ISPs and, 24
  laptops, 209
  link-local, 31

MAC addresses and, 95
multicast, 23, 31
outside global IP address, 140
private, 26
public, distribution, 27
RFCs, 26
route statements, 106–107
routing tables and, 105
spoofing, 345
SVI (Switched Virtual Interface), 109
SVI VLAN interfaces, 110
verifying, 32
IP packets, 97
IP services, RFC 1918 addresses, 138
IPP, broadcast addresses, 26
IPS (intrusion prevention system),
  160, 344–345
IPsec
  AH (Authentication Header), 387
  encryption, packets, 173
  site-to-site VPNs, 173, 353
IPv4, 28
  ARP process, 30
  record types, 145
IPv6, 267–268
  bits in address, 27
  connectivity verification, 29
  dual-stack hosts, 28
  duplicating, 210
  dynamic routing protocols, 103
  expansion, 29
  IPv4 ARP process and, 30
  need, 27
  network prefix, 29
  router interfaces, 28
  routes, 219–220, 315–316
  setting, 28
  shortened, 28
  solicited-node multicast message, 232
  static addressing, 28
  subnet quartet, 29
ISL (Inter-Switch Link), 284
ISPs (Internet Service Providers), IP
  addresses and, 24
IVR (inter-VLAN) routing, SVI IVR, 98

J

jitter, 340
JSON, 204–206, 376, 402

L

LACP (Link Aggregation Control
    Protocol), 289–290
LAG (Link Aggregation), 297
LANs (local area networks)
    controllers, wireless, 9
    DR (designated router), displaying, 127
    OSPF adjacency, 118
    switches, 208
LCP (Link Control Protocol), 258
    process, 14
Lean and Agile methodology, 363
leased lines, 208
line speed diagnosis, 18
link-local addresses, 31
link-state routing protocol, 97, 115
    networks, 116
LLDP (Link Layer Discovery Protocol),
    380
    advertisement interval, 64
    devices, viewing, 64
    holddown timer, 64
LLMNR (Link Local Multicast Name
    Resolution), 335
LLQ (Low Latency Queuing), 341
local addresses, unique, 30
Local mode, 83
logs, security incidents, 186
loop avoidance, 36, 89
loopback interfaces, 128
loops
    routing, 310
    switching, 35
LSAs (link-state advertisements), 325, 397
LSDB (Link State Database), 325
LSR (label switch router), 261
LWAP (Lightweight AP), 9, 255

M

MAC addresses, 35, 274–276
    aging time, 37, 38
    dynamic entries, 37
    flooding attacks, 244, 399
    IP addresses, 95
    ports and, 36
        security, 182, 357
    tables, 42, 233
        number of entries, 211
    verifying, 32
machine language, 198
malware, 224, 347
Meraki dashboard, 298
mesh topology, 296
    full-mesh, 10
Metro Ethernet, 231
MIC (Message Integrity Check), 361
microsegmentation, 6
Microsoft Azure, 14
MLPPP (multilink PPP), 13, 258
monitor filters, 163
MOTD (message of the day), 225
MPLS (Multiprotocol Label Switching), 9,
    254, 258, 386
    OSPF support, 129
    packet labels, 18
MTUs (maximum transmission unit)
    jumbo frames, 47
    SDN and, 196
multi-access networks, 119
multicast IP addresses, 23, 31, 270, 323
    OSPF and, 117
    protocols, 27
    RIPv2, 87

N

NA (Neighbor Advertisement), 269
NAT (network address translations), 140,
    141, 397
    deleting from table, 142

disadvantages, 242
dynamic, 142
IP addresses, 332
one-to-one mapping, 242
packet switching path delay, 397
pool, 141
private network interface, 223
static, 141
native VLANs, 61–62
changing, 162
NBMA (non-broadcast multi-access), 325
NCP (Network Control Protocol), 389
NDP (Neighbor Discovery Protocol), 269
NETCONF protocol, 364
NetOps, 363
network planes, 194–196
networks
advertisement, 102
answers to review questions, 250–276
authentication, selective access, 168
automation, 190
scripts, 190, 191
broadcast networks, 119
controller-based, 192–193, 365–366
design models, 10–11
discontinuous, 218
distribution layer, 194
domains
broadcast, 3
collision domains, 4
firewalls, 7
hubs, 5
mapping, 227
multi-access, 119
routers, 5
routing and, 102
SDN (software-defined networking), 365
segmentation, switches, 6
subnetworks, 24
switches, 5
terminal emulation, 79
topologies, 10
full-mesh, 10
hub-and-spoke, 12

hybrid, 10
trusted networks, 160
NHRP (Next Hop Router Protocol), 352
no switchport command, 108
nonces, 13
NS (Neighbor Solicitation), 269
NTP (Network Time Protocol), 143–145,
260, 333
default servers, 247
synchronization, 144, 398
NTP VNF, VMs, 209

O

ODL (OpenDaylight), 367
OIDs (object identifiers), 336
on-path attacks, 345
OSI (Open Systems Interconnection) model,
flow control, 21, 378
OSPF (Open Shortest Path First),
320–322, 368
AD (administrative distance), 129,
217, 328
advertising, 222
area borders, 122
Cisco metric, 93
default priority, 129
DR (designated router), 118–119
equal-cost routes, 120
interface bandwidth, 119
link-state advertisements, 123, 242
link-state routing protocols, 116
MPLS network, 129
multicast addresses and, 117
remote routers, 121
router priority, 327
routers, 242
OUI (organizationally unique identifier), 328

P

PaaS (platform-as-a-service), 259–260, 390
packet forwarding, 95, 240

packets
 ARP request packet, 96
 discarded, 340
 encryption, 173
 IP, 97
 local networks, 95
 network planes, 196
 path verification, 32
 remote networks and, 95
 routers and, 95, 96
 routing, 88
  ICMP and, 93
 routing endlessly, 240
 security, 173
 time, 243
PAgP (Port Aggregation Protocol),
  65–66, 289
passwords, 348–349
 attacks, 169
 commands, 164
 enable password, 164
 encryption, 167
 forgotten, 245
 routers, 164
 switches, 164
 Telnet, 164
pattern recognition, 197
PE (provider edge) router, 327
phishing, 162, 163, 346–347
physical data center, distribution switches, 6
physical security, 244, 399
ping
 break, 241
 dropped packet, 238
 extended, 242
 packets, 241
 return, 240
 sweep scans, 160
PoE (Power over Ethernet), switches, 64
PoP (point of presence), 378
Port Address Translation, 142–143, 222
port channels, modes, 68
port numbers, SMTP, 22
PortFast mode, 73–74, 215, 294

ports
 backup, 72
 blocking state, 73
 designated, 71
 err-disable state, 185
 GLBP (Gateway Load Balancing
  Protocol), 131
 MAC addresses and, 36
 PortFast mode, 73, 215
 repeaters, 208
 security, 181–184, 357–359
  switchport mode, 49
 static, 48
 status, inspecting, 183
 TACACS+, 79
PPP (point-to-point protocol), 230, 377, 389
 authentication, 12
  nonces, 13
 debugging, 17
 MLPPP (multilink PPP), 13, 258
 multilink connections, 13
privacy filters, 347
protocols
 Bell-Ford algorithm, 100
 connectionless, 209
 connectivity testing, 97
 distance-vector, 100
 dynamic routing protocol, 87, 93, 99
 EGPs (exterior gateway protocols), 101
 GLBP (Gateway Load Balancing
  Protocol), 131
 GRE, 169
 HTTPS transport and, 192
 hybrid, 100
 IEEE standards, 63
 IGPs (interior gateway protocols), 101
 interior gateway routing protocols,
  87, 101
 IPsec data packets, 225
 layer 2 traffic tunneling, 196
 load-balancing routers, 130
 lost segments, 21
 multicast IP addresses, 27
 network planes, 196

REST APIs, 198
routing protocols
    distance-vector, 97
    hop maximum, 99
    link-state routing protocol, 97
    topology tables, 88
SMTP, 22
SNMP replacement, 192
trunking protocols, 54
YANG data model, 192
provider responsibility, 18
PSK (preshared key), 362
PTR (pointer record), 334
public clouds, connectivity, 16
PVST+ (Per-VLAN Spanning Tree+), 290–291

Q

QoS (Quality of Service)
    Bronze profile, 300
    device trust boundary, 224, 299–300
    marking, 223
    packet marking, 244
    policing, 341–342
    queue starvation, 341
    queues, 153–154
    SDN controller, 365
    traffic classification, 153
    traffic policing, 154
    trust boundaries, 81

R

RADIUS (Remote Authentication Dial-In
        User Service), 299, 360
    ports, 185
    protocols, 185
reasoning display, 197
remote monitoring, 193
remote routers, 121
repeaters, 208
REST (representational state
        transfer), 364–365

REST APIs, 248, 371
    HTTP action verbs, 201
    protocols, 198
    response format, 205
RESTCONF, 200, 365, 372
reverse lookups, 145
RFC 1918 addresses, 138
RFCs, IP addresses, 26
RID, Cisco routers, 118
RIP (Routing Information Protocol), 309–310
    AD (administrative distance), 91
    hop count maximum, 87
    route entries, 115
RIPv2, 217–218, 383
    holddown timer, 238
    route calculation, 102
    route propagation, 114
RIPv2 advertisements, 87, 102
    multicast addresses, 87
ROAS (router on a stick), 98, 111, 286,
        316, 318
    ARP and, 112
    native VLANs, 109
root bridge, 292–293
round-robin scheduler, 154
route statements, 89–90, 106–107, 221, 384
route summarization, 112
routers, 5
    ABR (area border router), 326
    ASA (Adaptive Security Appliance), 253
    authentication, centralized, 185
    BDR (backup designated router), 326
    broadcast stopping, 389
    CE (customer edge), 327
    configuration automation, 190
    default gateway, 222
    DRs (designated routers), 325
        command, 126
        displaying, 127
        OSPF, 118–119
    dynamic routes, 97
    EXCHANGE state, 326
    EXSTART state, 326
    Fast Ethernet, 20

FULL state, 326
interior gateway routing protocols, 87
internal clock, 143, 145
IP address, 216
load-balancing, 130
LSA information download, 125
packets and, 96
passwords, 164
PE (provider edge), 327
remote, 121
remote monitoring, 193
security, 165
time synchronization, 223, 243
time zones, 144
VRRP (Virtual Router Redundancy
    Protocol), 328
routes
    configuring, 190
    destinations, 238
    scalability, 301
    static, 94, 303
        viewing, 113
routing
    administrator and, 98, 112
    automatic, 103
    bandwidth, 112
    configuration time, 99
    criteria, 94
    default, 114
    description, 97
    dynamic routing protocol, 87, 93, 307
    loop avoidance, 89
    loops, 310
    network administrators and, 94
    packets, 88
        ICMP and, 93
    S*, 89
    small networks, 219
    static, 105, 112, 305–309, 314, 319
    topology tables, 88
    verifying routes, 89
routing protocols
    distance-vector, 97
    exterior gateway, 101

hop maximum, 99
link-state routing protocol, 97, 115
network planes, 195
topology tables, 88
routing tables
    display, 103
    host route, 94
    IP addresses, 105
RSTP (Rapid Spanning Tree Protocol), 68–69,
    214–215, 293, 381
    alternate ports, 70
    backup ports, 72
    port transitions, 73
rxload counter, 263

S

SaaS (software-as-a-service), 259–260
    email, internal users, 16
SBI (southbound interface), 368
scalability, routes, 301
SCP (Secure Copy Protocol), 224, 394
SDM (Switching Database Manager), 317
SDN (software-defined networking), 365
SDN controller, 193, 194, 195, 247, 367
    MTU and, 196
    overlay, protocol, 247
    QoS, 365
SDN switches, 193, 366
    next-hop packet, 197
SD-WAN (Software-Defined Wide Area
    Network), 365, 367
SecOps, 363
security. *See also* attacks
    AAA authentication, 186
    administrative privileges, 163
    authentication
        limited, 162
        local, 167
        smartcards, 168
        types, 163
    connectivity, 173
    data in transit, 161

DHCP snooping, 162
encryption, key generation, 164
GRE (Generic Routing
        Encapsulation), 169–170
IDS (intrusion detection system), 160, 254
incident detection, 186
IPS (intrusion prevention system), 160
malware, 224, 347
monitor filters, 163
packet tampering, 173
passwords, 164
physical, 244, 399
ping sweep scans, 160
ports, 181–184, 357–359
routers, 164, 165
social engineering, 163
SOHO networks, 186
SSH, 165–166
switches, 164
tailgating, 163
WPA, 187
WPA2-Enterprise, 186–187, 361
WPA3-Enterprise, 186–187, 361
segments
    switches, 6
    TCP and, 22
serial connections, encapsulation, 208
serial links, encapsulation, 13
servers, in DMZ, 8
service providers, access point, 209
shoulder surfing, 347
site-to-site VPNs, 173
SLA (service-level agreement), 9, 254
SLAAC (Stateless Address
    Autoconfiguration), 152, 232, 269, 339
smartcards, 168, 351
SMTP (Simple Mail Transfer Protocol)
    port numbers, 22
    protocols, 22
sniffer attacks, 345
SNMP (Simple Network Management
    Protocol), 147–149, 336–337, 366
    automation, 364

Inform SNMP messages, 243, 337
    messages, 193
    polling from NMS, 223
    replacement protocol, 192
snooping, DHCP, 161, 226, 346
social engineering, 163
    shoulder surfing, 347
software development, 231
SOHO networks, 186
spanning-tree portfast default command, 74
speed and duplex negotiations, 21
Spine/Leaf networks, 366
    architecture, 193
    traffic flow, 194
spoofing, 161
SSH (Secure Shell), 298, 348
    encryption, 80
        key generation, 164, 166
    encryption key generation, 155, 156
    local user configuration, 156
    security, 165–166
SSID (service set identifier), length, 77
SSL (Secure Sockets Layer), 345
star topologies, 235, 255
    three-tier design model, 10
state, firewalls, 8
static access ports, 48
static routes, 94, 303
    AD (administrative distance), default, 91
    viewing, 113
static routing, 105, 112, 305–309, 314, 319
store-and-forward mode, 210, 273
STP (Spanning Tree Protocol), 68, 273, 393
    bridges
        port roles, 71, 72
        root bridges, 70
    broadcast storm, 379
    convergence, 72
    default, Cisco switches, 70
    designated ports, 71
    network plane, 194
    network topology changes, 69
    port transitions, 72

ports, blocking state, 73
    root ports, 71
straight-through cables, 17
subnet masks, 23, 24, 94
    CIDR notation, 23
    verifying, 32
    wildcard, 175, 176
supernet, 302
supplicant, 350
SVI (Switched Virtual Interface), IP
    addresses, 109
SVI IVR (inter-VLAN), 98
SVI VLAN interfaces, 110
switch modes, 36
switches, 5, 252, 377
    100 Mb/s hub and, 21
    802.1X, 168
    access layer, 11
    advantages, 6
    authentication, centralized,
        185
    bridge ID calculation, 71
    cable types, 16, 17
    Catalyst 9000-M, 80
    collision domains, 389
    core layer, 11, 256
    core switch, 252
    CRC checksums, 36
    devices, 236
    distribution, 6
    distribution layer, 11, 256
    forwarding, 211
    frames, dropping, 40
    internal clock, 143
    LANs, 208
    latency, 252
    layer 2, 6
    link configuration, 75
    loop avoidance, 36
    loop switching, 35
    microsegmentation, 6
    network segmentation, 6
    passwords, 164
    PoE (Power over Ethernet), 64

    remote monitoring, 193
    reprovisioning, 45
    root bridge, 70
    SDN switches, 193
    serial numbers, 212
    store and forward method, 210
    time synchronization, 223, 243
    trunks, viewing, 54
    virtual, 252
    wire speed, 6
switching office, 208
switchports
    traffic forwarding, 215
    VLAN information, 211
syslog, 149–150
    event logs, 243
    network planes, 195
    server verification, 223
SysOps, 363

T

TACACS+, 216, 382, 394, 400
    port, 79
tailgating, 163
TCN (topology change notification), 291
TCP (Transmission Control Protocol), 21
    segment delivery and, 22, 23
    sliding windows, 22
    three-way handshake, 231
Telnet, 79
    passwords, 164
terminal emulation, 79
Terraform, 202–203, 374–375
three-tier design model
    full-mesh topology, 10
    hybrid topologies, 10
    star topologies, 10
three-way handshake, TCP, 231, 264
time, details, viewing, 143
time synchronization, 223, 243
TKIP (Temporal Key Integrity Protocol),
    361, 362

topologies
  centralized switches, 10
  DMVPN, 172
  full-mesh, 10, 255
  hub-and-spoke, 12
  hybrid, 10
  limited cable access, 230
  star, 10, 235, 255
  WAPs, 208
traceroute, 240, 241
  ICMP packets, 242
traffic
  attacks, 160
  DMVPN connections, 172
  Spine/Leaf networks, 194
  wildcard masks, 175, 176
trunking protocols, 54
trunks, 58
  802.1Q protocol, 60–61
  viewing, 54
  VLAN interface, 54–55
  VLANs, 61
trusted networks, 160
TTL (time to live), 305–308, 320, 335, 395
two-tier design model
  collapsed core layer, 10
  layer switches, 11
txload counter, 263

U

UDP (User Datagram Protocol), 22, 263
unicast addresses, 30
unique local addresses, 30
URIs, firewalls, 208, 377
UTP (unshielded twisted pair), 261

V

virtual firewalls, 273
virtual switches, 252, 273
virtualization

cloud computing and, 15
  hardware, 35
VLAN IDs, 45, 48
VLANs (virtual LANs), 277–300
  attacks, 162
  benefits, 46
  converting to from flat layer, 45
  databases, 52, 234
  default, switch configuration, 49
  deleting, 46
  dynamic, 47
  frames and, 46
  global configuration mode, 233
  hopping attack, 244, 386
  interfaces, verification, 51–54
  name changes, 47, 49
  native, 59, 61–62
    changing, 162
  old, 45
  ports, verification, 50
  range
    extended, 45
    modifying, 46
  ROAS configuration, 109
  routers, 47
  routing between, 108
  running-config, 59
  spanning-tree instances, 69
  static, 46
  switched virtual interfaces, 239
  switchports, 211
  trunk interface, 54–55
  trunks, 61
  VoIP phones and, 47
  VTP VLAN pruning, 56–57
VM NIC, 35
VMs (virtual machines), 34, 272
  NTP VNF, 209
  synchronization, public to internal, 16
  VNF (virtual network function), 16
VNF (virtual network function)
  devices, 35
  VMs and, 16

VoIP phones, 47, 50
VPNs (virtual private networks), site-to-site, 173
VRRP (Virtual Router Redundancy Protocol), 328
VTP (VLAN Trunking Protocol), 54, 55
    VTP traffic forwarding, 56
VTP VLAN pruning, 56–57
VXLAN (Virtual Extensible LAN), 369, 401

W

WANs (wide area networks)
    hub-and-spoke design, 12
    multicast packets, 245
    overlay, 196
    private, 225
WAP (wireless access point), 8
    attacks, 161
    autonomous, 377
    debugging, 80
    device connection, 81
    independent operation, 76
    topologies, 208
    wireless controllers, 77
    WLCs and, 79
web browsers, web server requests, 22
web servers
    public, IP addresses, 27
    scaling, 35
WEP (Wired Equivalent Privacy), 272
wildcard masks, 175, 176, 354
wire speed, 6
wireless clients, 9
    density, 76
wireless controllers
    bandwidth, 77
    EtherChannel, 215

LANs, 9
link aggregation, 215
wireless networks
    5 GHz, 34
    authentication, 34
    Bluetooth and, 34
    encryption, 34
    frequency spectrum, 34
    signal drop, 77
    small, 79
WLANs (wireless LANs), 254
    QoS and, 81
    WAP list download, 82
    WLCs and, 77
WLCs (wireless LAN controller), 78, 254–255
    WAPs, 79
    WLANs and, 77
WMAN (wireless metro area network), 297
WPA (Wi-Fi Protected Access), security, 187, 387
WPA2-Enterprise, security, 186–187, 361
WPA2-LEAP, 401
WPA3-Enterprise, security, 361
WPAN (wireless personal area network), 297

X–Y–Z

X-Auth-Token, 199
XML (eXtensible Markup Language), 364
YAML (YAML Ain't Markup Language), 364
    configuration management and, 201
    files, 191
    key-value pairs, 191
YANG (Yet Another Next Generation), protocols, 192
zone state, 253

Online Test Bank

To help you study for your CCNA Certification exam, register to gain one year of FREE access after activation to the online interactive test bank—included with your purchase of this book! This test bank includes every one of the more than 1,000 questions found in the book.

The test bank also offers the two included practice exams, as standalone elements. Take these practice exams just as if you were taking the actual exam (without any reference material). When you've finished the first exam, move on to the next one to solidify your test-taking skills. If you get more than 90 percent of the answers correct, you're ready to take the certification exams.

To access our learning environment, simply visit www.wiley.com/go/sybextestprep, follow the instructions to register your book, and instantly gain one year of FREE access after activation.